Monitoring and Evaluation Training

SAGE was founded in 1965 by Sara Miller McCune to support the dissemination of usable knowledge by publishing innovative and high-quality research and teaching content. Today, we publish more than 850 journals, including those of more than 300 learned societies, more than 800 new books per year, and a growing range of library products including archives, data, case studies, reports, and video. SAGE remains majority-owned by our founder, and after Sara's lifetime will become owned by a charitable trust that secures our continued independence.

Los Angeles | London | New Delhi | Singapore | Washington DC

Praise for
Monitoring and Evaluation Training: A Systematic Approach
By Scott G. Chaplowe and J. Bradley Cousins

"This text is excellent for building the capacity of trainers and helping professionals and nonprofessionals to learn about program evaluation."

—Lori Bakken, Associate Professor and Evaluation Specialist,
University of Wisconsin–Madison

"This book reflects a meticulous review of the literature and discourse on evaluation capacity building and development to inform successful M&E training. It acknowledges the complexity of interdependent considerations, including larger organizational and societal contexts, to deliver not only effective M&E training, but also training transfer—the ability of trainees to apply M&E learning after training has been completed."

—Joseph Dickman, Deputy Director, Research, Evaluation,
and Learning, The MasterCard Foundation

"I often note that it seems like we're endlessly training NGO staff in M&E, and we can be frustrated with the mediocre work that results. Effective training is so much more than just delivering or facilitating good content. What is so essential about this book is that it fills a key gap on how to effectively train for M&E, and it does so in a thorough yet digestible format. In an era of increasing demand and need for evaluation capacity building, this book is a key tool for higher quality and more sustainable results."

—Christie Getman, Senior Director, Technical Support
and Program Quality Unit, Lutheran World Relief

"This is a very comprehensive and well-illustrated training manual which is grounded in modern theories and presents practical applications for all known M&E tools and methods. As a former trainer in project cycle management and facilitator of planning and self-evaluation workshops, I would have loved to have had such a book."

—Claude Hilfiker, Head of Evaluation,
World Intellectual Property Organization

"The book contains useful guidelines for designing effective M&E training, and for designing training generally."

—John Mathiason, Managing Director, Associates for International
Management Services, and Professor, Cornell Institute of Public Affairs

Monitoring and Evaluation Training

A Systematic Approach

Scott G. Chaplowe
International Federation of Red Cross and Red Crescent Societies

J. Bradley Cousins
University of Ottawa

Los Angeles | London | New Delhi
Singapore | Washington DC

Los Angeles | London | New Delhi
Singapore | Washington DC

FOR INFORMATION:

SAGE Publications, Inc.
2455 Teller Road
Thousand Oaks, California 91320
E-mail: order@sagepub.com

SAGE Publications Ltd.
1 Oliver's Yard
55 City Road
London EC1Y 1SP
United Kingdom

SAGE Publications India Pvt. Ltd.
B 1/I 1 Mohan Cooperative Industrial Area
Mathura Road, New Delhi 110 044
India

SAGE Publications Asia-Pacific Pte. Ltd.
3 Church Street
#10-04 Samsung Hub
Singapore 049483

Printed in the United States of America.

ISBN 978-1-4522-8891-8

This book is printed on acid-free paper.

MIX
Paper from
responsible sources
FSC® C014174

Acquisitions Editor: Helen Salmon
Editorial Assistant: Anna Villaruel
Production Editor: Olivia Weber-Stenis
Copy Editor: Karin Rathert
Typesetter: C&M Digitals (P) Ltd.
Proofreader: Alison Syring
Indexer: Scott Smiley
Cover Designer: Glenn Vogel
Marketing Manager: Nicole Elliott

15 16 17 18 19 10 9 8 7 6 5 4 3 2 1

Brief Contents

PLAN

DO

(Featuring

99

real-life
examples)

Contents

PLAN

Part 2—A Systematic Approach to M&E Training   135

(Featuring

99

*real-life
examples)*

List of Acronyms

A

ADDIE—training analysis, design, development, implementation, and evaluation

AEA—American Evaluation Association

C

CBO—community-based organization

CBT—computer-based training

E

ECB—evaluation capacity building

ECD—evaluation capacity development

ELT— experiential learning theory

I

ICT—information and communications technology

ILT—instructor-led training

INTRAC—International NGO Training and Research Center

IQ—intelligence quotient

ISD—Instructional Systems Design

J

JCSEE—Joint Committee for Standards for Educational Evaluation

K

KSAs—knowledge, skills, and attitudes

M

M&E—monitoring and evaluation

MBTI—Myers-Briggs Type Indicator

N

NCERT—National Council for Educational Research and Training

NGO—non-governmental organization

NTK—need to know

O

OECD—Organization for Economic Co-operation and Development

OER—open educational resources

OJT—on-the-job training

P

PME—participatory monitoring and evaluation

R

RBM—results-based management

ROLE—Readiness for Organizational Learning and Evaluation

S

SMART—specific, measurable, attainable/achievable, relevant, timely/time bound

SME—subject matter experts

SSA—Sarva Shiksha Abhiyan

SWOT—strengths, weaknesses, opportunities, threats

T

ToR—terms of reference

ToT—training of trainers

V

VAK— visual-auditory-kinesthetic

VfM—value for money

VLE—virtual learning environment

U

URL—uniform resource locator

Preface

Why did we write this book?

This book was written to address the increasing demand for monitoring and evaluation (M&E) training. It offers a systematic approach to M&E training for programs and projects, bridging theoretical concepts with practical, how-to knowledge to support M&E training that makes a difference.

If you were to do a keyword search for "M&E training" on the Internet today, you would be inundated with opportunities from an array of M&E training providers. In addition to university-based training programs, there exists an assortment of M&E certificate programs, continuing education courses, workshops, and seminars offered on-site and online. For example, one online training forum listed over 140 different M&E training events in 2014 (MandE, 2015). There is also a host of M&E resources available for self-learning, ranging from printed guidelines and books to online websites, learning platforms, blogs, and communities of practice. In addition to these public sources, organizations from the civic, public, and private sectors are increasingly providing their own M&E training to staff and stakeholders they work with. More than ever, people are seeking learning opportunities for M&E.

The demand for M&E training and other approaches to capacity building have steadily increased over the past twenty-five years. This trend reflects increasing expectations for performance accountability and delivery of results. Today, M&E capacity building is in the spotlight, with the United Nations declaring 2015 the International Year of Evaluation, adopting a resolution titled, "Capacity Building for the Evaluation of Development Activities at the Country Level." From community projects to large-scale, national programs, organizations are increasingly mainstreaming M&E as core competencies for their staff and volunteers. There is growing recognition that sustainable M&E practice requires an understanding that extends beyond specialists to include various people at various levels in program delivery.

With the increasing demand for M&E training, one would also expect an increase in the resources available to help guide people to prepare for and deliver M&E training. However, while there is a surplus of books, guidelines, and other resources on how to do good M&E, available resources giving advice on M&E training are relatively scarce. This book was written to help address this gap.

We would be amiss to imply there are no resources available on adult training in general and specifically for M&E. On the contrary, much of this book is informed by the existing scholarly literature and practical guidance that already exists in these areas. Anyone who even "dabbed" into the field of training will know that there is an array of books on adult learning and training facilitation. Related, the last couple of decades have seen a steady increase in scholarship and research on evaluation capacity building (ECB) and development (ECD).

However, more often than not, pedagogy is implicit rather than explicit in the literature for evaluation education (Trevisan, 2004), and we also contend for M&E training. As one article in the *American Journal of Evaluation* observed for teaching program evaluation:

> The existing literature provides some information concerning a practical application component; however, there is almost no discussion of pedagogy or, more specifically, the selection of teaching strategies for a program evaluation course (Oliver, Casiraghi, Henderson, Brooks, & Mulsow, 2008).

Furthermore, much of the existing M&E capacity building literature is rather academic, included as specialization within traditional fields of study (e.g., education, psychology, or public health) or more targeted toward training evaluators or M&E professionals versus others interested in understanding and participating in M&E: "limited attention has been paid to capability building for those working at a community level and for professionals with limited understanding of evaluation" (Adams & Dickinson, 2010, p. 422). It is worth noting that there are an increasing number of practical guidelines from various organizations in the public and nonprofit sectors for M&E training, but for the most part, they are largely tailored to specific organizational contexts and program areas.

Thus, we wrote this book to provide guidance for M&E training that can be tailored and adapted broadly to different training needs contexts, whether training for professionals or nonprofessionals, organization staff, community members, or other groups with a stake in M&E. The book benefits not only from our understanding of available scholarship and practical guidance but also from our collective fifty plus years of experience in M&E training and education as well as our considerable contributions to research on evaluation use, participatory evaluation, and ECB, including the integration of evaluation into the organizational culture. Much of our work has been interdisciplinary, inter-sectoral, and international.

Who this book is for and how to use it

In the broadest sense, this book is for anyone interested in M&E training. More specifically, it targets two principal user groups:

1. First, it can be used as a practical manual for M&E trainers and others involved in managing or supporting M&E training. Related, it can also be used by educators to teach M&E in settings that are not strictly

"training," such as formal education in postsecondary and continuing education contexts.

2. Second, this book can be used as a text in postsecondary educational settings for those needing to understand and support M&E capacity building as part of their career path or as a resource book for the training of trainers (ToT) to prepare people to provide M&E training to others.

We have organized this book into three parts. **Part 1** provides a conceptual foundation for M&E training as part of a larger system that includes other learning opportunities, contextual considerations that can support or hinder training outcomes, the learners themselves, and the trainer. **Part 2** outlines a systematic approach for M&E training, from training analysis, design, and development to its implementation and evaluation. **Part 3** focuses on practical methods and techniques for M&E training, profiling 99 example activities for training delivery to inspire readers.

We understand that readers' levels of understanding, interests, and needs vary, and we encourage you to navigate through the book accordingly. For example, some readers may choose to forgo the theory presented in Part I and go straight to the example activities presented in Part III. To assist with this, we begin each chapter with a brief introduction and summary of learning objectives and end each chapter with a summary of key points. Throughout the book, we also provide a variety of visual aids to highlight and summarize key topics.

This is an introductory book to M&E training, examining key concepts and practices from various fields, notably training and capacity building, adult learning, and M&E. As such, our ability to explore each topic in depth is limited—in fact, many of the topics in this book can be and, in fact, are books in and of themselves. Therefore, at the end of each chapter we list some recommended resources for further study.

Our primary focus is on M&E training rather than M&E itself. We do not expect readers will seek out such a book on training others in in M&E if they did not already have a basis in it themselves. However, our review of some key M&E concepts and practices is likely to be helpful to some.

A final note for readers—It would be presumptuous and inappropriate to present this book as a definitive blueprint of set practices or rules for M&E training. A key message throughout the book is that training should be adapted and tailored to its specific training context, including the individual learners, their culture, and the trainers themselves. Therefore, we encourage readers to keep an open mind and use the book according to their particular needs. Rather than providing a "definitive" answer for all M&E training challenges, we hope this book serves as a springboard for readers to further explore for themselves M&E training that makes a positive difference.

Acknowledgments

First and foremost, the authors would like to acknowledge the trainees, students, and colleagues whom they have worked with and learned from in the planning, delivery, and follow-up of training, workshops, classes, and e-learning over the past thirty years. Learning is truly two way, and these individuals provided a real-life laboratory in which to pilot, explore, and improve upon the concepts and practices contained in this book.

In the preparation of this book, we wish to acknowledge the contributions of Ben Mountfield for his initial input on the book's outline; Stephanie Evergreen for her feedback on the initial drafts of Chapters 2 and 4; and Sara Vaca for her feedback on Chapters 1 and 6 as well as her support in the design of the table of contents and selected diagrams for the book. We are also very grateful to have enlisted Jessie Mountfield to help add some "character" to the book with her illustrations. This book has also benefited from the helpful and constructive suggestions from the following reviewers: Lori L. Bakken, University of Wisconsin-Madison; John Mathiason, Cornell University; and Karen and Craig Russon, Evaluation Capacity Development Group.

Special thanks go to Hubert Paulmer, who brought the two authors together, and the dedicated support of the people at SAGE Publications, especially acquisitions editor Helen Salmon, who believed in the book from the start and allowed it to extend beyond the anticipated length.

Lastly, Scott would like to thank the International Federation of Red Cross and Red Crescent Societies (IFRC) for allowing him to take time off to work on the book, with special mention to Josse Gillijns for his confidence. He also wishes to express his deep gratitude to Maria Victoria Castillo Rueda for her patience, good humor, and loving support throughout, demonstrating that "unanticipated outcomes" can very much be positive and beautiful. Brad would like to acknowledge the University of Ottawa for its generous support and to express his continuing deep gratitude to his loving wife Danielle for her support and understanding.

About the Authors

Scott G. Chaplowe is currently a senior monitoring and evaluation (M&E) officer at the International Federation of Red Cross and Red Crescent Societies (IFRC), based in Geneva. In addition to M&E, he has over twenty years' experience in policy research and analysis, strategic planning, and capacity building and development for civil society and international organizations. He holds an MA in Geography from UCLA, with a focus on political ecology and natural resource management, and has authored articles on urban agriculture, civil society, and evaluation; coedited a book on sustainable agriculture; and developed an assortment of guides on M&E, program design, capacity assessment, and strategic planning. His initial experience in adult education was working with experiential learning and leadership with Outward Bound and the National Outdoor Leadership School (NOLS). He has since taught at universities in both the United States and abroad (China and Taiwan) and has extensive experience in the development, delivery, and evaluation of individual and organizational training (face-to-face, e-learning, and blended learning). He has provided training in M&E and related topics in North and South America, Europe, Africa, and Asia, including professional development workshops for the American Evaluation Association (AEA), the European Evaluation Society (EES), the South African Monitoring and Evaluation Association (SAMEA), the Malaysian Evaluation Society (MES), and the Sri Lankan Evaluation Association (SLEVA). For more information, visit www.ScottChaplowe.com.

J. Bradley Cousins is professor of Evaluation at the Faculty of Education, University of Ottawa. Cousins' main interests are in program evaluation including participatory and collaborative approaches, use, and capacity building. He received his PhD in Educational Measurement and Evaluation from the University of Toronto in 1988. Throughout his career he has received several awards for his work in evaluation, including the Contribution to Evaluation in Canada award (CES, 1999), the Paul F. Lazarsfeld Award for Theory in Evaluation (AEA, 2008), and the AERA Research on Evaluation Distinguished Scholar Award (2011). He has published many articles and books on evaluation and was editor of the *Canadian Journal of Program Evaluation* from 2002 to 2010. Throughout his career, Cousins has had considerable experience planning, delivering, and evaluating evaluation training and capacity building in Canada and abroad. Internationally he led evaluation capacity building in Central and West Africa and a major three and one-half year project in India. He is currently leading a nationwide evaluation of teacher in-service training in that country in collaboration with several of the people he had previously trained. Cousins completed a three and one-half year term as director of the Centre for Research on Educational and Community Services at the University of Ottawa in July 2015. He continues to be an active member of CRECS, which has a strong mandate for research and evaluation capacity building. For more information, visit www.crecs.uottawa.ca.

Key Concepts
for M&E Training

Part 1 of the book lays some conceptual groundwork for the more practical applications that we will be presenting in Part 2. Much of what we cover derives from the wider knowledge base, but to some extent we draw from our own practical experience. We begin in Chapter 1 with an overview of initial ideas for the book, including substantial consideration to the choices that we have made. In Chapter 2, we lay out our vision of what training is and what differentiates it from other professional learning opportunities, and then we discuss the array of options available for training delivery today. Much of what we describe in Chapter 2 could apply to training in any domain, but what sets this book apart is its focus on training for monitoring and evaluation (M&E).

In Chapter 3, we consider a range of issues associated with the larger capacity building context for M&E training. Our intention is to provide readers with an understanding of M&E as part of a larger systems, with key considerations at the levels of the individual, organization, and external environment that shape the demand for and potential success of M&E training. In Chapter 4, we then examine the learning or training participant. We cover a wide range of territory about adult learning and identify key principles to inform professional development, such as M&E training. Finally, we conclude Part 1 with some thought about the people providing M&E training. The role of the M&E trainer is demanding, and there are many requisite qualities to consider. Chapter 5 provides a detailed examination of these qualities as well as other considerations associated with training delivery and facilitation.

Part 1 is, in many respects, foundational, and it feeds nicely into the heart of the matter, a systematic approach to M&E training, which we detail in Part 2.

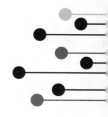

CHAPTER 1

M&E Training That Makes a Difference

One of the principles of adult learning we discuss later in the book is to respond to the "need to know" what, why, and how learning will happen. In short, adults learn better when they have a sense of direction of where learning is heading and for what reasons. That is largely the purpose of this introductory chapter. We expand upon the preface to clarify for readers what this book is about and how it can support monitoring and evaluation (M&E) training.

1.1 What is M&E Training That *Makes a Difference*?
....

As the title of this chapter suggests, this book was written to help readers provide M&E training that will make a difference. Readers familiar with the field of evaluation will know that "utility" is a core standard for program evaluation.[1] Likewise, we believe that if M&E training is to make a positive difference, it should be useful and used. In the vernacular of training, we refer to this as "training transfer" or the ability of trainees to apply learning from training after training has been completed. However, effective M&E training is more than just the ability of trainees to practice newly acquired learning; it makes a difference when it contributes to meaningful change at individual, organizational, community, and even societal levels.

_____

1. For example, see the *Program Evaluation Standards* of the Joint Committee for Standards for Educational Evaluation (JCSEE, 2015).

Learning Objectives

By the end of this chapter readers will be able to . . .

✓ Identify key factors that contribute to M&E training that makes a difference

✓ Explain what is meant by systems thinking as it relates to M&E training

✓ Define M&E and results-based management

✓ Explain the reasons for the increased demand for M&E training

✓ Describe who may be involved in providing M&E training

✓ Describe the kinds of M&E training this book can be used to support

An underlying premise of the book is that *the more training helps people understand M&E, the more capable they are to become involved in, support, and own M&E practices.* This, in turn, contributes to more effective and sustainable programming and results that make a difference. However, for many people M&E is not the most exciting or appealing training topic, and some even feel threatened by and are reluctant to participate in such training. Having solicited people's expectations prior to M&E training, we have found it is not unusual for them to anticipate it to be boring or technically intimidating and to negatively associate M&E with terms like "required," "mandatory," "controlling," "judgmental," "bureaucratic," "unnecessary," and "burdening." More often than not, we find resistance to M&E training heightened for the very reason people need it: they do not understand and value M&E.

This book was written to help redress such potential obstacles, so people are instead stimulated by M&E training and motivated to learn. Therefore, a second premise of the book is that *M&E training can be delivered in an enjoyable and meaningful way that engages leaners; such an approach helps demystify M&E so it can be better understood, appreciated, and used.* Among other things, this requires a sound understanding of adult learning principles and practical methods and activities to apply them in M&E training. In Chapters 4 and 9, we will take a look at adult learning and tips for effective training facilitation, and in Part 3 of the book we present a selection of activities to inspire active, engaging delivery of M&E training.

However, providing M&E training that makes a difference is more than just engaging facilitation during its delivery. It requires careful planning and consideration of the larger system or context in which M&E training is both provided and to be used. This includes a variety of different actors and factors specific to the training context, such as the individual learners and other training stakeholders, the identified needs and desired outcomes for M&E training, the training content, trainers and delivery system, and the available resources and support for training and its transfer.

It is not enough to design and deliver training that provides M&E learning, but it is also critical to identify key factors that can help or hinder its potential to be used. This requires understanding the demand and opportunity for M&E learning to realistically transfer after training into meaningful practice at the level of the individual, organization, or society. As Preskill and Boyle (2008, p. 453) underscore, "Unless people are willing and able to apply their evaluation knowledge, skills, and attitudes toward effective evaluation practice, there is little chance for evaluation practice to be sustained." Thus, another central premise for this book is that *if M&E training is to make a difference, it should be approached with careful attention to the larger system or capacity-building context in which training is provided.*

Finally, and as the book's subtitle conveys, a fourth premise for this book is that *M&E training should be approached in a systematic manner.* Therefore, it should be orderly planned to gather information and analyze training demand, needs, and resources and identify relevant objectives; and it should be designed to realistically achieve and evaluate these objectives. However, a systematic approach does not imply the development and use of a rigid blueprint to be followed blindly. Such practice can inhibit experimentation and the ability of training to adapt and respond to changing needs and unanticipated outcomes (whether positive opportunities or challenging obstacles). A systematic approach will recognize the dynamic and systemic nature of the training context, which will vary and change over time.

M&E training is a substantial investment in time and resources, for those providing as well as those participating in training. Careful, systematic planning, implementation, and evaluation helps ensure the return on that investment so that M&E training makes a positive difference.

1.2 Systems Thinking for Training

As we have suggested, if M&E training is to make a difference it is important that it is conceptualized as systematic. It is equally essential to approach training as part of larger system. In short, training does not occur in isolation, nor is it the only way to build M&E capacity, but it should be planned and delivered as a coherent approach that considers other factors that affect M&E capacity building. In the following chapters in Part 1 of the book, we provide the conceptual background to understand various aspects of the larger system for M&E training. At this point, we provide a brief introduction to the concept of systems thinking to inform this discussion.

The origins of systems thinking as a field trace back to the first half of the twentieth century and are associated with several disciplines, notably biology and engineering. As its name implies, it seeks to understand complex phenomena, such as a training event or a program being implemented and evaluated, as part of a larger system composed of interdependent parts. Therefore, to understand any one part of the system, it is best to examine it in relationship to the other parts of the overall system rather than in isolation (Ramage & Shipp, 2009).

Systems thinking has evolved as an increasingly influential, interdisciplinary perspective. It has given rise to an assortment of approaches and methods to study a range of systems, whether physical, biological, social, engineered, or conceptual.[2] It has had an especially significant influence on the understanding of how people and organizations learn, and during the 1990s, systems thinking received much attention when it was identified by Peter Senge (1990) as the "Fifth Discipline" that makes the other disciplines work. Readers familiar with the field of evaluation will know the concepts of systems thinking has had a growing influence on the understanding and practice of evaluation (e.g., Hargreaves, 2010; Morell, 2010; Patton, 2011; Williams & Imam, 2007).

---

2. For instance, Williams and Hummelbrunner (2009) summarize nineteen different approaches and methods for using systems thinking in a range of areas, from evaluation to teaching.

Systems thinking has also has had considerable influence on the field of training. During the 1970s, influential models for instructional design, such as Dick and Carey (1996) and Morrison, Ross, and Kemp (2011), popularized a more holistic approach to the entire training process and context. This systems emphasis has given rise to what is now commonly referred to as Instructional Systems Design (ISD), and a variety of models, frameworks, and approaches to guide training and other forms of education based on a systems approach.

In Part 2 of the book, we discuss ISD in more detail, presenting an approach to ISD for training consisting of five iterative phases commonly referred to in training circles as "ADDIE": training **a**nalysis, **d**esign, **d**evelopment, **i**mplementation, and **e**valuation. For now, these key phases or aspects of training will help us highlight two overall features of systems thinking that will be useful for the chapters to come, specifically (1) M&E training as a system within a system and (2) M&E as dynamic and changing.

1. M&E training as a system within a system

For some readers, it may sound very abstract to consider M&E training as a subsystem embedded in and interdependent on larger systems. In fact, it can even be counter-intuitive for those accustomed to "scientific reductionism" to understand things in this way. In contrast to breaking down what is to be understood into constituent parts and examining their properties, systems thinking explores the properties that exist when the parts are combined and functioning as a whole. To help better understand this for M&E training, we will use a metaphor of a chef preparing a meal to help explain M&E training as a system within a system.

2. M&E training as dynamic and changing

Our chef metaphor helps convey a second and related aspect of systems thinking: Reality is complicated, with multiple factors interacting over time, which means things are constantly shifting and may not always go as anticipated. Such a dynamic understanding takes one away from linear notions of change. For example, in our metaphor there may be unannounced guests who arrive for dinner or unexpected incidents, such as a spilt wine. Similarly, during training a variety of unanticipated encounters may occur, from unexpected questions to disruptive behavior. Related, there may be unintended outcomes resulting from training; for instance, while M&E training may improve performance among staff, it may also result in higher levels of staff turnover because they are more qualified and leave the organization for better-paying positions elsewhere.

Systems thinking draws upon the fields of systems dynamics and complexity theory to help understand the important role of feedback loops and emergent behavior that can occur when individual yet interdependent parts of the overall system interact. It is important to understand that the feedback or influence of one actor in the system

A "Chef Metaphor" to Understand System's Thinking for M&E Training

Just as trainers need to analyze the larger training context for M&E training, so must a chef to prepare a meal. For instance, the chef needs to consider the purpose of the meal, that is, whether it is for an event like a wedding banquet or to be served on a regular basis, such as a cafeteria at a workplace. How many people will be dining and are there any individual dietary preferences or restrictions, such as people who are vegetarians, do not eat pork, or have food allergies? Obviously, it is critical to identify such preferences, whether they are because of culture, religion, or individual constitution. Other questions to consider include, is there a limited budget for the meal, an equipped kitchen, an appropriate facility to serve the meal, and will multiple cooks and servers be needed or will it be a one-person operation? These various considerations mirror those during training analysis to determine what is realistic for training needs and purpose, time frame and setting, number and profile of trainees, and available resources for training.

Next, the chef will need to design a menu with recipes for each dish based on dietary preferences and needs, the available time, produce at the market, cooking facilities, and equipment. Then there is the actual preparation and serving of the meal. Whether the dining experience is a white-tablecloth affair or a picnic with paper plates, the utensils, presentation, and serving of the food should be tailored accordingly. Likewise, servers should observe proper etiquette appropriate for the event. Attention should also be given to whether diners need directions to the dining area, where they should park their cars, the location of toilets, and so forth. Such considerations reflect those during the training design, development, and delivery, including the training curriculum,

development of instructional aids, practical logistics, and the actual training facilitation.

Finally, throughout and after the meal, it will be important to monitor and obtain feedback from the diners. Did they get what they ordered (well done or rare), was there sufficient variety and quantities of food, were dishes on time, at suitable temperature, and were refills forthcoming? In short, were diners satisfied? Some of this monitoring occurs during the meal by observant servers, provided by unsolicited comments (compliments or complaints) from diners, and can also be solicited from diners—for example, many restaurants have a comment book or feedback forms, and people are increasingly using social media, such as websites, to rate restaurants.

Jessie Mountfield

These last considerations highlight the importance of monitoring and evaluating during and after a training event. However, as we will discuss, there may be longer term outcomes than just satisfaction, such as what difference has the training made for stakeholders? For instance, if it was a wedding banquet, did it provide a lasting experience and memories for all those attending? Similarly, did M&E training for an organization, for example, contribute to better M&E practice and organizational objectives in the long run?

can result in unanticipated outcomes (positive or negative) that can reinforce or hinder M&E training and its transfer. Recognizing such complexity, it is not always easy to map everything out in advance, as the different interactions may result in "emergent," unanticipated behavior within the system.

This does not mean that we "throw the baby out with the bathwater" and discard planning altogether. In fact, as Part 2 of the book reflects, just as projects and programs develop plans or frameworks to achieve their intended results, we recommend a *systematic* approach to identify and achieve training objectives. However, we humbly acknowledge the complexities of the training context and the need to remain flexible and open to multiple perspectives and possibilities in our approach. This underscores the importance of establishing feedback mechanisms within the training system itself, to "tune in" and listen to how things are going during training and went after training—hence, the ironic importance to apply M&E principles to training that also focuses on M&E.

Because our book is written at an introductory level, our treatment of systems thinking is limited and focused for the most part on M&E training. Hopefully, our discussion thus far underscores that successful training requires more than just good facilitation but encompasses a variety of considerations and related roles and responsibilities. Just as a chef may need to wear multiple hats, from researching the market to cooking, serving, cleaning up, and soliciting feedback, so must a trainer—which we will examine more closely in Chapter 5.

In fact, providing training can be much more complicated than providing a meal, and we understand that it might seem like a whole lot. However, we do not want to scare people off. On the contrary, we wrote this book to help readers successfully navigate the potential complexities of M&E training, and we adopted a systems approach for the very reason that it is useful for "addressing and resolving situations that are wicked, messy, and horribly tangled" (Williams & Hummelbrunner, 2009, p. 1).

We will revisit the systems perspective as it applies to M&E training throughout the book, but for now, let's take a closer look at what we mean by "M&E" and how we will be using it in the book.

1.3 Revisiting M&E

While we assume readers of a book on M&E training are already familiar with M&E, we nevertheless recognize it can mean different things to different people. For example, **Box 1.1** lists some of the acronyms/abbreviations used by different organizations that reflect the various practices and purposes associated with M&E. Therefore, we want to

- **DME** (design, monitoring, and evaluation)
- **DMEL** (design, monitoring, evaluation, and learning),
- **MEA** (monitoring, evaluation, and accountability)
- **MEAL** (monitoring, evaluation, accountability, and learning)
- **MEL** (monitoring, evaluation, and learning)
- **PARME** (program accountability, review, monitoring, and evaluation)

- **PMER** (planning, monitoring, evaluation, and reporting)
- **PM&E** (performance monitoring and evaluation)
- **PM&E** (planning, monitoring, and evaluation)
- **PM&E** (participatory monitoring, and evaluation)
- **SM&E** (strategy, measurement, and evaluation)
- **RM&E** (research, monitoring, and evaluation)

clarify how we are using M&E in relation to training. First, we will specifically look at *monitoring* and *evaluation*, and then we will explain how we will be using M&E broadly to encompass other related processes as part of a program's overall management system.

As its abbreviation reflects, monitoring and evaluation are closely related and often considered together as one process. However, it is important to understand they are distinct. A good starting point is to consider the definitions of the Organization for Economic Co-operation and Development (OECD). Although intended for international development, these definitions largely capture the purpose and use of M&E for most program contexts, whether domestic or international:

- *<u>Monitoring</u>* is a continuous function that uses the systematic collection of data on specified indicators to provide management and the main stakeholders of an ongoing development intervention with indications of the extent of progress and achievement of objectives and progress in the use of allocated funds (OECD, 2002, p. 27).

- *<u>Evaluation</u>* is the systematic and objective assessment of an ongoing or completed project, program, or policy, including its design, implementation, and results. The aim is to determine the relevance and fulfillment of objectives, development efficiency, effectiveness, impact, and sustainability. An evaluation should provide information that is credible and useful, enabling the incorporation of lessons learned into the decision-making process of both recipients and donors. (OECD, 2002, p. 21)

A couple of points are worth noting. First, although it is essential for M&E to focus on what is intended, it is also important to assess unintended consequences, positive or negative, of interventions. Second, it is helpful to understand the purpose of and relationship between monitoring and evaluation with regard to timing. Monitoring is ongoing to *describe* what is happening, whereas evaluation is periodic to *judge* how well it happened and what difference it made, intended or not. Monitoring happens throughout program implementation, providing information for program management and decision-making. Evaluation can occur during (formative) or after (summative) program implementation, but is less frequent, with the intention to "step back" for more in-depth assessment to judge the worth of programing. This valuation of programming is then used externally to uphold accountability to program stakeholders (e.g., intended program beneficiaries and donors) and to foster learning (internally and externally) to inform future programming, strategic planning, and best practices for the respective program area/s.

There are a variety of different types of program monitoring and evaluation (IFRC, 2011a, pp.12 & 15). Monitoring types include process (activity), performance, results, compliance, beneficiary, financial, and context monitoring. Evaluation types include those according to who conducts evaluation (e.g., self, joint, internal, external, or independent evaluations), when they are conducted (e.g., ex-ante, real time, midterm, final, or ex-post evaluations), or the evaluation's particular method or focus (e.g., meta-, impact, or participatory evaluation). Recognizing their differences, the distinction between monitoring and evaluation is not always "black and white." Monitoring typically provides data for evaluation, and elements of evaluation (assessment) can occur when monitoring. For instance, results monitoring can merge with evaluation to assess a program's efficiency and effectiveness during implementation.

With regards to training, it is important to recognize that the knowledge and skills required for evaluation can be more advanced than monitoring. For example, program monitoring typically focuses on tracking shorter-term outputs or deliverables that are easier to measure, such as the number of items or amount of service provided. On the other hand, evaluation often examines longer-term outcomes, such as changes in knowledge, attitudes, and practice that require more methodological rigor to assess causality and impact.[3] Consequently, instruction to prepare people to be "evaluators" is typically more demanding, requiring a longer period of training and/or formal education and practical experience:

---

3. Note that standards or rigor are independent of method in impact evaluation. Rigor is important regardless of whether a conventional social sciences approach (e.g., randomized control trials, [RCT]) or an alternative approach such as contribution analysis (Mayne, 2012) is employed.

Ultimately, nothing teaches how to do evaluations as well as direct experience in designing and running actual evaluations. (Rossi, Lipsey, & Freeman, 2004, p. ix)[4]

M&E and results-based management (RBM)

M&E does not happen in isolation but are two of many interrelated processes in a program management system. As such, M&E and its training often includes other processes that are not technically monitoring and evaluation but are very much part of an M&E system. For example, program design, data management, and reporting are often considered part of the M&E system and included as topics in M&E training (or M&E may be included as topics, [modules] in other program management training).

For our purposes, we consider the larger program management system for M&E from the perspective of results-based management (RBM). Also referred to as performance management, RBM is a management strategy based on clearly defined and measurable results (objectives) and the methodologies, processes, and tools to achieve those results (Görgens & Kusek 2009; Kusek & Rist 2004; OECD & World Bank, 2006; UNDG, 2011). RBM supports better performance and accountability by applying a clear, logical framework to plan, manage, and measure programming and its intended results.

The current practice of M&E largely evolved with RBM during 1990s, coinciding with the adoption of the logical framework approach to programming by the public sector and international development agencies (Edmunds & Marchant, 2008; Mathison, 2005). As we discuss below, it reflected the increasing demand for performance accountability. We believe the basic premise and practices of RBM applies just as well to smaller domestic programs as to larger international ones. It is based on a strong notion of causality or attribution of how various inputs and activities lead logically to higher orders of results (outputs, outcomes, and impacts) (OECD & World Bank, 2006, p. 8). By identifying in advance the intended results of a program and how to measure them, M&E becomes more straightforward, and related reporting becomes more relevant and useful.

It is helpful to conceptualize M&E as part of a RBM system by considering a generic project (or program) cycle. **Figure 1.1** represents a basic project cycle, reflecting four interrelated phases in a project, and **Figure 1.2** illustrates in more detail potential M&E activities that occur during the project cycle. An initial (needs) assessment is typically conducted first to determine if there are and the extent of any problems or needs to address. A variety of methodologies can be used at this stage, such as stakeholder, SWOT (strengths, weaknesses, opportunities, threats), and problem analysis (e.g., IFRC 2010; Watkins, Meiers & Visser, 2012). This is followed by a planning or design phase to prepare for project

---

4. As Rossi et. al. (2004, p. 27) point out, while "there are many evaluation tasks that can be easily carried out by persons of modest expertise and experience," the most complex evaluation activities "require the dedicated participation of highly trained specialists at ease with the latest in social science theory, program knowledge, data collection methods, and statistical techniques."

FIGURE 1.1   Basic Project Cycle

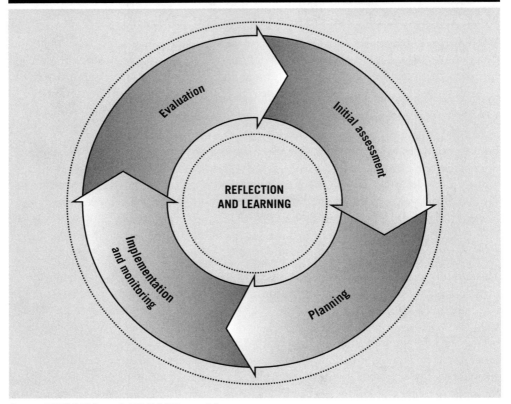

REFLECTION AND LEARNING

Evaluation

Initial assessment

Implementation and monitoring

Planning

Source: IFRC 2010, p. 6, IFRC 2011a, p. 10.

implementation. For M&E, this can include a logframe specifying the identified objectives, indicators, means of verification and assumptions, as well as a M&E plan, baseline study, reporting templates, and other tools and activities contributing to the M&E system.

Project implementation operationalizes the M&E system, which includes routine monitoring and reporting as well as any formative (e.g., midterm) evaluations or reviews to assess and inform ongoing program implementation. Summative evaluation after implementation is used to assess the project's impact (both intended and unintended) and what difference it made. Throughout the project cycle, data management and reporting is ongoing, sharing information to support learning, project management, and accountability.

The phases summarized in the project cycle are only illustrative and will vary according to the operational context and organizational culture. For example, programing in emergency contexts may begin with immediate implementation to provide services to

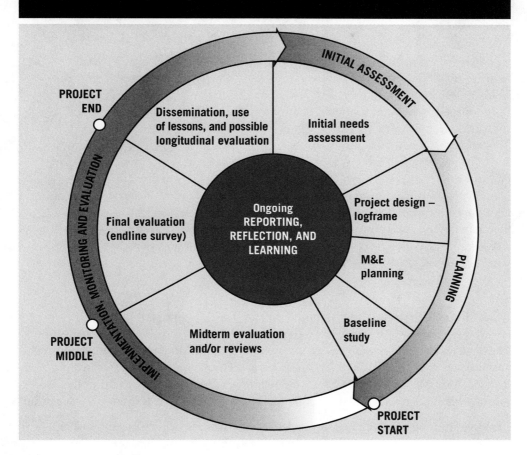

FIGURE 1.2 Project Cycle With Example M&E Activities

INITIAL ASSESSMENT

PROJECT END

Dissemination, use of lessons, and possible longitudinal evaluation

Initial needs assessment

IMPLEMENTATION: MONITORING AND EVALUATION

Final evaluation (endline survey)

Ongoing REPORTING, REFLECTION, AND LEARNING

Project design – logframe

M&E planning

PLANNING

Midterm evaluation and/or reviews

Baseline study

PROJECT MIDDLE

PROJECT START

people in need and later conduct more thorough assessment and planning to inform longer-term continuation of programing. The important point is that M&E consists of a variety of interrelated processes in the overall RBM system. Such a systems perspective approaches M&E as a subsystem that is interdependent on other program management systems. We adopt this broader interpretation of M&E, recognizing that training for it can be tailored according to different understanding of and needs for M&E practice.

As our above discussion suggests, this book is centered on what we consider to be a conventional conception of M&E. However, it is important to recognize there are alternative and emerging approaches, as **Box 1.2** highlights. Nevertheless, we believe the core principles and practices presented in this book apply to effective planning and delivery of training regardless of the specific M&E concepts and content (which should be tailored according to specific training needs).

BOX 1.2
Developmental Evaluation

Note that so far we have been talking primarily about conventional approaches to M&E, which are particularly appropriate when the program logic, theory of change, or intended results chain of an intervention's impact are well understood and explicated. However, many organizations embrace innovation and develop interventions in an incremental and evolutionary way. Such interventions are more suited to what Patton (1994; 2011) has dubbed "Developmental Evaluation." In this alternative approach, M&E is not structured in advance, but actually follows an intervention as it evolves. The evaluator participates as part of the program/administrative team and contributes to the enhancement of evidence-based decision-making along the way. For our purposes, and for reasons of simplicity, we will focus predominantly on conventional approaches to M&E in the present book. This is not to say, however, that many of the ideas that we have about training for M&E do not apply to those working in development evaluation contexts. It is to say, rather, that ideas about training for developmental evaluation remain relatively untested at present.

1.4 The Rising Demand for M&E Training

The demand for M&E training reflects the need for broader M&E understanding, support, and practice. Two parallel trends have played a particularly important role fueling this demand. One is an increased emphasis on performance accountability, and the other is a growing expectation for stakeholder participation in M&E to foster learning and ownership.

Increasingly, programs, projects, and related initiatives are being gauged by what difference they make. Stakeholders, whether program donors, management or recipients, want to be to be assured that interventions are well-planned and resources used efficiently and effectively to achieve longer-term outcomes that have sustainable impact over time. This trend has been heightened by economic pressures and increased competitiveness that has affected all sectors of the economy—private, public, and civic. For instance, in international development, public agencies and NGOs have increasingly been asked by donors to demonstrate their Value for Money (VfM) to maximize the impact of each dollar spent on programming (e.g., DFID, 2011; Emmi, Eskiocak, Kjennerud, Rozenkopf, & Schatz, 2011). As the World Bank conveys:

> There are constant and growing pressures on governments and organizations around the world to be more responsive to demands from internal and external stakeholders for good governance,

accountability and transparency, greater development effectiveness and delivery of tangible results. (Görgens & Kusek, 2009, p. 1)

As the demand for performance accountability has grown, so has the demand for more effective and efficient practices to assess the impact of programming. It is no longer enough to ensure that interventions are designed with frameworks to manage inputs, activities, and outputs. Expectations are high for M&E that provides reliable and useful information for performance feedback and reporting to demonstrate long-term as well as short-term results. Consequently, there has been an increased demand for improved capacity, such as M&E training, to meet these expectations for M&E.

The second trend for greater stakeholder participation in M&E has a historical precedence over the last 40 years of lessons from participatory research and practice in development and community-based initiatives: "Human development is development *of* the people *for* the people *by* the people" (UNDP, 1993, p. 3, emphasis in the original). It is now widely accepted that if social initiatives are to bring about meaningful change, they need to meaningfully involve the very people whose lives they seek to change. Building local capacity fosters greater understanding, ownership, and ultimately sustainability of public and social programs. In turn, this contributes to performance accountability to deliver lasting results.

The spotlight on participation has been unmistakable in both the literature and practice of evaluation.[5] It would be hard to find a book or guideline on evaluation that does not include a section on the importance of and recommendation for stakeholder consultation and involvement. Some of the most influential approaches to evaluation, such as Utilization-Focused Evaluation (Patton, 2012) and a range of collaborative approaches to evaluation (Cousins, Whitmore, & Shulha, 2013), are premised on the importance of stakeholder engagement in determining the questions and type of information gathered, its analysis, and how it can used in the future.

Likewise, the focus on greater participation has had a significant impact on the practice of M&E. As stakeholders take a more active role in decision-making and resource allocation, they have not only become more involved in identifying their own needs and designing interventions, but also in determining, monitoring, and assessing the measures of success. For instance, **Figure 1.3** illustrates a cartoon messaging a more inclusive approach to M&E in the M&E guidelines of the International Federation of Red Cross and Red Crescent Societies (IFRC, 2011a).

In international development, the attention on participation has given rise to what is called Participatory Monitoring and Evaluation (PME) (e.g., Estrella & Gaventa, 1998; Estrella et al., 2000). PME challenges the once conventional approach to M&E that is conducted by external experts and prioritizes accountability requirements of funding

---

5. It is beyond the scope of this book to do justice to the scholarly research and practical guidance in this area, but examples include works such as PRIA (1981), Feuerstein (1986), Guba and Lincoln (1989), Rubin (1995), Jackson and Kassam (1998). A comprehensive, scholarly review of research on participatory and collaborative approaches to evaluation can be found in Cousins and Chouinard (2012).

FIGURE 1.3 IFRC Cartoon for Participatory M&E

Source: Drawn by Julie Smith for IFRC. IFRC (International Federation of Red Cross and Red Crescent Societies). (2011). *Project/programme monitoring and evaluation (M&E) guide.* Geneva: IFRC Planning and Evaluation Department.

agencies and policymakers (Estrella & Gaventa, 1998, p. 12). When M&E becomes more inclusive it supports more than reporting and auditing; it builds social capital and responsibility as stakeholders reflect upon and learn from their own experience, using this to make and own decisions about their future.

> Participation is increasingly being recognized as being integral to the M&E process, since it offers new ways of assessing and learning from change that are more inclusive, and more responsive to the needs and aspirations of those most directly affected. (World Bank, 2014a)

The trend toward and lessons from stakeholder participation in M&E are not limited to international programming. The scholarly literature on capacity building and training related to M&E is growing,[6] and most would agree that M&E will be more effective when it is done *with* rather than *to* program stakeholders. Communities, community-based organizations, public agencies, elected officials, and other stakeholders in both "developed" and "developing" countries have long been involved

6. For example: Adams and Dickinson (2010); Bakken, Nunez, and Couture (2014); Barnette and Wallis (2003); Clinton (2014); Cooksy (2008); Cousins and Bourgeois (2014); Darabi (2002); Davis (2006); Kelly and Kaczynski (2008); Kingsbury and Hedrich (1994); LaVelle and Donaldson (2010); Lee, Wallace, and Alkin (2007); Orr (2010); Preskill and Boyle (2008); Preskill (2008); Rotondo (2012); Trevisan (2002; 2004)

in and developed systems to track and assess their work (whether or not they called it "M&E"). As Preskill and Boyle (2008, p. 443) express for ECB,

> Seeking to enhance stakeholders' understanding of evaluation concepts and practices, and in an effort to create evaluation cultures, many organizations have been designing and implementing a variety of strategies as a means of helping their members learn about and engage in evaluation practices.

Later in this book, we will look more closely at the demand for M&E training during the training analysis. While performance accountability and stakeholder participation are fundamental considerations, there can be other factors contributing to training demand according to the specific context. Whatever the reasons, the demand for M&E training is an important determinant of the potential for M&E training and its transfer: the higher the demand, the more likely stakeholders will be receptive to and supportive of M&E training and M&E practice afterward. It is worth noting that M&E training itself can help shape people's attitudes toward and thus demand for M&E.

1.4 Who Provides M&E Training?

Terminology Tip
Trainer or Facilitator?

We often use the terms "trainer" and "facilitator" interchangeably when, in fact, there are some differences. A trainer has expert knowledge and experience in a particular subject area that trainees need—for example, M&E knowledge and experience. A facilitator may not necessarily have that knowledge but helps trainees learn from each other and solve problems, drawing upon existing knowledge and skills within the group. Sometimes the difference is framed to say that trainer is a content expert, while a facilitator is a process expert (e.g., Barbazette, 2006, p. 85). However, we contend that it is not so black and white and will depend on the training context. *We chiefly use "trainer" in this book because people attending M&E training typically lack and thus are seeking M&E knowledge and understanding.* However, this does not discount that there may be experience within the group to draw upon, and good trainers use facilitation techniques to create an active learning climate in which knowledge is discovered through discussion and practical activities. Therefore, we will also use the term facilitation, as this is very much part of M&E training.

In Chapter 5 we will take closer look at what makes a good M&E trainer, but for now we want to clarify how we will be using "trainer" in the book. For the most part, we use trainer to broadly refer to those providing M&E training, recognizing that other terms are often used. Thus, we want to clarify that this usage is often for the sake of convenience and brevity. In actuality, those involved in providing training encompasses a wide range of people, as diverse as the contexts where M&E training is provided. Training providers come from the public, civic, and private sectors, including community, government, educational, nonprofit, health care, corporate, and professional organizations.

As we have already seen, there are various aspects of M&E training, and the people involved can range from one trainer who oversees the entire training process to a number of people who focus on different parts (i.e., in a large organization where a high degree of specialization is possible). While job titles may not literally include trainer or training and roles and responsibilities can vary, there is an assortment of people who participate in providing or supporting training. Even community members and other recipients of M&E training are increasingly included in developing training plans and other aspects of training. While not exhaustive, the word cloud in **Figure 1.4** provides a snapshot to remind readers of the breadth and diversity of people who can be involved in providing training.

FIGURE 1.4 People Potentially Involved in M&E Training

1.5 What Kind of M&E Training?

M&E training can take many shapes and forms. Ultimately, the kind of training provided will depend on a variety of contextual (systemic) considerations, such as the training needs, content, learners' profile, trainers' experience, available time, and resources. We will explore this in more detail in later chapters, but for now we want to look at five aspects of M&E training that will help clarify the focus and scope of this book for readers.

1. Program and project M&E training

This book focuses primarily on M&E for programs, projects, and related interventions. While there are differences between programs and projects, usually in relation to scale and scope (programs tend to be larger, consisting of multiple projects), the commonality is that they are planned interventions, typically with objectives, indicators, and within a defined time frame, budget, and other performance parameters. For our purposes, the basic principles for good M&E (and related training) are the same for programs and projects.

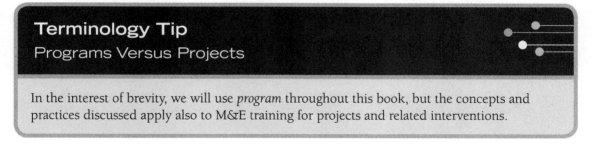

Terminology Tip
Programs Versus Projects

In the interest of brevity, we will use *program* throughout this book, but the concepts and practices discussed apply also to M&E training for projects and related interventions.

Programs are designed and implemented for different stakeholders and purposes in all sectors for society—public, civil, and private. This book was largely written with M&E training for social programs in mind, designed and implemented to improve social conditions, such as development, health care, and education. However, we believe the concepts and practices can be applied to a variety of program contexts where objectives need to be monitored and evaluated for effective service delivery.

2. Short-term and long-term M&E training

This book can be used to guide the planning and delivery of M&E training of different duration, ranging from single-event training delivered in hours or days to a longer training program with sequenced activities delivered over weeks or months. As we will discuss, training duration will depend on the training needs, content, available time, resources, and other factors. Single-event training is often used to introduce a particular M&E topic, raise awareness, or address an immediate need. Ongoing training can explore more complicated topics and provide more repetition, practice, and feedback to reinforce learning; understandably, it also requires more time and resources in planning and delivery.

3. Face-to-face versus distant (e-learning) M&E training

There are a variety of training delivery options (media) available today, foremost being traditional, face-to-face training (e.g., classroom based) versus training provided through e-learning (e.g., technology based, such as online training). We have written this book primary for in-person instructional settings, where face-to-face interaction is possible. However, many of the concepts we discuss are also useful for providing distance, e-learning training. While in-person training remains the most popular medium for training delivery (ASTD, 2013), to ignore the potential of e-learning in the 21st century would be a mistake. E-learning offers a range of possibilities for M&E training, whether as a complement to enhance in-person training delivery or an alternative that better meet training needs. Therefore, while our focus is largely in-person training, you will also find considerable attention given to e-learning in this book (especially in Chapter 2).

4. Organizational versus non-organizational M&E training

There is no one setting for M&E training, and throughout this book we will refer to two major types of M&E training contexts. **Organizational training** refers to M&E training provided to organizations, communities, or other group entities for a specific program or as part of their overall capacity building for future programming. In addition to individual learning goals, training objectives for organizational training also target outcomes for the specific organization or institution. **Non-organizational training** refers to M&E training provided to individuals who are independent of any organization or unaffiliated with the same organization or group (although a few may be from the same organization); for instance, independent learners attending training for their own personal development goals or coming from different organizations where they intend to apply what they have learned.

Figure 1.5 provides some examples of organizational and individual training. However, we want to stress that we use this distinction for the convenience of looking at M&E training in this book. In reality, the boundary between the two can be very blurred and fluid, with the outcomes of M&E training crossing over from organizational into individual training, and vice versa. For example, one of us

FIGURE 1.5 Organizational Versus Non-organizational M&E Training

Organizational Training

- A community workshop with a program implemented by a community-based organization.
- A training program for staff with a public agency as part of its human resource development strategy.
- As overview of M&E for school administrators supporting school programs in a school district.
- A series of training for program managers for a regional health care program implemented by an international NGO.

Non-Organizational Training

- A professional development workshop offered by a M&E professional, consultant, training company or firm.
- An online M&E certificate course offered by a training institute or learning center.
- Series of training workshops or short courses offered by a training institute, learning center, evaluation association (VOPE).
- Training program offered as part of a continuing education from a university or community college.

has been involved in extensive evaluation capacity building (ECB) work in India in recent years that took the form of an integrated approach involving workshops that were synchronized with ongoing evaluation work at critical junctures (e.g., planning, instrument development, data processing, and analysis). This multiyear initiative uniquely contributed to both organizational- and individual-level ECB because many of the individuals involved were not employed by the host organization.[7]

We distinguish these two types of training settings because they can have different and considerable implications for M&E training. For instance, in an organizational setting, training objectives and available information (e.g., about the staff and training needs) may allow for and require more detailed and elaborate planning as part of a larger capacity-building strategy to meet and sustain organizational strategic goals. In contrast, such information and the rigor required may not be available when planning training for individuals unaffiliated with the same organization (see **Box 1.3**). Related, the potential to evaluate and follow up training will typically be higher in an organizational setting, where it is often easier to access trainees after training versus training with individuals coming from different places. These and other differences between these two training types will be important to consider as they affect the planning and delivery of M&E training.

---

7. For more information, see http://www.ssatcfund.org/

5. Inclusive M&E training

> Training everyone accepts the premise that if we are to realize the promise of mainstreamed evaluation, everyone must have some basic knowledge and appreciation of evaluation. . . . We already have programs in place to teach evaluation skills for the select few who intend to conduct or manage evaluations, but that does not fully meet the need because these are not the only groups with a claim or responsibility to participate in or conduct evaluation. (Barnette & Wallis 2003, pp. 53–54)

Although the above quote speaks to evaluation, we believe it also applies to the M in M&E. As we have already discussed, there is a growing demand to build the capacity of different stakeholders to participate in M&E. Increasingly, M&E is evolving from a specialized pursuit of professionals or technical specialists to a more inclusive practice involving a wider assortment of stakeholders. Therefore, this book is written to support M&E training for a broad range of people, varying in level of M&E knowledge and experience from beginner to advanced and varying in motivation and purpose for training from people who need to perform M&E

BOX 1.4
Example Learners for M&E Training

- **Community members** or intended "beneficiaries" of a program intervention so they can better understand and participate in M&E processes

- **Project team members** or other partners who need some understanding of M&E to perform their responsibilities

- **Program management** who need to oversee and manage a program's M&E system, uphold quality assurance, and ensure reporting is evidence based and useful

- **Organizational senior leadership**, HR managers, or other members who need a better understanding and appreciation of M&E to support it within the organization

- **M&E experts** or professionals who needs an in-depth understanding to lead the development and implementation of M&E systems, conduct evaluations, and provide technical assistance

- **University or continuing education students** interested in M&E to complement their professional background for career purposes

- **Professional trainers** or facilitators who want to better understand M&E to train others

to those seeking an understanding to support others performing M&E. **Box 1.4** highlights some examples to illustrate the range of potential learners for whom this book can be used to provide M&E training.

Inclusive training encompasses not only trainees but also those involved in supporting M&E training. Stakeholder engagement is an important way to build demand so M&E training is owned and supported. Stakeholder participation is more than just consultation, but a meaningful opportunity for people to provide input and become involved in various aspects of M&E training. Who are M&E training stakeholders? They are the individuals or groups with a direct or indirect role or interest in M&E training. Foremost this includes the trainees but can also include a range of other people depending on the training context: for example, program managers and staff, volunteers, community members, sponsors and donors, support agencies and partner organizations, public workers, elected officials, and the general public. We will revisit the importance of engaging key stakeholders in training throughout this book.

1.6 CHAPTER SUMMARY

In this chapter we provided a road map for the book and laid out some foundational ideas that will be important as the reader moves forward. We will build upon and elaborate these ideas throughout the book, but some important summary points of this introductory chapter are the following:

- M&E training makes a difference when it is useful and used. Therefore, it is important to plan, deliver, and follow up training with attention to training transfer—the ability of trainees to meaningfully apply learning after training.

- Rather than threatening or boring, M&E training can be enjoyable and engaging, inspiring participants to learn and practice M&E.

- Training is likely to make a positive difference when it is systematic; planned, implemented, and evaluated in a coherent, ordered, cyclic manner.

- Systems thinking helps understand the interrelated and dynamic components of systematic training and the larger context in which it is provided. M&E training does not happen in isolation and will have a unique configuration of different factors that change over time and should be carefully considered to achieve and sustain training results. It is intentional and conducted to meet specific needs, yet it should remain flexible and adaptable to changing needs and unanticipated outcomes.

- Monitoring and evaluation are two distinct but interrelated processes. Monitoring is the routine collection of information to *describe* what is happening, whereas evaluation is episodic to *judge* how well it happened and what difference it made. Both contribute to learning, inform decision-making, and uphold accountability for effective program (and project) delivery.

- M&E is part of a results-based management (RBM) system, based on clearly defined and measurable results (objectives), and the methodologies, processes, and tools to achieve those results. Therefore, M&E training often includes other related processes as part of a program's overall RBM.

- Two important trends that have contributed to the demand for M&E training are increased expectations for performance accountability and greater stakeholder participation in M&E to support learning for and ownership of program goals.

- In addition to trainers who deliver M&E training, there are a variety of additional people who may support M&E training and therefore use this book, ranging from subject matter experts and instructional designers to program managers and donors.

- This book was written for M&E training of different duration for programs and projects, (which we will refer to as "programs" throughout the book for brevity). While the focus is on face-to-face training, we also give considerable attention to distance and e-learning because of their importance as a source of learning for M&E training.

- An important distinction to make for M&E training is whether it is organizational or non-organizational training. Organizational training is for organizations, communities, or other group entities, whereas non-organizational training targets individuals who are independent of or affiliated with different organizations or groups.

- When training builds understanding, people are more likely to become involved in, support, and own M&E practice. Therefore, this book is written to support M&E training for a broad range of people with different levels of understanding and involvement in M&E.

1.7 RECOMMENDED RESOURCES

For readers interested in learning more about systems thinking, Peter Senge is a prominent thinker in the field. In addition to his influential book, *The Fifth Discipline: The Art and Practice of the Learning Organization*, he has authored two field books on systems thinking, and there is a concise overview on the subject by Senge on the website of the Society for Organizational Learning (2015, webpage *Systems Thinking*) as well as other related resources. The website of the Free Management Library (2015) also provides a useful introduction to *Systems Thinking, Systems Tools and Chaos Theory*, and the website of the Donella Meadows Institute (2015) on *Systems Thinking Resources*.

We highly recommend the work of Bob Williams for understanding systems thinking, not only for its clarity but also its practical application to M&E, as Williams is himself an evaluator: *Systems Concepts in Action: A Practitioner's Toolkit* (Williams and Hummerlbrunner, 2009) and *Wicked Solutions: A Systems Approach to Complex Problems* (Williams and van 't Hof, 2014). For the field of evaluation, we recommend four books that incorporate a systems approach to evaluation: Hargreaves (2010), Morell (2010), Patton (2011), Williams and Imam (2007). USAID (2015a) offers a series of podcasts as part of their Systemic M&E initiative, and we also recommend *Dealing with Complexity Through Planning, Monitoring & Evaluation* (Ongevalle, Maarse, Temmink, Boutylkova, & Huyse, 2012). In Chapter 6, we summarize additional recommended resources related to systems thinking for instruction design and training.

On the topics of RBM, M&E, and participatory M&E, we recommend the following resources, all freely available online. For RBM, readers can refer to the comprehensive publication from the World Bank, *Ten Steps to a Results-Based Monitoring and Evaluation System* (Kusek & Rist, 2004) and the United Nations Development Group, *Results-based Management Handbook* (UNDG, 2011). On the topic of M&E, readers can refer to the concise overview by Chaplowe (2008), *Monitoring and Evaluation Planning*, which is also summarized in a 20-minute webinar available as part of the AEA Coffee Break Webinar series (Chaplowe, 2012). Also developed by Chaplowe, we recommend the *IFRC Project/Programme Monitoring and Evaluation Guide* for a more comprehensive but user-friendly overview on the topic (IFRC, 2011a). For further reading on participatory M&E (PM&E), we recommend *Who Counts Reality? Participatory Monitoring and Evaluation*, by Estrella and Gaventa (1998) and the edited volume, *Learning from Change: Issues and Experiences in Participatory Monitoring and Evaluation* for a more thorough discussion on the subject (Estrella et al., 2000). We also steer readers to the valuable web portal on PM&E from Wageningen University (2015).

Finally, we point out to readers that many of the online resources we recommend at the end of Chapter 2 for M&E training and capacity building will also lead to a host of publications on the topics of RBM, M&E, and PM&E.

CHAPTER 2

The Training Landscape

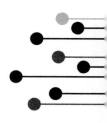

We could have titled this chapter, "The *Changing* Training Landscape," as technological innovations such as e-learning are dramatically transforming the training industry. Today there is an assortment of delivery options (media) for training, and we believe it is important to understand this menu of possibilities to make informed decisions that best cater to training needs. We begin by looking at what distinguishes training relative to other forms of education, situating it within an education continuum spanning formal, nonformal, informal, and incidental education. We then discuss three broad categories of training to consider for M&E according to how training is delivered:

1. Face-to-face training

2. Distance and e-learning training

3. Blended training

Our discussion is succinct, but we try to cover key considerations for different training delivery media, and we list at the end of the chapter additional resources and examples. As we shall see, different delivery options for training can be used in conjunction with or as an alternative to live, in-person workshops. A systems perspective to training acknowledges that trainings occur in contexts where multiple other sources of learning occur. This, in turn, can better inform an integrated approach to training as part of a larger capacity-building strategy to achieve training objectives.

Learning Objectives

By the end of this chapter readers will be able to . . .

✓ Describe what distinguishes training as a source of learning

✓ Explain training in relation to other sources of education (formal, nonformal, informal, and incidental)

✓ Compare and contrast face-to-face, distance and e-learning, and blended approaches to training delivery

✓ Identify synchronous and asynchronous approaches to distance training

✓ Explain the effect of e-learning in training today

2.1 What Is a Training?

To a large extent, training is defined by its content and focus. For example, a training on project design (e.g., logframes), M&E planning, osurvey design, or leading a focus group discussion will each have a relevant curriculum and purpose. But what distinguishes training from other forms of education?

The *American Society for Training and Development* defines training as, "A process that aims to improve knowledge, skills, attitudes, and/or behaviors in a person to accomplish a specific job task or goal" (ASTD, 2014). This definition highlights an important aspect of training: Training is intentional, meaning it is organized and planned with a specific purpose in mind. For program M&E, training seeks to build an understanding, appreciation, and ability to apply concepts, practices, and tools for measuring and assessing change, which is intended to contribute to improved service delivery and accountability. In other words, it could be said that M&E training seeks to build the capacity to *measure* change to *effect* change. However, as we point out in Chapter 1, M&E is interrelated with other components of a RBM system and training, for it typically includes a variety of related knowledge, skills, and attitudes (KSAs).

Another key aspect of training is that it develops specific KSAs to be used immediately upon completion of the training. Training is generally more vocational and applied than formal education—"Education focuses on learning *about*; training focuses on learning *how* [emphasis added]" (Milano & Ullius 1998). This is an especially important distinction for M&E, which has developed more as a field of practice than a traditional academic discipline. While there has been an increase in dedicated university programs for M&E (see, for example, LaVelle & Donaldson, 2010), M&E typically appears as a specialization within traditional disciplines and applied domains (e.g., psychology, education, public health) rather than as a discipline in itself.

Consequently, there exists no set standard curriculum leading to a recognized M&E credential. This is changing as professional networks and associations for evaluation have developed standards, principles, ethics, and guidelines to uphold quality M&E, (e.g., the African, American, and European associations). One notable example is the *Canadian Evaluation Society* (CES, 2014), which has developed a professional designation called the Credentialed Evaluator that centers on verification that persons have undertaken the necessary educational and practical experiences necessary to become an evaluator (as opposed to exam-based certification). Such developments are important, as they can have significant consequences for the content and process of future M&E training.

To date there remains a lack consensus and agreement on M&E competencies and curriculum that characterizes other more traditional disciplines and fields of study. Instead, M&E training and objectives tend to be more tailored and practical to the specific contexts served. It often arises to meet the demand for KSAs sought after and outside of the formal educational setting, in response to real-world, on-the-job needs. Next time you are at a gathering of professionals with M&E experience, ask around to see how many of them gained their M&E knowledge through formal education versus on-the-job training and skill building.

2.2 Formal, Nonformal, Informal, and Incidental Education

....

Education is a broad concept for different experiences in which people can learn. One useful categorization to help situate training within education is that of formal, nonformal, informal, and incidental education (see **Figure 2.1**). These terms have been in use since the early 1970s in global education (Coombs, Prosser, & Ahmed, 1973; Faure et. al., 1972), and remain influential today (European Commission, 2006; Werquin, 2010). These distinctions help cultivate a systems perspective of training as part of a larger education context in which other sources of learning can be considered for developing an integrated training program to best meet learning needs.

Formal education

Formal education refers to the organized, systematic educational model we are familiar with in the classroom setting of schools, using a standard curriculum leading to a recognized credential, such as a high school or university diploma or degree. Learners are usually referred to as students and educators as teachers rather than instructors. In the field of evaluation, there are increasing opportunities for education in the formal setting (LaVelle & Donaldson, 2010). The formal approach to education plays an important role in preparing evaluation professionals, and offerings differ depending on this educational program and often area to which the evaluation will be used—for example, community health.

FIGURE 2.1 An Education Continuum

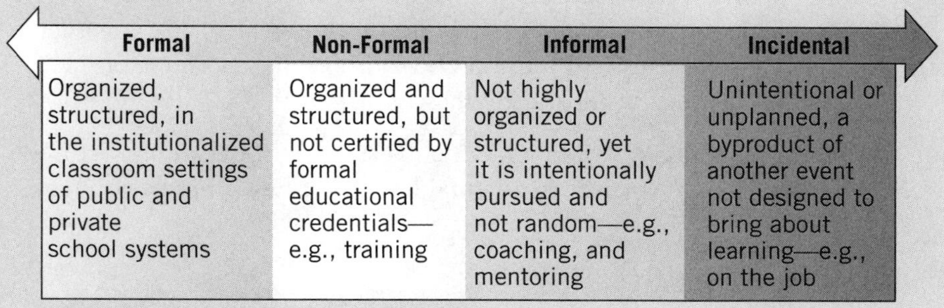

Formal	Non-Formal	Informal	Incidental
Organized, structured, in the institutionalized classroom settings of public and private school systems	Organized and structured, but not certified by formal educational credentials— e.g., training	Not highly organized or structured, yet it is intentionally pursued and not random—e.g., coaching, and mentoring	Unintentional or unplanned, a byproduct of another event not designed to bring about learning—e.g., on the job

Nonformal education

Nonformal education typically includes planned activities with learning objectives and timelines, but the curriculum is not as standardized as in formal education. Rather it is more adaptable to the learner's needs. Though the result is not a formal degree or diploma, nonformal education—such as professional trainings—can have industry recognition and often serves as a stepping stone for further formal education. Examples include training workshops, continuing courses, conference style seminars, and an array of e-learning options discussed later in this chapter. While nonformal education can be led by a qualified teacher, it can also include trainers, facilitators, instructors, and tutors with the appropriate and relevant experience. Related, recipients of nonformal learning are usually referred to as something other than students, such as trainees, participants, learners, and members.

Informal education

Informal education is not highly organized or structured and typically does not include formal curriculum and credits. However, it is important to stress that informal education is not random but intentionally pursued. Another important distinction is that the control of learning rests primarily in the hands of the learner (Marsick & Watkins, 1990). Examples include on-the-job self-training, coaching, and mentoring.

Incidental education

Incidental education refers to unintentional or unplanned learning that occurs as a byproduct of another experience not designed to bring about learning.[1] Also referred to as random learning (UNESCO, 1997), it is acquired through daily life experiences, whether at home, work, or play, and sources can range from a parent or peer to the mass media. It includes everyday observation, personal interactions, and problem solving that occur on-the-job or from supporting M&E processes.

As a nonformal form of education, M&E training often occurs after a break from formal education to acquire additional knowledge and skills for the real world, whether it be a specific job or volunteering for a community program. Formal education has broader goals, and the content covered is intended to be used in many different contexts. Some formal educational programs also refer to their evaluation course offerings as training, but for many people, especially non-M&E professionals, M&E education occurs through nonformal training outside the formal school system.

While the focus of this book is training, which is an intentional and structured approach to capacity development, incidental learning is increasingly receiving

---

1. Some include incidental learning as a type of informal learning (Marsick & Watkins, 1990), while others clearly separate the two (UNESCO, 1997). Whether taken together or separately, the distinguishing factor is the degree of intentionality; although unstructured, informal learning is usually intentional, whereas incidental learning is generally not, often being unconscious and taken for granted.

attention as an important source of learning not to overlook. Cousins and colleagues (Cousins, Goh, Clark, & Lee, 2004; Cousins & Bourgeois, 2014) make a distinction between direct (intentional) evaluation capacity building (ECB) and indirect ECB where learning occurs from actual involvement in evaluation processes (in contrast to planned learning events such as trainings). As Patton (2002) notes,

> Teaching isn't just a classroom activity, nor is training confined to workshops. Every interaction with an evaluation client, participant, stakeholder, and user is a teaching opportunity. (p. 93)

One popular concept that underscores the importance of incidental learning is the *70-20-10* model. Initially developed for business management (Lombardo & Eichinger, 2000),[2] this model posits that learning in the workplace is a blend based on a ratio of 70% from real life and on-the-job experiences, tasks, and problem solving; 20% from relationships, networks, and feedback; and 10% from training and other structured sources of learning (see **Figure 2.2**). This ratio is useful not as a rigid blueprint but as a reminder not to fixate on a unidimensional approach to capacity building

FIGURE 2.2   The 70-20-10 Learning Formula

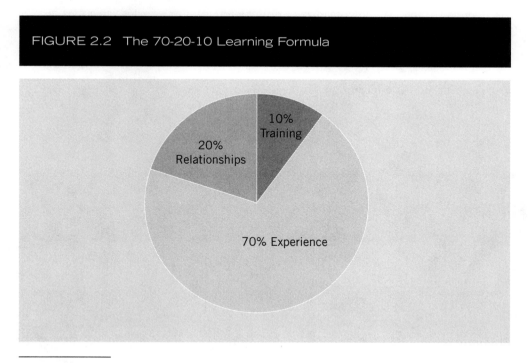

---

2. The 70-20-10 model was developed by was developed by Morgan McCall, Robert W. Eichinger, and Michael M. Lombardo at the Center for Creative Leadership, http://www.ccl.org/leadership.

(e.g., limited to episodic training) while overlooking other important sources of learning and knowledge.

Ultimately, the particular recipe or configuration for M&E learning will vary according to the specific capacity-building context and individual characteristics. The boundaries between formal, nonformal, informal, and incidental learning are often blurred, with important spillover for M&E learning. For instance, when training community members to enumerate household surveys using mobile phones, prior *incidental* familiarity with the mobile phone platform can be an important asset during the training. For our purposes, it is useful to consider these forms of education and learning as a continuum within which M&E learning can occur.

2.3 Training Types—A Brief Overview

Having discussed distinctions between education and training, we now turn to an examination of different options for training delivery. There is an array of training types available today according to the delivery medium, and a variety of ways to approach discussing the topic. We will organize our discussion into three major categories of training according to how they are delivered:

1. **Face-to-face (in-person) training**

2. **Distance & e-learning training**

3. **Blended training**

Terminology Tip
Training "Media" and "Medium"

Training or instructional media is the plural of medium and refers to the physical means or way of communicating learning to trainees. The primary medium is the instructional setting for training—for example, a physical classroom versus an online platform. Secondary training media refers to the particular technology used in training activities to communicate instructional messages to learners, such as PowerPoint slides, Prezi presentations, videos, or printed case studies.

Table 2.1 provides some examples of different training delivery media for each of these three instructional settings. It is worth noting that the tremendous diversity of training types requires a degree of flexibility in their presentation. Therefore, while we discuss e-learning with distance training, we should not equate the two. We look at them together because e-learning has had such a profound impact on distance learning, and it is really difficult to discuss the latter without also discussing e-learning. However, distance learning can occur without e-learning, and e-learning is often used in face-to-face training. We will take a closer look at this later in the chapter.

TABLE 2.1 Example Delivery Options for Training

Face-to-Face Delivery	Distance Delivery	
	Synchronous (real time)	Asynchronous (not real time)
• Instructor-led classroom • Training workshop • On-the-job training • One-on-one instruction • Coaching • Mentoring • Internships	• Video/audio conferencing • Teleconferencing • Online chatting • Interactive whiteboards (with sound) • Polling • Live webinars • Virtual (online) workshops	• Self-paced reading material (print or e-book) • Websites and online reading • Virtual presentations (slideshow) • Audio/video recording, podcasts • Recorded webinars (webcasts) • Automated mobile applications • Computer-based training (CBT) • Email and email lists • Online messaging • Online discussion & bulletin boards • Blogs & microblogs (Twitter) • Wikis
Blended Delivery = Combination of the Above Delivery Media		

In **Table 2.2**, we list key aspects of training to consider in relation to each of the three categories, reflecting how these primary delivery mediums affect key considerations for training. For example, the degree of interaction between trainees and trainers will have a considerable effect on the type of learning that can occur. During training analysis, such considerations will shape the training curriculum and activities selected to meet learning objectives.

TABLE 2.2 Comparing the Three Major Training Categories

Aspects	Distance Delivery—Asynchronous	Distance Delivery—Synchronous	Face-to-Face Delivery
Interaction	No real-time interaction—delayed questions and discussion	Real-time communication for questions and discussion	In-person, immediate interaction, with visual and linguistic cues
Hands-on learning	Low potential for hands-on, experiential learning	Higher potential for interactive and experiential learning	Most potential for hands-on, interactive, and experiential learning
Peer-collaborative learning	Lower potential for peer learning, building trust, rapport, and teamwork	Higher potential for peer learning, building trust, rapport, and teamwork	Highest potential for peer collaboration, building trust, rapport, and teamwork
Learning style	Greater appeal to people accustomed and with access to technology interface	Greater appeal to people accustomed and with access to technology interface	Greater appeal to people without familiarity or access to technology
Independent learning	Self-directed. Requires motivation and participation not guaranteed	Instructor-led, engaging, and higher potential to monitor participation	Instructor-led, engaging, and highest potential to monitor participation
Convenience	Participation at any time, place, and pace	Participation at any place, but restricted to scheduled time	Participation restricted in place and time
Cost	Cost includes delivery technology, which varies from low to high	Cost includes delivery technology, which varies from low to high	Cost includes travel, facility, and time away from one's job
Outreach	Greatest potential for outreach, access, and mobility	Greater potential for outreach, access, and mobility	Outreach and access limited to capacity of physical setting
Adaptability	Delivery is set in content, structure, and format	Delivery somewhat adaptable—for example, last minute changes	Delivery most adaptable—for example, last minute or on-the-spot changes
Duration	Typically delivered in shorter sessions or modules, for example, 10 to 60 minutes	Typically delivered in shorter sessions or modules, for example, 60 to 90 minutes	Typically longer in duration, for example, several hours to days

Blended Delivery = Combinations of the Above Delivery Options

It needs to be made clear that no method of educational provision is intrinsically better than another; rather, the appropriateness of a particular method or combination of methods selected is determined entirely by the context in which they are to be used and the educational needs they are intended to fulfil. (Butcher, 2011, p. 25)

As the above quote reflects, it is important to acknowledge there is more than one tool in the training toolbox. Showing up at the job with a large toolbox means that it will be easier to select the right tool for the specific job. Such an approach reinforces a systems outlook for training, where the selection of one or more delivery method is interdependent on a variety of context-specific factors, including the following:

- The M&E training content
- The trainees and their learning preferences and abilities
- The trainers and their facilitation preferences and abilities
- The available time and resources for training
- The particular setting for which training is to be used

The above considerations are largely addressed in the remaining chapters of this book, drawing upon principles of adult education, training analysis, design, and delivery. First, it is important to become more familiar with the various training types that populate the training landscape.

2.4 Face-to-Face Training

Face-to-face training, also called "in-person" training, is where the trainer and trainees are all physically together at the same place and time. There may be a temptation to refer to these as "live" training events, but as we shall see, with e-learning technology, distance training can also be live (synchronous). There are a variety of ways to deliver face-to-face training, and **Table 2.3** summarizes some key examples. We also note other sources of learning that relate to and can support face-to-face training.

The physical presence of everyone in face-to-face training, allowing for greater human interaction, is its main asset. Trainers and trainees can directly hear and see each other and thus better interpret and respond to body language and paralinguistic clues. Questions are often more forthcoming when people are present, and answers, discussion, and debate flow more naturally. Peer learning is reinforced when learners can hear and learn from each other questions and answers in person. Trainers can better

TABLE 2.3 Examples of Face-to-Face Delivery Options for M&E Training

Training workshop	Workshops are a form of interactive, group training that combines the strengths of an instructor-led, classroom-style training with hands-on, experiential learning opportunities. Emphasis is given to trainee participation, discussion, and applied, practical activities rather than passive listening to a lecture or presentation the whole time. In contrast to a lecture-style training activity, the workshop format usually takes more time to prepare and requires facilitation skills in addition to subject matter knowledge. There are a variety of methods for engaging participants—which we shall examine later in this book. Higher interaction requires smaller groups of people, for example, fewer than 50 participants.
Instructor-led classroom	Traditional, instructor-led training (ILT) in the classroom typically uses lecture, storytelling, slides, overhead projector, and blackboard and whiteboard, often accompanied by training materials in print. These are useful when one-way knowledge delivery is a priority, and participant interaction is usually limited to questions and answers. Limited interactions allows this format to accommodate larger groups of people, for example, 50 or more.
On-the-job training	OJT occurs while the learner is engaged in performing the actual tasks needed in the real world. It differs from on-the-job (incidental) learning because it is intentionally planned, provided under the guidance of an experienced colleague (often the supervisor). It can be very structured, as with a formal apprenticeship or internship, or limited to a period of planned observation and modelling. For our purposes, OJT is important to consider because it can complement and follow up an M&E workshop for learning transfer. Also, in addition to applying technical knowledge, it allows learners to cultivate "softer" skills, such as communicating with others and navigating political and organizational cultures inherent to any M&E context (Trevisan, 2002).
One-on-one instruction	One-on-one training is commonly used to teach specific skills new for the learner, such as how to use a software. It can be planned or occur when the particular need arises for the learner to apply the new skill. The delivery is tailored to the individual and specific task and is usually quicker than group training, but outreach is obviously limited to one learner. One-on-one instruction can be part of a coaching or mentoring approach and can be a useful supplement to group training when longer instruction is required.
Coaching & mentoring*	Both coaching and mentoring are intentionally planned, usually one-on-one and ongoing rather than a specific training event. Coaching tends to be short term and task oriented, providing constructive advice, feedback, and guidance for improving performance. Mentoring is longer term and more relationship orientated, emphasizing a relationship with the mentor that stresses mutual trust for more than task learning but also for personal and professional development for the future. Both coaching and mentoring can be valuable complements for training follow-up and also as a source of referral to training.
Other important sources	Some other sources of in-person learning that can complement or coincide with an organized training include (a) *apprenticeships*, a formal program of training in the

workplace, often meeting requirements for recognized licensing for a particular trade or career; (b) *internships*, which also provide job experience for professional careers but can be less structured and supervised; (c) *employee orientation* and *performance appraisals* to introduce employees to and appraise job responsibilities, organizational expectations, policies, procedures, and culture; (d) *technical assistance* to support specific needs of a program or site; and (e) *exchange visits* between M&E stakeholders to share experience, feedback, lessons learned, and new perspectives. Weaving such face-to-face approaches into an integrated approach to training can better ensure learning transfer and learner acquisition of KSA.

* We include coaching and mentoring in our discussion of face-to-face training, as this is a common means source of delivery, but it is important to recognize the it can also be conducted through distance delivery.

capture and hold someone's attention and see if trainees are confused, lost, or not paying attention (e.g., checking their email, twitter feeds, or texts). The physical proximity also allows trainees to demonstrate and trainers to verify if learning is occurring, allowing training to be more readily be customized on the spot to meet learners' needs.

Another key advantage of the face-to-face training is that it can provide a more hands-on, practical experience closer to the real world where the training is to be used. M&E can be theoretical, and it is helpful when training employs experiential methods that involve interaction and problem-solving learning (Lee, Wallace, & Alkin, 2007; Trevisan, 2002; see also discussion in Chapter 4). This includes interpersonal skills such as listening, explaining, and negotiation. Another feature of in-person training is that for many it is more motivating and engaging to learn with others present. They prefer the support and reassurance provided by the physical presence of a trainer and peers and can be more compelled to participate and perform well in front of others. Social needs are better fulfilled in person, and it is usually easier to build trust, rapport, and connection in a face-to-face setting.

The physicality of the face-to-face training is also its greatest shortcoming. Training delivery is restricted in time and place to the physical (classroom) setting. Not only might this be inconvenient to participants (and the trainer), outreach is also limited to the physical capacity of the room or physical learning setting. Therefore, the cost per trainee for an in-person training event is typically higher than most e-learning and other distance training options discussed below. Costs include those associated with the trainer, facility, materials, and may also include transportation, accommodation, and time away from the job.

2.5 Distance Training & e-Learning

In contrast to face-to face training, distance training does not need to take place in the same location as the trainer (Moore & Kearsley, 2012). It can be self-directed or instructor lead (directed) and can be a powerful complement to live, face-to-face learning. Distance education has been around for some time, including learning through self-paced print, correspondence courses, and the use of radio and television (Cuban, 1986). However, with computer and online technologies, the options and practice of distance training have skyrocketed with e-learning. In Appendix 2.1 for this chapter, we summarize some of the different possibilities available today for distance delivery of M&E training.

Terminology Tip
"Self-Directed" Versus "Directed" Learning

A "self-directed" approach to training, also called self-paced, is one where the trainees take responsibility for their learning, which can include the content, pace, time, and location of the learning. It is an important approach to learning for many types of distance training. "Directed" (or instructor-led) learning is when the trainer takes responsibility for the delivery of the training. In addition to face-to face training, this is also used for certain types of distance training, whether correspondence or online.

For many, e-learning means learning that occurs over the Internet. However, we adopt a more inclusive use of e-learning to include the range of possibilities to deliver training by combining electronic ("e-") media and information and communications technology (ICT) (e.g., ASTD, 2014; Naidu, 2006). Therefore, in addition to training that is delivered through the Internet, (i.e., online training; web-based training or WBT; and Internet-based training or IBT), we use e-learning to include other forms of electronic training delivery not reliant on the Internet: for example, computer-based training (CBT), digital recordings, teleconferencing, and television. As already noted, it is important to understand that e-learning does not equate with distance learning, but we discuss them together as it has become such an integral part of how distance learning is delivered. In short, whatever the technological interface, when it is the primary medium for training delivery instead of face-to-face instruction, it falls within the domain of distance training.

Technological innovation and training delivery

> Information technology is a game change. . . . Today's knowledge revolution isn't about how much information is available. It's about how fast knowledge can travel through vast, connected networks of people— and how it can grow exponentially. (Oblinger, 2012, pp. v & 4)

Indeed, technological innovation is rapidly transforming the field of training and education as a whole (e.g., Collins & Halverson, 2009; Oblinger, 2012). In his book *The E-learning Revolution*, Sloman (2002) presents 21 propositions for training in the era of e-learning, the first of which is, "The internet changes everything, including training." According to the *American Society for Training & Development*, there has been a steady increase in the adoption of technology for training delivery and a gradual decline in the use of traditional instructor-led classroom methods (ASTD, 2013).

As new technologies transform our daily lives, it is inevitable that they will likewise transform training, especially the appeal and progress in distance training. A new "always on" generation of adult learners has emerged that is always online and accustomed to learning on-the-go (Ally, 2009). For such people, the use of new technologies used in e-learning will not be alienating but a familiar format from both formal and informal learning that people come to expect. Technological innovation and its demand in today's lifestyle are pushing the boundaries of more traditional approaches to in-person training.

However, e-learning is not a technological "magic bullet" for training, nor is it a substitute for face-to-face training. Regardless of the technology, there are still important considerations regarding the quality of content and what delivery medium is best suited for the trainees, trainer, and the particular training context. In one study, *The No Significant Difference Phenomenon*, a review of 355 reports concluded that there was no significant difference on the quality of learning between distance and face-to-face approaches (Russell, 2001). There is often a "preoccupation" with new technological at the expense of how to best use technology (Moore & Kearley, 2012).

We will take a closer look at the pros and cons of e-learning and distance training as a whole, but first it is useful to familiarize ourselves with some of the major delivery options used in distance training.

Asynchronous and synchronous training delivery

The effectiveness of e-learning or any distance training varies largely according to the delivery technology used—that is, the difference between a correspondence training program through mail (postage) versus one delivered live, online, using video conferencing technology. **Table 2.4** lists some of the major delivery mediums that are often used for distance training and education and also to complement face-to-face training. In the Appendix 2.1 for this chapter, we provide more detailed descriptions of how each medium can be used for M&E training. While not exhaustive, this inventory reflects the wide range of options available for distance and e-learning training, and it is important to stress that these delivery media can and are also used in face-to-face training.

TABLE 2.4 Examples of Distance Delivery Media for M&E Training		
• Self-paced reading material	• Virtual presentations	• Computer-based training (CBT)
• Correspondence courses	• Virtual (online) workshops, webcasts, & webinars	• Social media and networking
• Digital audio/video recording	• M-(mobile) learning	• Websites, blogs, & microblogs
• Open educational resources (OER)	• Virtual learning environment (VLE)	• Virtual (online) communities

When considering the array of possibilities for distant delivery of training for M&E, it is helpful to understand the distinction between synchronous and asynchronous training delivery. These terms are commonly used with e-learning, but they are also helpful to categorize other distance learning methods.

- **Asynchronous training** refers to training with no real-time interaction between the trainer and trainees. It does not require people to be online or in-person at the same time. Trainees can access materials at any time, and participate at times and locations according to their own choosing. Asynchronous training includes self-paced lessons or instructor-guided assignments using printed materials, computer-based training (CBT), or online recordings of webinars, webcasts, and podcasts. While not real time, participant interactions and involvement can be supported through email, electronic mailing lists, discussion boards, blogs, and even wikis. Asynchronous learning can be used for stand-alone training, but it is also used to supplement synchronous and in-person training.

- **Synchronous training** is delivered in real time, with live interaction between one or more participant at the same time but not place. Participants can ask questions, discuss, share, and work collaboratively in real time. The level of interaction depends on the technology used and includes video and teleconferencing, webinars, virtual workshops, and chats with a messenger service. Synchronous online training resembles face-to-face training in that participants need to log in at the same time, but the meeting place is an online space rather than an in-person setting.

Ultimately, the appropriateness and utility of asynchronous and synchronous training delivery will vary according to the specific training context and needs. We examine this more closely below, highlighting some key considerations for both distance and e-learning.

Distance and e-learning advantages

Distance training excels in its flexibility and convenience for both the trainer and trainee. It helps overcome the restrictions of time and space, which is particularly appealing for the busy adult learners of today's fast-paced society. It allows people to pursue learning without having to be away from home and job responsibilities and is usually designed to be completed in short chunks of time that can fit around one's daily schedule. While asynchronous training can be done any time and from anywhere, synchronous training needs to be scheduled (which can be challenging across time zones, jobs shifts, and personal schedules). Both reduce travel time and costs, and enrollments fees are generally cheaper than in-person trainings. In the work setting, there is the added benefit that employees are not taken away from their jobs as with an onsite training workshop.

The convenience factor of distance learning today is epitomized by "m-learning" (see Appendix 2.1). In technologically equipped settings, mobile devices are beginning to replace books and notes, with the added convenience of a compact, portable space for what otherwise required book bags and bookshelves to transport and store. Coffee shops, hotel lobbies, stations and, airports are increasingly filled with people tapping away on their smartphones or tablets. As technology speeds up life, the "nomadic" learner and worker travelling frequently from place to place is turning to mobile technology to access information and learning materials according to their schedule and location (Ally, 2009).

Distance training is also a cost-effective way to increase training outreach across multiple locations at one time. It is particularly effective for reaching people living in remote locations where schools, training programs, expertise, and libraries may otherwise be unavailable. It can address issues of equity, providing access to disadvantaged populations, such as handicapped or disable people unable to access in-location training. However, while training registration and attendance costs may be lower, the cost of owning the technology (e.g., computer and Internet access) can restrict access. Yet the technology is become more inexpensive as it advances. In developing countries, mobile phone technology has jumped digital divides, being more affordable than computers and practical than traditional phones dependent on physical cables. Such trends hold promise for m-learning delivery of distance training.

Monitoring learner participation in distance training is not as direct as with the interactions with in-person training. However, certain types of e-learning nevertheless offer some convenient means to monitor and track trainee participation. Online connectivity allows such features as poll questions and pre- and post-tests to be conducted to check trainee understanding. Similarly, other statistics can be used for the trainer, such as online attendance as well as participation in discussion boards, study groups, and so forth. More sophisticated, automated programs can be used with the computer to assess a learners' level and assign an appropriate training progression.

Another important distinction of distance training is that it is more self-directed for the learner, with greater control over the learning process, both in the choice and use of different learning sources. Learners can skim over content already mastered and devote more time to other areas requiring more attention. Related, some people find distance training less stressful and like that it is "discreet." It is especially well suited to people who feel uncomfortable in large groups, allowing them to progress at their own pace without feeling they will hold others back or have to wait for them. People have different learning preferences (see Chapter 4), and advances in e-learning technology offer a variety of different options to suit different people.

For the trainer, content can be easily standardized and reused for different learning groups in the future, whether in print, recorded, or online. Learners can be directed to appropriate information based on their needs, and online materials can be easily updated and revised with learners able to see the changes at once. Because delivery is not limited to location, it is effective for a long-term M&E training program over months or even years, or it can be used for the timely delivery of short tutorials to update or introduce new M&E topics, tools, and techniques or refresher lessons and guidance tips.

Distance and e-learning disadvantages

The primary shortcoming of distance training is that it cannot provide the degree of human interaction possible in face-to-face training. Thus, it does not fulfill social needs and skills in the same way as face-to-face. As such, face-to-face M&E training may be a better choice for building trust, teamwork, and ownership when working with stakeholders, such as a community or project team.

Interaction is a critical element for learning, and the success in distance learning is largely a function of high levels of interaction among peers and the trainer (Swan, 2003) that, in turn, is largely determined by the delivery technology used (Anderson & Elloumi, 2004; Moore & Kearsley, 2012). Technology has advanced such that many aspects a face-to-face training can be recreated virtually. However, online streaming is only a partial substitute for in-person visual and verbal cues. It is still more difficult than in-person training to facilitate discussion, respond to questions, and gauge learning and how well material is understood, making it hard to anticipate and directly respond to learning needs.

Related, limited human interaction affects the content and type of activities that can be used in distance training. It is more challenging to provide applied, hands-on practice that is closer to a real-life, interpersonal, tactile setting. Therefore, distance training tends to focus on developing cognitive skills (knowledge and critical thinking). As we shall see, experiential methods that use hands-on learning are particularly useful for engaging M&E learning.

While distance learning affords greater control over the learning process, this requires a greater degree of self-motivation and responsibility from learners, and may not be the best option for the people who procrastinate and have bad study habits. Some learners prefer the support and reassurance provided by the physical presence of a trainer and colleagues, and the impersonal interaction of distance learning can feel isolating. Written information can be miscommunicated or interpreted, advice or timely response to questions delayed, and learners may be intimidated or frustrated by the remoteness and the delivery technology used. And while many people are becoming accustomed to the technology used in e-learning, there many remain others who may not be comfortable or even familiar with learning online with a computer or handheld device.

Additional considerations for technology-based training delivery

The technological costs for distance learning can vary, depending on the specific delivery technology used. For more traditional distance learning, costs involve the development, printing, and postage of training materials (which are now often shared electronically). For e-learning, costs range from something as inexpensive as posting a blog or a recorded video online to designing an expensive computer-based training (CBT) program or online learning platform with multimedia graphic, video, and auditory features that respond to spoken word. For e-learners, there may also be associated costs to access a computer or mobile device, software, and reliable Internet bandwidth to receive materials and instruction. Furthermore, there is the added cost of adapting to changing technologies, such as replacing outdated or incompatible hardware and software. Nevertheless, the potential of outreach with online e-learning can offset such costs.

Another important consideration for e-learning is that it requires a very different organizational program and approach to traditional face-to-face training. For example, the development of an e-learning course may involve a whole team of specialists, including instructional designers, subject matter (content) experts (SME), web developers and media editors, course administrators, online facilitators and tutors, and technical support specialists.

A final consideration is that as the market for e-learning increases, so will its technological potential. Investment and innovation in even newer technologies will add more options in the future. *Distance training may not be a substitute for face-to-face training, but it is the trend that will continue to evolve and have a tremendous impact on how training is delivered.*

2.6 Blended Learning

Blended learning combines different delivery options to best meet the needs of the particular training context. The concept of combining learning media and methods has been around since students brought home books and homework for self-study. However, blended learning is most commonly used to refer to traditional classroom, instructor-led training that is supplemented with e-learning formats. (Bersin, 2004).

For our purposes, we will use blended learning broadly to refer to any time different delivery options are combined for training, whether electronic, printed, or in person.[3] Such an expanded interpretation of blended allows for different combinations of media and methods for more effective trainings. **Figure 2.3** illustrates how different delivery options can be used for a blended training program for organizational training.

Blended learning acknowledges that there is no one "recipe for successful training delivery." Such flexibility in delivery allows the trainer to better utilize time and resources according to need. For example, it can be very useful prior to a live workshop (whether in person or online) to provide learning resources beforehand—for example, pre-reading PDFs, online slideshows, or recorded webcasts. This allows trainees to become familiar with basic content or a case study so that the live training can devote more time to complex concepts, discussion, questions, and hands-on work. After training, additional resources can be used to reinforce training content and allow trainees to bridge learning to related topics.

A blended approach for M&E training is highly advantageous, reinforcing a systemic approach to training that recognizes and utilizes different sources of learning. This allows greater flexibility to adapt to training needs. It is worth noting again that the configuration of blended methods will depend on the trainees, trainers, time/resources, and the ultimate setting for which the training will be used—all forthcoming topics in the remainder of this book.

---

3. For example, the International NGO Training and Research Center (INTRAC, 2014a) uses blended learning to deliver M&E and other course remotely, combining webinar technology, Skype, and an online learning platform. Courses include online presentations, discussion, peer sharing and learning, self-directed work, and one-on-one coaching with the trainer.

FIGURE 2.3 An Example of a Blended Training Program

Pre-Training	Training Workshop	Post-Training Workshop
Professional review process recommends training **Pre-reading** provided by email (PDF) or website link—for example, organizational M&E guidelines or case study for in-person activities **Online virtual presentation** (slideshow) pre-assigned on M&E topic	**Experiential, hands-on activities,** using the case study for problem solving **Engaging video** of expert presentation for discussion **Video-conferencing** with in-field colleagues with **interactive whiteboard** **Blogs** for homework assignments and peer review/feedback	**On-the-job learning** Continued **mentoring** with possible **coaching** for targeted skills Online **community of practice** or **study groups**, including **discussion boards** for additional sharing and peer support **Webinars/webcasts** for additional guidance tips, updates, and new material
Preparatory concepts/knowledge	**Applied understanding/practice**	**Transfer and support**

2.7 CHAPTER SUMMARY

In this chapter we identified what distinguishes training as a source of M&E learning and then examined the variety of options and related considerations for training delivery. In short, training is not the "magic bullet" for M&E capacity building, and whether and how to train will largely depend on the M&E capacity building context. Additional summary points include the following:

- M&E training is an intentional process to improve knowledge, skills, attitudes and behaviors for measuring and assessing change as well as related practices in the overall of the RBM system.

- It is helpful to understand M&E in relation to other sources of learning, for which we discussed the categorization of formal, nonformal, informal, and incidental education.

  - Formal education refers to the educational model we are familiar with in the classroom setting of schools.

  - Nonformal education, which includes training, is planned and structured with curriculum but it is not standardized and does not lead to formal degrees as with formal education.

- Informal education, such as mentoring, is intentional but less organized and structured than nonformal education (e.g. without curriculum).

- Incidental education is when learning is an unplanned byproduct of an experience not intended for learning.

- There are a variety of delivery options for M&E training, which can be divided into three primary categories: (1) face-to-face (in-person) training; (2) distance & e-learning training; and (3) blended training, which combines face-to-face with distance and e-learning.

- We devote considerable attention to e-learning in this chapter as it is having a profound impact on the training industry and therefore is an important consideration as an alternative to face-to-face M&E training or for a blended approach to M&E training that complements face-to-face

delivery. However, e-learning is not a substitute for the level of interaction and degree of hands-on learning offered by face-to-face training.

- An important distinction for e-learning and distance training is between asynchronous versus synchronous training. Asynchronous training does not involve real-time interaction between the trainer and trainees (i.e., people do not need to be online at the same time), whereas synchronous training does involve real-time interaction, (i.e., it is live and allows live questions and answers).

- Each of the three primary delivery options (instructional settings) for M&E training has different advantages and disadvantages that should be considered in relation to specific training needs and contexts. For instance, the level or interaction and degree of hands-on learning required for the training content; the specific trainees and learning preferences; the specific trainers and facilitation preferences; and the convenience, cost, and outreach of the training delivery method.

2.8 APPENDICES

Appendix 2.1 Examples of Distance Delivery Media for M&E Training

Self-paced reading material	Books, workbooks, and guidelines remain effective sources of learning (this book included). In addition to print, reading material includes e-books and PDF files that can be easily disseminated on websites and as email and chat attachments. Reading material provided through the Internet, such as PDFs, are particularly well suited for the self-directed learner, as is printed material when electronic alternatives are unavailable or unaffordable. Preparatory reading is useful with live training (whether in person or online), allowing participants to familiarize themselves with basic content or a case study and the trainer to devote more time to complex concepts, discussion, questions, and application of concepts. Post-training readings can help reinforce training content and allow trainees to bridge learning to related topics.

Correspondence courses	E-learning has reinvigorated this long-standing approach to distance learning, which involves the exchange of learning materials, assignments, and tests through the mail and increasingly online. Instruction is usually on an individual basis, and progress is measured through assignments and exams returned to the instructor at the trainee's pace. Completion of a correspondence course depends on the learner's speed in mastering the assigned materials.
Digital audio/video recording	Digital recordings include CD, MP3, DVD, podcasts, video clips, and screencasts. They are asynchronous and therefore effective for one-way delivery of training content. Learners can pause, rewind, and view the recording at their own pace. Many people find recordings more engaging than print; a short, fun, educational video can be shown during an in-person training to lighten the mood, shift gears, and grab people's attention. Digital recordings are relatively quick and inexpensive to develop and easy to disseminate online. For instance, a simple webcam or digital camera can be used to record a lesson, guest speaker, or lecture and immediately posted on a personal or social networking website (e.g., YouTube or Vimeo). Recordings are useful for sharing updates, orientation, guidance tips, and other key messages. Video recordings are particularly useful for providing virtual instructions and demonstrations, such as modelling how to obtain consent for a household survey interview. A *screencast* is basically a "moving" screenshot of actions taking place on the computer screen using software, which can be handy to demonstrate how to complete an M&E spreadsheet, logframe, or operate software. Digital recordings are increasingly popular with learners for their convenience to download onto handheld devices, allowing people to multitask while learning, whether they are running at the gym, commuting to work, or doing laundry.
Virtual presentations	*Virtual presentations* are online, self-running (asynchronous) slideshows, often with voice narration and hyperlinks to other learning sources. They are effective for short training tutorials or to introduce content that can be further discussed and practiced in a face-to-face or synchronous setting. Virtual presentations are easy to make (e.g., using PowerPoint) and to upload to the Internet onto a personal or a social networking website (e.g., on SlideShare) for timely dissemination. Virtual presentations blend well with face-to-face trainings, allowing the trainer to introduce basic concepts prior to the in-person training and spend more face-to-face time on practical understanding and working with the concepts.
Webcast & webinars	Online presentations are a popular and powerful delivery tool for M&E training, either as a stand-alone option or in combination with other training methods. *Webcasts* are one-way broadcasts (e.g., TV), while *webinars* are interactive, allowing for questions, discussion, and debate through voice, text-based messages, or video chat. They are both useful to stream in live seminars, lectures, panel discussions, guest speakers, and debates. The can also be recorded and uploaded to the Internet for asynchronous viewing at any time. A good example of M&E webinars is the Professional Development eStudy Webinars of the American Evaluation Association (AEA, 2014). These webinars are delivered in 90-minute sessions and allow for attendees to send in questions and comment via chat during the live presentation.

(Continued)

(Continued)

Computer-based training (CBT)	The term *CBT* is used in many ways in the training industry.[4] We use it to refer to the asynchronous training delivered on a computer or handheld device (e.g. tablet or smartphone) without relying on online connectivity to operate it (in contrast to web-based training using the Internet). CBT is installed on a computer and fixed in its format and content. It is asynchronous but can use interactive courseware, including drill-and-practice, simulations, educational games, and problem solving. It is typically designed in linear, sequenced training modules that can be stopped, resumed, and paced according to the user's need. It can involve simple text-based programs or more multimedia training programs with graphic, video, and auditory features that respond to spoken word. It can even employ more sophisticated, three-dimensional experience through virtual reality, such as a flight simulator (although we are not aware this yet for M&E training).
M-(mobile) learning	M-learning is a subset of e-learning that occurs on mobile, electronic devices, including handheld computers, PDAs (Personal Digital Assistants), tablets, and mobile and smartphones. It includes software and mobile applications (apps) that provide "just-in-time" knowledge, immediate answers to specific questions, guidance tips, and feedback in real time when the learner needs it (Ally, 2009; FAO, 2011). It can employ just about any of the e-learning deliver methods included in this table as well as the expanding area of mobile apps. Learners can review training materials or correspond with instructors and other learners while commuting to work or sitting in a café, unconstrained by the physical location of a desktop computer. Content can be tailored according to learner preferences, including navigation, highlighting, and notes. M-learning also includes embedded training where the instruction is integral for operation of the mobile device and the software/application installed on it (e.g., software for on a mobile phone for collecting monitoring data). Below, we discuss m-learning further.
Virtual learning environment (VLE)	VLEs provide online space as resource and activity centers for learning. *Virtual classrooms* and *learning platforms* are two widespread examples of VLEs. They can host a range of asynchronous, self-directed resources, such as training curriculum, content, homework, tests, and other activities. They can also be used synchronously to host training events such as virtual classes, workshops, webinars, and webcasts. Interaction is enhanced with the use of Internet forums, such as blogs and discussion boards and study groups. VLE are useful for both self-directed and directed training and are a valuable supplement to face-to-face training, offering additional online support for both trainees and trainers. Many of the specific resources offered through VLE are individually discussed separately in this table. Moodle (2014) is a free, open-source software popular for developing e-learning platforms and classrooms.
Open educational resources (OER)	OER are free educational resources that anyone can access without concern for royalties or license fees.[5] They can be a valuable source for training, and be reused and adapted without permission from the copyright holder (Butcher, 2011, p. 5).[6] They are a form of resource-based learning (RBL) that includes course materials, textbooks, curriculum, maps, lecture notes, video, audio recording, and a variety of multimedia. One notable example is the OER Commons (2015), on which a search using the keyword "evaluation" had over 800 results. While they are most common on the Internet, OER can be paper based or computer based. An important subset of OER for training is Open CourseWare (OCW, 2014), which is a platform for sharing digital educational courses,

	syllabi, textbooks, lectures, presentations, and notes. *Massive Open Online Courses* are a type of Open CourseWare that is designed to allow unlimited, open participation through the Internet. Refer to the recommended resources at the end of this chapter for some examples of online education resources for M&E training.
Virtual (online) workshops	We use *virtual workshops* to refer to the range of online learning events that are planned and facilitated live (synchronously) to mimic the traditional instructor-led class or workshop. They are also called virtual classes or trainings as well as online classes, trainings, or workshops. Rather than one-way lectures, the virtual workshop allows for more group interaction for questions, discussion, and collaborative work and problem solving. This is achieved by integrating different types of synchronous tools, such as audio and video conferencing (e.g., with Skype, chat), interactive whiteboard, and application sharing. Group interaction can occur in smaller, online break-out rooms, with break-out groups reporting back to the plenary group. As virtual workshops are less animated than their face-to-face counterpart, they are shorter, with content presented in sessions or modules about 60 or 90 minutes. Virtual workshops are often supplemented with online discussion boards, study groups, and communities of practice.
Social media and networking	*Social media* includes an assortment of web-based technologies useful for delivering and supporting training. It is the use of websites and applications for sharing user-generated content (UGC)—e.g., email and messaging, social networking (e.g., Linkedin, Facebook), Internet forums and online communities, weblogs, social blogs, microblogging (e.g., Twitter), wikis (e.g., Wikipedia), photographs (e.g., Picasa), music and videos (e.g., Youtube), podcasts, webcasts, rating, and social bookmarking. Indeed, social media is a vast category, and we discuss some specific examples as they apply to training elsewhere in this summary table. Social media tools such as forums and wikis can be useful for tasks that require reflection and time to accomplish them, and asynchronous discussions can be useful to engage learners who are shy or lack language fluency to collaborate effectively in real-time conversations. Social media in increasingly becoming integrated into our lives, and some element of social media is usually involved in both in-person and distance training. For example, email is often used to promote or enhance training with reminders for upcoming events, sending out resources and assignments, soliciting follow-up to questions, and conducting training evaluations online.
Websites, blogs, & microblogs	Websites, blogs, and microblogs are forms of social media that are especially useful for M&E training, whether in person, distance, or blended. Websites provide a wealth of resources for both the trainer and trainee, ranging from downloadable PDFs to blogs, bulletin boards and recorded videos and webinars. For example, the *Monitoring and Evaluation News* website (MandE, 2015b) has pages devoted to M&E resources, events, surveys, training, and jobs (to name a few). Blogs (online journal entries posted on a web page) and microblogs (e.g., Twitter) are effective tools for trainers and trainees to share opinions, experiences, lessons, feedback, and resources. Both also can contain hyperlinks to other websites and resources. Blogs can be used for learners to submit feedback on each other's assignments during a training. M&E websites and blogs can be found on personal, organizational, and public websites. We have listed some examples of them and other online M&E resources at the end of this chapter.

(Continued)

(Continued)

Virtual (online) communities	A virtual community uses social media for people to network and share common interests, ideas, resources, experience, and expertise. This includes online (virtual) forums, communities of practice, and study and discussion groups. Interaction can be asynchronous; For example, participants post messages and discussion online using email lists, discussion, and message boards. Interaction can also be synchronous via audio and video conferencing or a chat room. Virtual communities are a relatively easy and inexpensive way to extend the value of self-paced print, self-directed e-learning, as well as synchronous e-learning and in-person trainings. Members are able to discuss learning topics, find answers to questions, work together on exercises, and assess and provide feedback to each other. A virtual community can be as simples as an email list or a platform of social networking websites, such as LinkedIn and Facebook, where many communities are devoted to M&E, training, and related topics. An online study group can be used for M&E trainees to work on a project case study, collaborating virtually in the project design and development of the M&E system. We have listed some examples of virtual communities at the end of this chapter.

[4]Related terms include computer-aided instruction (CAI), computer-assisted instruction (CAI), computer-based instruction (CBI).

[5]The concept emerged arose from a 2002 at a UNESCO forum to reduce the commodification of knowledge.

[6]OER licensing mechanisms vary, with Creative Commons (2015) being the best known.

2.9 RECOMMENDED RESOURCES

Readers will note that recommended resources for this chapter is relatively long compared to other chapters. This is because we want to highlight many of the valuable resources for distance and e-learning M&E training, which is an important focus of this chapter. We will refer to many of these recommendations elsewhere in the book, as they are an important resource to complement face-to-face training for a blended approach to M&E training.

Training overview

There is a wealth of general resources available on training. Three recommended books include *Approaches to Training and Development* (Laird, 2003), which provides a comprehensive overview, albeit geared toward business organizations; *Training Fundamentals* (Chan, 2010), which provides a more basic introduction to training, and *Training in Organizations* (Goldstein & Ford, 2002), which offers a more scholarly discussion of organizational training. Readers can spend days perusing general resources on training available on the Internet: One comprehensive, online resource that we recommend is the website, *Big Dog & Little Dog's Performance Juxtaposition* (Clark, 2015a). The website for the American Society for Training & Development (ASTD, 2015) is another valuable resource, including its useful *Online Glossary* for training.[7]

For readers interested in a more in-depth discussion on formal, nonformal, informal, and incidental education or learning, we recommend the freely available publication, *Classification of Learning Activities—Manual* (European Commission, 2006). For another look at different training types, the Massachusetts Institute of Technology's training and development website

7. Note that the ASTD is in the process of changing its name to the Association of for Training Development (ATD).

offers a very user-friendly *Training Delivery Guide*, which includes a *training delivery method matrix* to consider many of the different training options discussed in this chapter (MIT, 2015).

Distance and e-learning

As its title implies, the book *Distance Education: A Systems View of Online Learning* provides a comprehensive look at distance learning stressing a systems perspective (Moore & Kearsley, 2012). We found the following books, all freely available under the Creative Commons License, useful resrouces on e-learning and the impact of technology on education: *E-Learning. A Guidebook of Principles, Procedures and Practices* (Naidu, 2006); *Theory and Practice of Online Learning* (Anderson & Elloumi, 2004); *Emerging Technologies in Distance Education*, (Veletsianos, 2010); *Game changers. Education and Information Technologies* (Oblinger, 2012). Also, *Mobile Learning Transforming the Delivery of Education and Training* (Ally, 2009) provides a comprehensive look at m-learning, although this field, like e-learning, is rapidly evolving. The College of Education at the University of Texas (2015) offers a useful online *Mobile Learning Portal* linking to a variety of books, journals, and other resources on this topic.

For a more hands-on guide for designing and developing e-learning courses, we recommend the very user-friendly guide, *E-learning Methodologies. A Guide for Designing and Developing E-learning Courses*, available online from the Food and Agriculture Organization (FAO, 2011). Both EdITLib (2015) and Edutech Wiki (2015) are useful online, digital libraries with resources on education and technology, and a list of additional, free books on e-learning can be found on the website of eLearning Industry (2015). Books for purchase to consider include *e-Learning by Design* (Horton, 2011) and *Teaching Online: A Practical Guide* (Ko & Rossen, 2010).

Open educational resources (OER)

In Appendix 2.1, we provide a brief overview of open educational resources (OER). For readers interested in a more detailed discussion on the topic, we recommend *A Basic Guide to Open Educational Resources* (Butcher, 2011). The websites of OER Commons (2015) and OpenCourseWare Consortium (2014) are useful resources for open education sources that can be used for M&E training, where users can search courses by subject area, material types, language, and institution. In addition, several websites offer aggregators (directories) of Massive Open Online Courses (MOOCs), including Coursea (2015), Free Online Education (2015), Coursetalk (2015), and MOOC List (2015).

M&E online resources[8]

There are an array of valuable online resources that offer resources for M&E training as well as sources of synchronous and asynchronous M&E training. While far from exhaustive, below we highlight some recommended examples.

---

8. Note that the availability and content of online resources are regularly changing, including the uniform resource locator (URL).

- **Websites—evaluation associations and societies.** Also called Voluntary Organizations for Professional Evaluation (VOPEs), evaluation associations and societies offer an array of resources to provide or support M&E training. For example, the American Evaluation Association (2015) offers *Coffee Break Webinars*, *eStudies*, and a *Thought Leader Discussion Series* from prominent evaluators. The websites of the International Development Evaluation Association (IDEAS, 2015) also has a wealth of resources for M&E capacity development and the International Organization for Cooperation in Evaluation (IOCE, 2015) provides a comprehensive listing of international, national, and regional evaluation organizations to consider. EvalPartners (2015), which we will revisit in Chapter 3, is a valuable resource for VOPEs and M&E capacity building in general.

- **Websites—universities and related partnerships.** In addition to being a valuable resource for M&E professional development and training (e.g., see the *University Programs* webpage on the AEA website), universities offer many free resources and opportunities for M&E training. For example, the Evaluation Center (2015) at Western Michigan University offers *Evaluation Checklists* on over twenty-five topics related to M&E; Oregon State University (2015) offers an online series of webinars with PowerPoint slides for program evaluation capacity building; the website of Claremont University (2015) offers free online training in international development evaluation; and the web portal on *Participatory Planning, Monitoring & Evaluation* developed by Wageningen University (2015) offers resources on related theories, methodologies, approaches, tools, videos, and other related resources. The International Program for Development Evaluation Training (IPDET, 2015a) has a

Resource Center with speaker presentations, publications, and other links useful for M&E training. The Evaluation Toolbox (2015) from Swinburne University of Technology has an assortment of resources (e.g., guidelines, tools, templates, and case studies) for community projects that aim to change household behaviors.

- **Websites—collaborative initiatives.** There are a host of valuable websites from collaborative initiatives related to M&E, offering a variety of resources, such as virtual libraries, toolkits, and e-learning opportunities—for example, webinars, blogs, email lists, communities of practice, and links to other websites and resources. Notable examples include BetterEvaluation (2015), Monitoring and Evaluation News (MandE, 2015), My M&E (2015), MEASURE Evaluation (2015), the Centers for Learning on Evaluation and Results (CLEAR, 2015), the Regional Platform for Evaluation Capacity Building in Latin-American and the Caribbean (PREVAL, 2015), InterAction (2015), and the Active Learning Network for Accountability and performance in Humanitarian Action (ALNAP, 2015). For instance, consider the six-module *Equal Access Participatory Monitoring and Evaluation Toolkit* (Lennie, Tacchi, Koirala, Wilmore, & Skuse, 2011) available from BetterEvaluation; the publication, *M&E Fundamentals: A Self-guided Minicourse* (Frankel & Gage, 2007), available from Measure Evaluation; the four-part webinar and guidance notes on impact evaluation available from InterAction; the *Interactive Course Manual. A Manual on Organizing and Running a Successful Training Course on Evaluation Methods* from CLEAR (2013); the *Evaluation of Humanitarian Action* guide in three languages; and the recently developed online course, *Introduction to Evaluating Humanitarian Action*, available from ALNAP.

- **Websites—international and national public agencies.** The United Nations system offers a host of useful resources for M&E training and capacity building and development. For example, the interactive M&E training modules from UNICEF (2015); the World Bank (2015) webpage, *The Nuts and Bolts of M&E System*; the *Monitoring and Evaluation Training Guide* from the UNDP (2015); and the useful webpage for the International Labour Organization (ILO, 2015), *External Resources*, with links to both UN agencies and other non-UN organizations for M&E related capacity building and development. Similarly, websites from other non-UN public agencies offer an assortment of useful resources. For example, the website of the Organization for Economic Cooperation and Development (OECD, 2015) includes its trilingual *Glossary of Key Terms in Evaluation and Results-Based Management*; USAID (2015b) offers a useful *Learning Lab* with guidance tools for M&E; the National Science Foundation has a very useful *Online Evaluation Resource Library* (OERL, 2015) with instruments, plans, and reports; the Corporation for National and Community Service (2015) provides an *Performance Measurement Module Series*; and the webpage of the Center for Disease Control and Prevention (CDC, 2015) offers a host of resources, with links to others external to CDC.

- **Websites—civic organizations.** The websites of many nongovernmental, nonprofit, and other civic organizations offer an assortment of resources that can be tailored and adapted for M&E training and capacity-building contexts. For example, we recommend the websites of Care, International Federation of Red Cross and Red Crescent Societies (IFRC), Mercy Corps, Oxfam, Save the Children, and World Vision. For instance, IFRC (2015) offers online, asynchronous and synchronous training in *Project/Programme Planning (PPP)* and *Introduction to Monitoring and Evaluation* on its learning platform and its publications on different M&E topics; these resource are freely available to the general public in Arabic, English, French, and Spanish.

- **Websites—individuals.** There are also a host of websites from individuals, ranging from professionals to academics, with a wealth of resources for M&E that can support training and capacity building. For instance, the Global Social Change Research Project (2015) by Gene Shackman offers free resources for program evaluation and social research, and the website by former AEA President Michael Trochim, Social Research Methods (2015), provides useful introductions and links to additional resources for evaluation and research.

- **Social media.** As discussed earlier in this chapter, social media platforms are a valuable complement to reinforce M&E training, which we also highlight in Part 3 of the book on training follow-up. These include online communities of practice, blogs, and social networking services such as Twitter. Smith (2003, 2009) provides a useful summary of the use of community of practice for learning and organization development. Many of the abovementioned initiatives have active listservs, such as Monitoring and Evaluation News. Some other notable examples of communities of practice include the Pelican Initiative (2015), listserv XCeval (2015), and AIMEnet (2015) for the M&E of HIV/AIDS. These each host discussion, debates, and Q&A and share M&E-related resources. The website of AEA (2015) has a webpage listing over 35 discussion lists and listservs related to M&E as well as another webpage listing numerous individual and organizational blogs and Twitter sources that readers can tap into for M&E training and capacity building.

3

The M&E Capacity Building Context

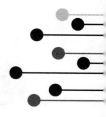

In Chapter 2 we examined training and the variety of ways that M&E training can be provided. In this chapter, we will step back and look at the bigger picture: the capacity building context in which M&E training is provided. M&E training does not happen in isolation but is embedded in complex social systems that affect training and its outcomes. Individual learners, organizations, external donors, and other actors and factors in the capacity building context can have a considerable impact on the supply and demand for M&E training. This affects not only the support for and availability of training opportunities but also training transfer and utility.

We will first discuss capacity building and lessons from research and practice in evaluation capacity building (ECB). We will then build upon our systems view of M&E training and look at three levels of analysis of the capacity building context: (a) individuals, (b) organizations, and (c) the external environment. It is important to note that much of what we cover has to do with understanding the capacity to *practice* M&E but that we also consider essential the capacity to *use* M&E. Generally speaking, we know much less about the latter, but it nevertheless remains an essential consideration (Cousins & Bourgeois, 2014). We end the chapter by taking a brief look at M&E capacity assessment and strategic planning to inform and support M&E training and other capacity building.

By the end of this chapter readers will be able to . . .

✓ Explain capacity building as it relates to M&E training

✓ Describe the use of levels analysis to the M&E capacity building context at the level of individuals, organizations, and external environment

✓ Explain the importance of and key considerations for M&E capacity assessment and strategic planning

We will revisit many of the points raised in this chapter elsewhere in the book, especially in our discussion of training analysis (Chapter 6). This is understandable because the entire training process and people involved operate in and interact with a larger system or context in which training is provided. Before we get started, reflect on the hypothetical scenario in **Box 3.1**.

BOX 3.1
A "Bad" Example

You are asked to provide a four-day, in-person workshop on project design and M&E planning for a program team. However, you are approached about this at the last minute, without any time to meet or discuss the training with key stakeholders. Based on a description of the target audience you get over the phone, you design an engaging, integrated workshop session that capitalizes on principles of adult education. Training facilitation goes well, and trainee feedback forms rate the workshop well.

However, the training did start with a stumble when you realized only two-thirds of the intended participants showed up, which you later discover is because of competing commitments within the organization, including another training in leadership and program management the same month. A couple of months after the training, you discover that the uptake and use of the M&E practices covered during training is minimal. Many of the targeted projects have not adopted logframes with measureable results and indicators to monitor and assess implementation. A project manager explains that the organization leadership does not require or provide any incentive for project teams, which are understaffed and have other obligations that take precedence over M&E. In short, your training seems to have made little difference.

This example is abbreviated, but it highlights an important lesson: **No matter how well training is delivered, it is essential to carefully consider the larger capacity building context.** If we want training to transfer or "stick," it should be planned as part of an integrated approach to M&E capacity building that considers multiple stakeholders, different demands, and potential roadblocks training may encounter. We now turn to an elaboration of what we mean by M&E capacity building.

3.1 What Is Evaluation Capacity Building?

In its broadest sense, capacity can be understood as "the ability of people, organizations and society as a whole to manage their affairs successfully" (OECD, 2006, p.12). Building these capacities involves improving the ability of people to solve problems, achieve objectives, and perform better over time. In turn, capacity building will be relative to whose capacity is being developed; that is, whether it is intended for individuals in a community, a project team with an organization, or professionals working with a national or international agency. As we shall see, these different stakeholders can be very much interrelated.

Since the 1990s, the concept and pursuit of capacity building has become increasing popular, reflecting growing recognition that technical assistance and funding is not always enough for sustainable change. It has been especially pronounced in international development, where increasing attention has been given to participatory versus top-down approaches to development (e.g., Chambers, 1997). In the introduction to this book, we briefly looked at how this trend has given rise to more participatory approaches to M&E and thus demand for training. People are increasingly viewed as *participants in* rather than *beneficiaries of* development (Sen, 1999). This trend is driven by the conviction that building local capacity and engagement in programs fosters greater understanding, ownership, and ultimately sustainability of the initiative—the biblical axiom is entirely relevant here: *Give a man a fish, and you feed him for a day; show him how to catch fish, and you feed him for a lifetime.*

With the start of the 21st century, capacity building likewise became a "hot topic" in the field of evaluation (Preskill & Boyle, 2008). In 2000, ECB was identified by the American Evaluation Association (AEA) as the overarching theme for its annual conference. Not long afterward, a volume of the journal, *New Directions for Evaluation* edited by Compton, Baizerman, and Stockdill (2002), yielded one of the earliest and most cited definitions of ECB:

> ECB is a context-dependent, intentional action system of guided processes and practices for bringing about and sustaining a state of affairs in which quality program evaluation and its appropriate uses are ordinary and ongoing practices within and/or between one or more organizations/programs/sites. (Stockdill, Baizerman, & Compton, 2002, p. 8)

In their review of the literature, these authors also identified seven lessons for ECB, which we summarize here (Stockdill et al., 2002, pp. 17–22):

1. **ECB requires a broad stakeholder base to create and sustain it.** If ECB is to make a difference and be used, "ECB practitioners must pay attention to all relevant systems and players as stakeholders."

2. **ECB requires broad-based demand.** If people value evaluation, they will seek out the capacities to support it; in turn, capacity building can build more appreciation and demand for evaluation and further ECB.

3. **Demand and purpose must be matched.** If ECB is to be effective, people's expectations for evaluation should correspond with the actual

use of evaluation. For example, do stakeholders understand and agree whether evaluation is for accountability, program improvement, and learning, or a combination?

4. **ECB operates on many levels.** ECB works best when it identifies and integrates multiple levels and systems in the evaluation context. This involves coordination between the different stakeholders at each level.

5. **ECB requires many methods.** If evaluation is to be adopted as a routine, everyday practice, it is best that it encompasses a wide variety of evaluation approaches and methodologies.

6. **ECB lacks resources.** The potential for ECB depends on a long-term commitment to human and financial resources; however such commitment and resources are often limited or missing.

7. **ECB must be flexible.** ECB is ongoing and needs to be adaptable to multiple contexts, continually adjusted and refined as these contexts change.

Jessie Mountfield

While ECB has since been defined, described, and applied in many different ways,[1] this "first mapping" of ECB provides a useful foundation to consider M&E training and the larger capacity building context. Firstly, the definition underscores that capacity building is context specific, and the seven lessons highlight considerations to best navigate this context. It is no coincidence that the key messages we summarize for M&E training in our introduction largely echo these lessons. They reflect and stress the importance of a systems approach that considers the larger picture, such as different stakeholders, demands, and resources, and the variety of methods and approaches to adapt according to specific contexts.

Secondly, capacity building is ongoing and should be adaptable to emerging needs. This reflects that capacity building happens in a dynamic system that is constantly evolving and changing. For example, at the organizational level, capacity building such as

1. For example: Preskill and Boyle, 2008; Görgens and Kusek, 2009; Labin, Duffy, Meyers, Wandersman, & Lesesne, 2012; OECD, 2014a, 2014b; Segone, Heider, Oksanen, Silva, & Sanz, 2013; Simister and Smith, 2010.

M&E training may lead to a "virtuous cycle," improving performance, which attracts more funding for additional programming, which in turn could stimulate further demand for M&E capacity building (Leviton, 2014). On the other hand, a *vicious cycle* may result in which funding causes the organization to scale up programming too rapidly and it "topples over" as a result, overextending itself beyond its capacity to effectively deliver services.

Related, when we view capacity building as ongoing, M&E training should be planned and implemented as part of a larger, sustained effort to build an M&E culture that can be continued over time. Training does not exist for its own sake but is a means to an end; it should complement other efforts contributing to higher goals, such as more effective and accountable programing that supports longer-term strategic objectives. Thus, it is essential to consider the larger context in which training is provided.

Another element in the definition provided by Stockdill et. al. (2002) is the intentionality of capacity building. We agree that for the most part capacity building, such as M&E training, is planned or *direct*. Thus, much of this book provides guidance to systematically approach M&E training, including consideration of the larger context in which it is provided. However, as we discussed in our prior chapter, capacity building may also occur incidentally, as a byproduct of another experience. M&E learning as well as the demand for or appreciation of M&E and related capacity building can be *indirect* and unplanned as a result from involvement in M&E processes, such as learning by doing as in participatory evaluation.

A "levels analysis" of the capacity building context

Another important ECB lesson identified by Stockdill et al. (2002) is that capacity building operates on many levels. In systems thinking, a *levels analysis* is often used to consider complex wholes that are made up of smaller subsystems. In international development, a levels analysis has been usefully applied to analyze capacity building and of national evaluation capacity development (ECD), see **Box 3.2**. A three-tier approach is often used to consider capacity building at the micro (e.g., individual), meso (e.g., organizational), and macro (e.g., societal) levels.[2]

For M&E training, levels analysis helps underscore that training is embedded in and interdependent on a larger, dynamic system and should thus be planned accordingly. Rather than approaching M&E training as simply building individual knowledge and skills, a levels analysis broadens the lens of training as nested within systems with cascading effects down the various levels of analysis for M&E capacity building. For example, government policies for greater accountability can have a profound impact on organizational demand and support for M&E training.

---

2. For example, Fukuda-Parr, Lopes, & Malik, 2002; Hieder, 2011; Horton et. al., 2003; OECD, 2006; Segone & Rugh, 2013.

In the remainder of this chapter, we will use a levels analysis to better understand capacity building context for M&E. As portrayed in **Figure 3.1** and following Horton et al., (2003), our discussion will focus on three levels: the individual, organization, and external environment. It is important to recognize that we use these levels for conceptual convenience and that in reality each level is complex and will vary greatly according to context.

We now consider each of these levels in turn.

3.2 M&E Capacity Building at the Individual Level

Capacity building is a complex human process heavily influenced by a range of people who bring to M&E training different values, beliefs, emotions, experience, and motives. For our purposes, we will consider this by distinguishing between those individuals who are directly involved in M&E training and those who are not so involved but indirectly affect M&E training.

Those directly involved in M&E training include the trainees as well as the trainers. For trainees, M&E learning needs and objectives will vary and as we discuss in Chapter 7, it is important to determine this early on to inform training design. In **Table 3.1**, we list some examples of different stakeholder groups and related M&E skills. It is especially important to pay attention to the personal motivation or reasons

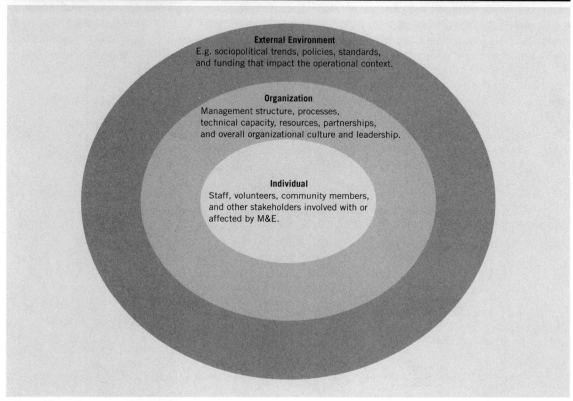

External Environment
E.g. sociopolitical trends, policies, standards, and funding that impact the operational context.

Organization
Management structure, processes, technical capacity, resources, partnerships, and overall organizational culture and leadership.

Individual
Staff, volunteers, community members, and other stakeholders involved with or affected by M&E.

Adapted from Horton et al., 2003, p. 30.

people are participating in M&E training. For example, they may be attending training on their own initiative, for professional or career development, or because it is required of them from the organization or program with which they work.

Related, trainee characteristics and personal circumstances will affect the training methods and delivery modes designed to best achieve learning objectives. This includes prior M&E experience, educational background, culture, age, gender, location, and availability for training. These and other considerations are a critical aspect of training analysis, which we will revisit in Chapter 7. Also, in the following chapter on adult learning we will look at the importance of tailoring training delivery accordingly to different learning styles, preferences, and other trainee characteristics.

Stakeholder group	Examples of relevant M&E skills
Independent learners	• This will vary according to the individual's profile—for example, they may seek an overview course on M&E or specific knowledge on logframes, survey design, or qualitative data collection.
Program target population (Intended "beneficiaries," e.g., members from a community, public school system, workers organizations)	• Understanding of M&E ethics, principles, and standards to inform individual rights as well as expectations and "surveillance" of M&E conduct. • Negotiation with external stakeholders on the program intervention and related. • Participation in initial needs assessment and program design. • Appropriate monitoring, data analysis, and reporting. • Participation in input into evaluations.
Program/project team (e.g., staff or volunteers)	• Practicing M&E ethics, principles, and standards. • Supporting needs assessment and project design. • Data collection and analysis for results monitoring and reporting. • Stakeholder monitoring and communication. • Data management. • Supporting evaluations, reviews, and related assessment exercises.
Program/project management	• Upholding M&E ethics, principles, and standards in programming. • Strategic and operation planning at the program level that supports M&E functions and capacity building. • Meeting M&E and accountability requirements—for example, to donor. • Managing and supervising M&E functions in the project/program team. • Itemizing and managing program budgets that include M&E. • M&E understanding for proposal writing and project design. • Preparing job descriptions and terms of reference (ToR) to recruit qualified M&E staff. • Managing evaluations, including the follow-up and use of findings and recommendations for programming.
Organizational leadership and management (e.g., senior management, including heads of M&E units or departments)	• Understand and use evidence produced by M&E systems for programming. • Upholding M&E ethics, principles, and standards. • Strategic and operational planning at the organizational level for M&E. • Securing adequate funding and other resources for M&E. • Supporting organizational learning and follow-up to program evaluations. • Conducting organizational/M&E capacity assessments. • Promoting external/public M&E communications and education. • Professional networking, partnerships, and exchange visits to support M&E.

Stakeholder group	Examples of relevant M&E skills
Policymakers	• Understand and use evidence produced by M&E systems in policy practice. • Know about the different kinds of evidence available, how to gain access to it, and how to critically appraise it. • Improve government infrastructure (agencies/ministries) by supporting relevant, coherent, and well-coordinated M&E practice.
Designated M&E expertise (e.g., M&E officers, technical advisors and consultants, personnel working in an M&E unit or department)	• Upholding M&E ethics, principles, and standards in programming. • Designing M&E systems for reliable data collection, analysis, and reporting. • M&E resource development and capacity building planning and delivery (e.g., trainings). • Leading or providing technical assistance for M&E exercises—for example, needs assessment, project design, M&E planning, household surveys, etc. • Understanding different evaluation designs, advantages, and limitations, etc. • Leading internal, self-evaluations and reviews (including evaluation follow-up and use within the organization). • Advising and supporting different data collection methodologies and analysis (quantitative, qualitative, and mixed methods). • Managing external consultants or teams for independent evaluations (e.g. commissioning, ToR development and recruitment, oversight of quality of field work, reviewing evaluation reports, etc.).
Funding agency or donor	• Incorporating M&E ethics, principles, and standards into program/project funding requirements. • Understanding of M&E funding and resource requirements (budget, time, human resources). • Assessing M&E components (e.g. logical framework and M&E plan) in submitted program proposals. • Coordination among funders to harmonize M&E requirements of grantees. • Reviewing and feeding back on M&E information in program reports. • Understanding of evaluation types, and challenges and limitations to impact assessment.

Adapted from Bamberger, Rugh, & Mabry, 2012, p. 467.

As with training participants, it is also important to consider the characteristics, background, and motivation of the trainers and others who may be directly involved in the training process, such as subject matter experts, designers, and evaluators. This includes a range of competencies, including technical skills, familiarity with the training context and trainee audience, interpersonal and management skills, and other personal attributes. There are also a range of influences, pressures, and incentives that affect those who provide training that are important to consider: "People who develop education and training programs for adults do not work in a vacuum" (Caffarella, 2002, p. 58). These various individual factors play critically into providing training that meets M&E needs, and in Chapter 5, we will take closer look at key competencies for good M&E trainers.

In addition to trainees and trainers directly involved in M&E training, there are other individuals indirectly involved who can have a considerable effect on training outcomes. This is particularly relevant for organization training, where organizational objectives and different stakeholders within the organizations can shape the demand for and use of M&E training. Examples range from those who commission M&E training to community members, program managers, and organizational leadership. These individuals will have their own personal motives, agendas, issues with others, and sometimes territorialism within the organization. M&E inherently involves power relationships between individuals that can affect the potential for transfer afterward:

> Whether in the locality, or when larger-scale institutions are involved, questions of who is accountable to whom, and who can voice concerns about performance, also involve questions of power. (Gaventa & Blauert, 2000, p. 233)

It is crucial to identify key individuals or "gatekeepers" who can support or hinder training goals, especially leaders or natural *champions* for M&E who have the ability to influence and inspire others to apply M&E learning into practice. Negotiating social dynamics among different individuals can be a difficult process, whether in a large organization or a single community project, but can have considerable impact on whether training makes a difference.

An investment in individual capacity is also an investment in a larger system. Depending on the training context, this can include organizations, project teams, communities, and other stakeholder groups. Ultimately, whether M&E training is organizational or for individuals unaffiliated with the same organization, it is an investment at a societal level, building a cadre of expertise in M&E and related capacities for evidence-based decision-making, performance management, results-based management (RBM), and the like. Trained personnel may move among different organizations and pursue different career opportunities and, in doing so, they bring with them capacities they have developed through training and other sources of learning.

3.3 M&E Capacity Building at the Organizational Level
....

Expanding our capacity-building lens, we use the organizational level broadly to include a wide range of groups where people work together to collectively achieve a given organization's immediate, intermediate, and long-term objectives. Examples range from national agencies and international organizations to nongovernmental organizations (NGOs), volunteer organizations, private organizations, and community-based organizations (CBOs). These entities can be healthy or sick—emerging, growing, or dying—and M&E needs will vary widely.

Organizations differ in purpose, scale, and scope, and so do their M&E and RBM systems. For example, **Figure 3.2** illustrates twelve interrelated components for a national M&E system that the World Bank identifies for governments and partners focused on development (Görgens & Kusek, 2009). (The figure is of particular interest in portraying the components as a system of interconnected processes.) Such a

FIGURE 3.2 Examples of Components of a Functional M&E System

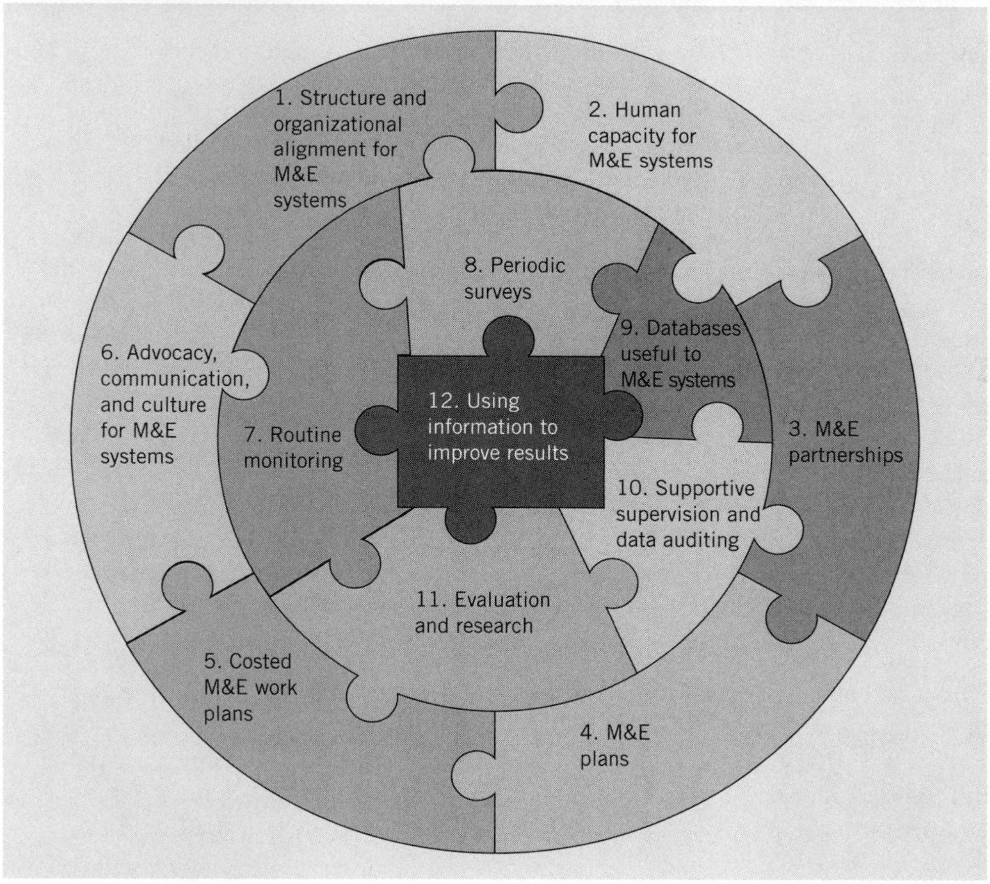

1. Structure and organizational alignment for M&E systems
2. Human capacity for M&E systems
8. Periodic surveys
9. Databases useful to M&E systems
6. Advocacy, communication, and culture for M&E systems
12. Using information to improve results
3. M&E partnerships
7. Routine monitoring
10. Supportive supervision and data auditing
11. Evaluation and research
5. Costed M&E work plans
4. M&E plans

Source: Görgens and Kusek (2009).

complex M&E system, however, would not be appropriate with a smaller organization, such as a CBO consisting of a 12-member committee and community volunteers. In some instances, M&E needs will require an M&E unit, officers, and others who specialize in technical assistance. However, in smaller organizational contexts, M&E may be one of many different responsibilities people have; for example, a director of a community-based nongovernmental organization (NGO) or program may have M&E responsibilities in addition to myriad administrative challenges.

Whatever configuration exists for an organization's M&E system, it is important to remember that it and capacity building for it are means toward an end that is relative to the organization's overall vision and mission. The M&E capacity to support this will depend on the resources, knowledge, and processes at its disposal and its ability to learn and adapt to change. Existing M&E capacity is the supply to conduct M&E but it is also essential to consider the demand to use it. The distinction between supply and demand is useful because it helps spotlight that demand can have a considerable influence on whether KSA from training transfers into meaningful practice:

> The stock of human capital and the supply of general and technical skills are important. However, a country's ability to use skilled personnel to good effect depends on the incentives generated by organisations and the overall environment. (OECD, 2006, p. 18)

As we have argued elsewhere (Cousins & Bourgeois, 2014), it is essential to consider not just an organization's capacity to use M&E to produce knowledge but also the extent knowledge is actually used by an organization. There will be those who practice M&E to produce sound evidence, and there are others who may not be "doers" of M&E but need to be able to understand and use the evidence it generates. The ECB literature tends to focus quite heavily on the M&E supply side, although many have acknowledged the need to educate, inform, and otherwise develop the capacity among organizational decision-makers to make good use of M&E results (Cousins & Bourgeois, 2014; Kusek & Rist, 2004; King, 2007; Loud & Mayne, 2014). Such a broadened perspective, we would argue, is part and parcel of a systems view of M&E capacity building.

Just as individuals have their own profile and character, so do organizations, which will also be central for training design. In the following discussion, we take a closer look at this, organizing our discussion into five broad areas—see **Figure 3.3**. Organizational systems and their subsystems can be conceptualized differently, according to the scale, scope, and complexity of its management and operation. These five categories emerge from our review of the literature,[3]

---

3. For example, Lusthaus and Murphy (1995); Horton et. al. (2003); Preskill and Boyle (2008); Cousins and Bourgeois (2014).

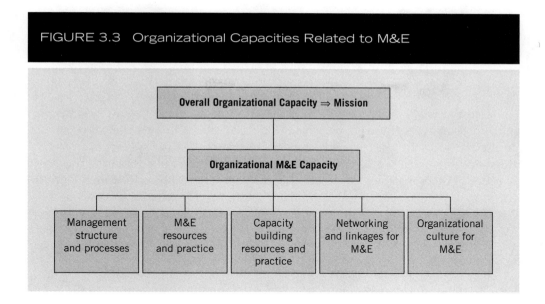

FIGURE 3.3   Organizational Capacities Related to M&E

Overall Organizational Capacity ⇒ Mission

Organizational M&E Capacity

| Management structure and processes | M&E resources and practice | Capacity building resources and practice | Networking and linkages for M&E | Organizational culture for M&E |

encompassing key organizational capacities we find useful to consider for M&E training. While we discuss each of these five areas separately, they are very much interrelated parts in the overall organizational system, each influencing and impacting the other. For example, organization leadership and decision-making personnel largely steer and manage available resources for ECB.

We will revisit these five areas again in Chapter 6 on training analysis, when it is important to focus inquiry on specific organizational contexts. For now, we briefly introduce them.

1. Management structure and processes

An organization's overall management structure and processes encompass the administrative structure as well as policies and procedures for managing human, financial, and other resources. This includes staff recruitment, roles and responsibilities, appraisal, training and support; budgeting; accounting; fundraising; information management, technology, and equipment; and infrastructure. The particular configuration of an organization's structure and where the oversight of M&E sits will vary according to its scale and scope of operations. M&E functions may be integrated as part of different program areas and managed by program staff along with other responsibilities or assigned to M&E officers/advisors; there may be a stand-alone department or unit within the organization supporting M&E across program areas; or M&E functions may be subcontracted externally. Whatever organizational management structures exists for M&E, it is imperative that M&E training takes this into account to ensure it is aligned and supports the existing M&E system and practice.

2. M&E resources and practice

An organization's capacity for M&E will greatly depend on the existing systems, guidelines, and procedures to perform M&E functions (in other words, the supply of M&E). This also includes related processes in a RBM system, such as program design, data management, analysis, and reporting. In addition to the presence of these management structures, there is also the degree to which M&E is incorporated and sustained as part of the overall program management and service delivery.

The best planning and structure for M&E will be of no avail if it is not adequately resourced. This includes M&E financial and human resources (and related capacity building expenses) as well as physical and technological resources for M&E (e.g., facilities, vehicles, computers, software). M&E capacity building requires a considerable up-front investment and must be maintained; ideally, this will be recouped by improved efficiency in service delivery and accountability to potentially attract funding.

However, inadequate funding is frequently noted as one of the greatest constraints for ECB (e.g., Horton et al., 2003; Johnson, 2000). Often M&E and its capacity building is not specifically itemized, but subsumed in the overall program budget or part of the organization's overhead (e.g., administrative costs). Consequently, the true M&E costs may not be adequately reflected and/or planned in the program. The predicament is complicated when M&E capacity and understanding is low to begin with and management underestimates adequate investment. For the M&E trainer, available funding and resources can serve as an important indicator for an organization's understanding and prioritization of M&E and the likelihood of support for its long-term development. Of course, it will also, to a large degree, determine M&E training possibilities.

3. Capacity building resources and practice

> It is now recognized that training programs are most successful when they are seen as having an integral role in the organizational structure, purpose and processes of the agency. (NSDTA, 2010, p. 9)

Effective training will depend on an organization's readiness and receptivity to capacity building. This includes the planning and resources available for M&E training but also following up after training to support and sustain training outcomes. A useful indicator is whether and organization has a capacity building strategy that includes M&E training in relation to other initiatives. Particular attention should be given to the space or barriers in organization for trainees to apply new skills or influence organizational decision-making. Training will be of little value if participants are unable to put their newly found knowledge and skills to practice.

In its guidelines for effective training programs, the NSDTA (2010, p.13) identifies five key "essentials" that are useful indicators for the potential of capacity building within an organization:

1. Administrative support

2. An organizational climate that permits looking at problems and the means to resolve them

3. Top staff commitment to the value of cooperative planning and the development of ways to work together to meet program and staff needs

4. A realistic understanding by management of what one can expect from a sound staff development and training program, namely, that it is not a substitute for good management or a cure-all for every organizational problem

5. Reinforcement and follow-up of training programs by the supervisory and managerial staff

4. Networking and linkages

The extent to which an organization can effectively network and link with external partners is an important consideration for capacity building (Horton et al., 2003). External partners can be valuable resources for M&E expertise, training, and guidance. One particularly noteworthy source for M&E networking and support is what has become known as VOPEs (see **Box 3.2**). For M&E, the operational context is becoming more complex and diverse with multiple actors holding strong accountability demands. Increasingly, an organization's performance depends on its ability to effectively navigate and utilize external resources and support. This includes funding, cooperation and knowledge exchange opportunities, and peer-to-peer collaboration. However, as external stakeholders become more involved in and affect the demand for M&E, there are important considerations for an organization's autonomy, which we will examine more closely in our discussion below on the external environment in which organizations operate.

BOX 3.2
Voluntary Organizations for Professional Evaluators (VOPEs)

Voluntary organizations for professional evaluators (VOPEs) are receiving increasing attention in the evaluation community and are a valuable source for M&E capacity building (Rugh & Segone, 2013; Segone & Rugh, 2013). VOPES are evaluation associations or societies operating nationally (e.g., AEA), regionally (e.g., African Evaluation Association, AfrEA), or internationally (e.g., International Organization for Cooperation in Evaluation, IOCE). Membership is open to all stakeholders involved in, supporting, or using evaluation, and the number of VOPEs has increased from 15 in the 1990s to more than 150 today (Segone, Heider, Oksanen, Silva, & Sanz, 2013, p. 19). VOPEs help establish and advocate for standards, principles, and guidelines that promote professional practice in M&E that contributes to accountability, learning, and public transparency.

5. Organizational culture and demand

Sometimes called the institutional climate, an organization's culture "reflects the traditions, values, and basic assumptions shared by its members and that establish its behavioral norms" (Bourgeois & Cousins, 2013, p. 301). For M&E, it is largely an outcome of how well the management and technical capacities, networking, and resource investment support M&E understanding and meaningful practice within an organization. As we have argued, meaningful practice extends beyond the capacity to just do M&E and includes the capacity to effectively put M&E knowledge to use.

An organization's culture is its unique "personality," and will vary subject to its history and traditions, mission and the adherence to fundamental principles and codes of conduct, leadership tone and management style, and any opportunities, incentives, and rewards for capacity development. These factors affect the motivation and demand for M&E and help shape an organization's "internal environment," including teamwork and cooperation (or, conversely, competition, territorialism, and hidden agendas). The extent of social cohesion within an organization can have considerable influence on the success of collective goals, such as the establishment of and reliance on M&E systems.

Ideally, an organization's culture encourages critical reflection on and innovation for M&E practice and training. As **Box 3.3** highlights, however, it is not always a given that an organization is receptive to and will embrace M&E capacity building. Organizations, after all, are not typically completely rational entities and are most often subject to nonrational or political forces.

> Building and sustaining such (M&E) systems is primarily a political process, and less so a technical one. (Kusek & Rist, 2004, p. 2)

BOX 3.3
Organizational Barriers to M&E Capacity Building

Organization culture can be resistant to M&E, which is perceived as a threat, a source of policing and judgment, and fuels competition within the organization (Taut & Alkin, 2003). When externally mandated and procedural, M&E may be perceived as a "hoop" of imposed requirements to jump through to guarantee funding but distracting valuable time and resources (Chaplowe & Engo-Tjega, 2007, p. 267). When there is a separate division or department dedicated to M&E capacity development, there is a risk of the "bureaucratization of training" into a separate administrative function that "will not be responsive to line operation needs, whether owing to benign ignorance, sinister empire-building interests, or both" (Brinkerhoff, 1989, p. 8). Institutionalized training may be perceived as an external agenda and have little credibility with the very program managers and teams it is meant to assist. Capacity building must be carefully approached to best assure buy-in and support and needs to consider attitudes as well as knowledge and skills.

Whether an organization's culture supports or hinders M&E training and practice will be largely shaped by its leadership. "It is not enough to train, educate, and engage staff in ECB (evaluation capacity building) activities; leaders must also learn to think evaluatively and support meaningful evaluation practice within the organization" (Preskill, 2014, p. 117). Leadership sets the organizational priorities, including the extent to which M&E is planned, resourced, encouraged, and used. Their commitment should not be underestimated, as it could have a multiplier effect on the potential for and uptake of the M&E capacity building efforts.

3.4 M&E Capacity Building in the External Environment

> The enabling environment for evaluation is determined by a culture of learning and accountability, meaning the degree to which information is sought about past performance, the extent to which there is a drive to continuously improve, and to be responsible or accountable for actions taken, resources spent, and results achieved. (Segone et al., 2013, p. 23)

The external environment includes the broader social, political, and economic systems in which programming occurs, extending across organizations to include other civic, public, and private stakeholders in society. M&E does not operate in a political vacuum, and initiatives for transparency and accountability are especially susceptible to explicit and implicit agendas and motivations (Bamberger et al., 2012). This external environment can have a considerable impact that enables or hinders M&E capacity for the various subsystems within it (individuals, communities, and organizations). For example, enabling factors could include sound policies, high levels of commitment, effective coordination, and a stable economic environment. On the other hand, economic and civil instability, poorly conceived policies, and high levels of corruption can make for a highly disabling environment for M&E capacity building.

Government agencies, international organizations, politicians, funding agencies, and other external actors can play a particularly significant role in shaping the overall demand for M&E and its capacity building. Expectations for program accountability are increasing, reflected in policy, laws, and standards as well as the funding and budgeting priorities of public, international, and private donors. How these demands translate and are conveyed within an organization will vary. **Box 3.4** highlights three types of incentives commonly employed to promote M&E. However, probably the most effective incentive is for decision-makers to experience firsthand the utility and benefits of M&E (Cousins & Bourgeois, 2014). This thinking aligns with the organizational change adage "belief follows practice." It is through firsthand experience with successful use that organizations come to appreciate the true power of M&E as a lever for change.

Building M&E demand, however, is complicated. Incentives and accountability requirements are not always enabling and can even constrain and compromise an organization's autonomy and ability to effectively deliver programs (e.g., Chaplowe & Engo-Tjega, 2007; Leviton, 2014). In their haste to obtain and satisfy M&E requirements and related funding requirements, organizations "may become more attuned and accountable to the donors' needs rather than the people they are meant to represent and serve" (Chaplowe, 2012, p. 267). The needs and interests of donors should not overshadow those of other stakeholder groups. A donor-driven agenda of imposed M&E systems and protocol may be incompatible with and burdensome for an organization's operational culture (and as noted above, this can heighten resistance to M&E within an organization).

Whether enabling or disabling, the external environment can have a considerable effect on M&E capacity efforts, such as training. Thus, those involved in supporting M&E should be attentive to these external factors and actors. Such awareness shares many elements with what the AEA refers to as "cultural competence" in its guiding principles for evaluators (AEA, 2004). Just as an evaluator "must have specific knowledge of the people and place in which the evaluation is being conducted," so must the people supporting M&E capacity building (AEA, 2011, p. 3). In Chapter 6 on training analysis, we revisit key considerations for the external environment when analyzing the training context. We now turn to some thoughts about sizing up capacity and planning the way forward.

BOX 3.4
M&E Incentives

Depending on the context, the motivation to adopt and practice M&E may not be forthcoming. Therefore, incentives are often used by organizations, donors, and other external actors to improve the uptake and practice of M&E. M&E training itself can be used as an incentive. Mackay (2007, p. 62) identifies three types of incentives commonly employed to encourage better M&E:

1. *Carrots* encourage and reward M&E practice, such as financial incentives, awards and prizes, career advancement, etc.

2. *Sticks* require M&E and penalize its poor practice, such as laws, decrees, regulations, financial penalties, naming and shaming, etc.

3. *Sermons* or positive messages endorse or advocate the value of M&E, such as high-level statements, awareness-raising initiatives, etc. These messages can underscore the benefits of M&E practice, such as organizational learning and improvement.

3.5 M&E Capacity Assessment and Strategic Planning

M&E training is most effective when planned as part of an integrated strategy that takes into consideration the program and organization's strategic objectives, resources, and other factors in the M&E context. Strategic planning provides a road map to identify, prioritize, and communicate M&E capacity building priorities, contributing to the organizational understanding and culture for M&E. It also helps mobilize and manage M&E resources and ensures M&E training and other capacity building approaches are coordinated and reinforce each other.

It is beyond the scope of this book to examine in detail M&E capacity assessment and its strategic planning.[4] However, these can play an important role determining M&E training objectives and help ensure they are planning and implemented as part of a coordinated approach. When capacity building efforts complement each other and work in synch with other knowledge management systems, they can reinforce learning transfer collectively.

---

4. Each of these topics merit and have an assortment of treatises devoted to them, some of which we have listed at the end of this chapter.

M&E trainers are often asked to support and maybe even lead capacity assessment and strategic planning exercises. In addition to their experience with capacity building, M&E trainers often offer expertise in assessment and design, which lends itself well to capacity assessment and strategic planning. Therefore, we have briefly summarized some key considerations on these important topics to conclude this chapter, with additional resources suggested as further reading for tis chapter.

M&E capacity assessment

Strategic planning, whether for M&E or overall organization objectives, is best informed by a realistic and comprehensive assessment of an organization's strengths and limitations. Depending on the scale and scope of the organization, M&E capacity assessments may be part of a larger organizational assessment exercise, or it may be done separately, focusing on M&E or RBM. If conducted separately, it is important it complements and feeds into any existing organizational assessment processes.

In its guide on M&E capacity development, the World Bank identifies seven useful steps for Human Capacity Development Assessment for M&E systems, which we summarize in **Box 3.5** (Görgens & Kusek, 2009).

The guide also identifies two approaches for an M&E assessment exercise (Görgens & Kusek, 2009). A bottom-up approach asks the stakeholders involved in the M&E

BOX 3.5
Seven Key Steps for an M&E Capacity Assessment

1. Plan the capacity assessment—concept note and project plan
2. Obtain political and senior management buy-in and approval
3. Determine the M&E competencies required
4. Design the assessment data collection instruments and train team members
5. Collect data for the capacity assessment
6. Analyze data and prepare a capacity assessment report
7. Present human capacity development assessment results in a report

Source: Görgens & Kusek, 2009, pp. 101–105.

system to assess their capacity, which is advantageous for understanding and ownership of the assessment for participatory planning. However, stakeholder understanding and capacity may be low in M&E, limiting their ability to critically assess M&E systems and processes. In contrast, with a top-down approach, assessment of M&E capacity is made by comparing criteria with the capacity that exists in those participating in the M&E system. "A top-down approach does not mean that capacity building needs are imposed in any way but rather that the starting point is what the system requires and not what stakeholders believe they need" (Görgens & Kusek, 2009, p. 100).

There are a variety of other tools and methods for organizational capacity assessment and specifically for ECB. Bourgeois developed a profile tool for organizational self-assessment of evaluation capacity that warrants consideration (Bourgeois & Cousins, 2008; 2013; Bourgeois, Toews, Whynot, & Lamarche, 2013). Although developed in the context of public sector governance, the tool is empirically grounded and comprehensive in its coverage of organizational capacity to do evaluation (human resources, organizational resources, evaluation planning, and activity) and capacity to use evaluation (evaluation literacy, integration with decision-making, learning).

Another approach is the Readiness for Organizational Learning and Evaluation (ROLE) instrument, "designed to help an organization determine its level of readiness for implementing organizational learning and evaluation practices and processes that support it" (Preskill & Torres, 2015, p. 1). ROLE groups 78 assessment items into six areas to identify existing learning capabilities as well as those capacities that need to be developed: (1) Culture, (2) Leadership, (3) Systems and Structures, (4) Communication, (5) Teams, and (6) Evaluation.

However M&E capacity assessment is conducted, it is best to plan it in conjunction with strategic planning. When strategic planning occurs in a timely manner after capacity assessment, the results are more likely to be used.

M&E capacity strategic planning

Strategic planning for M&E capacity building should include specific, measureable objectives and the allocation of resources for their accomplishment. It may be prearranged as part of an organization's overall strategic and operational planning or *ad hoc* and opportunistic in response to M&E needs and demand in program implementation. Related, M&E strategic planning may be integrated with and cut across program areas, or it may be specific to one program area or department overseeing the M&E function in the organization.

Table 3.2 summarizes some key considerations for developing an M&E capacity building strategy. The process will vary according to the organizational context and focus and should be aligned with and support the long-term capacity building

TABLE 3.2 Strategic Planning for M&E Capacity Building

1. **Consult with key stakeholders,** especially field staff knowledgeable of M&E realities, as well as senior management necessary for approval and support of strategic objectives.

2. **Identify a team (task forces) to develop the strategy.**

3. **Conduct or review an M&E capacity assessment.**

4. **Prioritize identified M&E capacities areas**—existing individual capacity assets and deficits.

5. **Identify constraints to addressing the M&E capacity gaps**—for example, lack of funds or management support.

6. **Identify the most suitable M&E capacity building objectives and strategies for achieving them.**
   - ✓ Identify objectives that are realistic and measureable, contributing to overall organizational strategic objectives.
   - ✓ Develop or build upon standardized M&E guidance and training resources for a consistent approach to M&E best practices.
   - ✓ Identify funding and resources to target for M&E capacity building objectives.
   - ✓ Itemize program budgets for M&E capacity building rather than subsumed (and assumed) as part of overall operating costs.
   - ✓ Identify specific capacity building activities to address objectives—for example, training workshops, distant e-learning, mentoring, and on-the-job training.
   - ✓ Sequence and schedule M&E capacity building activities to ensure an integrated (blended) approach that reinforces long-term M&E learning transfer into practice.
   - ✓ Establish a strategic selection process for training participants according to their level and needs.
   - ✓ Identify M&E training sources (internal expertise or external consultants) for capacity building objectives.
   - ✓ Prepare skilled M&E trainers (training of trainers) to ensure a consistent and organizationally compatible approach to capacity building.
   - ✓ Develop a network of M&E support for ongoing capacity building—professionals, mentors, partner organizations, consultants, sector specialists, and others to support M&E capacity objectives.

7. **Draft the M&E capacity building strategy** (or plan), as a stand-alone document of embedded objectives as part of a larger organizational strategy.

8. **Communicate and advocate the M&E strategic objectives**, building understanding and ownership for their achievement, with particular emphasis on leadership and potential M&E champions.

9. **Implement, regularly monitor, assess, and report on M&E capacity building performance.**

10. **Review and revise the M&E capacity building strategy on a regular basis**—at a minimum, it is recommended that strategic plans are reviewed and revised every three to five years.

Adapted from Görgens & Kusek, 2009, pp. 100 and 107.

objectives of the program/organization. In some organizations there may be a stand-alone document for M&E capacity building, while in others M&E capacity building objectives may be embedded within a more global organizational plan.

Stakeholder participation is again critical for the success of the exercise, ensuring ownership and support necessary to achieve and sustain identified M&E objectives. The wider the stakeholder involvement, the higher the potential for eventual ownership. Two groups of stakeholders are especially important to involve in the planning process. First, senior management and key decision-makers are essential for the approval, funding, and resources of the strategic plan, as well as leadership support and motivation. Second, it is important to include organization members with practical M&E knowledge to inform realistic planning—not just from a headquarters' perspective but also from the field where programs are conducted.

The scope and rigor of strategic planning for M&E capacity building will vary greatly between organizations, as will the time and resources required for the exercise. The process should be tailored so it is relevant and realistic to specific organizational needs. Stakeholder involvement is critical for ownership and meaningful follow-up.

3.6 CHAPTER SUMMARY

In this chapter, we have given close consideration to a variety of aspects of M&E capacity building and the larger context in which M&E training is provided. Important summary points include the following:

- Capacity building involves improving the ability of individuals, organizations, and societies to successfully manage their affairs and achieve goals. M&E training is one of an assortment of capacity building options for M&E. Whether it targets the specific needs of a particular organization or individuals unaffiliated with the same organizations, it is important to understand the various factors and actors in the capacity building context that affect M&E training outcomes.
- The scholarly research on evaluation capacity building (ECB) underscores key considerations for M&E training, including the importance of stakeholder engagement, demand, resources, utilizing multiple approaches, and recognizing and remaining flexible to the multiple levels and changes in the capacity building context.

- A levels analysis is a useful way to consider the capacity building context (system) in which M&E training is provided. Drawing upon the valuable research in evaluation capacity development (ECD), three interdependent levels are identified:

  - The individual level includes those directly involved in M&E training (e.g., trainees and trainers), as well as those indirectly involved who can support or hinder training efforts (e.g., organizational leadership). It is important to consider the personal motives, experience, background, and other characteristics of these individuals.

- At the organizational level, it is not only important to identify the capacity to practice M&E but also the degree M&E information is actually used to inform decision-making. We identify five broad, interrelated areas to consider organizational capacity for M&E and training to support it: (1) management structure and processes, (2) M&E resources and practice, (3) capacity building resources and practice, (4) networking and linkages, and (5) organizational culture and demand.

- The level of the external environment includes broader social, political, and economic factors that can support or hinder M&E capacity building, such as policies, laws, and funding priorities. External actors, such as politicians, government agencies, international organizations, and donors, can have a significant effect on the demand for M&E capacity building efforts, such as training.

- In an organizational context, M&E capacity assessment and strategic planning helps ensure the M&E training is planned as a coordinated approach that considers other strategic priorities, resources, and contextual factors as a return on the investment of training:

  - M&E capacity assessment can be conducted as a stand-alone exercise focused on M&E or as part of a lager organizational assessment. An important consideration is stakeholder understanding of M&E and their ability to critically assess M&E systems and processes.

  - Similarly, M&E strategic planning can result in a targeted plan focused on M&E or part of a larger strategic planning exercise, with M&E objectives embedded in an overall organizational strategic plan. Ultimately, the scope and rigor of M&E strategic planning will depend on organizational needs, resources, and other specific considerations outlined in our discussion of the levels analysis of organizations.

3.7 RECOMMENDED RESOURCES

In the preparation of this chapter, we relied on scholarly articles on ECB, especially from the *American Journal of Evaluation* and *New Directions for Evaluation*. A good place to start is the 2002 NDE issue, *The Art, Craft and Science of Evaluation Capacity Building* (Compton, Baizerman, & Stockdill, 2002) and then jump ahead twelve years to the 2014 NDE issue, *Organizational Capacity To Do and Use Evaluation* (Cousins & Bourgeois, 2014) and the 2014 AJE issue with a forum on *Evaluation Capacity Building* (Rallis, 2014).

We also relied heavily on and recommend several freely available publications on ECD. Foremost, we found extremely useful the publication by Horton

et al. (2003), *Evaluating Capacity Development: Experiences from Research and Development Organizations around the World*, which provided much of the organizing framework for this chapter. This was complemented by *Evaluation and Civil Society. Stakeholders' Perspectives on National Evaluation Capacity Development* (Segone & Rugh, 2013), especially its useful overview of a framework for the capacity building context. Related, we also recommend the publication, *Building Better Policies: The Nuts and Bolts of Monitoring and Evaluation Systems* (Lopez-Acevedo, Krause, & Mackay, 2012). For a practical look at strengthening evaluation capacity at the agency and national level, we also recommend Chapter 18 in the book

Real World Evaluation (Bamberger et al., 2012), which also includes additional recommended resource on the subject.

The websites of several international organizations have further guides freely available ECB and ECD, including the *Evaluation Capacity Development* webpage of the Independent Evaluation Group with the World Bank Group (IEG, 2015), and the OECD (2015) webpage, *Developing Evaluation Capacities*. On the website for UNEG (2015), readers can freely download the trilingual publication, *National Evaluation Capacity Development: Practical Tips on How to Strengthen National Evaluation Systems*. The website of the Evaluation Capacity Development Group (ECDG, 2015) also hosts a variety of useful resources, including their ECD Toolkit, with user-friendly tools, such as one for assessing the organizational culture for evaluation.

The website of My M&E (2015) has several publications for free download related to ECB and ECD; in addition to the publication edited by Segone and Rugh (2013) identified above, we also recommend *Advocating for Evaluation: A Toolkit to Develop Advocacy Strategies to Strengthen an Enabling Environment for Evaluation*. My M&E also hosts the website for EvalPartners (2015), a global partnership to enhance the capacities of civil society organizations (CSOs), focusing on strengthening the institutional capacity of Voluntary Organizations of Professional Evaluators (VOPEs); we recommend the recently developed EvalPartners Toolkit to develop advocacy strategies to strengthen an enabling environment for evaluation.

On the topics of M&E capacity assessment, we highly recommend the comprehensive (493 pages) capacity development toolkit from the World Bank, *Making Monitoring and Evaluation*

Systems Work (Görgens and Kusek, 2009). We also recommend the profile tool for organizational ECB by Bourgeois and Cousins (2008) and Bourgeois et al. (2013) as well as the Readiness for Organizational Learning and Evaluation (ROLE) instrument by Preskill and Torres (2015). There are a variety of other tools and checklists, such as the *M&E Capacity Assessment Tool* from Capacity for Health (2015), the *Checklist for Building Evaluation Capacity* by Volkov and King (2007), and the *Institutionalizing Evaluation Checklist* by Stufflebeam (2002). The McKinsey 7-S Framework, available from Mind Tools (2015), is useful for overall organizational assessment. Finally, we refer readers to Table 7.2 in Chapter 7, which includes key questions we identify for analyzing the context for M&E training in an organizational context.

For M&E strategic planning, we again recommend Görgens and Kusek (2009). MIT (2015) offers a concise list of key considerations available on its website for training and development: *What Makes an Organization's Training Plan Strategic?* Other useful examples of more generic guidelines freely available for strategic planning include the following: *How to do Strategic Planning: A Guide for Small and Diaspora NGOs* (James, n.d.); *Developing Your Nonprofit Strategic Plan* (McNamara, 2015); *Ten Keys to Successful Strategic Planning for Nonprofit and Foundation Leaders* (Mittenthal, 2015); and *Strategic Planning Guidelines for National Societies* (IFRC, 2012). The trilingual website for Capacity .org (2015) is a general "gateway" for capacity development on a variety of topics, including M&E-related topics as well as access to 15 years and 47 issues of www.capacity.org journal. Lastly, Chapter 7 of this book will look further at more practical application of ECB during training analysis, with related recommended resources.

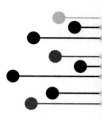

CHAPTER 4

Adult Learning

We have taken a look at the context for M&E training as a system, and to a large degree, Chapter 4 informs training delivery for the learners or trainees in this system. An understanding of adult learning is central to designing and delivering effective curriculum and activities for M&E training. However, adults are indeed complex systems, and no one explanatory model or theory is fully satisfactory. The body of work on adult theory is tremendous, with a variety of different opinions and perspectives:

> The fact that so many people have thought about, investigated, and written about the process of learning over the years suggests the complexity of the topic. Learning defies easy definition and simple theorizing. (Merriam, Caffarella, & Baumgartner, 2007, p. 275)

Therefore, any attempt to summarize such a topic as adult learning is far from exhaustive, and it is certainly beyond the scope of this chapter to provide more than a brief overview of some of the key concepts and considerations for M&E training. To complicate matters, there is considerable disagreement and divergence between the different adult learning theories and concepts. Nevertheless, we have tried to identify some common threads (themes) to guide us through our discussion.

Much of the discussion is theoretical, and the key adult learning principles in the last section drill down to concrete practices to inform training, which we will discuss in Parts 2 and 3 of the book. Some readers may prefer to come back to the theoretical background and read over the adult learning principles first.

Learning Objectives

By the end of this chapter readers will be able to . . .

✓ Explain what is learning and why it is hard to verify

✓ Explain Bloom's three learning domains

✓ Identify the key characteristics of adult learning from andragogy

✓ Describe Kolb's experiential learning cycle

✓ Compare and contrast a "four learning styles" approach with the "visual-auditory-kinesthetic" or VAK perspective for understating learning styles

✓ Explain what is differentiated instruction and why it is important

✓ Compare and contrast learner-centered with trainer-centered approaches to training

✓ Summarize the key adult learning principles identified for M&E training

4.1 What Is Learning?

Before we examine what makes learning distinct for adults, it is important to understand what we mean by "learning" itself. This is not as simple as it may seem, because learning is complicated and not fully understood. It is complex because people are complex, each with different sets of values, preferences, priorities, and experiences that affect the learning process. However, we feel that two key ingredients of learning are (a) it is a *process*, and (b) it involves a *change* in knowledge, attitudes, or skills (KSA). Therefore, for our purposes, we will adopt the definition offered by the educational theorist David Kolb (1984), known for his work in experiential learning:

> Learning is the process whereby knowledge is created through the transformation of experience. (p. 38)

This definition highlights two defining features in the history of learning theories (Merriam et. al., 2007). First, there is a notion of change—either in knowledge, attitudes, or behavior. However, learning is more than just a product (change), it is also a process concerned with what occurs during learning to cause a change in the individual learner. Importantly, the process of learning is not directly observable and verifiable but instead *inferred*. As evaluators, we can appreciate the implications this has for measuring learning outcomes (discussed in Chapter 9). In some instances, learning may become immediately discernible (e.g., one's ability to calculate a percentage); in other instances, it may be a considerable amount of time before learning becomes apparent (e.g., one's ability to facilitate a focus group discussion). Therefore, "learning" is a slippery concept when closely examined. It is one thing to define learning in a sentence, but it is another to operationalize and measure it.

Bloom's Taxonomy

In Chapter 2, we looked at an educational continuum from formal to informal education to help understand training relative to other sources learning. Another useful way to understand learning is according to **what** people learn. Developed in 1956, Bloom's Taxonomy classifies learning into three domains, as summarized **Figure 4.1**.[1] While other classification systems have been followed, this time-honored taxonomy remains widely accepted and used today.

Bloom's three learning domains underpin the classical "knowledge, skills, attitude" (KSA) structure so influential in training and education today. They are useful to better understand the training content and select the best instructional methods. The three

---

1. Bloom's taxonomy further subdivides the cognitive and affective domains from more simple to complex behaviors, and while the psychomotor initially did not have subcategories, these were later created by other educators.

FIGURE 4.1   Bloom's Three Learning Domains

Cognitive	• Knowledge and comprehension, including the ability to recall, analyze, and use information.
Psychomotor	• Physical movement, including coordination and the ability to physically manipulate a tool or instrument.
Affective	• Emotions, values, opinions, and attitudes, including the ability to interact with others.

domains are not absolutes nor mutually exclusive. For M&E training, the cognitive and affective domains typically take precedence, whereas the psychomotor domain, which was initially established for motor skills to operate equipment, has evolved to include modern day skills such as the use of a computer, software, or mobile device for M&E.

Of the three domains, the cognitive domain is typically the first domain to be addressed before the others. It occurs when trainees are presented with new information and concepts, such as how to select or design a SMART indicator. Knowledge can be further classified in many ways according to content, which will be discussed in Chapter 7 on training design, but two general categories include declarative and procedural knowledge. Declarative knowledge concerns learning about something, for example, facts, concepts, and principles. Procedural knowledge is when people learn how to do something. In an M&E training, defining different data collection methods would be declarative knowledge, whereas the recommended steps or procedures for facilitating a focus group discussion would be procedural knowledge.

Among the three learning domains, affective learning can be the greatest challenge. Unlike facts, they involve personal values, judgments, and beliefs that can be deeply embedded and culturally reinforced. Furthermore, attitudes are internal states that a trainer cannot directly monitor to know if a change has occurred. One approach for affective change is the use of peer learning—see **Box 4.1**.

It is worth noting that the three learning domains also apply to the trainers and their learning process. As we shall see, a distinction can be made between the *hard skills* comprised of the technical knowledge trainers need of the subject matter (cognitive domain), versus the *soft skills* comprised of interpersonal abilities that are essential to

BOX 4.1
Peer Learning for Affective Change

Peer learning involves sharing knowledge, ideas, and experience between learners.* People's opinions are highly influenced by peers, and learners can be motivated by the attitudes of other learners (Beasley, Valerio, & Bundy, 2008). For example, rather than a trainer "preaching" about why reliable monitor data is important for reporting, trainees can discuss this in small discussion groups, listing key reasons (e.g., on a flipchart) for reliable reporting and the consequences of misreporting. Such engagement is likely to instill more meaningful reflection and potential affective change than a trainer trying to convince trainees.

---

* Peer learning should be distinguished from peer education in that the latter is a type of formalized peer learning in health promotion for health-enhancing change among peers.

successfully facilitate trainings (affective domain). Both are critical for effective M&E trainers, and we discuss them further in Chapter 5.

4.2 How Adults Learn

If you were to design a lesson for children, you would probably select instruction and exercises methods quite different than for training adults. Adult learning is premised on the belief that adults learn differently than young learners. A child typically enters learning because it is required and expected, whereas an adult usually assumes their own responsibility and initiative for learning. Adults bring with them a whole different set of past experiences, values, opinions, expectations, and priorities that shape why and how they learn and the methods that best help them achieve their learning goals.

There are many schools of thought for adult learning, with seemingly more debate than consensus (e.g., Davenport & Davenport, 1985). However, virtually all theoretical attempts to understand adult learning are grounded in philosophical and theoretical orientations that have been around for many years. Typically, they embrace the concepts of behavioral change and experience. John Dewey, for example, wrote extensively on the use of experience for learning (e.g., Dewey, 1938). B. F. Skinner stressed that learners must engage in behavior to learn new behaviors (Skinner, 1974), and Carl Rogers emphasized that learners must participate in the learning process for meaningful learning to occur (Rogers, 1969). Other prominent theorists for adult learning include Kurt Lewin, Jean Piaget, William James, Carl Jung, and Paulo Freire.

Our focus in this chapter will be limited to two prominent influences in adult learning: andragogy and experiential learning. We have selected these two from other schools of thoughts and theoretical models of adult learning because we feel they provide a good overview of key considerations for M&E training. However, it is important to acknowledge the rich theoretical heritage that informs the field of adult learning. Merriam et. al. (2007, p. 275) identify five theoretical orientations to learning— behaviorist, humanist, cognitivist, social cognitive, and constructivist. While space prevents us from exploring these foundational *metatheories* in detail, **Table 4.1** provides a snapshot summarizing their key aspects.

It is worth noting that these metatheories are not age specific (e.g., childhood versus adulthood) and certainly not exhaustive. Some theorists contend that adult learning is not so distinct, but rather learning is a single fundamental human process regardless of age, underpinned by the principles of these metatheories (Davenport & Davenport 1985). Certainly, there are certain learning principles that are the foundation for

TABLE 4.1   Five Metatheories of Learning

Theory	Example Theorists	View of the Learning Process	Example Methods
Behaviorist	Pavlov (1849–1936) Watson (1878–1958) Skinner (1904–1990)	Learning is caused by external stimuli and positive reinforcement, and can be observed and measured. Learner is more passive.	Lecture, drill and practice, repetition, multiple choice tests
Humanist	Maslow (1908–1978) Rogers (1902–1987)	Learning builds on personal experience and perspectives, leading to fulfill one's potential.	Discovery, discussion, problem solving, self-directed and collaborative
Cognitivist	Piaget (1896–1980) Miller (1920–) Neisser (1928–)	Learning is an internal, mental process, involving insight, information processing, and memory. Learner is active.	Lecture, visual tools, multiple choice and essay assessment
Social Cognitive	Bandura (1925–) Rotter (1920–2014)	Learning is relative to social context, stressing interactions and relationships between people and the environment.	Peer learning, collaboration, games, role playing, other group activities
Constructivist	Dewey (1859–1952) Kolb (1938–)	Learning occurs as an individual's personal interpretation and reflection from experiential, real-life experience.	Discovery, hands-on activities, problem solving, self-directed and collaborative

Source: Adapted from Merriam et. al., 2007, p. 295.

any learning experience, and are applicable to both adults and children in general. However, we believe that there are also important distinctions for adult learning that are worth noting for M&E training.

4.3 Andragogy

Popularized by the educational theorist Malcolm Knowles, *andragogy* is "the art and science of helping adults learn" (Knowles, 1980, p. 43). The term first appeared in Europe in the 1800s, and it evolved as a concept in the United States during the 1900s. As adults increasingly sought learning opportunities beyond their formal schooling years, it became apparent that they required different instructional approaches than used in the classroom setting.

Andragogy emerged in response to the traditional pedagogical methods used in child education. While the broader definition of *pedagogy* refers to the art, science, or profession of teaching, its Greek origins literally mean the teaching of children. Andragogy was presented as a more adult-focused alternative to pedagogy to emphasize that adults should be taught differently from children (Knowles, 1970). Subsequently,

> Andragogy became a rallying point for those trying to define the field of adult education as separate from other areas of education. (Merriam, 2001, p. 5)

Depending on which source is consulted, andragogy is conceptualized and presented in different ways. It has fueled much research and controversy, and Knowles himself refined his thinking over the years. However, the key elements of the andragogy remain the same. At the core of Knowles' andragogical model is the premise that adults are self-directed learners who bring to learning a different set of experiences, priorities, opinions, and values than children. Unlike children, who have not been around as long, adults do not passively accept learning but more readily question it relative to their prior experience and how they can apply it to their immediate needs. Knowles summarized the distinct characteristics of adult learners in what are today his six key assumptions of adult learning (Knowles, Swanson, & Holton, 2005). **Table 4.2** lists these assumptions, and they are very much reflected in the adult learning principles we propose in the last section of this chapter.

Knowles elaborated a holistic model for andragogy, for which the adult learning assumptions provide the foundation, including an eight-step process to apply his andragogical principles (Knowles, 1995). As with his assumptions, these steps have evolved in the field of adult learning. In our discussion of experiential learning below, we will look more closely at the stages in the experiential learning cycle, and in Chapter 8 we will discuss Gagné's nine events of instruction to inform training design.

TABLE 4.2   Knowles's Six Assumptions of Adult Learning

1. **The need to know**—Adults want to know the reasons why to learn something before undertaking learning.

2. **Self-concept**—Adults want to take responsibility for their own learning.

3. **Experience**—Adults bring considerable experience to inform their learning.

4. **Readiness to learn**—Adults become ready to learn when they experience a need to learn.

5. **Orientation to learn**—Adults are problem centered and interested in the practical application of learning.

6. **Motivation to learn**—Adults are responsive to some external motivators (e.g., better job or higher salary), but respond better to internal motivators (e.g., increased self-esteem, confidence, and job satisfaction).

As noted earlier, adult learning is a very contentious field, and Knowles' model of andragogy is not without its critics (e.g., discussed in Brookfield, 2005; Davenport & Davenport, 1985; Merriam et al., 2007; Taylor & Kroth, 2009).[2] Criticism notwithstanding, the underlying premise that adults bring different experiences, preestablished beliefs and dispositions to learning than children has had considerable influence (e.g., Laird, 2003), and therefore we felt relevant for an introductory book on M&E training. Knowles' emphasis on adult learning needs has also contributed to the learner-centered approach to training (and education as a whole) that we will discuss later in this chapter.

4.4 Experiential Learning

As the name implies, experiential learning theory (ELT) holds that individuals learn best through direct experience. It is a learning theory that draws upon the principles of andragogy: Individuals learn when actively engaged in their learning with relevant experiences (Beard & Wilson, 2006; Kolb, 1984). It is important to note that the theory is not restricted to adults but includes learners of all ages. Also, it is not restricted to organized learning, such as trainings or classroom instruction, but also includes learning

---

2. One overall criticism is that it lacks the scientific rigor of a theory with limited empirical evidence. Consequently, it makes certain assumptions, foremost being that the principles apply to all "adult" learners. For instance, adults may not always be internally motivated to learn but may be externally motivated—that is, for increased earnings, job opportunity, and social capital. Related, the principles may also apply to children. For example, some children may also be self-directed in their learning and want to understand the reason for learning. Further criticism is that andragogy does not consider the distinct social, political, and cultural factors of adult learners and is limited to western notions of adult behaviors and motivations for learning. In response to the criticism, Knowles has acknowledged that these characteristics are "assumptions" and do not apply solely to "adult" learners (Knowles, 1989).

I hear and I forget, I see and I remember, I do and I understand.
(Confucius, 450 BC)

Tell me and I forget, teach me and I remember, involve me and I will learn.
(Benjamin Franklin, 1706–1790)

There is an intimate and necessary relation between the process of actual experience and education.
(John Dewey, 1859–1952)

Knowledge is experience. Anything else is just information.
(Albert Einstein, 1879–1955)

All learning begins with experience. Real learning begins when a response is called for in relation to an experience.
(Jarvis, 1987, p. 16)

from the experiences of daily life, such as incidental learning (Houle 1980, p. 221).

The principle that people learn by doing and direct discovery has intuitive appeal and has been used in trainings by many who may have never known it as a formalized learning theory. Most of us have experienced the difference between sitting down and listening to a boring lecture ("death by PowerPoint") versus being actively engaged in a group activity. Experiential instruction methods are learner centered, stressing the process of learning over the content.

Experiential learning has had wide influence in adult learning, including evaluation training and education. Trevisan's (2004) literary review of evaluation training concludes, "One of the most enduring recommendations in literature about the teaching of evaluation is that students receive hands-on or practical experiences during their education" (Trevisan, 2004, p. 256). The evaluation training and education literature includes numerous references and recommendations for experiential learning approaches.[3] As Kelly and Kaczynski (2008) note, practical experiences in evaluation education helps the adult learner connect theory and practice. M&E training is especially well suited to learning from authentic, relevant experience that translates into the real world:

> Such (evaluation) training must involve real-world experiences or simulations that reflect reality of settings, dynamics, and interactions. Building in such training experiences requires creativity and capitalization of opportunities for real-world involvement. (Barnette & Wallis, 2003, p. 61)

Kolb is one of the most influential proponents of experiential learning, and his experiential learning cycle is a useful way to take a closer look at its underlying principles (Kolb & Fry, 1975). Developed with Fry, the cycle summarizes four primary stages of learning (see **Figure 4.2**). In essence, the cycle portrays an intuitive theory of change for learning involving having an experience, followed by reflection and drawing conclusions, and then practicing or applying the learning for reinforcement and preparation for use in the real world.

---

3. For example, Adams and Dickinson, 2010; Barnette and Wallace, 2003; Davis, 2006; Kelly and Kaczynski, 2008; Lee, Wallace, and Alkin, 2007; Orr, 2010; Preskill, 1992, 1997.

FIGURE 4.2 Kolb's Experiential Learning Cycle

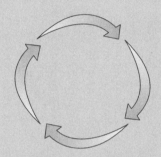

Experiencing—Provide an experience that actively engages, preferably self-directed, with little or no guidance or supervision from the trainer. Activities can include solving problems, playing games, role plays, etc.

Experimenting (applying)—Learners critically test what has been learned in new situations, reinforcing and internalizing learning by working directly with the concepts themselves.

Reflecting—Learners pause to observe and think about their experience. Can be facilitated or independent, done individually or with others. Framed with questions such as, "What just happened?" "How did you feel about it?" "What worked well and didn't?" "What did you learn?"

Conceptualizing—Learners draw generalizations and conclusions, and how it can apply to the real world. Typically involves active facilitation with leading questions and activities to consider learning as it applies to real life.

The learning cycle as an integrated process with each stage mutually supportive in a continuous spiral of learning (Kolb & Fry, 1975). Thus, the learner can enter the cycle at any stage, and no one stage is effective as a learning procedure on its own. Different versions of the cycle exists (e.g., experience—reflect—conclude—apply and activity—discuss—apply). But no matter how often the conceptual model is adapted, the essential elements remain: experience—reflect—conclude—practice/apply (Beard & Wilson, 2006).

4.5 Learning Styles and Preferences

Learning in adulthood is an intensely personal activity.

(Merriam et al., 2007, p. ix)

Everyone does not learn in the same way; consequently, there is no one recipe for adult learning. People have different ways of receiving, processing, and retaining information—learning preferences. For instance, some people like to be challenged and learn best diving right in, actively engaged. Others are more reserved, preferring to be thoroughly briefed and reflect before proceeding with their learning.

The concept of different learning styles may sound like common sense, but research into this area is relative young, tracing back to the 1970s (Pashler, McDaniel, Rohrer, & Bjork, 2008). Increasing attention paralleled that given to experiential learning and learner-centered approaches to training and education. If learning is experienced, each experience is influenced by the individual's past and current circumstances of the learner (Beard & Wilson 2006).

Today there are an assortment of publications on adult learning styles and an array of methods and questionnaires to assess them. For instance, Kolb (1984) developed a Learning Styles Inventory in his work on experiential learning. Below we take a look at two prominent approaches that we feel are helpful to frame this topic for M&E training: Honey and Mumford's four learning styles and VAK (visual, auditory, and kinesthetic). Each is quite different, but together they can complement one another, providing different perspectives to consider adult learning styles.

Four learning styles

Drawing upon Kolb's experiential learning cycle, Honey and Mumford (1992) identify four primary types of learners. They point out that their learning styles are not static and can change for individuals depending on their circumstances. They also highlight that understanding the learning style not only benefits the teacher/trainer but also helps the learner become more aware of and pursue their personal learning. Following we briefly summarize each style as it relates to training:

1. **Activists** are "doers" and prefer to be directly involved and immerse themselves in an experience. They like taking the initiative, problem solving, discovering, exploring, confronting challenges, and experimenting. They are quick to speak up and get up to test new knowledge and skills, learning by doing. On the other hand, they are quick to get restless and bored when inactive for too long or the novelty of an activity wears off. Engaging activities that involve the learner are best for activists, such as role playing, puzzle/problem solving, and discussion or debates.

2. **Reflectors** or "reviewers" prefer to carefully gather and consider information before offering opinions or conclusions. They are thoughtful and cautious and inclined to listen, observe, and deliberate before testing or applying new knowledge or skills. They prefer ample background information and time to ponder and consider different perspectives and implications before making a move. To no surprise,

reflectors are inclined toward reflective activities, often self-paced, such as journaling or participation in an online forum, allowing them time to pause to consider new ideas.

3. **Theorists** prefer to step back and build a larger picture (theory) about what they are learning. They are conceptual, systems thinkers and like to logically analyze learning content in a coherent, organized manner. For M&E, they may gravitate to concepts such as a theory of change and approaches such as logic modeling. They like clear goals, objectives, and order. They can ask a lot of questions and challenge not only the information and concepts presented, but also the manner (processes) in which it is presented. It is helpful to have well-organized trainings for theorists, which clearly explain the rationale for the learning content and process.

4. **Pragmatists** are "realists" and prefer to test and apply what they learn to real-world situations. They like to solve problems and prefer to put theory to practice over excessive theorizing and discussion. They tend to be practical and goal-oriented, and learning content needs to make sense so they can see how it can help them outside of the training. Therefore, they like to know why they are learning something and how they can use it. Applied training works well with these learners, such as real-life case studies, fieldwork, and observations, accompanied by feedback and coaching.

You may be interested to reflect on your own learning style (see **Box 4.2**).

BOX 4.2
What Learning Style Are You?

Pretend that you just received a large box containing a new bicycle that you ordered. Inside you find parts to be assembled as well as detailed instructions and tools for assembly. What do you do?

1. If you rip open the box and immediately assemble and ride the bike without reading the instructions, you are likely an **activist**.

2. If you carefully open the box, set out the pieces, and think on it a day before assembling, you are likely a **reflector**.

3. If you find yourself critiquing how well (or not) the instructions are written, you are likely a **theorist**.

4. If you enjoy assembling the bicycle correctly and give it a test run to ensure it works as expected, you are likely a **pragmatist**.

VAK—visual, auditory, and kinesthetic

VAK classifies learning styles based on the three primary sensory receivers. Although we use all three senses when we learn, VAK holds that one or two is usually dominant. It is associated with Neil Fleming's work on VARK (Visual, Aural, Read/write, and Kinesthetic) which expanded on earlier neuro-linguistic programming (NLP) (Fleming & Baume, 2006). Its simplicity and intuitiveness makes it one of the most widely used models for learning styles in education.

VAK acknowledges that learning is "multimodal" and not strictly limited to one domain. Therefore, it recommends learning methods that involve all three senses. Such a multimodal approach also allows the trainer to better involve learners regardless of individual sensory preference. Of the three senses, vision is especially influential for adult learning (Constantinidou & Baker, 2002; Ware, 2013). Therefore, rather than classify leaners by one of the three senses, we prefer to use VAK to look at three important *ways* people learn:

1. **Visual learning** involves learning content presented through pictures, diagrams, demonstrations, or other visual media. For the visual learning, it is important to see the speaker, as well as what they are saying—that is, with a whiteboards, flipcharts, or PowerPoint slides. Other examples of visual aids include outlines or handouts of key learning points, summary tables (e.g., logframes), agendas, charts, Gantt and flowcharts, graphs, cartoons, and illustrations. Visual learning is also reinforced by taking notes to visually organize and support understanding; therefore, it can be helpful for trainers to emphasize key points to cue note taking.

2. **Auditory (aural) learning** involves listening or speaking and includes activities using verbal exchanges, stories, anecdotes, discussion, brainstorming, lectures, and so forth. People inclined toward auditory learning may move their lips and read aloud and welcome the opportunity to orally repeat or review key learning points. Therefore, involving them in question and answer sessions, where they either articulate or respond to questions, can be effective. Pneumonic devises are also useful to reinforce memory of key points.

3. **Kinesthetic learning** involves moving and touching. This includes concrete experiences where people learn from doing, such as problem

solving. The more the learner is standing up and using their body, the higher potential for kinesthetic learning. Someone inclined toward kinesthetic learning may lose concentration and get bored if there is little or no external stimulation or movement. Therefore, kinesthetic learning is reinforced when learners get up, move around, and try things out themselves rather than watch a demonstration. They prefer to stand around flipcharts to summarize points, draw diagrams, pictures, or simply doodle on a notebook.

Jessie Mountfield

Using color highlighters when reading can also be helpful for the sake of attaching a movement to what people are hearing or reading. For kinesthetic learning, such movement can reinforce understanding and memory of information.

Our overview of Honey and Mumford's four learning styles and VAK is brief, but we feel it highlights key considerations for an introductory book of this nature. As mentioned, there exists an assortment of other models on the subject (e.g., see **Box 4.3**). One commonality they all share is that they acknowledge that their categories of learning styles are not absolutes; learners may have a preference for a single style, but they do not rely on that to the exclusion of others. So what does this mean for M&E training? While it may not be possible to definitively assess,[4] never mind address, all the different learning styles one may encounter in M&E training, it is important to develop an informed awareness of them. This can help trainers to better adapt instructional methods, activities, and material that deliver to achieve learning objectives.

---

4. There exists an array of methods and questionnaires to assess people's learning styles and personalities. For instance, the prominent Myers-Briggs Type Indicator (MBTI) personality inventory bases its assessment on sixteen distinct personality types (Myers McCaulley, Quenk, & Hammer, 1998), while the Hermann Brain Dominance Instrument (HBDI) is based on a classification according to four quadrants of the brain (Herrmann, 1999). Each approach has its merits, but there remains little consensus or convincing evidence on how to best determine and measure learning styles (e.g., Pashler, McDaniel, Rohrer, & Bjork, 2008).

BOX 4.3
Multiple Intelligences & Emotional Intelligence

Another influential model for learning styles is Gardner's (1983) theory of multiple intelligences. Gardner refutes the idea of one type of intelligence; he initially identified seven intelligences, later added an eighth, and acknowledges that there may be more (Gardner, 1983, 1999). However, his theory has not been well accepted within academic psychology (Klein, 1997; Smith, 2002, 2008). Nevertheless, we mention it here as it has had considerable influence in the education community, challenging the dominant approach to measure on intelligence—the intelligence quotient (IQ). Related, Goleman, a friend and former classmate of Gardner at Harvard University, popularized the concept of emotional intelligence in his 1995 book of the same name. He also criticizes conventional measures of intelligence as being too narrow; for instance, explaining why people with high IQs sometimes struggle to learn, while those with modest IQs do remarkably well. Like Gardner's theory of multiple intelligence, it is worth mention because it also has had considerable influence, especially in training, organizational management, and human resource development.

4.6 Differentiated Instruction

In addition to *how* people learn (learning styles and preferences), there are other important individual differences to consider among trainees. Differentiated instruction stresses different ways to meet the needs of different learners. It offers "a systematic approach to planning curriculum and instruction for academically diverse learners" (Tomlinson & Strickland, 2005, p. 6). As discussed in Chapter 3, individual learners bring different abilities and experience, values, beliefs, emotions, and motives to the M&E capacity building system. Trainees can vary in gender, ethnicity, culture, language, and socioeconomic status. Rather than a "one size fits all" approach, training should be tailored to different learner profiles.

Differentiated learning has received increasing attention, coinciding with equal access to individuals with disabilities and public school initiatives, such as the American *No Child Left Behind* policy in 2000, and a growing body of literature supports it benefits (Huebner, 2010; Nunley, 2006; Tomlinson & Strickland, 2005).[5] In their resource guide for curriculum differentiation, Tomlinson and Strickland (2005) summarize five useful elements to distinguish and modify for differentiated learning, which we adapt and summarize here:

---

5. ASCD (2014) provides free sample chapters, study guides, and author interviews on differentiated instruction.

1. **Content**—the subject matter and learner access to information and ideas that matter

2. **Process**—how learners come to understand and own the necessary KSA for training objectives

3. **Products**—how learners demonstrate learning objectives in practice (assignments, performance reviews)

4. **Affect**—affective needs include safety, positive reinforcement, and a sense of belonging

5. **Learning environment**—includes the physical space in which learning occurs as well as the learning atmosphere (pace, group dynamics, space, distractions)

As is often the case, these elements are interrelated; for example, a comfortable and affirming learning environment can help different learners feel secure and uninhibited in the learning process. Affective needs are especially important during the learning process, and includes social cohesion, kinship, and affirmation that learners, "are valuable just as they are" (Tomlinson & Strickland, 2005, p. 11). Learners need to be recognized and know they can succeed. Those who are struggling need to feel a sense of belonging with their peer learners. There are a variety of activities and facilitation techniques to help "fringe" learners meaningfully participate in the learning process. For instance, learners can be flexibly grouped by shared interests, topics, learning styles, or abilities.

Differential instruction requires a good understanding of the target learners for training. This is best considered during training analysis so the curriculum can be designed to help different types of learners accomplish learning objectives. The degree to which training instruction can be differentiated will depend on factors such as access to trainees and information about them prior to training, the number and diversity of trainees, and the length and duration of the training. A more rigorous approach to differentiated instruction may be more suitable for longer-term training programs, working with cohorts of trainees with varying experience and abilities that will change over time during training.

Much of the guidance in Part 2 and 3 of this book can be used to support differentiated instruction: that is, for instance, the trainee analysis, selection of the training facility, seating arrangements, and the types of learning activities and facilitation used for training. We identify differentiated learning as an adult learning principle later in this chapter and provide examples of how it can be supported for M&E training. It is very much a cross-cutting principle with respect to the others, as we shall see.

4.6 Learner-Centered Training

The concepts of self-directed, individualized learning we have discussed thus far are at the core of a *learner-centered* approach to learning. For training, a learner-centered approach stresses that learning is more successful when it is individualized and self-directed, and when the learners are more intrinsically than extrinsically motivated to take responsibility for their own learning. It challenges the dominant-teacher and dependent-learner relationship and advocates for a more participatory, empowering approach to learning.

Table 4.3 compares key aspects of a trainer-centered versus learner-centered approach to training. Training content is important, but learner-centered training stresses the importance of the learning process (activities and facilitation) to achieve learning objectives. It shifts the focus from the trainer to the learner's needs, experience, abilities, interests, and learning styles. Trainers should not simply plan the training based on what *they* think learners need to know but instead find ways to understand and incorporate the *trainee's* needs and prior experience so that trainings are more accessible and meaningful. As we shall see in Part 2 of this book, such considerations are critical for training design, delivery, and evaluation.

In her insightful book, Weimer (2002) identifies five changes needed in instructional practice to be learner centered: the balance of power, the function of content, the role of the teacher, the responsibility for learning, and the purpose and processes of evaluation. It is no coincidence that Weimer identifies first the balance of power. The more the learner participates in the learning process, the more power shifts from the trainer to the trainee. Rather than taking center stage all of the time, the trainer relinquishes control and allows trainees to take a more active role in their learning. Readers can refer to Box 10.7 in Chapter 10 for an example of a shift in the balance of power to learners when they challenged a training activity.

Prominent educational theorists, notably Paulo Freire (1970), have stressed the importance of changing the power-relationship in education, treating learners as subjects rather than objects. Instead of "depositing" information into learners as if they were passive "receptacles," learning is successful when the teacher/trainer and learner are equal, working alongside, supporting and learning from each other. Such perspectives have helped to move trainings away from the conventional lecture format that treats the learners as docile listeners. It inverts the traditional teacher/trainer role, putting the learners in more control of the learning process.

However, in learner-centered instruction, "power is shared rather than transferred wholesale" (Weimer, 2002, p. 28). Trainers will still make key learning decisions and not always with trainee input. Nevertheless, a learner-centered approach entails a different role for the trainer, emphasizing the trainer's role as a facilitator (Heron, 1999).

TABLE 4.3 Comparing Trainer-Centered and Learner-Centered Approaches

Learner-centered	Trainer-centered
Trainer brings M&E knowledge and experience, but empowers learners to explore, question, and participate in the learning process.	**Trainer** is the expert and repository of M&E knowledge and transmits it to the learner; they know best.
Learners are a valuable source of knowledge and experience to contribute to learning.	**Learners** are passive, listening, taking notes, and memorizing information.
Both trainees and trainer learn together.	*Only trainees are viewed as learners.*
Responsibility and power for learning is shared between the trainer and learners.	**Responsibility and power** for learning rests with trainer.
Training content and flow is adapted to the learners and their learning process.	**Training content and flow** is dictated by the trainer according to their agenda.
Interaction draws upon a wide range of activities to encourage learners to discuss, practice, experience, reflect, share, and critically question training content.	**Interaction** is typically limited to questions and answers and related discussion.
Activities are more interactive with learners, stressing active participation, critical thinking and questioning, collaborative, and peer learning.	**Activities** tend to be more one-way from trainer to learner, stressing trainer presentation of content, for example, lectures.
Atmosphere is more empowering, engaging, uninhibited, supportive, cooperative, and fun.	**Atmosphere** is more controlled, restrained, supervised, individualistic, and can be competitive.
Feedback is provided by the learners themselves as well as the trainer.	**Feedback** is provided only by trainers.
Assessment is incorporated into learning and involves the learner to enhance their potential and promote leaning; consequently, they tend to be more motivating and part of the learning process.	**Assessment** is separate from learning and done to the learner, stressing objectively scored tests with right/wrong answers; consequently, they tend to be stressful.

Sources: Beard and Wilson (2006); Huba and Freed (2000); Weimer (2002); Chatty, Baas, & Fleig (2003).

As we will discuss in Chapter 9, training facilitation stresses participatory, empowering approaches to learning, where participants actively learn and critically question, drawing upon their own shared experiences. The trainer is not the sole knowledge provider, nor are trainees submissive recipients. Trainees learn not only from the trainer but also from each other as equal participants in learning, and in this process the trainer/facilitator often learns from the trainees.

4.7 Adult-Learning Principles for Effective M&E Training

If you have read through the prior sections of this chapter, maybe you are a theorist learner and appreciated the overview of key adult learning concepts. Or maybe you are a pragmatist learner and have skipped the previous sections, choosing to "cut to the chase" to the applied principles we outline in this section. However you arrived here, let us first say a few words about the origin of the fourteen principles we identify for adult learning (summarized in **Table 4.4**). As our foregoing discussion highlights, there is a wealth of scholarship and research on adult learning. We draw upon this body of information to identify these principles. The underlying rationale is not original, but we have assembled and expressed the principles in a way to highlight those practices for adult learning we believe are important for M&E training.

Our suggested principles are about human learning behavior, so they are not absolutes nor are they exhaustive. They apply generally but not to all people under all conditions. For example, certain cultures may prefer a more structured, controlled delivery of trainings than a fun and active format. Therefore, these principles should be adapted and tailored accordingly to specific training contexts.

These principles not only are important for training facilitation but also inform other processes in the training system, such as analyzing trainees, identifying appropriate learning objectives and activities, and assessing learning and other indicators of training performance.

The principles are interrelated and illustrate the interdependence of different elements in learning systems, each principle complementing and reinforcing others. For example learning that builds on prior experience (Principle 4) can help ensure the training is relevant and meaningful to real-world application (Principle 5). Another example is that training that is fun and active (Principle 7) can support multisensory delivery (Principle 9) that allows participants to learn by doing (Principle 6) and sharing for peer learning (Principle 10).

In the remainder of this chapter, we will look at each of the fourteen principles, followed by tips and examples of how to support the principle in practice. This guidance will be supplemented in Part 2 of the book, where we provide more detailed guidance for the application of the adult learning principles for specific M&E training activities.

TABLE 4.4 Summary of Key Adult Learning Principles for M&E Training

1. **Establish a safe and respectful climate**—Adults learn better when they feel safe and respected.

2. **Respond to the "need to know" (NTK)**—Adults prefer to know *what*, *why*, and *how* they are learning.

3. **Provide a structured yet flexible progression**—Adults prefer learning that is well organized.

4. **Empower with genuine participation**—Adults want to share full responsibility for their learning.

5. **Incorporate past experience**—Adults prefer learning that builds upon their prior experience.

6. **Keep it relevant and meaningful**—Adults prefer practical learning that meets their needs.

7. **Provide direct experience**—Adults learn best by doing.

8. **Make it active, fun, and challenging**—Adults learn more when it is engaging and enjoyable.

9. **Use mixed/multisensory methods**—Adult learners require a mixture of learning approaches.

10. **Differentiate instruction**—Adult learning is more effective when instruction is tailored to different learners' needs.

11. **Utilize collaborative, peer learning**—Adults effectively learn from each other.

12. **Include practice and repetition**—Adult learning is enhanced by repetition.

13. **Design for primacy and recency**—Adults remember best what they learn first and last in sequence.

14. **Provide feedback and positive reinforcement**—Adults want to know if they are learning and to be encouraged in the process.

1. Establish a safe and respectful climate—Adults learn better when they feel safe and respected.

Adults learn best in a relaxed and friendly atmosphere, where they do not feel threatened. Tension is not conducive to learning, and a comfortable person will learn more readily than one who is fearful, embarrassed, nervous, or angry. Adults may feel vulnerable learning new topics such as M&E, outside their "comfort zone," where they are no longer in control. Therefore, M&E training should be structured to provide support and acceptance and to reduce the fear of judgment. Adults bring ego to their learning interactions with others and want to be valued and treated as an adult, not patronized or disciplined as can occur in child education. Good manners and courtesy are indispensable, and it is essential to establish rapport with and among trainees based on mutual respect and trust. It is important to cultivate a learning environment that positively acknowledges accomplishments and to help "save face" and preserve self-respect (image) when mistakes are made.

Tips for M&E training

- Agree upon ground rules for group work at the start of the training, so positive behaviors can be acknowledged and practiced from the start, and post them in a public space (flipchart or blog post) as a reminder that can be referred to as needed.

- Provide opportunities for trainee feedback on the training facilitation and their comfort level.

- Model responsible and respectful behavior as a trainer—that is, actively and carefully listen to questions, acknowledging and allowing for difference of opinion.

- Utilize individual coaching/feedback opportunities to establish rapport with trainees, connecting and relating to them as individuals.

2. Respond to the "need to know" (NTK)—Adults prefer to know what, why, and how they are learning.

Adults are self-directed and their understanding and buy-in is essential for eventual ownership and use of the learning. For example, when individuals seek training on their own initiative (as opposed to training required at their workplace), they often devote considerable energy exploring the benefits before investing valuable time and money. Adults prefer to decide for themselves what to learn. Therefore, it is important that they understand the reasons for learning something like M&E and how it will benefit them. Adults also want to know how the training will be conducted so they can better prepare for and participate in the training.

Tips for M&E training

- Clearly frame the purpose, specific learning objectives, and learning progression of M&E training.

- Help trainees become aware of their need to know, allowing them to ask question and express any concerns about M&E training content, progression, and relevance—that is, have trainees identify expectations prior to training.

- Ensure trainees understand why M&E training is relevant and related to real-world needs, and how it can help them.

- Make use of pre-training communication and an agenda/schedule to inform trainees about what to expect.

- Anticipate and answer the "So what?" or "What's in it for me?" or WIIFM questions.

3. Provide a structured yet flexible progression— Adults prefer learning that is well organized.

As self-directed learners, adults learn better when they have a sense of direction of where the learning is heading. The trainer needs to understand and anticipate learning pathways to help ground the training and then provide this "mental scaffolding" to help adult learners organize and understand the interconnections between different M&E topics. It also helps them anticipate what is ahead, satisfying their "need to know" what is expected of them and what they can expect of the training. This can reduce anxiety and empower them to assume more responsibility for their learning. However, it is important to remember that a well-structured progression should not equate with a rigid blueprint. It can serve as a road map, but there can be different routes to take you where you want to go (and sometimes the unexpected can take you right off the map). Therefore, it is also important to allow for flexibility and improvisation in training, accommodating emergent learning needs and opportunities to build meaning.

Tips for M&E training

- Design and communicate coherent lesson plans, ideally with trainee input and buy-in, clearly sequencing learning topics that mutually reinforce learning objectives.

- Communicate and validate the organization of the training using an agenda/schedule, identifying key learning objectives and the expected time to be allocated to each lesson/session.

- Periodically revisit the training agenda (i.e., the end of each day) and discuss in a participatory manner with trainees, adjusting according to training realities and trainee needs.

- Introduce learning topics and objectives in a consistent manner at the beginning of each lesson, realigning it to prior topics and the overall learning progression.

- Be ready to adapt to and accommodate emergent learning needs and opportunities that inevitably arise in training—that is, responding to questions about how M&E topics apply to trainee's particular context.

4. Empower with genuine participation—Adults want to share full responsibility for their learning.

Adults are independent learners and do not want things done *to* them but *with* them. They need to be the origin of their own learning and may resist approaches that do not meaningfully involve them. Adults think independently, and learning is more effective when people are actively involved as partners for whom their opinions, experience, and knowledge is just as valid as the trainer's. Participatory facilitation requires M&E trainers to relinquish some control over the learning process. The degree to which this is possible will depend on the level of interaction the specific training delivery allows (e.g., live, in-person training versus asynchronous online training), but the more adults are treated as equal participants rather than passive recipients, the more likely they will be motivated to learn.

Tips for M&E training

- Consider a sequenced learning progression that moves from more to less structure and supervision, relinquishing more responsibility at an appropriate pace that is challenging yet not overloading for trainees.

- Build into training regular feedback opportunities for trainees to reflect upon and express their opinion on M&E training content and facilitation.

- Delegate responsibilities in the training to the trainees themselves, such as conducting day reviews or energizers, managing a "parking lot" for follow-up ideas, and presenting out on appropriate topics.

- Lead toward inquiry before supplying too many facts, asking questions that allow trainees to explain training content themselves, for example, "Is there anyone who understands or can explain this?"

- Facilitate learning activities that are more self- or group-directed—for example, debates, discussions, and role-playing.

- When possible, actively involve trainees in the design and delivery of the training, which will enhance their understanding, involvement, and ownership.

5. Incorporate past experience—Adults prefer learning that builds upon their prior experience.

Adults bring a wealth of experience, prior knowledge, and priorities to learning that should be recognized and utilized as a rich resource and opportunity for training. They interpret new information according to their personal values and experiences. Therefore, adult learning should draw upon existing knowledge and experience. Adults will be more motivated to learn and trainings will be more effective if trainees can relate new knowledge to a familiar frame of reference, drawing upon their own experience.

Tips for M&E training

- Conduct training needs assessments and preliminary trainee consultation that not only determine subject matter familiarity but other prior experience and knowledge that may reinforce and enhance learning.

- Assist trainees to reflect and draw on past experience when problem solving; that is, while they may not have formally evaluated a program, relating it to another way they have been involved in assessment, such as rating a dining experience at a restaurant.

- Use questions to elicit and elaborate trainee prior experiences, relating it to the new learning content—for example, "Have any of you experienced this before?"

- Consider sequencing M&E training topics from the known to the unknown, beginning with trainees' existing knowledge and experience.

6. Keep it relevant and meaningful—Adults prefer practical learning that meets their needs.

Adults are goal-oriented and more motivated when learning immediately applies to their real-world needs. They are problem centered and interested in the immediate application of learning to solve problems relevant to their lives. Adults want to be assured that what they learn is worthwhile (value for money) and learning will be more meaningful when they see how they can realistically put it to use after the training.

Tips for M&E training

- Explain and show how M&E training content is useful and applicable to specific, realistic needs, and can help trainees achieve their goals.

- Design learning content that utilizes plenty of real-life examples, case studies and scenarios, and analogies that allow the trainee to more readily relate and transfer their learning to the real world.

- Link new concepts and theories to the real world by asking questions such as, "How does this fit with what you need to do now?" or "How do you see using this in the future?"

> All modern learning theories stress that adults must have a degree of ownership in the learning process and that they want to invest their previous experience in those processes (Laird, 2003, p. 151).

- When possible, conduct training as close as possible to real-life scenarios, which will be easier for trainees to transfer into real-world situations.

- Consider field trips to where M&E is being practiced or show videos of M&E activities being performed (e.g., a focus group discussion).

7. Provide direct experience—Adults learn best by doing.

Adults generally prefer hands-on learning with concrete experiences, experimentation, and problem solving. They like a challenge—to roll up their sleeves and get their hands dirty. Experiential learning from trial and error reinforces the meaning and intensity of learning. It also helps to build practical skills, confidence, and competence. Learning by experiencing is most effective when it is relevant to actual M&E situations encountered in the real world, and there is no substitute for learning from the real thing. For example, it is one thing to discuss how to design a project using a logframe but another to actually design one based on a real-life case study/scenario.

Tips for M&E training

- Provide hand-on learning opportunities rather than just observing, listening, and reflecting.

- Encourage problem solving and experimentation, allowing trainees to learn from trial and error.

- Utilize problem-solving activities, such as case studies and scenarios, allowing adults to discover firsthand solutions to their challenges.

- Provide plenty of practice time for trainees to practice and test their new skills/knowledge, reinforcing their learning from the experience of repetition (see below).

- When possible, provide learning experiences that incorporate actual tasks or skills that will need to be performed in real life.

8. Make it active, fun, and challenging—Adults learn more when it is engaging and enjoyable.

A dynamic, pleasing learning experience teaches more than a routine or boring experience. As Mary Poppins aptly expressed, "In any job that must be done, there is an element of fun. Find the fun and, snap, the job's a game!" Indeed, fun is not limited to children, and adults also learn best when they are enjoying themselves. Learning is more than sitting still and listening to a PowerPoint presentation, but should employ a variety of methods that make the learning more lively and engaging. However, fun does not mean less rigor. Active engagement and challenges are key ingredients that complement fun. Adults like to make demands on themselves and test their abilities. Learners of all aptitudes and abilities should experience an appropriate level of challenge, to enable each individual to achieve his or her potential. Why can't this be fun too?

Tips for M&E training

- For face-to-face training, keep people moving—when possible, have trainees get up out of their seats, for example, standing discussions around a flipchart, posting ideas on a wall, standup debates, role playing, or other group activities.

- Make learning into a game or contest—that is, teams can be used and points awarded during question or review sessions, puzzles or matching games can be used for key terms or concepts, contests can be used to see who can complete activities first or according to best criteria.

- Utilize "energizers" to give people a break from the lesson and reenergize them doing something else for a change.

- Switch seating arrangements (for face-to-face training) and have trainees change into different working groups (online or face-to-face training), encouraging interaction with different people that can be more dynamic and interesting.

Terminology Tip
Active Learning Versus *Action* Learning

While *active learning* refers to learning that is engaging, it is sometimes used to refer to a specific training approach based on experiential methods, "to systematically influence trainees' cognitive, motivational, and emotion self-regulatory processes" (Bell & Kozlowski, 2009, p. 265). In either case, active learning stresses dynamic methods that engage learners. In evaluation, this can include simulations, role playing, single course projects, and practicums (Oliver et al., 2008 p. 332). *Action learning* is a specific learning method involving small teams working on a real problem or project. Developed in the 1940s, various approaches have appeared, but the core elements remain the same (Revans, 1982). Action teams confront a problem (project, challenge, issue, or task), use insightful questions, and develop and implement an action plan. Planned reflection (individual and group) is used throughout the process, with facilitation from an action learning coach. In M&E training, such an approach can be used with developing project logframes or M&E plans. Already, an action learning approach is reflected in evaluation capacity building with organizations such as the World Bank (Mackay, 2002, p. 94).

9. Use mixed/multisensory methods—Adult learners require a mixture of learning approaches.

People learn differently, and therefore it is important to adapt and combine a variety of materials, mediums, and delivery methods that do not cater to one particular learning style. Some adult learners prefer to have information presented to them as a whole while others will want the details; some prefer text or speech while others want pictures and visuals; some prefer to learn by doing while others prefer to reflect before acting. Learning is multisensory, with vision recognized as most influential; therefore, it is good practice to include visuals as a core instructional method. However, adults learn faster when they are using two or more senses. A mix-methods approach to instruction can be multisensory, including visual, auditory, tactile, and kinesthetic methods. It is unlikely, in time as well as cost, to train in a way that satisfies everyone's learning style fully. However, a mixed-methods approach is more likely to at least partly address individual learning preference.

Tips for M&E training

- Acknowledge different learning styles rather than catering toward one—consider a questionnaire to identify preferred learning styles, which can be discussed with the trainees (as part of the trainee analysis, discussed in Chapter 6).

- At a minimum, incorporate visual aids to reinforce the spoken word and key learning points, as sight is the dominant sense used in learning—that is, flipcharts, PowerPoint slides, pictures, models, summary tables, agendas, charts, flowcharts, Gantt charts, graphs, cartoons, and illustrations.

- Balance time spent in training using active methods (e.g., debates, role play) with reflective, self-directed activities (e.g., case study reading, note taking).

- Ensure that trainees can see and hear clearly what is being done and said—pay particular attention to the seating arrangement or the Internet connectivity for online training.

- Regularly check whether the lesson is audible and the pace is not too fast—it is especially important when speaking in a non-native language that pronunciation is clear and deliberate.

10. Differentiate learning—Adults learning is more effective when it is tailored to different learners' needs.

Rather than a "one size fits all" approach, training should cater to different types of learners. This principle overlaps with others, but the emphasis is on adjusting training to best meet the needs of learners who have different levels, abilities, and individual circumstances. Instruction can be differentiated in content, process, products, affect, and learning environment according to the students' readiness, interests, and learning style. The goal of differentiation is to move *all* learners to a higher level of achievement. Differentiated learning is learner centered and is reflected in the other adult learning principles—for example, the use of mixed/multisensory methods and building upon learners' prior experience. Below we offer some other considerations.

Tips for M&E training

- Get to know your trainees—conduct trainee analysis, which can include pre-training assessment, reading staff performance reviews, and direct communication with prospective learners.

- Individually connect with individuals during training breaks and take other opportunities to monitor how the trainees are doing.

- Offer choices and flexibility for leaners to focus on topics they find interesting and use a range of media or formats for them to participate in learning and express themselves.

- Tier activities and resources to progress with increasing complexity, catering to different levels of understanding.

- Incorporate into training content examples and illustrations for both genders, different cultures, and varying levels of experience and abilities.

- Group people to support engagement and input from learners who would otherwise be shy or reluctant to participate in group activities.

- Use smaller groups with mixed abilities so less advanced learners can take advantage of peer support and larger group discussion for advanced learners to review and voice ideas.

- Provide materials in the primary language for second language learners and use more visual learning aids.

- Use ongoing learning assessment to help both trainers and trainees better respond to individual needs and learning goals.

- Provide feedback opportunities to monitor how learners feel about the pace, group dynamics, and overall facilitation—and adjust accordingly.

11. Utilize collaborative, peer learning— Adults effectively learn from each other.

Adults respond well when they learn from and with each other as equals, sharing knowledge, ideas, and experience (Boud, 2002; Damon, 1984). When peers examine issues together, the level of discussion and the learning pace is often more appropriate, according to shared experience, culture, language, age, and gender. Peers often feel more comfortable asking and clarify questions among themselves, and their explanations can be more suitable to the level and understanding of the questioner. Learners are challenged to interpret and articulate key points, rewarding their own understanding, while helping others with theirs. As noted in Box 4.1, peer education can be especially effective when the learning objective involves affective (attitude) change.

Tips for M&E training

- Provide opportunities for trainees to work in pairs or groups to share ideas and experiences rather than being talked at by the trainer—that is, break-out discussion groups, role playing, debates, problem solving.

- Frame activities so they allow trainees to generalize their learning experiences with each other, reformulate what they learn in their own words, discuss their leaning experience, question it, direct it, and apply it together.

- Use interactive, group activities, such as problem solving, group presentations, scenarios, and roles plays.

- Design the curriculum with activity debriefs that allow participants to reflect and process their learning experience.

- Make learning into a game or contest, where teams discuss and solve problems with each other (Principle 7).

- Capitalize on peer learning when the primary language used is not shared by all participants, allowing those with more fluency to assist others.

Terminology Tip
Collaborative Learning Versus Cooperative Learning

Collaborative learning is synonymous with how we use "peer learning" (learning from each other). It can be formally structured into training or can happen as a byproduct of group activities. *Cooperative learning* is a more structured approach using group-based instructional methods (Johnson & Johnson, 1999). It is largely a response to individual learning, which can be competitive in nature. Learners work in groups or teams to collectively complete learning tasks, for which successful completion and grades are dependent on group success. Clearly, cooperative learning shares many of the benefits of peer learning, capitalizing on each learner's resources and skills. It is more commonly used in formal educational settings, including evaluation education (Oliver et al., 2008).

12. Include practice and repetition— Adult learning is enhanced by repetition.

Adults retain new knowledge better when provided ample opportunity to review and practice. Often referred to as "over learning," learning that is reinforced by repetition is best understood and remembered. This is the basis of drill and practice; frequent attempts at recall improve retention, moving learning from short-term to long-term memory. Practice and repetition also builds learner's confidence and competence. However, the practice must be meaningful, with the learner's memory actively engaged. Therefore, it helps if it employs a variety of methods to involve the learner. The adult learner may not master each lesson completely, but repetition helps to reinforce the key learning points and skills. Lastly, repetition is reinforced with praise.

Tips for M&E training

- Practice and review can be done many times, in many ways—for example, questions and knowledge checks, lesson summaries, review periods, and self-assessment.

- Build redundancy into the lesson plan, where key learning points are repeated, restated, and reorganized—reinforcing learning and providing opportunities for further clarification.

- Utilize daily and/or session reviews to organize key learning points— that is, at the start and/or end of each day to review what has been covered and to frame what is ahead.

- Employ instructional techniques that force trainees to recall previously learned material rather than the trainer leading the review—for example, frequent and random questions.

- Combine practice and review with feedback activities—for example, small group or individual quizzes.

- Enliven practice and reviews with active and fun games, awarding points for correct answers.

13. Design for primacy and recency—Adults remember best what they learn first and last in sequence.

The concept of *primacy* is that information learned first creates a strong impression that is difficult to erase. The learner's introduction to learning content will lay the foundation for subsequent learning. It helps to frame, organize, and set the tone of what is to follow. It is much easier to teach right initially, than to "unteach" content later. Initial learning that is poorly designed or taught with incorrect content is confusing and complicates the learning process; it also instills bad habits and impressions that are hard and time consuming to correct. Related, the concept of *recency* is that information most recently learned is generally best remembered. Learning occurring last can sum-up and "fix" in the mind key learning points to emphasize. Recency also includes timing training in relation to when the trainees will need to apply what they have learned. Learning will be more successfully reinforced when training is timed with when new knowledge or skills need to be used.

Tips for M&E training

- Teach content right the first time, so the trainees learn it correctly from the start.

- Carefully prepare how you will introduce the training as well as individual sessions, as this establishes the tone and helps frame learners' expectations.

- Provide a clear summary of learning objectives and content and the order they will be introduced.

- Review at the end of the training and individual lessons key learning points that have been covered, and remind trainees of the sequence they have learned a topic.

- Accompany lesson introductions with a handout listing key learning points and refer to this when conducting lesson reviews, visually reinforcing and organizing lesson content.

- Structure essential material toward the start and end of the training when possible.

- Schedule trainings so that they can be immediately applied and thus the learning reinforced.

14. Provide feedback & positive reinforcement— Adults want to know if they are learning and to be encouraged in the process.

Adults learn better when they can see evidence of their progress and identify areas to improve. Feedback should be both timely and regular. Specific feedback, whether corrective or approving, is best provided when the learning moment is immediate and fresh. Regular opportunities should also be structured into trainings that allow trainees to practice the learning and receive structured, helpful feedback. In turn, this allows trainees to monitor and take responsibility for their learning progress. Feedback should also be supportive. Adult learners like to be recognized when they have performed well. Even when corrective feedback is required, it should be pitched in a positive, encouraging tone, helping to cultivate a safe and supportive learning climate. Learning that is rewarded is more likely to be retained. As the renowned psychologist B. F. Skinner (1974) stressed, learning is strengthened when accompanied by a pleasant or satisfying feeling, and it is weakened when associated with an unpleasant feeling.

Tips for M&E training

- Focus feedback on what was done well rather than criticizing what was done poorly—adults generally know (and do not need reminding) when their performance or contribution was not successful. At the same time, adults prefer candid honesty and do not want to be patronized with superficial praise.

- Acknowledge and praise trainees for trying, regardless of accomplishment, as long as they are learning in the process.

- Compliment correct answers, and if incorrect, find a way to be corrective in a positive manner.

- Employ repetition (see above), reviews, and knowledge checks (e.g. quizzes) to allow trainees to assess and monitor their own learning progress.

- Use group feedback opportunities that encourage peer reflection and discussion as well as individual feedback opportunities to discuss more constructive and targeted comments; this is more appropriate for a one-on-one exchange.

- Conduct reviews and conclude training highlighting learning accomplishments as well as areas to improve; this can be facilitated in a participatory manner with trainees assess their performance.

- Avoid "talking down" to trainees, whether correcting or praising them; adults resent being belittled and treated as a child and should be treated and respected as mature adults.

4.8 CHAPTER SUMMARY

That this chapter is among the longest in the book is no accident. Adult learning is a vast, evolving, and contentious field, with an array of theories as to what it is and how to best approach it. We have focused our discussion on what we identify as key considerations to understand adult learning for M&E training. Important summary points include the following:

- Learning is more than just a change in knowledge or behavior but also includes the process by which that change occurs.

- Bloom's taxonomy identifies three learning domains (cognitive, psychomotor, and affective) that underpin the popular knowledge, skills, and attitudes (KSA) used in training and education today.

- Andragogy is one influential theoretical approach to adult learning based on the premises that adults are self-directed and autonomous learners.

- Experiential learning is another influential theoretical approach that stresses the importance of learning from direct experience—learning by doing. Kolb's experiential learning cycle identifies four primary stages of learning: (1) experiencing, (2) reflecting, (3) conceptualizing, and (4) experimenting (applying).

- Learning styles and preference encompass a variety of theories that emphasize that people learn differently; two influential and useful models are Honey and Mumford's four learning styles (activists, reflectors, theorists, pragmatists) and VAK (visual, auditory, and kinesthetic learning).

- Learner-centered training embodies key features of andragogy, experiential learning, and learning styles, shifting the focus from the training to learner's needs, interests, experience, and abilities.

- Differentiated instruction supports a learner-centered approach to training, stressing the importance of addressing the different learners' needs as they relate to training content, process, products, environment, and the affective requirements of learners.

- We conclude our discussion framing 14 adult learning principles to guide M&E training. These principles draw upon the prior discussion and our understanding of what is important for M&E training. They are interrelated and complementary and should be adapted and tailored according to specific training contexts.

1. Establish a safe and respectful climate
2. Respond to the "need to know" (NTK)
3. Provide a structured yet flexible progression
4. Empower with genuine participation
5. Incorporate past experience
6. Keep it relevant and meaningful
7. Provide direct experience
8. Make it active, fun, and challenging
9. Use mixed/multisensory methods
10. Differentiate instruction
11. Utilize collaborative, peer learning
12. Include practice and repetition
13. Design for primacy and recency
14. Provide feedback and positive reinforcement

4.9 RECOMMENDED RESOURCES _____

As we acknowledge at the start of this chapter, there is a wealth of literature on the topic of adult education. Three books from prominent thinkers in the field include, *The Adult Learner: The Definitive Classic in Adult Education and Human Resource Development* (Knowles, Swanson, & Holton, 2011); *Adult Education and Lifelong Learning: Theory and Practice* (Jarvis, 2004); and *Experiential Learning: Experience as the Source of Learning and Development* (Kolb, 1984). We also found the book by Beard and Wilson (2006), *Experiential Learning: A Best Practice Handbook for Educators and Trainers*, very useful, with an insightful conceptual framework (diagnostic tool) of different aspects of the overall learning system.

As its title states, the book, *Learning in Adulthood. A Comprehensive Guide*, provides a thorough treatment on the topic that we found very useful to synthesize our thinking for this chapter (Merriam, Caffarella, & Baumgartner, 2007). Related, we also recommend the book, *Understanding and Facilitating Adult Learning* (Brookfield, 2001). The *International Encyclopedia of Education* is a comprehensive eight-volume, edited set useful as a background resource on key topics in this chapter (Penelope, Baker, & McGaw, 2010).

In our discussion on learner-centered training, we briefly highlighted the political/power dimension of adult education. In addition to *Learner-Centered Teaching: Five key Changes to Practice* (Weimer, 2002), we also recommend *The Power of Critical Theory: Liberating Adult Learning and Teaching* (Brookfield, 2005). Although written for media trainers, we found the learner-centered manual from AIBD and UNESCO user friendly in both

concepts and practice on the topic (McDaniel & Brown, 2001). For further reading on adult education and development, social inequality, and aid, we recommend the classic book, *The Pedagogy of the Oppressed* (Freire, 1970) and more recently, *The Political Economy of Adult Education* (Youngman, 2000). In the field of evaluation education, the article by Thomas and Madison (2010) is a compelling argument for the inclusion of social justice in evaluation education.

In addition to Wikipedia and WikiBooks, the online encyclopedia for informal education, Infed (2015) has cited summaries on key adult learning topics. The online book, *Emerging Perspectives on Learning, Teaching, and Technology* (Orey, 2001) has a variety of "short" articles by different authors on topics such as Bloom's taxonomy, learning-centered theories, and experiential learning. On his website, Big Dog & Little Dog's Performance Juxtaposition, Donald Clark (2015a) has a wealth of entries related to adult learning (as well as overall training); for instance, his webpage on *History of Learning and Training* has many summaries of major educational theorists and theories related to adult education. ERIC (2015) offers over 1.5 million bibliographic records on education research and information, and WikiEducator (2015) has links to various content supporting the planning and development of educational programs, including a community portal.

Lastly, many of those recommended at the end of chapters 6 and 10 are also useful for further information on adult learning topics and the application of adult learning principles for M&E training.

CHAPTER 5

What Makes a Good M&E Trainer?

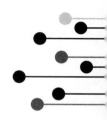

We usually discuss knowledge, skills, and attitudes (KSA) as it applies to trainees. In this chapter, we redirect this focus onto M&E trainers, providing an overview of key competencies they need for M&E training. An understanding of the key skill sets and characteristics for trainers can help inform key processes for M&E training, such as

- **Recruitment of training staff or consultants**—those managing trainings are better equipped to prepare trainer job descriptions and terms of reference (ToR) and assess the skills and abilities of candidates when recruiting trainers. We will elaborate on this in the last section of this chapter.

- **Trainer self-assessment and professional development**— trainers are more capable of identifying areas to improve through courses, training, mentoring/coaching, and other forms of professional development.

- **Trainer performance appraisal and management**—those managing trainers are more capable to assess trainer performance, provide feedback, set expectations, and support the trainer's professional development.

- **Curriculum development**—those who train or support the training of trainers (ToT) are better prepared to consider and design curricula based upon competencies needed for M&E trainers.

As we shall see, M&E trainers wear several hats and play a variety of roles in addition to training facilitation. In Part 2 of this book, we outline specific guidelines for M&E training that reflect the range of competencies and related knowledge and skills we summarize in this chapter.

Learning Objectives

By the end of this chapter readers will be able to . . .

✓ Identify some key sources for professional standards, competencies, and ethics for M&E training

✓ Explain the importance of the six key competency areas identified in this chapter as they relate to the roles and responsibilities of M&E trainers

✓ Describe the generic steps to recruiting a trainer and key considerations for each step

✓ Explain the advantages and disadvantages of recruiting an internal versus external trainer

5.1 Trainer Competencies

Just as the M&E training context is diverse and multifaceted, so are the skills, expectations, and responsibilities of the trainer. In addition to sound communication and a knack for explaining, trainers also provide problem solving, planning, counseling, leadership, and management. They need to interact with a variety of stakeholders in addition to trainees, such as other trainers, program and organization managers, administrators, and human resource personnel. Furthermore, trainers need to remain informed of the rapidly evolving field of training and human resource development as well as trends in M&E.

In short, training is not a "short order." For example, the National Staff Development and Training Association (NSDTA, 2004a) identifies 29 competency areas with over a 110 specific competencies in its *Instructor Competency Model*. It is beyond the scope of this book to go into such detail, but we do want to highlight key competencies for M&E training. Following a review of sources on training and M&E standards, principles and ethics (see **Box 5.1**), we have summarized key competencies we believe are critical to highlight, organizing them into six core areas:

1. Standards & ethics
2. Technical skills
3. Context familiarity
4. Interpersonal skills
5. Management skills
6. Personal attributes

While it is unlikely a trainer will "master" all of the competencies identified, successful trainers possess most of them to some degree, and they work to improve or compensate for those which they are deficient. In Appendix 5.1, we also provide a summary checklist of trainer competencies that can be used when recruiting trainers and inform a similar tool to assess trainers' performance during and after training.

1. Standards & ethics

Standards, principles, and ethics are fundamental for any profession. However, for

BOX 5.1
Industry Standards, Competencies, and Ethics for M&E Trainers

As with the field of evaluation, there is no universally recognized source for professional standards, competencies, and ethics for training. Instead, this will vary according to country and organizational context. Nevertheless, M&E trainers should be well informed of industry standards, competencies, and ethics for both training and M&E. Below we have listed notable sources for both fields:

- The American Society for Training & Development's *Competency Model* (ASTD, 2013)

- The National Staff Development and Training Association's *Instructor Competency Model* (NSDTA, 2004a)

- The National Staff Development and Training Association's *Code of Ethics for Training and Development Professionals in the Human Service* (NSDTA, 2004b)

- The Academy of Human Resource Development's *Standards on Ethics and Integrity* (AHRD, 1999)

- The *Code of Ethics of the National Association of Social Workers* (NSAW, 2008)

- The American Evaluation Association's *Guiding Principles For Evaluators* (AEA, 2004)

- The Joint Committee on Standards for Educational Evaluation's *Program Evaluation Standards Statements* (JCSEE, 2015)

trainers this straddles not only the field of training itself but also the field for which people are being trained—in our case, M&E. As we note in Box 5.1, there are different sources for professional standards and ethics for both training and M&E. Nevertheless, the actual contents share many of the same elements because training and M&E both involve interacting with stakeholders to help them achieve their goals. Below we have summarized ten critical training standards and ethics that should familiar to those working in the M&E profession:

- **Legal compliance**. Understand and observe laws and regulations governing commerce, individual rights, and client expectations.

- **Respect for people**. Reserve and promote the security, dignity, and welfare of all stakeholders, for example, establishing a safe and respectful learning environment.

> *Inherent within the work of both human services practitioners and those who promote their training and development are two central concepts: care and control. Developing caring relationships and valuing people are balanced with providing the right amount of control (structure/ influence/authority) to promote human change and development.*
> (NSDTA, 2004b, p. 3)

- **General welfare**. Consult with, design, and conduct trainings to fulfill the interests and needs of all stakeholders, providing opinion, guidance, and leadership to achieve longer-term objectives.

- **Utility**. Ensure that the training serves its intended purpose, addresses legitimate training needs, and is not being used when other non-training interventions are more appropriate.

- **Feasibility**. Ensure that the training is realistic to the training context (e.g., organizational culture and budget) and uses resources in a responsible and efficient manner.

- **Integrity/honesty**. Maintain a constant commitment to being truthful, that is, when framing expectations, providing feedback, conducting assessment, and representing credentials and experience.

- **Fairness.** Remain objective and impartial in training assessment/ evaluation, making judgments, and handling difficult issues.

- **Confidentiality**. Maintain confidentiality of personal information shared during training (e.g., assessment and evaluation data), and if shared, consent should be obtained.

- **Informed consent**. Ensure trainees understand and accept the intended training objectives, their expectations as participants, and any risks or consequences involved (i.e., use of training assessment and evaluation data at their workplace).

- **Professional conduct**. Monitor and check personal behavior and impulses to maintain professionalism, for example, trainers should observe appropriate boundaries between themselves and others so that working relationships are not confused with personal relationships.

2. Technical skills

M&E trainers need technical experience not only in M&E but also in training itself. Both areas of knowledge and experience are vast, and the specific technical skills required will depend on the individual training context and needs. Below we summarize five broad technical areas for M&E trainers (which can also be referred to as *hard* skills—see **Box 5.2**):

- **Subject matter knowledge and experience.** You can't teach what you don't know. Therefore, it is essential that M&E trainers have an appropriate level of understanding and command of M&E required for the training program. This will largely depend on the training focus, that is, an introductory versus a more advanced training. M&E knowledge is not enough, and it needs to be matched with practical experience to draw upon to respond to those difficult questions and to embellish instruction with useful examples to make the learning more meaningful as it applies to real-life situations.

- **Adult learning principles.** M&E trainers need to understand and apply principles of adult learning to training design, development, and delivery. They should be well versed in adult learning theory and approaches to appeal to and actively engage different learning styles. This is the focus of Chapter 4, and we summarize key adult learning principles for effective training on page 98.

- **Instructional design and development.** M&E trainers need to be able to use training assessment data to articulate M&E training objectives and outcomes, design the curriculum, and select appropriate training methods. This requires a sound understanding of adult learning principles, instructional strategies, and how different instruction methods affect how people learn. The training needs to be designed with an instructional progression that is sequenced according to the level and needs of the trainees. Related, training materials need to then be developed that are appropriate to learners' level, culture, and other attributes. These various skills are discussed in further detail in Chapter 7.

- **Assessment**. Assessment skills are indispensable at all stages of training: during the initial needs assessment, while monitoring participant learning and feedback during the training, and for post-training evaluation to assess learning transfer and related training outcomes (Chapters 8 and 9). Assessment may also involve supporting a larger organizational capacity assessment (Chapter 3). Trainers need to be well versed in qualitative and quantitative data collection and analysis methods that are practical to the training context. For instance, an organization may require very thorough learning assessments prior to, during, and after training to support individual performance development. Whatever context, the trainer should be able to interpret and communicate results to stakeholders for effective follow-up and use of assessment findings. Assessment should also uphold evaluation principles and ethics, with which an M&E trainer will hopefully be competent.

- **Technological literacy.** M&E trainers need to be able to use technology across different areas of expertise. As we discussed in Chapter 2, this includes an understanding of the various training technologies available and effectively incorporating them into M&E training to best achieve learning objectives. Technological competence is also indispensable for the development and dissemination of training materials, from training announcements to handouts and presentations. Knowledge of computer and analysis software is a valuable asset for collecting and analyzing data for pre- and post-training assessment. It is also essential for information management associated with the training (to efficiently organize, share, and use information). Finally, it is worth noting that software and applications are increasingly being developed for doing M&E, from program logic modelling to survey design and enumeration (e.g., see MandE, 2015). With such trends, technological competency for M&E training is becoming more prerequisite than optional.

3. Context familiarity

As discussed in Chapter 3, trainings are embedded in complex contexts, with different actors and factors that impact the training and its potential contribution to capacity building. A trainer's prior experience with the context in which M&E training is to be used can be a valuable asset and go a long way to establish credibility and legitimacy among stakeholders. This includes familiarity with the individuals, communities, organization, or program involved with the training as well as the larger sociocultural and political setting. For instance, knowledge of an organization's culture, management structure, and policies and procedures can help a trainer better understand and interact with stakeholders to meet training needs. In training where trainees come from a range of organizations, it may be more appropriate for the trainer to have experience with a wide array of organizations or the types of communities and initiatives in which trainees will use their M&E knowledge and skills. Familiarity with the local context contributes to cultural competence, including knowledge of local language, customs, and other dynamics with which a trainer may need to contend. However, it is worth noting that there may be instances when it is preferable to enlist an external trainer who is unfamiliar with the operational context—for example, perceived neutrality or credibility among stakeholders.

4. Interpersonal skills

Technical proficiency is not enough for good M&E training. M&E trainers need to be able to effectively interact and relate to people. This is important not only with learners during training delivery but also with other key stakeholders during training planning and follow-up. Furthermore, interpersonal skills themselves can be a learning objective for trainees that trainers need to model and impart; there is growing attention of the importance of interpersonal skills as a core competence area for program evaluation (Christie, 2012; Ghere, King, Stevahn, & Minnema, 2006). We can consider interpersonal abilities as a type of *soft* skills (see Box 5.2), and we identify four key areas to consider them:

- **Communication skills.** The essence of a trainer's job is to effectively communicate information to others for learning. Good communication skills are also essential for stakeholder consultation during training planning and follow-up. Trainers need to be able to communicate well verbally, visually, and in writing. They need to convey information in a concise, coherent, and clear manner, so others can understand the training content, rational for decisions, recommendations, and opinions. Spoken word should be loud and clear, and the speed and emphasis adjusted according to the audience. Body language, gestures, movement, and eye contact all play an important role to engage listeners and emphasis key points. Good communication also includes knowing when and how to use appropriate visual aids (e.g., flipchart diagrams or slides) to help trainers explain or summarize concepts and ideas. A final but critical point is that communication is a two-way street, and a good communicator knows how to actively listen, solicit feedback, and respond to questions and input from others.

- **Stakeholder consultation skills**. Stakeholder consultation and collaboration is essential to ensure that M&E training is tailored to stakeholder needs. It is used to identify M&E needs, frame expectations, and help builds mutual understanding and ownership necessary to support training and sustain longer-term objectives. M&E trainers need to identify, consult, and engage the appropriate people at the right time, whether it be senior management for approval and funding for training or project field staff to realistically understand M&E practice at the operational level. In organizations, it is often necessary to carefully consult with human resources (HR) to incorporate M&E into career planning and professional development. Stakeholder consultation is closely aligned with good facilitation and includes the ability to anticipate and negotiate various interest groups to encourage cooperation and collaboration.

- **Cultural competence skills**. Cultural competence is the ability to recognize and interact effectively with people of different cultures and socioeconomic backgrounds. It is related to context familiarity but specifically focuses on oneself as we relate to others who are different:

"Cultural competence requires awareness of self, reflection on one's own cultural position, awareness of others' positions, and the ability to interact genuinely and respectfully with others" (AEA, 2011, p. 3). A trainer should recognize and validate differences because of culture, ethnicity, gender, religion, or sexual preference. Training content, communication, and behavior should be adapted to best accommodate cultural difference—for example, anticipate linguistic differences with translations, visual aids, and appropriate activities. Trainers should be able to quickly identify and respond to any conflict or discrimination that may arise because of cultural differences. (We revisit cultural considerations in Box 9.2 in Chapter 9.)

- **Facilitation and group management skills.** Facilitation involves the management of group processes and dynamics to help different people achieve common goals, whether it is learning or strategic planning. This is an important skill not only for training delivery and adult learning but also for other aspects of training, such as stakeholder consultation and decision-making for training. A good facilitator engages and involves participants, building understanding and ownership to support and sustain training objectives. They know when to speak and offer opinion and when to remain silent and encourage others to express themselves. They also know how to summarize/synthesize key points for consensus and decision-making. Such skills should be familiar to M&E practitioners experienced in focus group discussion and participatory evaluation. Facilitation is a core skill for training delivery to support trainee engagement in and responsibility for their learning; therefore, we will revisit facilitation again in Chapter 9.

5. Management skills

Trainers need to plan, schedule, and manage a host of tasks throughout the training cycle, from the initial training analysis and design to training delivery, follow-up, and evaluation. Making all the pieces fit together in a cost-effective and timely manner requires a considerable degree of organizational and management skills. The trainers' role in management will vary according to context; that is, whether they are providing training alone or with others to delegate responsibilities. Management can involve resourcing and budgeting for M&E training, oversight of contractual and legal agreements with clients, and the recruitment and supervision of administrative and training personnel supporting training. It also includes overseeing training logistics, such as advertising training, recruiting trainees, and arranging for the training venue, transportation, accommodation, security, refreshments, and so forth. Management can include a lot of the behind-the-scenes activities that need to be done for a training to be successful, and follow-through is essential.

BOX 5.2
Hard Versus Soft Skills

It can be useful to look at training skills as either "hard" or "soft." Hard skills refer to trainers' technical knowledge and experience—for example, M&E, adult learning theories, organizational development, and management. Soft skills refer to how trainers relate to themselves and others (largely reflected by one's interpersonal skills and personal attributes). They include the ability to internalize values and principles, effectively facilitate, and build and sustain trusting relationships, commitment, and respect. Successful M&E trainers need a balance of both skill sets; soft skills allow the trainer to more effectively put the hard skills to use.

6. Personal attributes

In addition to the competencies outlined above, there are a variety of personal characteristics that are important for trainers. These are very closely related to a trainer's interpersonal skills but also include their personal work ethic and ability to do a good job in a timely and responsible manner. Personal attributes fall within the soft skills category (Box 5.2), and we highlight ten personal attributes we believe are especially important for M&E training.

- **Organized and prepared.** Much of this book is about how to best prepare to provide effective training. Training can encompass much, and a well-planned, systematic approach helps get the job done. This is also important for the delivery of training topics in a coherent, comprehensive manner. It is typically a challenge to cover all the learning topics in the time allotted for training delivery, and an unplanned or "off the cuff" approach does not work.

- **Results oriented**. Just as adult learners are goal oriented, such qualities also apply to the trainer. This includes not only designing training with concrete, realistic results that meet training needs but also the work ethic and perseverance to follow through and achieve identifiable results. Training is a considerable investment in time and resources, and the trainer should be capable to lead the process and ensure there is a return on investment.

- **Versatile and flexible.** As this chapter reflects, there is an array of different competencies, characteristics, and responsibilities that a trainer juggles.

Jessie Mountfield

Therefore, it is helpful when the trainer can adapt to the various roles they play. Related, adaptability is also the ability to think on one's feet and respond quickly to the unexpected. It is important to know when and how to "let go" and "go with the flow." Things do not always go as planned, and if everything is set in stone, it will eventually crack. With some flexibility and openness to change, a trainer may find the unanticipated is actually an opportunity (teachable moment) rather than a hindrance.

- **Patient and accepting.** Learning takes time and adults learn better in a calm environment where they do not feel rushed or imposed upon. Patience is closely related to being accepting and respectful of others and how they learn, communicate, and operate, whether in the training itself or with other aspects of the training. Patience and acceptance start with oneself, and trainers need to also remember not to be too hard on themselves when the inevitable "hiccup" occurs.

- **Energetic and enthusiastic**. Effective trainers are not only interested in what they do but passionate about it—both the subject matter and helping other learn it. Training is demanding, and a high level of enthusiasm helps sustain energy for its tedious aspects, for example, administrative hassles. Dynamic trainers know how to make learning active and fun, and a positive attitude is contagious, engaging learners and other stakeholders to support training.

- **Humorous and fun**. Trainers do not have to be comedians, but it is helpful if they can lighten up the atmosphere, especially when tense or difficult situations emerge. Humor is a useful tool to connect with people, and it is not limited to jokes, but also pointing out silly things, being playful, and having the humility to laugh at oneself. Such qualities can go a long way to gain rapport and earn respect with trainees.

- **Creative**. Effective training that engages learners with participatory, experiential, hands-on activities requires innovation and creativity. Rather than a pre-packaged lesson plan, successful trainers can customize and tailor it to engage the particular audience. Like a creative chef, it is important to be able to mix ingredients and spice it up rather than serve the same dish regardless of who sits down to dine. Creativity also helps with problem solving and to better respond to the unexpected.

- **Empathic**. Trainers work with and for people, therefore, it is important that they can relate to them. Successful trainers are able to bond and establish rapport, respect, and understanding with others. They are able to sense and respond to changes in feelings and emotions, show compassion when others are down, and celebrate when they are up. However, empathy needs to be genuine, and good trainers are authentic and truly connect with trainees.

- **Authentic**. People relate to and trust trainers who are authentic. In his book *The Skillful Teacher*, Brookfield (2006, p. 77) refers to "personhood" as the ability for a teacher to move out from behind their formal role as instructor and to reveal themselves as "flesh and blood human beings with lives and identities outside the classroom." Related, successful trainers practice what they preach. Nothing undermines trainer credibility more than contradicting the very principles or commitments they expose—for example, framing a lesson as participatory and then dominating it with lecture.

- **Responsive**. The best trainers take the time to provide extra attention and assistance. They empathize with people who are struggling and will go the extra distance to help them. When trainers make themselves available to provide individual attention and feedback, it reinforces their credibility and respect—learners are assured that the trainer is genuinely concerned for their welfare.

5.2 Recruiting a Trainer

The success of training depends largely on the trainers, so it is important to carefully plan their recruitment when required. Whether recruiting for an organization or a community group, one should not underestimate how much is involved and consequently rush the process. Training consultants are often booked well in advance, and a last-minute rush to locate someone can reduce the pool of qualified candidates. Hiring an M&E trainer follows a similar procedure as recruiting any staff or consultant. Below we have outlined eight generic steps that we feel are worth considering for recruiting M&E trainers. We frame this process for training within a given organization, but it would apply similarly to recruiting trainers for other types of M&E training for individuals unassociated with the same organization.

1. Consult with stakeholders

It is a good idea to first consult with key stakeholders to ensure buy-in and support for the training exercise. Key considerations include the intended purpose of the training, alignment with overall capacity-building objectives, available resources, political support for the training, and the time frame. It is also important to ensure that roles and responsibilities are identified for managing the recruitment process and the trainer once engaged. This may involve engaging a hiring committee or taskforce.

2. Identify M&E needs

It is important to first consider the overall training needs. An organization may have prior capacity assessment information to inform this (e.g., from staff performance reviews) or it may conduct its own training needs assessment at this stage. Oftentimes, however, training needs assessment is identified itself as a need, for which the recruited trainer will be responsible. Another important consideration is whether the training need is met by recruiting internally or externally. Using someone already with the organization or program may be preferable as part of an overall capacity-building strategy to prepare a trainers to meet long-term training needs. However, this may involve additional time and investment in a training-of-trainers (ToT) context. **Box 5.3** summarizes other key considerations for recruiting internal versus external trainers.

3. List trainer qualifications and prepare terms of reference (ToR)

A list of trainer qualifications and traits should be tailored for the specific training needs. This will also inform the scope of work (SOW) or terms of reference (ToR) for the particular training exercise or a job description for a permanent position. Also, Appendix 5.1 at the end of this chapter provides an example of a trainer competency checklist that can be used to inform this process, and following are some useful elements for the ToR or job description:

- **Purpose of the training position/assignment**. Specific technical sector or program area, trainee profile, and so forth. Ideally this can and should include the training objective, but this can later be developed with selected trainers.

- **Scope of the position/assignment**. For example, stakeholders, regions, and programs involved and whether M&E training is for organizational-wide needs, a newly established M&E unit, and so forth.

- **Training location/s, time frame and duration**.

- **Organizational overview**. For example, background information on the organization/program's history, mandate, guiding principles, existing M&E capacity assessments and objectives.

BOX 5.3
Recruiting Internal Versus External Trainers

Internal Recruitment	External Recruitment
Pros	**Pros**
• Internal trainer is already familiar with the organizational structure, policies, culture, and priorities.	• Provides outside experience and fresh perspective/insights that may be unavailable within the organization.
• Organization is already familiar with the trainer's qualifications and job performance.	• Larger talent pool could attract skilled applicants suitable for particular training needs.
• Typically less costly and time consuming than going outside the organization.	• Can provide a sense of external neutrality and credibility to better navigate organizational politics.
• Internal trainer has a long-term stake in the organization and will be around for training follow-up and support.	**Cons**
• Vertical or horizontal movement within the organization can boost staff morale and retain staff.	• External consultant fees are typically higher than staff salary.
Cons	• Administratively time consuming to recruit and contract.
• Expanding organization or new program may not have the capacity to meet increasing training needs.	• External consultant may not be familiar with organizational culture, systems, and processes.
• Internal politics—the selection of one trainer may cause resentment; staff may challenge trainer's credibility and authority.	• Risk that training content may be pre-package and not tailored to the specific organizational/program needs.
• Diverts trainer from normal responsibilities (unless it is to be a full-time position).	• May upset staff morale and be a disincentive to not utilize internal human resources.
• May entail additional time and costs for training-the-trainer (ToT).	• Current organization members may resent and challenge external authority.

- **Primary responsibilities**. Estimated amount of time to be dedicated to different training tasks, for example, training analysis, design, development, and evaluation, and any travel time involved.

- **Training methodologies.** Identify any preferred training delivery technology and approaches—for example, face-to-face, distance, e-learning, and combinations of each; participatory, experiential learning versus lecture and presentation.

- **Key working relationships.** Identify who the trainer will report to and key stakeholders to consult and work with, including whether the trainer is a team leader, team member, or will be training independently.

- **Trainer qualifications.** Required and preferred competencies and experience, including language(s) and other qualifications relevant to the specific training responsibilities.

- **Application procedures.** Where to submit the application and the materials to be included—for example, resume, cover letter, technical and financial proposal (if necessary), examples of relevant training reports and evaluations from prior trainings, and references.

See **Box 5.4** for further considerations about working with an external trainer.

4. Advertise the training consultancy or position

Post the ad for the training assignment or position to the outlets most likely to reach your potential candidates (often, an abbreviated announcement is used to direct interested candidates to the full description on the organization's website). Potential outlets for external trainers include M&E websites and listservs, training websites and listservs, appropriate program area/sector websites (e.g., community health, education), universities, think tanks, VOPEs (voluntary organizations for professional evaluators, see Box 3.2 in Chapter 3) and other professional organizations.

5. Screen and shortlist applicants

It is useful to develop a recruitment checklist to rate candidates, ensuring standard criteria and fairness in the assessment of applicants—see the example in the Appendix 5.1 for this chapter. It is also important to identify a selection committee with the adequate knowledge/experience with the organization and capacity building priorities to make informed decisions (ideally, they were identified in Step 1 and involved early on in the recruitment process). These people should also be involved in the interviews, ensuring consistency in the assessment of candidates. It is important to check references to assess past trainer performance and also review prior records of post-training reports and evaluations from training activities for which the candidate has led or participated.

6. Interview candidates

Interviews can be conducted through teleconferencing or in person; often teleconferencing will be used to identify who to shortlist for an in-person interview. The degree of rigor will depend on the particular training context—for example, location of the candidates, training budget, and duration of position. As mentioned above, it is important to have a qualified selection committee who will participate in all of the interviews. Related, interview questions should be developed beforehand based on the ToR/job description to ensure a structured interview for evaluating candidates equally. In addition to speaking to a candidate about their work experience and background, an assessment exercise can complement the interview:[1]

- *Written feedback*. Provide an example of an M&E area to provide feedback on, for example, a logframe or M&E plan.

- *Hypothetical training design*. Provide a hypothetical training topic prior to the interview and ask for a short outline of how the applicant would design the training.

- *Mini-presentation*. Arrange for each candidate to demonstrate their training approach and delivery to assess their planning, communicating, and facilitation skills. This can be a mini-presentation over the Internet (e.g., with a slide show) or an in-person training session with a representative sample of trainees.

7. Hire and orient the trainer

Ensure the decision-making process is well documented, transparent, and accountable, so you can explain the criteria and process if questioned. Follow other standard hiring procedures, for example, background checks, and when the offer is made, clearly outline expectations, agreements, rates of pay, and all other relevant information so that the trainer can make an informed decision. Be sure to follow up and inform other applicants of your decision and retain their application records in case the selected trainer needs to withdraw their application. Finally, it is important to work with the trainer to develop a comprehensive training plan that goes beyond the ToR or job description and details training needs, schedule, curriculum design, and assessment. Like an inception report for an evaluation, this is important to ensure a clear understanding and realistic plan of work, checking that the training plan is in agreement with stakeholder expectations.

---

1. An assessment rubric should be developed of criteria for consistent and fair rating of candidate's performance for any assessment exercise used.

BOX 5.4
Working With an External Trainer

What is the ideal relationship for working with an external training consultant? Margerison (2001, p. 85) proposes four useful consulting roles to help consider this question:

1. The *doctor* is where the client has a problem and the consultant needs to diagnose and find a prescription to cure the illness.
2. The *detective* is where somebody is responsible for the problem and the consultant needs to identify and deal with the culprit.
3. The *sales model* is where the consultant has a product or service (bag of tricks) to help the client achieve its objectives.
4. The *travel agent* is where the consultant serves as an advisor to help the client on a journey toward achieving its objectives.

Like Margerison, we feel that the travel agent role is optimal. This approach allows the external consultant to truly "consult" with the client to determine needs, priorities, and solutions that are compatible to stakeholders' realities (operational context, strategic direction, organizational culture, etc.). A partnership that actively involves the client in analyzing M&E training needs and solutions also builds needed stakeholder ownership and support to achieve and sustain training objectives. We are particularly wary of the sales model approach, where an external training consultant comes in with pre-packaged training curriculum and materials that are not tailored to specific stakeholder training needs. Such an approach should only been used if it has been well reviewed to ascertain that it is indeed in line with and will achieve the learning objectives.

5.3 CHAPTER SUMMARY

In this chapter we outline *key competencies for good M&E trainers* and briefly look at good practices for recruiting M&E trainers. Important summary points include the following:

- Understanding M&E trainer key competencies can assist with trainer recruitment, self-assessment and professional development, performance appraisal and management, as

well as the development of curriculum for training of M&E trainers.

- There are a wide range of roles and responsibilities for M&E trainers. We have outline key competencies into six core areas:

  1. Standards & ethics
  2. Technical skills
  3. Context familiarity

4. Interpersonal skills

5. Management skills

6. Personal attributes

- There is no one recognized set of standards for M&E trainer competencies, and our list summarizes skill sets and characteristics that we believe stand out from *both* the field of M&E and the field of training.

- To a large degree, the specific recipe of competencies for a "good trainer" will depend on the particular training context. For example, a trainer working with a team or organization may be able to share training responsibilities with colleagues (e.g., managerial tasks) and therefore may not be required to be proficient in all competency areas.

- When recruiting a trainer for an organization, there are key considerations as to whether to recruit external or internal to an organization. For example, it may be preferable to use someone already familiar with the organizational culture who can support

training transfer after training. On the other hand, it may be necessary to recruit outside experience and fresh perspective/insights unavailable within the organization.

- We outline seven steps for recruiting a trainer, similar to recruiting any staff or consultant (and refer readers to the Example Trainer Recruitment Checklist in Appendix 5.1):

1. Consult with stakeholders

2. Identify M&E needs

3. List trainer qualifications and prepare terms of reference (ToR)

4. Advertise the training consultancy or position

5. Screen and shortlist applicants

6. Interview candidates

7. Hire and orient the trainer

- When working with a training consultant, we recommend a partnership ("travel agent") relationship to tailor training solutions that best meets training needs.

5.4 APPENDICES

Appendix 5.1 Example Trainer Recruitment Checklist

Trainer's name:	
Training/Position:	
Date completed:	Reviewers:

Instructions

The purpose of this checklist is to provide a consistent, transparent, and accountable rubric to recruit a training consultants or staff/employee. This is only a generic example and the identified criteria should be aligned to the specific training needs per terms of reference (scope of work) or job description. A rubric can be developed to consistently rate candidates on each criteria according to training/job needs. It is recommended that a review committee with adequate knowledge/experience of the training context and capacity building priorities complete the checklist together.

(Continued)

(Continued)

Assessment Criteria	Candidate A	Candidate B
Date completed for candidate		Add additional columns as need
Dates candidate is available		
Application materials, e.g.,		
• Complete and on time?		
• Example of relevant prior training reports		
• Example of relevant prior training evaluations		
Reference check, e.g.,		
• Referee A		
• Referee B, etc.		
Costs/fees (for training consultants)		
Academic qualifications		
Training experience—for example, . . .		
• Training background—e.g., number and type of relevant trainings		
• Adult learning principles		
• Training needs assessment		
• Instructional design and development		
• Training monitoring and evaluation		
Technical literacy for training—e.g., familiarity with various delivery options (media) to support training		
Training management experience—as appropriate—e.g., resourcing and budgeting, recruitment and supervision of personnel, logistics and administration		
Subject matter (M&E) experience— for example, . . .		
• Program design (logframes, results framework, outcome mapping, etc.)		
• M&E planning		
• Data collection and analysis (qualitative and quantitative)		

Assessment Criteria	Candidate A	Candidate B
• Baseline/endline studies (e.g., household surveys)		
• Managing and conducting evaluation		
Context familiarity—for example, . . .		
• Organization: e.g., management structure, culture, policies and procedures, etc.		
• Program or project		
• Community—cultural		
• Local language/s, culture, customs, (potential for cultural competence)		
• Probable legitimacy/credibility among stakeholders		
Interview performance How did the applicant come across in the interview? Did they communicate clearly? Did they exhibit desired personal attributes such as enthusiasm or professionalism? Gut feelings?		
Assessment exercise Note that a separate assessment rubric should be developed of criteria for consistent and fair rating of candidate's performance for any of the above assessment exercises—see Appendix 11.4 in Chapter 11 for an example of a trainer assessment form.		
• Example of written feedback		
• Hypothetical training design		
• Mini-presentation		
TOTAL		

Additional comments—Use this space to record any additional points worth noting, etc.

1. **Candidate A:**

2. **Candidate B:**

3. **Etc.**

5.5 RECOMMENDED RESOURCES

In Box 5.1 earlier in this chapter, we identified some key resources to consider professional standards, competencies, and ethics related to both training and evaluation for M&E trainers (each freely available online). For the field of evaluation, the website of IDEAS (2015) has a comprehensive listing of *Competencies for Development Evaluators*, with links to frameworks, reviews, and other related resources. The book by Yarbrough, Shulha, Hopson, & Caruthers (2011), *Program Evaluation Standards*, discusses in detail the thirty JCSEE standards that support core attributes of evaluation quality. Related, we also recommend the book, *Fieldbook of IBSTPI Evaluator Competencies* (Russ-Eft, Bober-Michel, Koszalka, & Sleezer, 2013), for additional information and resources to train others in this area.

Three additional resources we found useful background reading for evaluation competencies include: the discussion of standards and ethics in Chapter 9 in *Real World Evaluation* (Bamberger, Rugh, & Mabry, 2012); the 2004 issue of *New Directions for Evaluation* (Russon & Russon, 2004) on international perspectives on evaluation standards; and the article "Establishing Essential Competencies for Program Evaluators" (Stevahn, King, Ghere, & Minnema, 2005), which formed the basis for the *Competencies for Canadian Evaluation Practice*.

We will revisit cultural competence in Chapter 10 on training implementation and refer readers to Box 10.4, which highlights the useful workbook, *Culture Matters* by the Peace Corps (2014). Other resources we recommend on this topic include the *American Evaluation Association Statement on Cultural Competence in Evaluation* (AEA, 2011); the evaluation guide by CDC (2014), *Practical Strategies for Culturally Competent Evaluation*; and the article, *Cultural Competence in Evaluation: An Overview* (SenGupta, Hopson, Thompson-Robinson, 2004).

In addition to the two resources identified from the National Staff Development and Training Association in Box 5.1, NSDTA (2015) produces a useful series of competency guides to support effective staff development and training programs. Additional resources for training competencies include the competency model and related resources on the website of the ASTD (2015); the Experiential Training and Development Alliance (2000), which provides a concise discussion on the definition and ethical practices for professionalism in experiential training and development; *Ethics for Training and Development* (Gordon & Boumhart, 1997); the statement on the *Code of Ethics* by the National Education Association (NEA, 2015); and the checklist, *Duties of the Teacher*, from prominent evaluator Michael Scriven (1994).

Two books that we found useful to consider key competencies for trainers and education include *The Skillful Teacher* (Brookfield, 2006), with a very insightful Chapter 4 on what students value in teachers, and the book by Heron (1999), *The Complete Facilitator's Handbook*. Lastly, we refer readers to the recommended resources identified in Chapter 10 on training facilitation and the freely available training of trainer (ToT) guides recommended in Chapter 10.

A Systematic Approach to M&E Training

*"Give me six hours to chop down a tree and
I will spend the first four sharpening the axe."*

Abraham Lincoln

As Mr. Lincoln underscores, careful preparation can be more than half the work in getting the job done well. This is certainly true for successful M&E training. Relative to actual training delivery, the time and effort spent preparing for training can be exponentially greater, playing a critical role in "setting up" training for success. Thus, the primary objective of this second part of the book is to provide practical guidance to systematically plan the effective delivery and follow-up to M&E training, the overarching goal being the integration of M&E into organizational and program systems.

In Chapter 6 we present an overview of the ADDIE framework to systematically approach M&E training: **a**nalysis, **d**esign, **d**evelopment, **i**mplementation, and **e**valuation. In the remaining five chapters of Part 2, we address each of these ADDIE phases in sequence. Our approach is intended to provide an in-depth and practical look at each these phases, but it is essential to understand that they are all part of a larger, cyclic system and that it may be problematic to consider them independently. Thus, while our approach is *systematic*, it is also *systemic*, reflecting the principles of systems thinking introduced in Part 1 of the book; decisions during the different phases of M&E training are based upon and have implications for other elements in the training system.

We want to provide practical fodder for consideration in Part 2, and we attempt to make explicit many of the elements of a training system that may be taken for granted. Part 2 relies heavily on our own practical wisdom, but we draw heavily from myriad practical resources available for those interested in designing, delivering, and analyzing training; our goal is to orientate them toward M&E training. Our focus is primarily on live, face-to-face M&E training, but we believe much of the discussion is also useful for distant and e-learning training for M&E. While readers will no doubt find Part 2 of the book more practical than Part 1, the same can be emphasized even more for Part 3. In that concluding section of the book we share some practical examples activity types to consider for M&E training design and delivery.

An Overview of the ADDIE Framework for Training

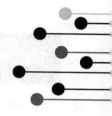

This chapter introduces the five interrelated phases of the ADDIE framework for training: **a**nalysis, **d**esign, **d**evelopment, **i**mplementation, and **e**valuation. We first discuss ADDIE as a systematic *and* systems approach to training, and then explain why we have selected the ADDIE framework for M&E training. We then conclude the chapter outlining some overall considerations for managing the ADDIE process. In the appendices to this chapter we provide a more complete overview of the ADDIE framework in the form of a checklist for M&E training organized by each of the five phases. It will be complemented with additional checklists and resources elaborating key process for each ADDIE phase. It is also worth noting that the checklist can be used to inform areas to evaluate training processes during the evaluation phase of ADDIE.

Learning Objectives

By the end of this chapter readers will be able to . . .

✓ Summarize the key phases of the ADDIE framework for training

✓ Explain how the ADDIE framework can be used both systematically and systemically

✓ Identify some overall consideration for the management of the ADDIE process

6.1 ADDIE as a *Systematic* and *Systems* Approach for Training

Figure 6.1 summarizes the five phases of the ADDIE framework for training. ADDIE is often referred to as Instructional Systems Design (ISD) because it offers a more holistic or systems approach to the entire training process, from analysis to evaluation.[1] It is also systematic because it is intentional, providing an orderly process for gathering information and analyzing training needs and resources, identifying training objectives, and designing a training intervention to achieve these objectives. For example, during the analysis stage, one should not assume that training is the answer to all needs but first determine that it is an appropriate (and feasible) solution before progressing to training design.

---

1. ISD can be contrasted with Instructional Design (ID), which focuses primarily on the analysis and design phases of training; as such, ID is typically used in conjunction with ISD (Clark, 2015b).

FIGURE 6.1 The ADDIE Training Cycle

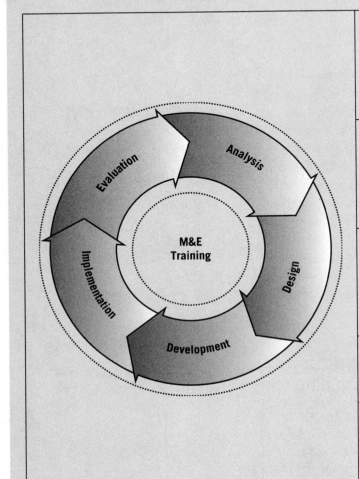

1. **Training analysis:** Determine whether M&E training is needed and if so, the overall purpose and recommended type of training to deliver based on training needs, audience, and available resources.

2. **Training design:** Draws upon the information gathered during training analysis to design training objectives, content, and curriculum for training implementation, evaluation, and follow-up.

3. **Training development:** Based on the training design, this stage involves the preparation of materials and other practical logistics for training implementation, evaluation, and follow-up.

4. **Training implementation:** Brings together the investment made thus far to deliver, evaluate, and follow-up M&E training.

5. **Training evaluation:** Includes the analysis and reporting of data collected prior to, during, and after M&E training for its evaluation.

While the stages of ADDIE discussed in this book are presented as an orderly progression, it is more than the sum of isolated parts. The ADDIE approach is sometimes criticized for being linear and simplistic, with pre-determined stages that straightjacket training planning into artificial steps (Gordon & Zemke, 2000). However, such criticism is warranted only if the framework is used in such a limiting manner—which we do not recommend. Instead, we stress that the phases in ADDIE are iterative and should be approached with careful attention to the interrelationship between each phase. The potential of the ADDIE approach depends on recognizing the importance and interdependence of each component in the framework: the training context, audience, content, and instructional and evaluation methodologies are all interrelated and inform training delivery and follow-up.

Rather than linear processes, each ADDIE phase should interact with and inform the other phases—thus, we represent the ADDIE framework in **Figure 6.1** as a continuous training cycle. For example, we will discuss how backward planning can be used to consider training evaluation early in the analysis and design phases to help identify desired results that will inform the design of realistic, measurable training objectives. Similarly, formative evaluation is conducted throughout the implementation phase to inform training delivery—for instance, in Chapter 8 we will discuss the importance of piloting training for continual, formative feedback.

6.2 Why Have We Chosen the ADDIE for This Book?

The origins of ADDIE trace back to the U.S. armed forces work in ISD during the mid-1970s, but there is no single author; instead, it has evolved informally over time to refer to a generic process for ISD (Molenda, 2003). It has become one of the most widely recognized and used approach for designing training. However, the field of ISD is huge (as you can discover with a simple web search), and there is an assortment of alternative approaches to ISD used for training.[2] For example, two other influential approaches to ISD worth noting are the models of Dick and Carey (1996) and Morrison, Ross, and Kemp (Morrison, Ross, Kemp, & Kalman, 2011, also known as the "Kemp Model"), both also developed in the 1970s. The Dick and Carey model is noted for its systems-oriented emphasis, and the Kemp Model for its holistic, learner-centered approach to classroom-oriented instruction design.

So, why have we selected ADDIE framework to guide M&E training? Foremost, we believe the ADDIE framework provides a sound foundation that covers the basic components to consider M&E training as a whole system. While the specific combination and complexity of procedures offered by other ISD approaches vary—for example, the models of Dick & Carey and Kemp each have nine components—for the most part, they reflect the underlying processes outlined by the ADDIE framework (Gustafson & Branch 2002; Reiser, 2001). The ADDIE framework can be used to incorporate critical considerations and elements offered by other approaches to ISD, such as the systems and learner-centered perspectives of Dick and Carey and Morrison et al.

---

2. For a more comprehensive look at instructional design theories and models, consider Reigeluth and Carr-Chellman (2009).

Second, the ADDIE framework is intuitive and easy to understand, which is one of the reasons it has been so widely embraced. It offers a basic approach to consider six "W" questions for training: Who? What? When? Where? Why? and How? For M&E trainers, the ADDIE phases should be especially familiar as they largely mirror the same stages of the project cycle often used in M&E training: project (needs) assessment, design or planning, implementation and monitoring, and evaluation.

Third, the ADDIE framework is flexible and can be used in different training settings for M&E. It can be adapted for narrow training needs, such as a single training event focusing on one M&E learning objective, or an entire training program over months addressing a variety of M&E learning objectives. It is used for both face-to-face training (e.g., Chan, 2010; Hodell, 2001) as well as distance, e-learning training (e.g., FAO, 2011; Shelton & Saltsman, 2007). The specific selection and configuration of practices we discuss for each ADDIE phase reflect this flexibility as we interpret the framework for discussing M&E training in this book.

Ultimately, whether one uses the ADDIE framework or some other approach, it should be adapted according to the particular M&E needs, learners *and* trainers, and what is realistic to the specific training context. As Morrison et. al. (2011, p. 12) point out, "There is no single best way to design instruction." Therefore, we encourage trainers to keep an open mind and tailor training to best meet M&E training objectives. ADDIE can be used in combination with other instructional design approaches, and the order of and emphasis on the different processes we discuss can be reconfigured as needed. Thus, we stress that the ADDIE framework should not be used as a rigid blueprint for planning and delivering M&E training. For this reason, we refer to it as a framework rather than a model (as the latter may imply reality prototype that should be closely followed).

6.3 Planning to Manage the ADDIE Process

Before looking at the first ADDIE phase, training analysis, the reader might be wondering about practical management considerations for training. There is no one-size-fits-all approach for this. In Chapter 8 on training development, we discuss how a training strategy or plan may be developed to manage the specific M&E training that has been designed, based on the training analysis. However, prior to the training design it will be necessary to consider the who and how for training analysis and design. In short, consideration should be given early on to the management of the overall ADDIE or planning process so that M&E training can realistically meet its objectives in a timely and efficient manner.

Just as evaluators need to consider the evaluability or feasibility of evaluation, those involved in training planning need to likewise consider what resources are available

BOX 6.1
What About Stakeholder Participation?

Just as stakeholder engagement is critical for M&E, it is likewise essential throughout training. This is especially true for training analysis. If M&E training is to meet the needs of its intended users, it is essential to involve a wide range of stakeholders at this stage. This not only helps cross-check (triangulate) training needs and underlying causes, but builds ownership to support training recommendations, planning, delivery, and use. It is important to understand their interests and expectations and how they will be involved in and affected by training. How is training perceived by the intended trainees? Are they receptive, seeking training on their own initiative, or is training seen as a requirement and threat? Who are the likely champions for M&E training, and who may resist it?

However, stakeholder participation is not limited to training analysis and should also be considered for other training processes. For example

- Training design. Stakeholder input can include examples or case studies and M&E tools that are relevant to the learning objectives and context for training.

- Training development. Stakeholder feedback can be provided on the training strategy, content and lesson plans, and the review and pilot of training.

- Training implementation. In addition to active participation in training reflection and feedback, trainees (and other stakeholders) can be involved in training facilitation.

- Training evaluation. From the design to participation in assessment and identifying recommendations, the utilization principles of evaluation underscore the importance of stakeholders' participation in evaluation, which we revisit in Chapter 10 (Box 10.3).

Access to training stakeholders will vary depending on the context, but it is best to consult a wide range of different groups when possible. In additional to the intended trainees, examples of other key stakeholder groups include community members, organizational management, partner organizations, and donors.

to practically plan for and manage training. This includes the availability (supply) of human, financial, and capital resources for M&E training (which, in turn, can reflect the demand and support for training). For example, human resources for a large training program may require M&E subject-matter experts (SMEs) to inform training content and resources, instructional designers to develop training curriculum, evaluators to develop assessment tools and lead training evaluation, trainers to facilitate training, and administrative personnel to handle training logistics. On the other hand, for a single training of short duration, a single trainer may be sufficient to manage and handle all aspects of a training process.

Clearly, the resources required *and* available to manage training will depend on the given training context and needs. Similarly, the extent these critical questions can be answered up front, prior to training analysis, will also be context specific. In certain settings, resource and management questions will need to be answered when training analysis is conducted. Therefore, we discuss this further in the following chapter on training analysis, and in Chapter 8 we look at the development of plans and other resources for training management. Nevertheless, we wanted to "flag" these important considerations now as they should indeed be deliberated early on. Whenever sufficient information is available to inform decision-making, careful attention should be given to the details of training management—for example, activities, budgets, timelines, roles, and responsibilities.

6.4 CHAPTER SUMMARY

This is the shortest chapter in the book because we will examine each phase of the ADDIE framework in more detail in the following chapters in Part 2 of the book. Important summary points at this stage include the following:

- The ADDIE framework is a form of Instructional Systems Design (ISD) that stresses an systematic and systems approach to training based on five interdependent phases: analysis, design, development, implementation, and evaluation.

- ADDIE is systematic because it is an intentional orderly approach to providing training; however, each phase interacts with and informs the other, reinforcing a systems perspective of the training process.

- We recommend the ADDIE framework for M&E training because we believe it (a) includes

the key components to comprehensively and holistically approach training, (b) it is intuitive and easy to understand, and (c) it is flexible and adaptable to different M&E training needs and contexts.

- The remaining chapters in the book will elaborate management considerations for the ADDIE process, but some key, overall considerations include the availability (supply) of human, financial, and capital resources for M&E training. Resources requirements and availability and the ability to assess this upfront or after initial analysis will be context specific.

- As we will reiterate in the following chapters, stakeholder engagement is a critical consideration throughout the ADDIE process, especially during training analysis, to ensure support for and use of M&E training.

6.5 APPENDICES

Appendix 6.1 Checklist for a Systematic Approach to M&E Training

Training Analysis

Have you . . .

- ☐ Identified and gotten input from stakeholders for M&E training?
- ☐ Determined whether training is needed and will be useful? What evidence exists that training is warranted?
- ☐ Considered the demand and support for M&E training?
- ☐ Identified the desired outcomes for training?
- ☐ Determined whether there are any specific M&E or other requirements that need to be considered for M&E training?
- ☐ Identified specific M&E tasks and KSA performance gaps and causes?
- ☐ Analyzed trainee (learner) profiles to inform training design?
- ☐ Analyzed the training context (e.g., organizational support) to inform training potential and design?
- ☐ Identified and considered other potential sources of learning that can meet or complement M&E learning objectives?
- ☐ Identified any existing and obtainable resources for M&E training (e.g., human, financial, and material)?
- ☐ Identified a primary delivery medium, location, and time frame for M&E training?
- ☐ Identified people responsible for the management of M&E training?
- ☐ Identified any potential training constraints or problems that may arise?
- ☐ Prepared a training analysis report to inform training development and communicate with key stakeholders?

Training Design

Have you . . .

- ☐ Identified training objectives that are relevant and realistic to address training needs?
- ☐ Designed SMART (specific, measureable, achievable, relevant, timely) learning objectives with clear links to KSA and expected M&E performance?
- ☐ Identified assessment methods for the learning objectives?
- ☐ Organized the instructional content (M&E topics) into a coherent training progression most suitable to the learner profiles, e.g., prior M&E knowledge and experience?
- ☐ Designed a training curriculum with activities and methods that are suitable for the learning objectives, trainee profiles, training time frame, and delivery medium/s?
- ☐ Ensured the training content and curriculum (activities and methods) incorporate and support the principles of adult learning?

(Continued)

(Continued)

- ☐ Designed training evaluation in tandem with training objectives to ensure they are relevant for desired results and measurable for assessment?
- ☐ Designed training follow-up to support training transfer after training?

Training Development (& Preparation)

Have you . . .

- ☐ Developed an overall training strategy and budget to efficiently manage M&E training and achieve training objectives?
- ☐ Confirmed stakeholder commitment and approval for the M&E training?
- ☐ Developed, adapted, or modified suitable training materials to implement the training curriculum?
- ☐ Ensured that training materials are simple, organized, and user friendly, appropriate for both trainees and trainer/s?
- ☐ Developed any pre-training materials (e.g. questionnaires, personal learning plans) to be provided to trainees prior to training?
- ☐ Developed training assessment and evaluation tools so they are ready for use prior to, during and after training?
- ☐ Identified supplementary training materials and resources to complement M&E training and follow-up?
- ☐ Reviewed training and evaluation materials/resources and piloted the training?
- ☐ Scheduled the training, and identified and prepared a suitable training facility?
- ☐ Selected and prepared trainees for the M&E training?
- ☐ Prepared training materials (e.g., copies), supplies, instructional media, electrical equipment, and so forth?
- ☐ Prepared other practical logistics for training; for example, transportation, accommodation, refreshments, and meals?

Training Implementation

Have you . . .

- ☐ Ensured that the trainer/s, training setting (e.g., facility), materials, equipment, and other aids are ready for training?
- ☐ Facilitated the M&E training with effective
  - o Communication, presentations, and explanations?
  - o Use of questioning and listening?
  - o Cultural competence to best interact with people of different cultural and socioeconomic backgrounds?
  - o Use of different (mixed) training aids in both instructional delivery by trainers and learning by trainees?
  - o Discussion and activity debriefs?
  - o Co-facilitation for training with more than one trainer?
  - o Handling of any disruptive behavior?
  - o Time management?

□ Ensured that training facilitation supports the 14 Principles of Adult Learning identified in this book:

1. Establish a safe and respectful climate?

2. Respond to the "need to know" (NTK)?

3. Provide a structured yet flexible progression?

4. Empower with genuine participation?

5. Incorporate past experience?

6. Keep it relevant and meaningful?

7. Provide direct experience?

8. Make it active, fun, and challenging?

9. Use mixed/multisensory methods?

10. Differentiate learning?

11. Utilize collaborative, peer learning?

12. Include practice and repetition?

13. Design for primacy and recency?

14. Provide feedback and positive reinforcement?

Training Evaluation

Have you . . .

□ Meaningfully involved stakeholders in training evaluation to ensure understanding, support, and use of evaluation?

□ Designed and developed evaluation and assessment tools early as part of the overall training design and development?

□ Developed an evaluation plan to guide training evaluation and communicate with others?

□ Identified suitable evaluators to lead the training evaluation?

□ Clearly defined the evaluation purpose and objectives to meet stakeholder needs?

□ Ensured that training evaluation gives attention to different levels of results?

□ Ensured the evaluation and its scope is practical and realistic for available resources, time frame, and capacities (evaluability)?

□ Identified evaluation questions and criteria to focus the evaluation?

□ Designed the evaluation to use mixed methods and triangulate data sources, with attention to potential unanticipated outcomes?

□ Identified methodological limitations for the training evaluation?

□ Upheld evaluation principles and ethics?

□ Articulated evaluation recommendations that focus on specific, practical actions for training follow-up?

□ Identified key audiences to disseminate evaluation findings and tailored reporting formats accordingly?

□ Identified lessons to inform the processes and methodologies for future training evaluation?

6.6 RECOMMENDED RESOURCES _____

There is a body of literature on instructional systems design for both education and training, ranging from chapters to books devoted to the topic. Foremost, we recommend the influential books by Dick & Carey (1996), *The Systematic Design of Instruction*, and Morrison et. al. (2011), *Designing Effective Instruction*. Although designed for graduate-level education, the article in the *American Journal of Evaluation* by Abbas Darabi (2002) provides an example of a framework for a systems approach for teaching program evaluation. For distance education and e-learning, we recommend the book by Moore and Kearsley (2012), *Distance Education: A Systems View of Online Learning*, which we also found useful for considering ISD for any training context.

We recommend the book, *Training Fundamentals* (Chan, 2010) for a clear, user-friendly overview of the ADDIE approach to training. The website of Donald Clark (2015a) provides useful historical and practical overviews on ADDIE, instruction design, and instructional systems design. For readers looking for more in-depth resources on instructional design, we recommend two books: *Survey of Instructional Development Models* (Gustafson & Branch, 2002), and Reigeluth and Carr-Chellman (2009) have a comprehensive three-volume series on instructional design theories and models. For a more concise overview of the history of instructional design, we recommend the 10-page article by Reiser (2001).

We found a variety of examples of checklists for instructional design when preparing that which we present in **Appendix 6.1.** Two that we found especially useful are the checklist and tool from IntraHealth International (2012), available in three languages, and the guide by UNAIDS (2010), *Standards for a Competency-based Approach to Monitoring and Evaluation Curricula & Trainings*.

In the following chapters, we recommend additional resources for specific stages of training planning. For now, we recommend two freely available resources to support the overall process: *Training that Works* (USAID, 2003) provides a very user-friendly summary of key components of training, and while it is health-focused, the website from I-TECH (2015) has a training toolkit that offers useful resources for each stage of training with guidance, worksheets, forms, and questionnaires available for free download.

Lastly, we encourage readers to explore the wealth of additional resources available online to support M&E training for particular contexts and needs. For example, a key word search for "training evaluation" resulted in over 300,000 results for presentations on the slide hosting website, SlideShare (2015). In addition to Clark's website identified above, four other interactive websites we recommend for training include Businessballs (2015), the Free Management Library (2015), the U.S. Office of Personnel Management (2015), and the *Instructional Design Knowledge Base* on the website of George Mason University (2015).

CHAPTER 7

Training Analysis

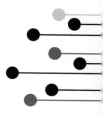

The purpose of the training analysis, the first step in the ADDIE framework, is to gather information to determine whether M&E training is needed, and if so, the overall purpose and recommended type of training based on available resources. Thus, the training analysis is more than a needs analysis, it is also a solution analysis. In addition to training needs, it examines opportunities and resources as well as limitations and constraints to make informed and justified recommendations regarding what should be done—whether it includes M&E training or some alternative intervention.

The training analysis should provide sufficient information to make an informed decision about how to respond to identified needs, and if it includes M&E training, the overall instructional approach (primary delivery medium) recommended to design and develop in the next stage of training planning. Later in the design phase, when specific learning objectives have been design and M&E topics sequenced, individual training activities and media can be detailed for the training curriculum.

Before we embark on our discussion, we want to highlight two overriding points. First, the scope and rigor of training analysis will vary according to the training context. Therefore, the utility of many of the approaches we present in this chapter will likewise vary, which we highlight in **Box 7.1**.

Second, training analysis should be exploratory, involve multiple perspectives and sources of information, and consider a range of alternative solutions to address identified needs and desired outcomes. Therefore, we once again stress the importance of

Learning Objectives

By the end of this chapter readers will be able to . . .

✓ List key questions to guide the training analysis

✓ Explain the importance of the needs and outcome analysis

✓ Summarize a backward design approach to determining training objectives

✓ Discuss how a trainee analysis can contribute to training planning

✓ Discuss how a context analysis can contribute to training planning

✓ Describe when and how a task analysis can contribute to training planning

✓ Describe when and how a gap and causal analysis can contribute to training planning

✓ Outline the key components of a training analysis report

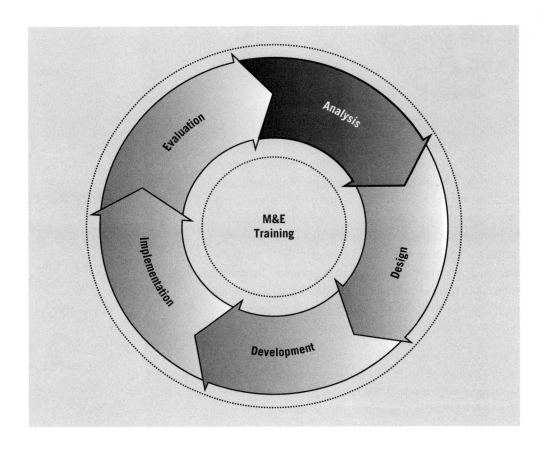

stakeholder involvement to inform this process. At this stage, initial stakeholder consultation largely sets the tone for their involvement in training and ideally builds stakeholder rapport, trust, and support.

When providing training to a specific organization, consider Box 5.4 in Chapter 5 and the ideal working relationship with an external training consultant. Like a travel agent helping a client plan a journey, training analysis and planning should be done in partnership with program stakeholders. It may be appropriate to establish a team (or committee) to conduct the training analysis, with representation from different stakeholder groups. This will not only help ensure understanding and ownership of the process but also provide multiple perspectives in the analysis of the training needs and solutions. Furthermore, this group can be used to guide and support stakeholder input during subsequent phases in the training cycle.

BOX 7.1
A "Light" Versus "Heavy" Training Analysis

This chapter provides a range of considerations for and approaches to training analysis, some of which will not be appropriate to particular training settings and should therefore be tailored accordingly. For example, in an organizational setting, there may be specific performance problems, such as the lack of evidence-based data in reporting, for which a more heavy analysis is appropriate. This can involve a detailed task, gap, and causal analysis, providing baseline data for ongoing staff performance reviews after training as part of a sustained capacity building strategy. On the other hand, such rigor may be unrealistic for M&E training for professional development offered to the general public (e.g., as part of a learning center), in which case there is not a specific problem to analyze. Related, pre-training access to trainees and other stakeholders where M&E is to be practiced may be limited or impractical for training analysis given the available time and resources. In such settings, a light training analysis focusing on key topics may be sufficient and best return on investment. As we flagged in the introduction to this book (Box 1.5 in Chapter 1), depending on the context, training analysis and design may require a more elaborate approach (luxury Mercedes Benz) or one that is simpler (basic Volkswagen).

7.1 Solution Analysis

Before looking at different approaches to gathering information for analysis, it is helpful to pause and consider what we want to get out of the exercise. Thus, we will begin with what we call the "solution analysis," which draws upon the gathered information during training analysis to examine whether training is recommended and if so how to best provide it. To a large degree, the questions posed during the solution analysis summarize the guiding questions to be answered during to overall training analysis—we lay out these questions below.

The solution analysis is not necessarily a discrete step or stage of training analysis, because the questions asked are answered as an ongoing process as more information is collected and analyzed during training analysis. At this stage of the planning for training, the level of detail of any proposed solution or approach for training delivery will be preliminary. The goal is not to design the solution but to propose the solution to design during the next phase of the ADDIE framework.

One way to consider the extent of the solution analysis is whether it is possible to recommend an overall instructional setting or primary delivery medium for training by the end of the analysis exercise. As discussed in Chapter 2, this can include

- Face-to-face, classroom-based training (e.g., training workshops)
- On-the-job training and learning (including mentoring and coaching)
- Distance, independent, or self-guided learning (e.g., asynchronous e-learning and self-tutorials)
- Distance, facilitated learning (e.g., synchronous e-learning and correspondence courses)
- Blended learning combining different delivery options

However, it may be the case that it not be possible or appropriate to determine the primary delivery medium at this stage of the training planning. Instead, it may be better to do so *after* learning objectives are prepared during the training design (Chapter 8). In this case, many of the questions and data collected to answer them during training analysis is used to inform decision-making for the primary instructional setting during the design phase. This illustrates the importance of approaching the ADDIE cycle as interdependent and iterative phases rather than rigid steps.

The fifteen questions that we summarize below are not exhaustive, and additional questions inevitably arise. Related, some questions may not be applicable for the particular training context. However, we believe they are a good starting place to consider the potential scope of inquiry during training analysis. As often is the case, the questions are also very much interrelated and iterative, and their answers come from a combination of the different approaches to data collection that we will discuss.

1. What are the needs and desired outcomes of M&E training?

A clear understanding of the desired outcomes or results for whatever intervention is proposed reflects the training need. We will discuss how backward design can assist with this as well as a task/topic and gap analysis. At this stage, it may be enough to just identify the overall learning goal for training (e.g., the M&E focus).

2. What are the underlying causes for the current situation?

It is important to verify whether there is a genuine need for M&E training. For example, there may be other factors contributing to M&E underperformance (performance gap). Is training needed to address an existing problem in an organization, to address anticipated need for programming, or to simply offer professional development opportunities to the general public? A causal analysis can assist answering such questions.

3. What would happen if nothing were done?

In a way, this question is a reality check or part of a risk analysis of what would be the consequences if M&E training did not occur. It helps ascertain how M&E training is critical.

4. What other sources of M&E learning are already available?

Other sources for learning may be able to meet M&E needs. Developing M&E training takes considerable time and resources, and it is important not to duplicate existing M&E learning initiatives. Related, it may be possible to utilize existing sources of learning in a blended approach to M&E training (discussed in Chapter 2); that is, face-to-face training complemented with M&E online tutorials, communities of practice, job aids, or M&E modules/content embedded in other trainings offered in an organizational context (e.g., in a program management training).

5. Is M&E training the best solution?

If there is a genuine M&E need, can the desired outcomes be achieved through another less costly and more effective intervention? Depending on existing sources of M&E learning, there may be alternatives to training that better guarantee return on investment—for example, individual mentoring/coaching or improved HR practices that recruit pre-trained staff?

6. What is the demand and support for M&E training?

Do people see the value of M&E training? Are they motivated to participate in it or support it? Such considerations are essential to sustain learning transfer and use afterwards. This applies to both organizational settings as well as training to the general public; if there is not an interest in M&E training, it will affect the market and participation in what is offered, and there may be a need to convince (motivate) the target audience.

7. Are there any specific training requirements?

In addition to the training itself, which may be required (e.g., by a donor), there may be other requirements that affect the type of training delivery, that is, accessibility requirements and legal obligations or the training content. This will be governed largely by the training demand and stakeholders.

8. *How urgent is the training need?*

Oftentimes, how quickly the situation needs to change will dictate the learning intervention. When M&E training needs to begin and be completed can have practical implications for what is feasible for training delivery. For instance, if the need is immediate, time and resources may not be available to develop an elaborate self-directed training program. Instead, an in-person workshop may allow trainees to better focus and achieve objectives in a shorter period of time. Training urgency will be relative to demand.

9. *How many people need to be trained and where are they located?*

The number of expected trainees will have an impact on the space, duration, budget, and resources required for training, and thus the instructional setting realistic for training delivery. For instance, individual or small-group learning needs may be best addressed by one-on-one or targeted training, whereas with a large group of trainees, training may need to be repeated on a rolling basis in multiple locations. If trainees are numerous and geographically dispersed, it may not be feasible to transport and accommodate them for an in-person training, and a distance option may be preferable.

10. *How might the trainee profiles affect training delivery?*

In addition to number and location of trainees, the M&E background, experience, and cultural characteristics of the target audience can have a considerable effect on the most appropriate way to deliver training. For example, whether they are literate, have worked with M&E before, or have access and ability to use technology will affect the choices made for training delivery. Also, as discussed below, there may be preferences for a particular type of training delivery. A trainee analysis can assist answering such questions.

11. *What is the expected duration of training?*

It is important to realistically consider how many hours are required to deliver M&E content—that is, whether it will be sequenced over a day, week, or months. This will depend on the scope and complexity of M&E learning objectives identified for training. For instance, it may be more suitable to cover training content in a single in-person workshop over a day or more, or it may be better to deliver training over a longer duration with mini-workshops and/or e-learning modules. The time frame will also depend on the available resources to sustain training.

12. *What level of interaction is most suited for training?*

Related to training duration, the level of interaction will depend on the type of M&E knowledge and skills identified for training and how much hands-on practice is required in a face-to-face setting. For instance, if the learning objectives are primarily related to knowledge, such as an overview of basic M&E concepts, a self-guided asynchronous e-learning tutorial may meet training needs. In other instances, deeper learning may require in-person training (e.g., developing an M&E plan or enumerating a household survey) where trainees can practice and use knowledge and skills and get individual feedback.

13. *What resources are available for training delivery?*

Delivery options will depend to a large extent on the available expertise and the financial and material resources required to develop and provide training. This includes qualified trainers, instructional designers, subject matter experts, administrative personnel, and material resources, such as existing M&E training materials, training equipment/media, and facilities. For example, resources and expertise may not be available to develop an e-learning training program, and it may be more affordable to provide a targeted face-to-face training. However, as noted above, if the target audience is large and dispersed, it might not be affordable to transport and accommodate trainees, and outreach will likely be limited when compared to online, e-training options. It is important to ensure existing expertise and material resources match training needs, and that expertise is not only present but also has time available to actually support training. Clearly it may be hard to predict the exact resources required for training at this stage, but it is helpful to know what resources are available *or* the prospect of obtaining them for M&E training.

14. *Is there a strong preference for a particular type of training delivery?*

Related to demand, a fundamental consideration is whether there is a strong market or organizational preference for a particular delivery medium for M&E training. The context and trainee analysis will be important to determine this. For example

- Trainees may prefer the convenience, flexibility, and control over the learning process offered by more self-guided delivery options, such as e-learning. On the other hand, they may find distance learning impersonal and isolating and instead prefer the support, motivation, and reassurance provided by the physical presence of a trainer and peer learners. Related practical considerations include access to Internet technology for e-learning or transportation and trainee resources to attend a face-to-face training.

- For an organizational M&E training, e-learning options may already be available and managers or decision-makers may prefer an in-person training event where staff can interact directly with an experienced

M&E trainer. Related, there may be a preference for an external training event away from the workplace, where staff can spend time outside their normal context, contributing to team building and other objectives. On the other hand, there may be costs associated with staff absence from regular job duties, and a self-guided, e-learning option may be preferable. Stakeholder consultation during the trainee and organizational analysis will help identify any strong preferences for training delivery.

15. *What potential problems or constraints might training encounter?*

Just as it is important to identify assumptions during project design that should be monitored for successful implementation, it is important to anticipate potential roadblocks or challenges that can arise and impact training delivery and desired outcomes. Related, consideration should be given to actions that can be taken to respond to and mitigate identified problems (e.g., a contingency plan). For example, if the context analysis reveals that political instability is an important factor, this can have considerable consequences for training delivery. In our discussion of a causal analysis, we highlight potential causes for performance gaps that can also come into play and affect how training is delivered and its outcomes.

7.2 Needs and Outcome Analysis

> The motivations, assumptions, and expectations of any ECB effort need to be fully thought through and articulated prior to taking any of the next steps in designing and implementing an ECB effort. (Preskill & Boyle, 2008, p. 447)

It is essential to understand why M&E training is being considered, what it seeks to achieve, and by whom and for what reasons it is being considered. At this stage, it is helpful to view identified training needs as a working hypothesis: There is a difference between the *perceived* needs and *actual* needs. For example, in an organizational context, those commissioning M&E training may feel it is needed to address poor M&E practice because of a lack of knowledge and skills, when in actuality people may have adequate knowledge and skills, but there may be low motivation and incentives to put them to practice—the causal analysis (discussed later in this chapters) assists with determining the underlying needs for training. As the above quote from Preskill and Boyle reflects, training analysis is like detective work, and it is necessary to investigate and verify the stated needs for training and whether training is indeed the best solution.

The motives for M&E training will vary according to context. Specific reasons can include the following:

- For professional development for individuals working with different organizations, programs, or initiatives for which M&E knowledge and skills are required

- To build M&E understanding, involvement, and ownership among stakeholders involved in a public (e.g., school), civic (e.g., community), or private (e.g., corporate) program or initiative

- For new hires, positions, or ongoing professional development within a program or organization

- In response to performance gaps, complaints, or some other shortcoming in an existing program and/or organization

- For a new program or the start-up of a new phase or initiative in an existing program

- Because it is required or mandated—that is, to meet compliance standards

- Because it has been budgeted, or it is important to spend unused program funds before the fiscal year closes

One helpful way to consider the needs analysis is whether requested M&E training is *reactive* to address an existing problem, *proactive* to identify anticipated needs and opportunities to improve performance, or *continuing* as part of ongoing program improvement (Watkins, Meiers, & Visser, 2012). Typically, when there is an existing problem, the training need will be more urgent, which will inform the solution analysis. Often there are multiple training needs, and it is useful to characterize and prioritize them. For instance, are M&E needs similar or different and do they overlap with other non-M&E program or organizational needs? The other components of training analysis discussed below help to characterize and better understand M&E training needs.

Identifying the desired outcomes for training

The flipside of training needs are the desired outcomes for M&E training or longer-term objectives or results that training seeks to accomplish. At the stage of training analysis, it may not be possible or recommended to prepare a detailed design of training objectives, which we will discuss during our next chapter. However, the training analysis is a good place to start considering what are the intended results or changes that M&E training is to bring about.

The level of understanding of the desired training outcomes can vary greatly. As Goldstein and Ford (2002, p. 42) summarize, it can range from among the following:

1. Training goals and options to achieve them are clear and understood.

2. Training goals are clear but not the option to achieve them.

3. Training goals and options to achieve them are unclear and not well understood.

One useful approach to identify or verify training outcomes and related objectives is "backwards design" or planning, which examines the intended training results prior to curriculum design (Wiggins & McTighe, 2005). This approach should be familiar for M&E practitioners working with program designs that use a results hierarchy to summarize how a program will bring about change and how to measure it (Chaplowe, 2008). Using the program design (or theory) it is possible to work backwards from the overall program and organizational objectives to consider training needs and later design training objectives.

The use of backwards design will vary greatly and should be tailored to specific training contexts. For our purposes, we will take a look at how it can be used by focusing on the context of an organization commissioning M&E training for program implementation. Ideally, the organization has an existing program theory (e.g., logic or conceptual model) to assist with backwards design, identifying intended results, indicators, and their means of verification. However, this is not always the case, and it may be necessary to construct one from stakeholder consultation and a review of existing data (e.g., program proposals or an organization strategic plan). Even when a program theory is provided, trainers need to carefully consult with stakeholders to determine whether intended results and measures remain relevant and realistic.

We will borrow from Kirkpatrick's four levels of training evaluation to illustrate how backwards planning can be approached for an organization implementing health programming (Kirkpatrick, 1996).[1] As summarized in **Figure 7.1**, Kirkpatrick identifies four levels to assess training effectiveness. Working backwards, the fourth level, Results, concerns longer-term program or organizational outcomes, such as improving community health. The third level, Behavior, relates to the required M&E tasks to support achievement of the program objectives. For example, developing logframes with reliable indicators to guide and measure community health programming. At Level 2, Learning, specific learning objectives can then be identified for required M&E tasks, for example, "After the M&E training, participants will be able to design logframes. . . ." At Level 1, Reaction, learner needs can be identified

---

1. Kirkpatrick is one of many approaches to training evaluation, which is discussed in further detail in Chapter 11.

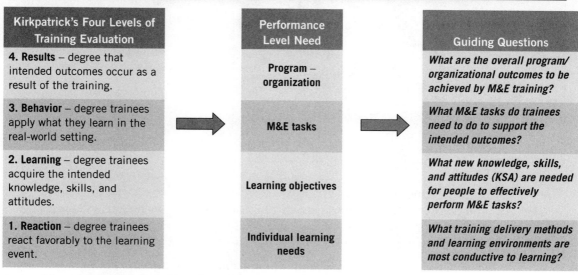

FIGURE 7.1   Backwards Planning Example for Organizational Training

Kirkpatrick's Four Levels of Training Evaluation	Performance Level Need	Guiding Questions
4. Results – degree that intended outcomes occur as a result of the training.	Program – organization	*What are the overall program/ organizational outcomes to be achieved by M&E training?*
3. Behavior – degree trainees apply what they learn in the real-world setting.	M&E tasks	*What M&E tasks do trainees need to do to support the intended outcomes?*
2. Learning – degree trainees acquire the intended knowledge, skills, and attitudes.	Learning objectives	*What new knowledge, skills, and attitudes (KSA) are needed for people to effectively perform M&E tasks?*
1. Reaction – degree trainees react favorably to the learning event.	Individual learning needs	*What training delivery methods and learning environments are most conductive to learning?*

Source: Adapted from Clark (2015b), Kirkpatrick & Kirkpatrick (2009).

to address and support achievement of learning objectives, for example, interactive exercises for learners who are not fluent in the same language.

In summary, meeting the individual learning needs (Level 1) helps achieve the learning objectives (Level 2) to achieve the M&E tasks (Level 3), thus contributing to the training outcomes at the program and organizational level. Our example is simplified and only one way to approach backward design. It encourages a levels analysis from organizational/program objectives down to the individual. Whatever approach is adopted, the important point to remember for training analysis is that M&E training needs and related outcomes are best identified and understood when considered in relation to the longer-term results that training is intended to support. We will revisit this in Chapter 8 on training design.

7.3 Trainee Analysis

A crucial element of training analysis is understanding the very people for whom training is intended. Also called a *learner analysis*, the trainee analysis drills down inquiry to the specific characteristics of the intended trainees as well as their personal

ANALYZING TRAINEES' NEEDS

Jessie Mountfield

learning environment—the setting in which they will use M&E learning. When a task and gap analysis is conducted (discussed below), the gathered information can complement the analysis of existing and desired trainee M&E performance.

In Chapter 3 we looked at individual learners as one level in the M&E capacity building context and identify different categories of potential trainees. In **Table 7.1**, we drill down the analysis of individual learners, listing key considerations that can be used to create trainees or learner profiles. During the solution analysis, information such as the number of expected trainees, their location, background and experience, motivations, expectations, and preferences will all have bearing on what, how, and where training will occur.

Again, the ability to access and obtain information about individual trainees will vary. For instance, with a training offered to the general public, the trainer may not know who exactly will attend the training and will need to base the trainee analysis on secondary data and consultation with those knowledgeable about the target audience and how they may use M&E training. On the other hand, when training for a specific organization or community program, it may be possible to directly consult with the prospective trainees, their managers, and others working with them.

In situations where access to trainees is limited, a representative sample can be used. In-person consultation can be one-on-one or through focus groups, and surveys may be most efficient if learners are geographically dispersed (and have reliable access to Internet/mail). It is also important to triangulate data sources and methods. This includes consultation with other relevant stakeholders, such as managers and supervisors, HR personnel, and others working with or supporting the trainees. Data collection can also include reliable secondary sources, such as job descriptions, appraisals and performance reviews, resumes/CVs, program performance monitoring, and review and evaluation reports that reflect personal performance.

Whether data collection is qualitative or quantitative, it is an opportunity to explore not only *what is* but also how people feel about it—for example, utilizing open-ended questions and rating scales. For instance, if there are existing M&E job aids, resources, or learning opportunities, probe to understand how often are they used, whether they are perceived as helpful, and why?

TABLE 7.1   Example Considerations for a Trainee Analysis

Key Factors	Key Considerations
Anticipated # trainees	What is the scope of participation in any learning intervention?
Trainee location	How might training location (including time zone differences) affect choices for training delivery—for example, costs associated for travel for in-person versus e-learning options.
Trainee availability	Can learners free up large blocks of time (days) or only hours?
Individual constraints	In addition to availability, what other potential barriers might affect learner accessibility and receptivity to training—for example, physical disabilities, restricted access to the Internet?
Demographic characteristics	What is the age range and gender ratio, and how might this affect training delivery?
Language & cultural characteristics	How will language and other sociocultural differences affect training delivery?
Technological literacy	What prior experience do learners have with computers, Internet, and software required for M&E tasks and training?
Educational background	What is the educational level, and how could it affect training delivery—for example, literacy, prior leadership or management training, and so forth?
Prior M&E training and experience	Prior exposure to M&E—for example, on the job, formal education; training (in-person or e-training); coaching; internships and mentorships? Be sure to note duration and M&E area/responsibilities. Has an individual skills assessment been done (related to M&E appraisal and feedback, below)?
Program involvement	What is the current and prior involvement in the program? What are people's roles, and to what extent is and how long has M&E been part of their responsibilities?
Motivation	How do learners perceive the prospect of M&E training? Is the M&E training required, recommended in a performance review, or optional? Are M&E skills part of the individual's current job requirements and appraisal or is it for future career development? Would certification or some form of recognition be a learning incentive?
Current and future M&E responsibilities	What particular M&E skills are needed—for example, field M&E or management of M&E staff? This complements the task analysis (see page 164).

(Continued)

TABLE 7.1 (Continued)

Key Factors	Key Considerations
Current M&E performance level	Refer to discussion of gap analysis, p. 169
Expected M&E performance level	Refer to discussion of gap analysis, p. 169
Learning style/preferences	How might individual learning preferences inform decisions for the most effective training delivery? (Refer to the discussion on learning styles in Chapter 4.) Depending on the context, a learning styles questionnaire may be administered at this stage in the training planning (for example, Soloman & Felder, 2014; LDPride.net, 2014).
Personal Learning Environment	
Program work environment	What is the workload and pace, the division of M&E and related responsibilities, individual or collective teamwork, collaboration and support from colleagues/coworkers, and so forth?
M&E appraisal and feedback	Does it occur, how often, is it helpful, used, and why? Who is responsible for this and how does it occur—for example, are there any guidelines, systems, checklists for supervising and appraising M&E performance?
Available M&E resources	Are they available, helpful, used, and why—M&E resource personnel, job aids, guidelines, manuals, templates, tools, and so forth?
Available M&E learning opportunities	Are they available, helpful, used, and why—on the job opportunities, formal education, training (in-person or e-training), e-learning (e.g., a learning platform), coaching, and mentorships?
Opportunity to apply M&E learning	To what degree will individuals be able to put to use M&E KSA—are supervisors receptive, is there opportunity for career advancement, and so forth?

7.4 Context Analysis

In our discussion of a levels analysis in Chapter 3, we stressed a systems understanding that training does not occur in isolation but in relation to the larger context in which it is provided. During the training analysis, this context needs to be examined more closely as it affects the specific M&E training being considered. Just as an evaluator needs to plan and conduct program evaluation with a realistic understanding of the people, institutions, politics, history, needs, interests, assets, and deficits in the program context (Patton, 1997), so must the M&E trainer for the design and eventual delivery of effective and useful M&E training.

In **Table 7.2** we summarize considerations for the training context. First, we take a look at considerations for training when it occurs in an organizational context. An *organizational analysis* for training is "an examination of system-wide components of the organization that may affect a training program beyond those ordinarily considered in task and person analysis" (Goldstein & Ford, 2002, p. 41). It is important to determine not only the organizational need but also its readiness for M&E training (Cousins, Goh, Clark, & Lee, 2004; Preskill, Torres, & Martinez-Papponi, 1999).

The organizational analysis involves detective work to find out more about the organizational culture and history to pinpoint capacities, constraints, and where there may be support and/or resistance to M&E training. As described in Chapter 3, M&E training may conflict with the organizational structure and practices, and some may find it threatening and may resist and make it difficult to adopt new M&E practices. "So much training effort is wasted because there is too little support from the relevant, usually powerful people, who could provide incentives for the participants to change their practice when they return from the course" (Pretty, Gujit, Scoones, & Thompson, 1995: 115). Therefore, particular attention should be given to the political climate in an organization. In addition to potential roadblocks (resistance) to training, identify potential *champions* (key supporters) that shape the demand and can help steer resources and support for the uptake of M&E training.

In the second part of Table 7.2, we list key considerations for the external environment. Whether M&E training targets an organization, community, or the general public, it is essential to identify specific actor and factors in the external environment that can influence training and its transfer into practice. As discussed in Chapter 3, this includes broader social, political, and economic forces, such as the demand for accountability, M&E expectations and standards, donor M&E and reporting requirements (format and frequency), funding availability, and other resources for M&E capacity building. In addition, there are practical considerations, such as the public infrastructure, facilities, transportation, and access to Internet, which can have a pervasive impact on M&E training delivery.

There are a range of secondary and primary sources of data that can be consulted for the context analysis. This can include people in an organization requesting M&E training, community members, partner organizations, donors, government agencies, and officials. For M&E training in an organization, trainers may be called in when M&E capacities have already been analyzed; in which case it is important to understand who made the analysis and how it was conducted. As with the other components of the training analysis, who and what is consulted will depend on the training needs stakeholders involved.

TABLE 7.2 Example Considerations for a Context Analysis

Key Factors	Key Considerations—Organizational
Management structure & processes	• What is the overall management structure (organogram), and where do M&E functions sit? • What are the organization's strategic objectives, and how do they relate to M&E training? • How might organizational policies, procedures, and other administrative processes affect M&E practice? • Are there well-defined roles and responsibilities for M&E—who is accountable for what? • How is M&E reflected in job descriptions and staff recruitment? • What incentives are used to promote M&E (*carrots* to encourage and reward M&E practice; *sticks* to require M&E and penalize poor practice; *sermons* that endorse or advocate the value of M&E)? • Are individual assessments conducted for M&E and related skills sets? • Is M&E included in performance appraisals and supported by career development—for example, coaching or mentoring?
M&E resources & practice	• What is the current M&E capacity of the organization—for example, is M&E information timely, reliable, and useful for the organization? • Has an organizational assessment been conducted for M&E (separately or as part of an overall organizational assessment)? • What are the gaps in the current M&E system that need to be addressed—for example, is there an adequate analytical capacity for decision-makers to interpret and use evidence? • Is there a strategic plan or objectives for M&E and its capacity building, and to what degree is it followed, monitored, and evaluated? • What existing guidelines, tools, templates, and other resources are available for M&E functions? • What is the current level of human, financial, physical, and technology resources for M&E? • Is M&E specifically itemized in program budgets, or is it subsumed (assumed) as part of the overall operational budget? • What are the funding prospects for sustaining or improving the M&E system?
Capacity building resources & practice	• What is the current "capacity for capacity building" within the organization? How often does it occur, and what is its uptake? • What M&E-dedicated training, resources, and other capacity building activities are currently available (either internal or external to the organization)? • What M&E-dedicated training, resources, and other capacity building activities have been available in the past? Have they been effective and why?

Key Factors	Key Considerations—Organizational
	• What non-M&E learning initiatives/training already exist? What is their timing and frequency? Do these trainings incorporate any M&E content? • How will the requested M&E training be complemented and supported by existing capacity building activities and systems? • What is the availability of funding for capacity building and specifically for the requested M&E training? • What is the availability of human resources for the requested M&E training—for example, for training development, facilitation, follow-up, and administration? (Note: consider not only their presence but availability for supporting the training.) • What material/physical resources are available for the requested M&E training—for example, existing M&E *training* materials (curriculums and content), equipment and technology, and training?
Networking & linkages	• What systems are established for advocacy, resource mobilization, and partnership engagement for M&E? • Are there potential public agencies, VOPEs, research centers, universities, and so forth that could serve as reliable partners for M&E capacity objectives? • How well does the organization identify and leverage autonomy in its partnerships for M&E and its capacity building? • Are there exchange visits, communities of practice, or other opportunities for M&E sharing and capacity building that can complement and should be planned with M&E training?
Organizational culture & demand	• What is driving the demand for M&E within the organization—for example, internal or externally (donor) driven? • What is the overall climate or perception of M&E capacity building? Is it perceived as top-down and mandated, or is there buy-in and understanding of its value within the organization? • Is there leadership/senior management support for M&E capacity building within the organization? • Who, specifically, is requesting M&E training and why? • What is the specific commitment for (or resistance to) the proposed M&E training? • How will training transfer and return on investment from training be sustained? • Who are the key decision-makers, potential champions, as well as roadblocks for M&E training? • Are there trusting relationships, teamwork, and collective responsibility in the organization/program? • What are the pressures and responsibilities faced by managers and staff that affect M&E functions within the organization? • What incentives and disincentives are there for M&E at the organizational level?

(Continued)

TABLE 7.2 (Continued)

Key Factors	Key Considerations—Organizational
Sociocultural setting	• What historical, demographic, and other cultural factors are relevant for M&E capacity building—for example, mores, values, and ways of knowing as well as holidays and customs that can affect training delivery and scheduling?
Political and economic trends	• What political and economic factors affect the priorities and funding for accountable M&E—for example, stability, crisis, corruption, changing political leadership, and agendas?
Regulatory environment	• What policy, laws, and administrative and bureaucratic systems affect the operational environment for organizations? • Are there M&E standards, norms, and requirements established and promoted through accrediting and public agencies and VOPEs? • Are M&E standards, norms, and requirements upheld? Are they externally monitored and assessed?
Demand and funding	• What funding as well as other resources are available from public, international, and private donors for M&E capacity building and the specific training being considered? • To what degree does external funding dictate M&E and overall programing priorities within the recipient organization? • What are donor/partner M&E expectations and requirements for M&E and reporting format, content, and frequency? • What degree are external incentives commonly employed for M&E?
External support/ resources	• What is the availability of external research and technical support for M&E—for example, from research institutes, universities, think tanks, VOPES, and other professional organizations? • What is the availability and reliability of public statistical information and the management systems to access and use M&E—for example, from government ministries or international organizations such as UN agencies? • What is the public infrastructure and technological options available for M&E and training—for example, Internet access in a less versus more developed country? • Are there mechanisms to support communication, coordination, and collaboration across organizations (civil, public, or private) for M&E?

7.5 Task Analysis[2]

A *task analysis* systematically documents the actions and decisions that are required to achieve desired M&E practice. It helps us better understand what and how things *should*

---

2. Often called a "job analysis" in an organizational context.

BOX 7.2
An Abbreviated Topic Analysis

How do you identify M&E topics if you are unable to conduct a task analysis? For instance, consider a three-hour introduction to M&E to the general public for which you are unable to determine who will be attending beforehand, never mind conduct a task or even an individualized trainee analysis. Typically, this scenario will involve a *topic analysis* that draws upon the experience of the trainer or subject matter expert and their familiarity with M&E area (subject) identified for training. Training topics would then be largely dictated by the allotted time and based on any general trainee characteristics that can be safely inferred— that is, whether the audience is comprised of educated professionals versus less educated and potentially illiterate community members. For instance, a three-hour introduction to M&E can include topics on the difference between monitoring and evaluation, different types of each, and how they can contribute to reliable reporting and decision-making. When posted or advertised, the training description helps attract suitable trainees. Thus, in this scenario the training analysis is determined less by the information gathered but is largely based on subject matter expertise and analysis of the M&E subject identified for training.

be done and ultimately what trainees should know and be expected to perform as a result of training. For example, people may need to know how to develop an evaluation terms of reference (ToR), program logical framework, or how to use an indicator tracking table to record indicator performance. The task analysis feeds into the gap and causal analysis and helps identify M&E topics for training (see **Box 7.2** for when a task analysis is not possible or appropriate). In turn, this will inform various stages in training planning, providing the groundwork to prepare learning objectives, designing the training curriculum, and post-training comparison for training evaluation.

A task analysis is more commonly used for organizational training, where access to trainees and longer-term organizational goals warrant the individual attention to M&E task performance. Despite its potential contribution to training, the task analysis is often neglected under the misassumption that it is already understood what people need to know and do. However, such understanding is not always shared, and there are different opinions of required tasks. A task analysis helps to make explicit any implicit understanding, supporting a shared understanding to focus the training analysis and subsequent design.

There can be several levels of inquiry during the task/topic analysis, and the rigor will depend on training needs and availability of existing information on M&E tasks and responsibilities. Data collection can involve stakeholder consultation, document review, as well as direct observation of people performing M&E related tasks in their work or simulated setting. It is important to consult with stakeholders with direct, practical knowledge of required M&E tasks. This includes the targeted trainee population, managers and supervisors, and M&E subject matter experts. It is also helpful to speak with any people who may have participated in similar trainings to determine which skills and knowledge (topics) has been useful and why. Secondary sources of data include M&E guidelines and standards, job descriptions, performance review criteria, and organizational policies and procedures.

Key questions to consider during a task analysis include

- What are the components of the task and how does it interrelate with other tasks/subtasks?

- What type of learning (KSA) does the task entail (Table 7.3)?

- Who is expected to perform the task?

- How often is the task expected to be performed?

- How long should it typically take to complete the task?

- How critical is the task to achieving program outcomes—for example, is it a *must do*, *should do*, or *could do* task?

- What is the consequence if the task is performed incorrectly or omitted?

- To what degree is the task completed individually or collectively?

- Is the task measurable and to what degree is it appraised and feedback provided?

- Who supervises or oversees individual performance of the task?

- What sources/resources are available for the task requirements—for example, supervisor, guidelines, standards, organizational procedures?

- Have relevant people been trained or do they have prior experience in the task area?

- Is there underperformance for the task (see gap analysis on page 169)?

- What recommended actions can improve task performance?

Table 7.3 is an abbreviated illustration of how a task inventory can be structured to record key areas of analysis. It is meant to be tailored accordingly—for example, we included columns for the gap and solution (recommended action/s) analysis, discussed below. Anticipating training content, task areas can be first organized by topic areas, such as, "Conducting a focus group discussion," and then broken down from high

TABLE 7.3   Example Headings for a Task Inventory Table

Task Description	Subtask/s (training topics)	KSA Type	Individual or Collective	Person/s Responsible	Frequency
Conducting focus group discussions (FGDs)	– Consult with stakeholders and confirm purpose of and approval for FGDs – Draft a FGD work plan and budget – Identify FGD locations and length – Recruit FGD participants and obtain informed consent – Develop FGD questionnaire guide – Train FGD facilitators and pilot FGD – Facilitate FGDs – Record FGDs responses and observations – Debrief FGDs and analyze information – Disseminate (use) FGD information and analysis	Encompasses knowledge, skills, and attitudes	Collective with project team	Project manager	One month period during project midterm review

Completion Time	Priority	Measurable Feedback	Sources & Resources	Prior Training Experience	Performance Gap	Recommended Action/s
30 days for each series of FGD	High	Currently not provided	Absent	No	Yes—project manager and team unprepared to conduct FGD	Develop FDG management checklist and facilitation guidelines. Provide training on FGD management and facilitation. Establish quality feedback during FGD process.

level (primary) into subtasks (secondary and tertiary)—for example, individuals may (or may not) be expected to design the questionnaire, determine the sample size, obtain informed consent, enumerate survey, and analyze the results. If M&E tasks are complicated, a separate column for subtasks can be added.

The task analysis is an especially good opportunity to begin to clarify the specific KSA required for M&E training. In Chapter 4 on adult learning, we introduced Bloom's taxonomy of learning domains. For example, the task of conducting an interview may require an understanding (knowledge) of the difference between closed-ended and open-ended questions, the ability (skill) to enumerate a household survey, and an appreciation (attitude) of the importance of confidentiality of survey data. Below, **Table 7.4** breaks down KSA into content areas or dimension, which can be useful when considering exactly what type of KSA is required for identified tasks/topics. For instance, the task of developing an evaluation strategic plan can involve concepts (knowledge), procedures, and decision-making (skills). This more detailed categorization of the type of KSA required for different tasks can come in handy later during the training design (see Box 8.3 in the following chapter on training design).

Clearly, a task analysis can be a considerable undertaking, meeting with and observing different people, and if time and access to people is limited, it may be necessary to

TABLE 7.4   KSA Types

Knowledge	• **Facts**: Remember and recall specific information that answers what, who, where, when? • **Concepts**: Understand, organize, and interpret concrete and abstract ideas and communicate them in one's own words. • **Principles**: Understand and apply guidelines, rules, and standards that guide good practice. • **Processes**: Understand the relationship between events/activities and how they work together (rather than how to do them).
Skills	• **Motor skills**: Execute a series of movements needed to perform a task, such as using an M&E software application. • **Procedures**: Understand and perform tasks by applying a procedure of sequenced steps, such as the steps to commission an evaluation. • **Decision-making & problem solving**: Interpret and draw conclusions, applying skills and knowledge to real, new, or complex situations. • **Interpersonal skills**: Communicate and interact with other people, including listening, consultation, facilitation, and negotiation.
Attitudes	• **Personal values**: Predispositions to behavior, including opinions and motivations.

Source: Adapted from FAO (2011, p. 34) and Goldstein and Ford (2002, p. 103).

consult secondary resources. However it is approached, it is recommended to avoid adding nonessential tasks and related KSA to the analysis, which can later complicate and confound training design.

7.6 Gap and Causal Analysis

Needs are the difference between the current situation or state of affairs and your desired situation. The *gap analysis* helps identify M&E underperformance and the KSA needed to address it (**Figure 7.2**).[3] It will not tell us what to do but will help us understand what warrants attention to bridge the gap between the existing and desired situation. In turn, this will help verify training needs, guide decisions, prioritize objectives, and frame realistic training expectations and performance targets. Later, it can also serve as a baseline to help to measure, monitor, and evaluate progress in M&E performance and achievement of desired training outcomes. Therefore, it is especially important to document any gap analysis information for later use that contributes to overall training objectives.

A gap analysis requires access to the targeted trainee population to determine performance gaps and is therefore, like the task analysis, more often used in an organizational training setting. Drawing upon the task analysis, the gap analysis begins with a list of M&E responsibilities and/or required KSA. These can then be analyzed to estimate the current M&E performance or existing KSA as well as the desired performance level for each task or KSA for each skill area. As the columns in Table 7.3 (shown earlier in this chapter) illustrate, the gap analysis can be combined with the task analysis to more efficiently use time and resources.

Relevant secondary sources, such as M&E standards and criteria, organizational assessments, performance appraisals, and program monitoring and evaluation

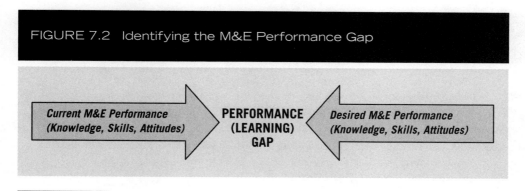

FIGURE 7.2 Identifying the M&E Performance Gap

Current M&E Performance (Knowledge, Skills, Attitudes) → PERFORMANCE (LEARNING) GAP ← Desired M&E Performance (Knowledge, Skills, Attitudes)

---

3. When there is no performance to measure, such as the start of a new program or in a nonorganizational training context, the gap analysis may focus on the estimated current level of KSA versus the desired level of KSA.

reports, can be particularly useful and save time. However, it is critical to also consult with and involve stakeholders with direct, practical knowledge of M&E performance and required KSA to verify any secondary sources. This includes the targeted trainee population, their managers and supervisors, HR personnel as well as any M&E personnel working with or supporting programming. In addition to qualitative data collection (e.g., interviews and group discussions), quantitative methods can also be useful. If a survey questionnaire is used, consider a dual-response survey format to collect information about the current and desired performance—for example, **Figure 7.3.** Direct performance observations may also be used, in which case it is recommended that a checklist is used to record performance levels for observed tasks.

The *causal analysis* is an extension of the gap analysis, examining the underlying reasons for identified gaps and related underperformance. Like the gap analysis, causes relevant to specific tasks can be noted when they are examined during the task analysis (reflected in the columns in Table 7.3, shown previously in this chapter). There is no one method for causal analysis, and it does not necessary occur as a discrete step but throughout the training analysis phase, drawing upon information gathered about the trainees, program/organization, and external environment. Stakeholder consultation and probing is essential, and there are a variety of tools and techniques ranging from SWOT analysis to fault (problem) tree analysis (e.g., see Watkins et al., 2012). When interpreting this information, stakeholder engagement is especially important to provide multiple perspectives and insight, and it can go a long way to build ownership and support for whatever is recommended.

However the causal analysis is conducted, it will be important to characterize the performance gap (need), and it is a good opportunity to explore solutions and the type

---

FIGURE 7.3   Example of Dual-Response Survey

Agreement: *1 = Strongly Disagree; 2 = Disagree; 3 = Neutral; 4 = Agree; 5 = Strongly Agree*

Current performance	Survey question	Desired or optimal performance
① ② ③ ④ ⑤	I am able to write SMART indicators for project design.	① ② ③ ④ ⑤

Source: Adapted from Watkins et al. (2012, p. 119).

of training or other intervention that can help remedy underperformance. Some key questions to consider include

- Why have the performance gaps occurred (see Table 7.5)?

- Are there any trends in and/or clusters of performance gaps and why? This can help uncover priority M&E areas or groups of people responsible for related tasks.

- How significant are the performance gaps? Consider to what degree underperformance affects achievement of program objectives.

- How urgent are the performance gaps? Consider whether they are immediate, intermediate, or long-term needs.

- Are there any performance gaps that should be prioritized? Consider their urgency and relevant to program objectives.

- What can help close the gaps, and what support is needed to do so? This will inform the solution analysis (discussed earlier in this chapter).

When considering the underlying causes, it is important to determine and not assume whether underperformance is because of a genuine KSA deficiency versus other factors. This will help determine whether training is really the best solution, versus some other form of intervention. There are a variety of reasons why underperformance may occur, and we have summarized some key examples in **Table 7.5**. Underlying causes are typically interrelated and complex. For example, insufficient KSA may require M&E training, but it may also be because of the recruitment of unqualified personnel, which may be related to inadequate HR management processes. It is important to maintain such a systems perspective that acknowledges the complexity and interconnectedness of the M&E capacity building context.

7.7 Training Analysis Report

As one conducts the training analysis, a report can be useful to synthesize findings, conclusions, and recommendations. This can then be shared with key stakeholders to guide decision-making and reinforce understanding, contributing to ownership and support for the eventual training or other interventions recommended. **Box 7.3** is an example of the content for such a training analysis report based on the information gathered from the various forms of analysis discussed in this chapter (and as expected, it should be tailored to the particular training and stakeholder needs). Typically, the report is a preliminary overview for training, and the understanding and recommendations will be refined during the later stages of the training planning, such as the development of a training strategy, discussed in the following chapters.

TABLE 7.5 Potential Causes for Performance Gaps (needs)

Causes	Considerations
Inadequate skills/knowledge	Is this because of unfamiliarity with M&E, neglect, or forgetfulness? Is it because of an absence of available learning and practice opportunities, motivational issues (below), or a combination of these factors? Was M&E performance adequate in the past, and if so, why is it no longer? Related, would remedial and/or a skill maintenance program be appropriate?
Inadequate motivation/incentive	There may be no deficiency in M&E knowledge and skills, but instead people are not compelled to put them into practice—for example, they think it makes no difference, is not worthwhile or beneficial. What is the source of the attitude problem—for example, do people lack conviction because they feel M&E is a bureaucratic burden? What incentives may address this—for example, positive messaging from credible/respected people (*sermons*) or procedural requirements within the organization (*sticks*)? Related, if training is provided, affective learning will likely be an important element to value the importance of desired M&E tasks.
Inadequate expectations	Regardless of the level of existing KSA, people simply may not be aware of M&E tasks expected of them. Is there a shared understanding of M&E standards, roles, and responsibilities? Has M&E been incorporated into job descriptions and appraisal processes?
Inadequate feedback	Are people informed in a timely manner and provided constructive feedback when they are underperforming? How well is M&E incorporated into regular performance reviews/appraisals? Is mentoring or coaching used and does it include M&E?
Inadequate labor supply	People may have adequate KSA, but their numbers or allotted time may be inadequate to meet M&E demands. Is the underlying performance because of staff turnover or insufficient resourcing and priorities at the management level? If additional people are need to be located, will they already be M&E qualified or will they need M&E training?
Unqualified personnel selection	Is there a problem with the recruitment, appointment, or promotion of people required to perform M&E? Are the wrong people in in roles expected to perform M&E tasks? In this case, it may be necessary to discharge or transfer personnel and/or reconsider HR processes for recruitment—that is, better incorporation of M&E into job descriptions.
Inadequate physical resources	Insufficient equipment or technologies can hinder M&E—that is, Internet access to use an online project management system. It is important to itemize budgets for essential M&E-related equipment and technology and to be ready to justify with program/organization management, donors, and so forth.
Inadequate management/leadership	Poor decision-making, strategic direction, and leadership can have a multiplier effect on all the above factors—for example, insufficient resourcing for or utilization of M&E capacity building. Often, management positions are based on seniority or research ability rather than management skills. In response, it is helpful to identify existing champions who understand and can promote M&E and capacity building. Related, consider options to "convert" other decision-makers into champions—for example, incorporate M&E into management leadership training.

Adapted from IntraHealth International (2007, p.19) and Pretty et al. (1995, p. 113).

BOX 7.3
Example Training Analysis Report Format

1. **Training analysis background**
   - **Commissioner**
   - **Program**
   - **Training analyst/s** (conducting the training analysis)
   - **Date**

2. **Executive Summary**

3. **Needs analysis**
   - **Need/problem statement**
   - **Tasks/topic analysis summary**
   - **Gap and causal analysis**
   - **Risk analysis**: consequences if the identified needs were left unaddressed

4. **Trainee analysis**
   - Identify any key demographic, cultural, or other background characteristics pertinent for training planning—for example, trainee location, literacy, educational level, M&E experience, and so forth.

5. **Context analysis**
   - **Organizational analysis** (when applicable): identify key factors in the organization, such as M&E resources, capacities, and overall climate and demand for M&E training.
   - **External environment:** identify external factors that can impact training, such as the demand for M&E, available resources, the sociocultural and political setting, and regulatory environment.

6. **Solution analysis**
   - **Learning goals:** for example, the overall learning goal
   - **Recommended actions/training**

(Continued)

(Continued)

- **Alternatives**: any alternatives to the recommended actions/training to address the learning goals

If M&E training is recommended, a preliminary training description can include

- **Training location—instructional setting** (primary delivery medium)
- **Trainee number**
- **Trainee requirements:** any knowledge, skills, or other prerequisites needed for training participation
- **Time frame:** recommended duration and frequency of training
- **Resource requirement:** human, material, and financial resources required for training
- **Management**: who will be responsible for the management of the training
- **Potential training constraints**: potential problems or limitations for the proposed training

7.8 CHAPTER SUMMARY

In this chapter, we have taken an up-close look at training analysis. It is interesting to note that such analyses are highly interrelated with what an M&E specialist would be expected to do. We differentiated heavy from light-duty training analysis and suggested that the decision will depend on context and circumstances. Heavy analysis approaches are only really appropriate for contexts where training will be developed and implemented for a specific or given organization. Light-touch approaches might be more sensible for contexts where trainees originate from a wide range or organizations. Additional summary points include

- Use a comprehensive set of questions to guide the training analysis; this will help ensure analysis feeds into solutions, whether it is training or some other intervention.

- It is important to distinguish the underlying needs for M&E training, and how they relate to longer-term training goals. Consider using a backward design approach to assist with this process and identify training objectives as part of training analysis. This will help develop a good image of where you would like the learner to be following training.

- Conduct trainee analysis to ensure training planning is evidence based and informed by a good understanding of who will be trained and the context they will be expected to apply acquired KSA.

- While the rigor of a task (or topic) analysis will vary, it helps to better understand what is expected of targeted trainees and informs any gap and casual analysis that may be conducted.

- A gap analysis helps identify M&E underperformance and specific KSA to address in M&E training. The casual analysis examines the underlying reasons for identified gaps and sharpen understanding of potential contributions of training.

- It is useful to capture training analysis in a training report to share with key stakeholders, building understanding and ownership for training (or other) solutions proposed.

7.9 RECOMMENDED RESOURCES

Many readers already supporting M&E will likely be familiar with resources for initial analysis and needs assessment from program and project planning, which are also useful for considering training analysis. For example, we recommend the World Bank's guide for a comprehensive overview of methods for needs assessment (Watkins et al., 2012). Another useful, online guide we recommend for generic needs assessment can be found at the website for the NOAA Office for Coastal Management (2015). Readers can refer to the recommend M&E resources in Chapter 2 to explore other guidelines for analysis and assessment that can transfer to training contexts.

In the preparation for this chapter, we found the books by Laird (2003) and Goldstein and Ford (2002) both useful background reading on organizational and individual needs assessment for training. For a more basic overview, we recommend the chapter in *Training Fundamentals* (Chan, 2010). On the use of backward design during training analysis, we found the discussion by Donald Clark (2015b) brief but useful, and we recommend the book *Understanding by Design* (Wiggins & McTighe, 2005) for a more thorough treatment.

Although developed for health worker training and education programs, we recommend the freely available guide from IntraHealth International (2007), *Learning for Performance*, which has many practical guidance tips, templates, and tools for training analysis that can be used for M&E training. Two other free publications we recommend include the *Training Package Assessment Materials Kit* from the Australian National Training Authority (Commonwealth of Australia, 2001) and *Methods for Consulting Educational Needs Assessment* from the University of Idaho (McCawley, 2009).

The training and development website from MIT (2015) is a user-friendly resource for training analysis, especially their interactive and downloadable *Key Questions Form*. We also recommend the webpage on *Assessing Your Training Needs: Needs Assessment to Training Goals* from the Free Management Library (2015). Lastly, we refer readers to the recommended resources for M&E organizational capacity assessment identified in Chapter 3, especially the checklists and tools in toolkit by the Evaluation Capacity Development Group (ECDG, 2015) and the World Bank's guide on M&E systems by Görgens and Kusek (2009).

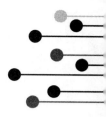

CHAPTER 8

Training Design

Training design, the next step in the ADDIE sequence, builds upon the information gathered during the training analysis to define specific training objectives, content, and instructional design (curriculum) to deliver training to achieve the objectives. Building on principles of backward design (Wiggins & McTighe, 2005) through training analysis informs in concrete ways an explicit representation of the intended results of training. Having developed such a vision, the training design phase helps us to plan and structure the training so as to enable the achievement of intended results. This includes the selection of methods, activities, and training materials most suitable for the specific training needs, audience, resources, and instructional setting identified during the analysis stage. Once these have been determined, then you are ready to start developing the training and preparing for implementation, the next phase of the ADDIE sequence.

The amount of time needed for this phase of training, who is involved, and the specific designed will vary according to particular M&E training being considered. For example, with a longer training program to be sustained over months in a large organization, it may require people specializing in instructional design working together with M&E subject matter experts for weeks to design the training. On the other hand, a three-hour introductory training on M&E to the novice evaluators or senior managers from a variety of organizations will not require as much time or people to prepare.

The five components we outline in this chapter for training design are inherently useful steps for most training types for M&E—for example, whether face-to-face training or e-learning.

Learning Objectives

By the end of this chapter readers will be able to . . .

✓ Explain the value and limitations of using objectives for training

✓ Write SMART learning objectives for M&E training

✓ Specify assessment methods for M&E learning objectives

✓ Organize instructional content for M&E training

✓ Design well-sequenced training curriculum for M&E training

✓ Identify key activity types and related considerations for the M&E training curriculum

✓ Discuss key considerations for including training evaluation and transfer as part of training design

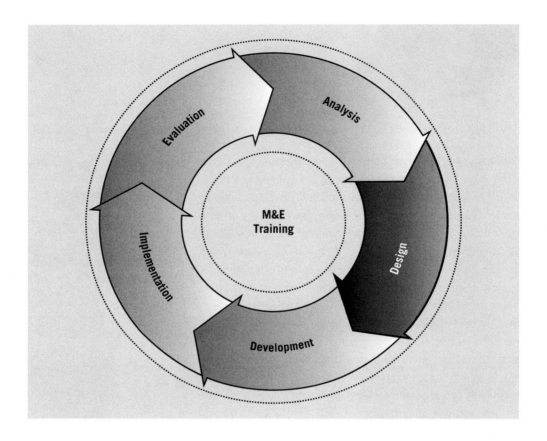

However, due to the broad scope of training delivery options, our discussion on curriculum design and the selection training activities is primarily geared toward the face-to-face workshop setting, where live, in-person interaction is possible. Nevertheless, many of the concepts and activities we discuss can also apply other training settings.

8.1 Identify Training Objectives

It is important to understand the intended results before proposing solutions. Just as a program evaluator must first understand a program's desired outcomes (program theory) to measure and evaluate performance (Funnell & Rogers, 2011), so must a trainer to design training that contributes to identified results. During training analysis, we looked at backward design (Wiggins & McTighe, 2005) to understanding of training need and desired outcomes. The training design expands upon this initial thinking to detail a hierarchy of objectives for training. Clarifying these objectives will provide a useful road map to

Jessie Mountfield

- Ensure training is relevant to the longer term training outcomes (whether organizational or for individual learners)

- Select and sequence training content (topics) in a coherent progression to support learning objectives

- Provide a basis to measure, monitor, and evaluate training

- Communicate to trainees and other stakeholders what to expect from training

Designing training objectives draws upon information gathered during the training analysis and requires careful consideration and time to develop. **Table 8.1** provides an example of four levels of objectives for M&E training; we include training materials to illustrate inputs for activities. Starting from the learner, learning objectives draw from the training analysis (e.g., analysis of topics, tasks, and gaps) to specifically identify what trainees need to learn to contribute to the overall learning goal. For M&E training, this typically refers to the specific KSA required for M&E but may include other learning objectives, such as teamwork.

The learning goal is the overall set of KSA or competency area identified for M&E training. It is the subject area that encompasses the various M&E topics targeted for training. In turn, it contributes to the longer-term outcomes for M&E training. Depending on training needs, a learning objective may require secondary learning objective/s (sometimes called *enabling learning objectives*) to complete subtasks or understand subtopics. Training activities and materials are used to deliver training to achieve the learning objectives.

As **Box 8.1** highlights, the use of pre-determined training objectives is not without its drawbacks. Furthermore, it is worth noting that there are an assortment of other design terms and formats used in training and education, ranging from learning outcomes and outputs, to performance objectives and educational aims. This can be confusing, especially for M&E practitioners, who themselves may use these terms differently in program design. Indeed, just as there is no consensus within the M&E

TABLE 8.1 Example Training Objectives[*]

Term	Definition	Example
Training outcomes	The longer-term results or desired changes training seeks to accomplish	Organizational: effective program design for program implementation, M&E, and reporting. Individual: professional development or personal interest.
Learning goal	The purpose of the training, identifying the overall M&E area to improve for training outcomes	Prepare trainees to design a program using a logical framework approach.
Primary learning objectives	What trainees are expected to achieve as a result of training	By the end of the training, trainees will be able to select the most appropriate data collection methods (means of verification) for their program.
Secondary learning objectives	What trainees (learners) are expected to achieve from training to accomplish the primary learning objective	By the end of training, the trainee will be able to explain what it means to triangulate data collection sources and why it is important.
Training activities	Activities planned in the training curriculum to achieve the learning objectives	Paired work in which trainees partner up to match provided data collection methods with appropriate indicators.
Training materials	The material inputs needed to conduct the training activity	PowerPoint presentation of instruction and handout for matching exercise.

[*]As we explain below, there is no consensus for results hierarchy terminology for training, which varies according to context and user.

community for the terminology in and the approach to program design, consensus is also absent in the terminology for training design.[1] Differences aside, the important point is to trace a logical train of thought (theory of change) of how training will bring about change. Ultimately, the training design should be tailored according to the training needs, and other terms as well as additional levels of objectives (results) may very well be appropriate.

---

1. For example, *learning outcome* is sometimes used instead of *learning objective*. We have adopted what we consider the most popular usage of the term, where "An objective describes an intended result of instruction rather than the process of instruction" (Mager, 1984, p. 5). This use of learning objectives was pioneered by Ralph Tyler (1949), an influential American educator/evaluator in the 1940s, and later popularized by the Robert Mager (1984) in the 1960s.

BOX 8.1
Blueprint or Road Map?

As we have discussed, a systems approach to training acknowledges training occurs in a dynamic context, and it is not always easy to plan for everything in advance. Despite best intentions, unanticipated learner needs and outcomes arise during training. For example, team-building and social networking among trainees may not be anticipated, but emerge as important outcomes for people. Brookfield (1986, p 267) warns that the use of pre-determined objectives is "school based," discourages flexibility, and may not account for differences in experiences, interests, and abilities in an adult setting. However, he also acknowledges there are instances when predefined learning objectives may be appropriate when specific learning content is to be covered.

We believe much of M&E training lends itself well to pre-determined learning objectives, and it is important to identify priorities to guide M&E training. As Preskill and Boyle (2008, p.449) explain: "Without having a clear sense of what it is we want people to learn from their engagement in evaluation activities and processes, it is difficult to design effective learning strategies. As is made clear in the instructional design literature, a program's design, implementation, and evaluation should flow directly from the desired goals and objectives." However, training objectives should not be a blueprint, but rather a road map. They provide direction to guide training, but one may need to change course and select a different route according to learners' need and opportunities that may arise during training.

8.2 Preparing Learning Objectives

Of the training objectives we have identified, designing learning objectives receives considerable attention, as they are the basis for identifying what people are to learn and how they are to put their learning to use. Once identified, they help prioritize and organize training content (topics) and guide training delivery and evaluation. If the training design is a road map, the learning objectives are the signposts that provide direction for training and the mile markers to measure progress. Below, we outline four steps to guide the preparation of learning objectives for M&E training.

1. Review M&E topics/tasks to prioritize for learning

Developing learning objectives takes time, and the effort should focus only on those essential M&E topics meeting training needs. Training topics represent content areas needed to accomplish the KSA identified for M&E training. The topics focus on what will be learned, whereas the learning objectives identify what the trainee will be able to achieve from learning the M&E topics. Sometimes this will be a particular M&E skill or task, like managing an evaluation, while other times it may just be knowledge and understanding, such as the difference between monitoring and evaluation.

Identifying the learning topics is an iterative process. A preliminary list of M&E topics may have already been identified during the training analysis (e.g., a task analysis). It is also useful during this stage to check with M&E subject matter experts (SMEs) and any relevant M&E technical resources (e.g., guidelines, policies, and standards) to ensure that the topics are indeed relevant. Preliminary M&E topics can be used to guide the preparation of learning objectives, and then later they can be cross-checked and sequenced once learning objectives have been finalized.

One way to take inventory of M&E topics is to create a table (**Table 8.2**) where M&E topics and related KSA can be listed. This can be used to draft learning objectives and note prerequisite knowledge and assessment for each objective, which we discuss below. As our example reflects, the learning objective will often represent the overall M&E topic or subject area (selecting appropriate data collection methods); specific topics covered to achieve the objective (e.g., triangulation) may be listed as secondary learning objectives.

2. Write the learning objective

Like indicator statements used in M&E, the wording of learning objectives is specific and precise to make expectations and measurement clear. There is no one recipe for writing learning objectives and the degree of detail will vary according to training and

TABLE 8.2 Example Template for Preparing learning Objectives

Learning Objective	KSA	Topics	Prerequisites	Assessment
By the end of the training, trainees will be able to identify the most appropriate data collection methods for their program.	• Knowledge: concepts • Skill: decision-making	• Primary/ secondary data • Quantitative/ qualitative methods • Triangulation	None	• Pre-/post-tests • Quiz • Post-training review

assessment needs. Below we will outline four steps to consider when writing M&E learning objectives, using the following example learning objective:

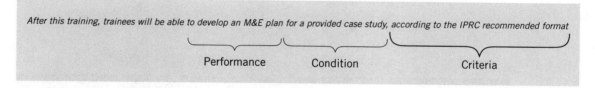

After this training, trainees will be able to develop an M&E plan for a provided case study, according to the IPRC recommended format

Performance   Condition   Criteria

1. **Specify when the learner is expected to achieve the learning objective.** As learning objectives identify what is to be performed as a *result* of training, they often begin with phrases such as, *By the end of this training . . .* , *After completing this training (lesson, session, etc.). . .* , *Three months after completing this training. . .* , and so forth.

2. **Identify the learner.** Learning objectives are learner focused, and the trainee is the subject of the statement. They express what the trainee is expected to do as the result of training rather than what the instructor does during training.

3. **Identify what is to be performed as a result of training.** Learning objectives focus on the consequence of learning rather than what or how trainees are learning. For example, rather than stating that trainees will learn about M&E plans, this is conveyed by stating that they will be *able to develop* an M&E plan. This later helps in the assessment of the learning objective; learning or understanding is not always directly observable or measurable, but it is possible to measure results through performance. Therefore, when writing learning objectives, much attention is given to the selection of the action verb used in the objective statement. The action verb is used to convey the KSA being performed and how it will be observed/measured.[2]

Table 8.3 lists example verbs to consider for learning objectives. In our example, *develop* is used to convey the knowledge and skills to be performed (creating an M&E plan). One useful question to help write objective statements is, *Given an M&E task and the required KSA to perform it, what behaviors indicate it is being performed correctly?* It is important to ensure that performance is realistic (achievable) for the trainee after the training. For example, there is a difference between *explaining* what is logic model and actually *developing* one. When preparing the learning objective, consider

---

2. Writing learning objectives is often based on the three learning domains identified in Bloom's Taxonomy (discussed in Chapter 4), providing a more detailed consideration than KSA categorization.

- The complexity of the KSA to be performed

- The training audience and their prior level of M&E understanding and experience

- What instruction is feasible within the given training duration and resources

	TABLE 8.3 Example Verbs for Writing Learning Objectives
Knowledge	define, list, recall, repeat, name, identify, recite, state, outline, recognize, explain, express, describe, discuss, review, compare, contrast, summarize, distinguish, provide an example, infer, select, prioritize, discriminate
Skills	apply, demonstrate, perform, prepare, operate, follow, display, arrange, assemble, construct, inspect, organize, draft, trouble-shoot, insert, inspect, place, point to, remove, coordinate, produce, develop
Attitudes	explain, demonstrate, model, support, defend, justify, display, initiate, comply, choose, influence, convince

4. **Specify any conditions and/or criteria for performance**. When possible, including any conditions, standards, or criteria for performance helps to further refine the learning objective. In our example, "for a provided case study and logframe" is the condition, and "according to the IFRC recommended format" is the criterion. Depending on the training context and KSA to be performed, it may not always be possible or necessary to specify performance conditions and criteria in a learning objective.

In summary, just as the acronym "SMART" is often used to guide the development of indicator (and objective) statements in project design, it likewise applies to learning objectives (IntraHealth International, 2007, p. 36):

- **Specific**. Use an action verb that precisely describes the desired behavior from training.

- **Measurable**. Ensure the verb that describes an observable action/ measurable action.

- **Attainable/achievable**. Ensure that it is realistic given the circumstances and resources.

Vague learning objective	Improved learning objective
By the end of training, participants will have a better understanding of M&E planning.	By the end of training, participants will be able to . . . • Develop an M&E plan (primary learning objective). • Explain the key criteria for secondary data (secondary learning objective). • Compare and contrast quantitative, qualitative, and mixed methods (secondary learning objective). • Explain triangulation and its importance (secondary learning objective).

- **Relevant**. Ensure that it pertains to specific M&E tasks desired and the setting in which they will be used.

- **Timely/time bound**. Specify a realistic time frame for performance when appropriate.

Similarly, just as indicators often need to be reconsidered and rewritten to be "SMARTer," this is often the case when designing learning objectives. For example, consider the difference between the learning objective statements in **Box 8.2**. The vague learning objective is very broad and does not provide a clear indication of what will specifically be achieved by training. While only illustrative, the improved learning objectives show how primary and secondary statements can be used to refine and specify the learning objective.

For some readers, the process we outline above may seem like "overkill," with excessive detail, while others may feel there should be more rigor—that is, indicators developed to measure each learning objective. Writing learning objectives can sometimes feel like a balancing act between providing detail and keeping it simple. More detail helps identify what to measure to evaluate learner performance and training impact. However, when too detailed and technical, statements can seem convoluted, especially communicating training content to stakeholders (i.e., to advertise and frame expectations for training).

Ultimately, the level of detail for learning objectives will depend on the degree to which individual performance will need to be assessed for job performance monitoring and/ or training evaluation (discussed in Chapter 11). Consider the example statements in

BOX 8.3
Example M&E Learning Objectives

By the end of the training, trainees will be able to . . .

Knowledge objectives

- Differentiate monitoring and evaluation

- Compare and contrast quantitative and qualitative data collection methods (for a given case study on impact evaluation)

- Identify the seven principles of good data management

- Describe the major types of bias to avoid in data collection and analysis

- Explain how politics can affect the independence of evaluations (for the provided case study or scenario)

- Distinguish important differences for primary versus secondary data

- Identify the key elements of an M&E plan (according to "X" organization's format)

- Compare and contrast logic models, results frameworks, and conceptual frameworks

Skill objectives

- Demonstrate how to obtain informed consent for a household survey (during an actual field visit)

- Draft an evaluation terms of reference (within three months of training completion)

- Write SMART indicator statements (for a provided list of objective statements)

- Determine a household sample using stratified random sampling (for a given case study)

- Conduct a stakeholder analysis for evaluation (for a given case study)

- Develop a community scorecard for program M&E (for a given case study)

- Prepare an evaluation strategy (for a given evaluation case study)

Box 8.3; parentheses have been placed around the conditions and criteria, which may or may not need to be included depending on training assessment needs. If assessment is a priority, but it is felt objective statements are becoming increasingly cumbersome, conditions and criteria for rating performance can be separately identified as well as specific indicators for learning assessment. Another option is to develop detailed learning objectives to assist with training design and assessment, while more user-friendly statements can be used to communicate with trainees and other stakeholders for whom such detail may be excessive.

The number of learning objectives required for a particular training will also vary according to training assessment needs (and of course, the training length and amount of content covered). If assessment is a priority, there may be secondary learning objectives for every topic covered; if it is not, only primary learning objectives may be adequate. For instance, in Table 8.6 (later in this chapter), the primary learning objective for the example training session is "develop an M&E plan." We also provide three related secondary learning objectives and over eight topics. Depending on the particular training, it may be sufficient to have just one (overall) learning objective (develop M&E plans), and the training topics can serve to communicate to others what type of learning is to occur.

3. Specify Learning Prerequisites

While preparing learning objectives, it is a good opportunity to also consider any prerequisite knowledge required for the objectives. Depending on the thoroughness of the training analysis, this may have already been noted, but at this stage of training design it is recommended to specifically note prerequisite knowledge for each learning objective that is developed. This can help match training with appropriate trainees and determine whether any pre-training assignments will be necessary. It also assists in determining the level of training—for example, introductory, intermediate, or advanced. For example, training on quantitative methods may have certain learning objectives that require statistics, whereas an introductory course on evaluation principles and ethics may not assume any prior knowledge. Table 8.2 (earlier in this chapter) illustrates how learning prerequisite can be noted when preparing the learning objectives.

4. Specify Assessment Methods

> The complexities of (training) evaluation should not be underestimated: however, the most serious problem has been the failure to always consider evaluation an ordinary part of the instructional design process. (Goldstein & Ford, 2002, p. 141)

While we will discuss training evaluation later in Chapter 11, as the preceding quote from Goldstein and Ford reflects, if assessment is to be conducted, it is best planned for early as part of the training design process. In fact, as our prior discussion underscores, planning for training evaluation actually starts with writing SMART learning objectives that support performance measurement and assessment. While preparing the learning objectives, it is efficient to also note the specific assessment methods and techniques to ensure they are indeed realistic and appropriate for the objective. This will also inform the development of assessment tools (e.g., pre-tests and quizzes) prior to training. If you have ever taken a test or quiz that did not assess the material presented during instruction, you understand how frustrating that can be. Such incongruence undermines not only the utility of the test/quiz but also the overall credibility of the training and trainer. In **Table 8.4**, we present some example methods and techniques for assessing learning objectives, which can be added to Table 8.2 (earlier in this chapter) as appropriate for the specific learning objective being considered.

The few days set aside for the workshop seem to be insufficient for all the topics one may want to offer to the trainees. In this context, it is better to reduce the number of topics than to overload the workshop. In either situation you will eventually have to leave out certain inputs, which you might feel are important. If you do this during the planning of the schedule, you have control over what gets left out. If however, you create an overcrowded schedule, you will simply have to leave out which ever inputs fall at the end of your programme when you run out of time. (Chatty, Baas, & Fleig, 2003, p. 18)

Our discussion on preparing learning objectives has focused on four steps. However, there is no one formula, and the process should be tailored to training needs and the particular person/s designing the

TABLE 8.4   Example Assessment Methods/Techniques

Example assessment method/technique	Knowledge	Skills	Attitudes
In-training written tests/quizzes	√		
Learner presentation or performance	√		√
Individual or group assignment	√	√	
Learner self-assessment	√	√	√
Peer assessment/review	√	√	√
Learner interview	√		√
Learner questionnaire or attitude survey			√
Supervisor interview		√	√
Supervisor questionnaire		√	√
Observation (simulation)		√	
Observation (practice)		√	
Post-training or staff performance review		√	√
Learner contract or action plan		√	

Adapted from IntraHealth International. (2007, p. 42).

training. Whatever approach is used, careful attention should be given to the learning objectives early in the training design phase, as they play a pivotal role in subsequent training design, development, delivery, and evaluation.

8.3 Organizing the Instructional Content

Once learning objectives have been prepared, you are ready to refine and organize M&E topics to be covered by training. This is a critical phase of training design as it provides the overall structure for the M&E content for the curriculum design and training activities that will be used to deliver training.

One of the biggest challenges in training is to cover the content in the allotted time. Therefore, before sequencing M&E topics, it is important to first ensure that each topic is really necessary for training. This will depend on two key factors. First, the topic should be relevant to the respective learning objective. For example, if the training in an introduction to evaluation, it may not be timely to also go into designing program logic models. Second, the appropriateness of a topic will also depend on the prior knowledge and experience of the trainees. For example, if trainees are already familiar with the major evaluation types, it may not be necessary to focus on this in a training event on preparing evaluation terms of reference (ToRs). When cross-checking the M&E topic, consider whether it is essential, recommended, or optional.

After M&E topics have been confirmed, the next step is to consider how to best sequence them into a coherent progression suitable for the training audience. There are a variety of interrelated approaches to order training topics, of which we list some of the more common ones here:

- **Prerequisite knowledge**. Topics are arranged according to the knowledge or skills needed first before progressing to another topic.

- **Performance order**. Topics are arranged in the order that skills need to be performed to complete a task.

- **Problem based**. Topics are arranged according to how to solve a problem.

- **Complexity**. Topics are arranged from simple to complex.

- **Generality**. Topics are arranged from a more general overview to specific or visa versa.

- **Familiarity**. Topics are arranged from known to unknown.

- **Importance**. Topics are arranged according to their priority, either relative to other topics or urgency in time.

- **Relationship**. Topics are arranged or grouped together based on their commonality in relation to the learning objective.

The above approaches to sequence topics are not exhaustive and typically are used in combination. For example, if a learning objective is to prepare an evaluation plan, topics may be arranged according to *performance order*, which is based on *prerequisite knowledge* needed to progress to the next topic. In situations where topics are not necessarily dependent on each other for order, they can be grouped together according to *relationship* and then introduced according to *complexity*. For instance, the difference between primary and secondary data can first be introduced, then the concepts triangulating data sources, and then more complex topics can be covered, such as the strengths and weaknesses of different data collection methods. Complexity is also related to *familiarity*, and if information is available on the learner's profile (e.g., from training analysis), it may be possible to organize topics from known to unknown (familiarity).

Whichever approach is used to sequence topics, it is important to avoid duplication and inconsistencies. (We distinguish duplication from planned repetition that is structured into the training curriculum to reinforce understanding—discussed below).

In **Appendix 8.1** for this chapter, we provide a several examples of different topics and their sequence used for M&E training curriculum. Rather than attempting to provide a "generic" sequence of M&E training topics, we purposefully chose to highlight examples because the topics and order in which they are presented should inevitably be adjusted to the particular training context and needs.

8.4 Designing the Training Curriculum

Having prepared the learning objectives and refined the M&E topics and sequence, you are ready to design the training curriculum. This is a detailed agenda or outline for trainers, providing a session-by-session summary to guide training delivery. It encompasses the planned interaction of learners with the training content and reflects the underlying methodology guiding how instruction, activities, materials, and secondary media are used in training.[3] Therefore, we recommend careful consideration to the design of the training curriculum.

By the time you reach this stage of training design, you should already have a good idea from the training analysis what is the preferred instructional setting for training (Chapter 7). Below we take a further look at some overall methodological considerations for designing the training curriculum and then the selection of specific activities (methods) for training delivery. Due to the broad scope of training delivery options, the following discussion will largely apply to methods and activities for the training workshop setting, where live, in-person interaction is possible. However, many of the concepts and activities we discuss can also apply to other training settings.

Identify an overall sequence for training methods

Just as M&E topics need to be sequenced, the training activities selected for the training curriculum should also reflect a coherent learning progression that will meaningfully engage trainees and support learning. In Chapter 4, we looked at some of the many theories and methods for adult learning, such as andragogy, experiential learning, and learner-centered approaches to training. Of particular importance is the experiential learning cycle, which identifies four primary stages to learning: (a) provide

---

3. For some, training curriculum is used to refer to a list of subjects or topics to be included in training.

an experience, (b) observe and reflect, (c) generalize and conclude, and (d) apply new KSA. The learner can enter the cycle at any stage, and how this is reflected in the curriculum will vary according to the content, learner, and context.

As a whole, the training curriculum should be comprised of activities that will meaningfully engage trainees and support learning. One of the more influential approaches to instructional design is the work of Robert Gagné's, who identified "nine events of instruction" to guide instructional design (Gagné 1985; Gagné & Driscoll, 1988).[4] Often referred to as "steps," they are based on a hierarchy of conditions/events that should be met to facilitate learning at each stage. We have summarized Gagné's nine events in **Table 8.5**, and in Chapter 10 we show how elements of these steps inform facilitating a training workshop introduction, activities, and closing.

Gagné's nine events of instruction are not prescriptive, and they were developed with in-person training in mind, well before the arrival of e-learning.[5] Nevertheless, they remain a useful model to consider, and the underlying methodology should be modified and adapted according to training needs. For example, it may be more engaging to first provide an opportunity (experience) to engage learners and explore learning content themselves so that the eventual presentation of key learning points is more relevant and meaningful. The importance of Gagné's model is to remind us that instruction can be well designed when considered in terms of a planning process to support learning.

Another way to consider the instructional design is presented by Heron (1999), which we want to briefly summarize as it illustrates an alternative structure based on increasing power and control that learners have during training implementation. John Heron (1999, pp. 8 &10) identifies three stages of facilitation based on increasing levels of trainee participation in training facilitation:

1. **Hierarchy early on**. The facilitator directs the learning process as learners do not yet have the required knowledge and abilities to orientate themselves for learning.

2. **Co-operation mid-term**. The facilitator shares power and control over the learning process with the learners, as learners have acquired a foundation of knowledge, ability, and confidence to orientate themselves for learning.

3. **Autonomy later on**. The facilitator relinquishes control over the learning process, as learners have a sufficient competence and confidence to exercise their own judgment to guide the learning process.

---

4. Gagné is a behaviorist with a focus is on the outcomes—behaviors—that result from training. His seminal book, *The Conditions of Learning*, originally published in 1965, is largely based on his work with the United States Army.
5. Gagné 's nine events are not without its critics. In his blog, "Gagné's Nine Dull Commandments," Clark (2006) criticizes Gagné's model as an "instructional ladder that leads straight to Dullsville."

TABLE 8.5 Gagné's "Nine Events of Instruction"

1. **Gain attention**	Present a stimulus or attention grabber to capture the learner's attention and interest in the M&E subject.
2. **Introduce the training objectives**	Identify the specific KSA trainees are to learn and be able to do as a result of training. This is also a good opportunity to discuss how learning topics will be approached, the training agenda, and learner expectations to reinforce buy-in and ownership for the learning objectives.
3. **Stimulate recall of prior learning**	Assist learners to associate new information with prior knowledge and experience. Learners understand and remember learning when there are links to personal experience and knowledge.
4. **Present the content**	Introduce new M&E content and material, which will become the basis for what is to be discussed and practiced afterward.
5. **Provide learning guidance**	Provide further support to assist learners to understand and apply M&E learning, using examples, case studies, metaphors, and other techniques to clarify complex concepts and help learners integrate and organize new knowledge.
6. **Elicit performance**	Provide a direct experience for learners to practice what they have learned and confirm their understanding. There is no substitute for learning from doing, and it helpful when practice is relevant to actual M&E situations encountered in the real world.
7. **Provide feedback**	Provide timely and specific feedback on performance to reinforce learning—that is, correct and learn from any mistakes while the learning moment is fresh. This helps both the trainees and the trainer gauge and monitor learning and understanding.
8. **Assess performance**	Conduct formal assessment of performance to verify that learning has occurred. In addition to monitoring learning and evaluating the effectiveness of the training, assessments can also reinforce key learning points.
9. **Enhance retention and transfer**	Identify strategies to help trainees internalize and apply M&E learning over time, after the training is completed.

Heron's approach is useful to consider for a more learner-centered approach to training. Like Gagné, each stage is graduated, informed by prerequisite knowledge, but the determining factor is the level of participation learners have in leading their learning process. Such an approach is empowering, recognizing that adults are self-directed learners and stressing the learning process as much as the training content. However, it will depend on a variety of factors, including the size and length of the training as well as the learners' background and experience in both the subject matter as well as learning management and facilitation.

In Chapter 10, we will revisit some of the key elements introduced above as they relate to training implementation—for example, setting the training climate, providing feedback, and facilitating training activities.

Select and schedule training activities

Training activities operationalize the methodology to achieve training objectives. They may use different training media, such as slide presentations and flipcharts, and materials, such as case studies and lesson handouts. Training activities not only include those for learning but also activities to create a supportive atmosphere for learning (e.g., ice breakers and energizers) as well as other potential training objectives (e.g., team building and networking). Each training activity reflects one or more methodological approach, such as experiential learning through problem-solving, peer learning, repetition, and positive reinforcement. In Chapter 4 we identified fourteen principles for adult learning. We recommend trainers consult these when selecting activities for the curriculum design (see Table 4.4 in Chapter 4).

There is an assortment of different types of activity that can be used for M&E training, which is good as it allows trainers to tailor training delivery to different training needs and audiences. **Table 8.6** lists twenty-one major activity types that can be used for M&E training, which we examine more closely in Part 3 of the book. The training literature is abound with books, articles, websites, and other sources with examples of activities and techniques for facilitating adult training—for example, see Recommended Resources at the end of Chapter 10 as well as Part 3. Likewise, there is growing attention within the evaluation community to the use of specific activities for evaluation capacity building (ECB), ranging from

TABLE 8.6 Example Activity Types for M&E Training*

1. Icebreakers	8. Guest Speakers	15. Practicum Experiences
2. Energizers	9. Panel Discussions and Debates	16. Independent Learning Activities
3. Lectures	10. Role Playing	17. Review Activities
4. Discussion Activities	11. Simulations	18. Learning Assessment Activities
5. Subgroup Formations	12. Demonstrations	19. Training Monitoring and Evaluation Activities
6. Case Studies	13. M&E Software Activities	20. Training Closing Activities
7. Learning Games	14. Learner Presentations	21. Training Follow-up Activities

*These are discussed in more detail in Part 3 of the book.

BOX 8.4
Guiding Questions for Activity Selection

- Are activities relevant to and do they help achieve learning objectives?

- Are activities meaningful and relevant to learners and real world needs?

- Do activities build on learners' prior experience and knowledge?

- Are activities within the ability of the learners, providing an appropriate level of challenge?

- Are activities fun, active, and varied to engage learners?

- Do activities use participatory and experiential methods, empowering learners to be actively involved in their learning?

- Do activities incorporate a variety of media and methods for different learning styles?

- Are activities culturally appropriate and nonthreatening, and will people be comfortable and willing to participate?

- Are review, repetition, and feedback built into the activities at regular intervals to reinforce learning?

- Are activities suitable for the number of trainees and the instructional setting?

- Are activities appropriate for and within the capacity of the trainer to facilitate?

- Are activities practical given the amount of time available for training?

- Are activities realistic given the amount of resources and time to develop the activity?

case studies and role playing to simulations and brainstorming (e.g., Adams & Dickinson, 2010; Lee, Wallace, & Alkin, 2007; Orr, 2010; Preskill & Russ-Eft, 2015; Trevisan, 2004).[6]

As with other aspects of training planning, activity selection will vary according to training context and purpose. **Box 8.4** summarizes some important questions to guide the selection of training activities, drawing upon the adult learning principles we identify in Chapter 4 as well as other practical considerations for training typically

6. Of particular note is the book, *Building Evaluation Capacity: Activities for Teaching and Training*, by Preskill and Russ-Eft (2015), which describes ninety activities for the teaching and training for evaluation.

answered during training analysis. Of particular importance when selecting training activities is variety. For longer training events, routine activities using the same method can be boring versus a wide range of methods and media—for example, group discussion, individual work, case studies, problem solving, brainstorming, guest speakers, games, and videos.

It is also critical to consider the level and type of interaction most suited for the learning objectives. For instance, the degree of hands-on practice and feedback required to develop an M&E plan or evaluation terms of reference, or conduct an interview. Related, certain activities and their type of interaction may be appropriate for different learning styles. For example, some group and peer learning activities, such as role plays or debates, may be more appropriate for active and outgoing learners, while they may cause anxiety and discomfort for more reflective and soft-spoken learners.

Another critical aspect of activity planning is time management. The number of activities planned and how they are developed and the time allotted to them will depend on the overall training duration. (For this reason, we adopt a broad usage of "curriculum" to include and plan for learning as well as other training activities, e.g., energizers, breaks, and the training introduction and closing.) Planning activities for a three-hour workshop will be much different than a five-day residential workshop or a series of workshops spread out over a year. Similarly, the time allotted to unpack one activity in a six-hour workshop will vary depending on whether there are two or twelve additional activities to plan around. Therefore, we recommend scheduling training activities as you design them in order to realistically consider and plan for time management.

As with other processes we have discussed, there is no "one way" to design a training curriculum. In **Table 8.7** we provide an example template for planning the training curriculum. The level of detail should be adapted to the training context and trainer, and later it can be simplified into a training agenda that can be shared with trainees and other stakeholders. We provide three example training sessions: two related to M&E learning (M&E plans and Evaluation principles & ethics) as well one session (training introduction) illustrating activities that are not lessons but serve other training needs

The options for M&E training activities are endless, depending on the creativity of the trainer/designer. In Chapter 9 we will take a closer look at considerations for facilitating training activities, and Part 3 of the book is devoted to a closer look at M&E activities for training. As we shall see in our next chapter, trainer guidelines, facilitation note, or lesson plans can be developed once activities have been selected and scheduled and the amount of allotted time for each session and its activities is known.

TABLE 8.7 Example Curriculum Template for Training Planning[1]

Session[2]	Time	Session Objectives[3]	Session Topics	Methods/Activities	Material/Media	Trainer/s	Additional Comments
Introduction	9:00–10:30 am	1. Stimulate interest in M&E planning 2. Identify and validate trainee expectations 3. Satisfy trainee "need to know" what will be included in the training and how it will be facilitated 4. Establish a positive learning environment 5. Assess trainee KSA prior to training	1. Welcome (training importance) 2. Introductions 3. Trainee expectations 4. Learning objectives (LO) 5. Training agenda and materials 6. Training ground rules and logistics 7. Pre-test	• Engaging story • "M&E experience tree" activity • "Expectations post-it" activity • Presentation and discussion • Individual work (pre-test) • Q&A and clarification throughout session	• Facilitator's notes, guide, or lesson plan • Name tags • Handouts: trainee packet, participant list/contacts, agenda, trainee guide, M&E guide • PowerPoint slides • Parking lot table (on flipchart) • Ground rule table (created on flipchart) • Written pre-test • Equipment: post-its, flipchart & markers, whiteboard & markers, PowerPoint projector & computer	List trainer/s' name	Consider having trainees identify expectations prior to training.

(Continued)

TABLE 8.7 (Continued)

Session[2]	Time	Session Objectives[3]	Session Topics	Methods/Activities	Material/Media	Trainer/s	Additional Comments
Break	10:30 – 10:50 am	• Replenish, toilet break, network, relax		Five-minute warning prior to end	Water, juice, coffee, tea, cookies, fruit, glasses, napkins, etc.		
Example session— M&E Plans	10:50 am–12:00 pm	**By the end of the training (session), trainees will be able to . . .** **Primary learning objective** 1. *Develop an M&E plan* **Secondary learning objectives** 2. *Explain the key criteria for secondary data* 3. *Compare and contrast quantitative, qualitative, and mixed methods* 4. *Explain triangulation and its importance*	1. Logframe review 2. Indicator criteria 3. M&E plan template overview 4. Indicator definitions 5. Data collection a. Primary and secondary data collection b. Qualitative, quantitative, and mixed methods c. Triangulation 6. Data collection frequency 7. Data collection responsibilities 8. Information use/ audience	• Small-group discussion of logframe • Group game— "SMARTer Indicator" • Presentation and discussion • Paired work— identifying and classifying data collection sources and methods • Group work/ practice—teams complete columns in M&E plan for given indicators with peer feedback	• Facilitator's notes, guide, or lesson plan • Handouts: example logframe, indicator criteria handout, M&E planning template, data collection sources, and methods handout • SMARTer indicator game pieces • PowerPoint slides • Equipment: flipchart & markers, PowerPoint projector & computer	List trainer/s' name	

Session[2]	Time	Session Objectives[3]	Session Topics	Methods/Activities	Material/Media	Trainer/s	Additional Comments
Lunch	**12:00 – 1:00 pm**	• Replenish, toilet break, network, relax		Five-minute warning prior to end	• Training facility cafeteria		
Example session— **Evaluation principles & ethics**	**1:00– 2:30 pm**	**Learning objective** *By the end of the training, trainees will be able to explain how the American Evaluation Association's five guiding principles of evaluation apply to evaluation.*	1. AEA five guiding principles a. Systematic inquiry b. Competence c. Integrity/honesty d. Respect for people e. Responsibilities for general and public welfare	• Partner game—definition matching cards • Presentation and discussion • Case study—individuals read and note issues/questions • Case study—small groups discussion and record issues to report in plenary • Plenary discussion/debate	• Facilitator's notes, guide, or lesson plan • Handouts: AEA guiding principles for evaluation, AEA case study • Definition game pieces • AEA PowerPoint slides • Equipment: flipchart & markers, PowerPoint projector & computer	List trainer/s' name	Consider sending out case studies prior to training for pre-reading.
Etc. . .							

1. A simplified version can be developed into a training agenda that can be shared with trainees and other stakeholders.

2. Other terms, such as *lesson*, *unit*, or *module*, can be used according to context; we use *session* to include activities that may or may not be related to a learning activity (lesson).

3. Objectives may be related to learning or other aspects of the training. *Learning objective* is abbreviated to LO. Secondary learning objectives will depend on the training context and assessment need; it may be sufficient to convey them by the session topics, depending on the training needs.

8.5 Designing Training Evaluation and Follow-Up

In addition to the training curriculum, training evaluation and any follow-up activities for training transfer should be designed *prior* to training implementation. When training evaluation and transfer are planned in tandem with the training curriculum, it helps support a coherent approach to achieving training objectives. Also, it will be necessary to develop resources for training evaluation and transfer prior to training delivery, for example, pre-/post-tests, quizzes, tests, and feedback forms used for training evaluation. Similarly, some activities for training transfer, such as the use of trainee development plans or contracts, are best communicated and initiated with trainees before and/or during training implementation.

While training evaluation and transfer serve two separate purposes, they are related and can be mutually supportive (Hutchins, 2009, p. 86). For example, post-training assessment of trainee learning and performance not only contributes to training evaluation but can also support the review of M&E content for trainees, reinforcing learning objectives. Similarly, any arrangements for training transfer, such as trainee logbooks and portfolios of M&E work, can also provide evidence that can be used for training evaluation.

The extent to which training evaluation and transfer should *and* can be planned will (again) vary according to context. For instance, if training is to certify achievement (versus certification of participation), there will be a much stronger need for learning assessment to score or grade individual performance. Another consideration is access to trainees. For example, with M&E training for an organization, training follow-up is typically a priority for its transfer into the workplace and contribution to longer-term M&E and strategic objectives for the organization. On the other hand, for M&E training of individuals unassociated with the same organization, access to trainees may be limited and the follow-up necessary to evaluate longer-term impact and support learning transfer may not be practical in time and cost.

There is a wealth of research on training transfer (e.g., see Baldwin & Ford, 1988; Burke & Hutchins, 2007) and for good reason: We want training to be used afterward and to make a difference. The "set-up" for training transfer begins with the training analysis, providing an understanding of how training is to be used, and the factors that can support or hinder its transfer. There are often existing practices or opportunities to establish new ones that can be used to support the transfer of M&E learning from training. In Chapter 2, we discussed the varied training landscape and the range of resources and approaches that can be used for *or* to complement training. In **Box 8.5** we look at other considerations for sustaining learning and practice from training.

However, the opportunity to pursue such activities and ultimately use newly acquired M&E knowledge and skills will largely depend on the demand for M&E practice. For instance, in an organizational setting, training transfer can be greatly influenced by such factors as leadership, institutional policies, and procedures that support human, financial,

BOX 8.5
Making Learning Last

To a large degree, planning to support training transfer is where M&E training overlaps with other processes identified for capacity building. For example, alternative learning interventions that can complement a training workshop include online e-learning modules or webinars, professional development meetings with supervisors, and on-the-job mentoring or coaching. Another avenue for sustaining learning is to encourage post-training interaction between trainees as well as with trainers. Continued interaction can be fostered through the use of social media, such as blogs, discussion boards, chat rooms, wikis, and similar technologies to share M&E tips and tools, to mutually review work and address challenges, and to provide other means of support for learning and practice. Whatever approach may be adopted to support learning transfer, it is important to remember it will not be possible to prescribe exactly how transfer will unfold. After training, when learners are no longer participating in the planned curriculum, emergent opportunities may arise that can foster continued learning, especially when learners interact. Even more so than the training itself, it should be fluid and responsive to emergent opportunities.

and other resources necessary to use and sustain M&E. As discussed in Chapter 3, a systematic understanding of such contextual factors helps better plan for M&E training transfer as part of a coherent strategy for M&E capacity building. Of particular importance is stakeholder involvement. When both trainees and other stakeholders supporting M&E training consider the use of M&E training and how to realistically integrate it into post-training practice, the more likely training transfer will occur.

There are a wide range of approaches and activities to support training transfer and evaluation. In Chapter 11 we take a closer look at training evaluation, and in Part 3 of this book we summarize examples of specific activities that can be used to support training follow-up.

8.6 CHAPTER SUMMARY

Training design is a considerable investment in time, but it provides the conceptual and practical foundation to achieve desired training results. In this chapter we highlight the main elements of the design process, and key summary points include

- While terminology may vary and needs change, identifying immediate and longer-term objectives for training helps ensure that training is designed with specific results to inform training design, evaluation, and follow-up. As discussed in Chapter 7, backward planning is a useful starting point for identifying training objectives.

- Formulating learning objectives for the training is a key aspect of training design, which should be based on observable changes in performance and practice behaviors. This informs the design of not only the training curriculum but also learning assessment.

- Therefore, concerted consideration should be given to the assessment methods concerning KSAs expected to arise from the training early in the planning process during training design.

- Plan the scope and sequence of instructional content to ensure relevance and progression of learning topics that supports learning objectives and intended KSAs.

- The training curriculum provides a detailed road map for M&E training, reflecting the underlying methodology guiding how instruction, activities, materials, and secondary media are to be used.

- The actual content of the curriculum will vary according to training needs, but two overarching models we discuss for considering the design of the curriculum include Gagné's Nine Events of Instruction and three stages of facilitation based on increasing levels of trainee participation proposed by Heron (1999).

- As we will revisit in Chapter 10 on training implementation, careful attention should be given to activity selection for the training curriculum, which should not only be appropriate for the learners and their profiles (e.g., level of understanding) but also take into consideration time management so that learning objectives can be realistically achieved.

- Training design is not limited to the curriculum to implement during training delivery but also includes careful attention to the training evaluation and follow-up (discussed further in Chapter 11 and Part 2 of this book). Post-training assessment and learning are related in that they can be mutually supportive when planned accordingly.

8.7 APPENDICES

Appendix 8.1 Example Topics for M&E Training Curriculums

Core course topics for the International Program for Development Evaluation Training (IPDET, 2015b) Introduction to Development Evaluation 1. Understanding the issues driving development evaluation	2. Building a results-based monitoring and evaluation system 3. Understanding the evaluation context and the program theory of change 4. Considering the evaluation approach	5. Developing evaluation questions and starting the design matrix 6. Selecting designs for cause-and-effect, normative, and descriptive evaluation questions

7. Selecting and constructing data collection instruments
8. Deciding on the sampling strategy
9. Planning data analysis and completing the design matrix
10. Evaluating complex interventions
11. Managing an evaluation
12. Presenting results
13. Looking to the future of development evaluation

Topics for Centers for Disease Control and Prevention (CDC) evaluation framework (Davis, 2006)

1. **Introduction**
   - Purpose of evaluation
   - Evaluation principles and standards
2. **Engaging stakeholders**
   - Evaluability assessment
   - Program analysis
   - Reaching consensus on evaluation purpose
3. **Defining the program**
   - Logic models
4. **Focusing the evaluation design**
   - Designing research/ evaluation questions
   - Needs assessment
   - Formative evaluation process and performance evaluation
   - Impact evaluation
5. **Gathering credible evidence**
   - Quantitative and qualitative mixed methods
   - Pilot testing/validating methods evaluation plan Implementation
   - Data collection, analysis, and storage

- Institutional review board issues
6. **Justifying conclusions**
   - Organizing evaluation data
7. **Ensuring use**
   - Reporting results

Topics for "Easy Evaluation" (Adams & Dickinson, 2010)

1. **Program planning (day one)**
   - Needs assessment
   - Stakeholder review
   - Identification of relevant evidence
   - Program logic
   - Introduction to theory-driven evaluation
   - Uses of program logic
2. **Evaluation approaches and forms of evaluation**
   - Evaluation theory tree
   - Selected evaluation approaches
   - Forms of evaluation (formative, process, and outcome)
3. **Ethics and evaluation practice (day two)**
4. **Evaluation priorities and questions**
5. **Evaluation criteria and standards**
   - Developing outcome criteria and standards (success in achieving outcomes)
   - Developing process criteria and standards (quality of activity/intervention)
6. **Data collection and analysis (day three)**
7. **Evaluative conclusions**
8. **Reporting and dissemination**

Topics for M&E blended learning training (INTRAC, 2014a)

1. Definitions used in M&E
2. Purpose of doing M&E
3. How it fits into the project cycle
4. Hierarchy of objectives (including log framing)
5. Developing Indicators
6. Approaches and methods to M&E
7. How to select and use various methods and tools for data collection
8. Basic skills required for effective M&E
9. Drawing up a terms of reference
10. Effective and purposeful reporting
11. Ensuring M&E leads to organizational learning

Topics for advanced M&E training (INTRAC, 2014b)

1. Clarifying different use of M&E terms
2. Issues to consider when designing an evaluation process
3. A structure for identifying issues to be addressed in M&E
4. The components of a good project or program M&E
5. Indicators and how to identify them
6. Tools to understand the logic of the interventions
7. Case studies that illustrate some of the challenges in conducting evaluations and introducing M&E systems
8. Quantitative and qualitative data collection methods/tools
9. Some newer tools to collect outcomes and impact data

(Continued)

(Continued)

10. Examination of recent methodologies, e.g., contribution analysis, outcome mapping, and most significant change

11. Some challenges with logframes (particularly recent donor requirements) and how to overcome them

12. Principles and strategies to support staff teams and partners to improve the evaluation of their projects/program

13. Strategies and tools to help participants to act as "agents of change" within their own organizations

14. Reflection time on course input and application to real life case study and think through what needs to happen on return to implement the learning from the workshop

Topics for Project Design (IFRC, 2015b)

1. **Results-Based Management (RBM)**

   - Project cycles—initial assessment, planning, Implementation & monitoring, evaluation

2. **Initial Assessment**

   - Vulnerability & capacity assessment
   - Field assessment & coordination team (FACT)/ emergency assessment
   - Participatory rapid assessment
   - Stakeholder analysis—who is involved
   - Strengths, weakness, opportunities, threats (SWOT) analysis
   - Problem analysis

3. **Planning**

   - Logical framework
   - Objective hierarchy
   - Indicators
   - Means of verification
   - Assumptions
   - Logframe limitations

Topics for M&E Planning (IFRC, 2015b)

1. **Basic M&E Concepts**

   - Difference between M and E
   - Common types of types of monitoring
   - Common types of evaluation
   - Baseline—endline study or surveys
   - ME standards and ethics
   - Minimize bias and error
   - Data management and quality control

2. **Determine the Purpose and Scope of the M&E system**

   - Review the project/ program's operational design (logframe)
   - Identify key stakeholder informational needs and expectations
   - Identify any M&E requirements
   - Scope major M&E events and functions

3. **Plan for Data Collection & Management**

   - Develop an M&E plan table
   - Assess availability of secondary data
   - Determine the balance of quantitative and qualitative data

   - Triangulate data collection sources and methods
   - Determine sampling requirements
   - Prepare specific data collection methods/tools
   - Establish stakeholder complaints and feedback mechanism
   - Establish project/program staff/volunteer review mechanisms
   - Plan for data management
   - Use an indicator tracking table (ITT)
   - Use a risk log (table)
   - Plan for cost contingency

4. **Plan for Data Analysis**

   A. Develop a data analysis plan, identifying the

      - Purpose of analysis
      - Frequency of analysis
      - Responsibility for analysis
      - Process for analysis

   B. Follow the key data analysis stages

      - Data preparation
      - Data analysis
      - Data presentation
      - Data verification
      - Recommendations and actions

5. **Plan for Information Reporting and Utilization**

   A. Anticipate and plan for information needs

      - Reporting needs
      - Reporting frequency
      - Reporting formats
      - Reporting responsibilities

B. Plan for information utilization

- Information dissemination
- Decision-making and planning

6. **Plan for M&E Human Resources and Capacity Building**

- Assess the projects/program's capacity for M&E
- Determine the extent of local participation
- Determine the extent of outside expertise
- Define the roles and responsibilities for M&E
- Plan to manage project/program team M&E activities
- Identify M&E capacity building requirements and opportunities

7. **Prepare the M&E Budget**

- Itemize M&E budget needs
- Determine which M&E costs are included in the overall project/program budget

- Review any donor budget requirement

Topics for Managing an Evaluation (IFRC, 2015b)

1. Evaluation types
2. Evaluation criteria, standards, and ethics
3. Stakeholder assessment and consultation
4. Identify management for the evaluation
5. Plan for potential challenges or constraints
6. Prepare and approve evaluation TOR
7. Disseminate TOR
8. Draft evaluation management plan, including budget, and timetable
9. Recruit the evaluation consultant
10. Identify any internal evaluation team members
11. Prepare project documentation and secondary data for consultant/s

12. Capture staff impressions prior to project end (when applicable)
13. Review evaluator inception report
14. Ensure compliance with IFRC Evaluation Policy
15. Plan for data collection logistics
16. In-person briefing at field office with evaluators
17. Gatekeeper visits—inform, permission, arrange
18. Data collection—individual and group interviews
19. Initial evaluation findings workshop/s
20. Prepare initial draft report
21. Stakeholder review of draft report
22. Final evaluation report approved
23. Prepare management response to recommendations
24. Trouble shooting

8.8 RECOMMENDED RESOURCES

In addition to those resources recommended in Chapter 6 on instructional systems design, three additional books we recommend are *ISD from the Ground Up: A No-nonsense Approach to Instruction Design* (Hodell, 2011), *Mastering the Instructional Design Process* (Rothwell & Kazanas, 2008), and *Designing Powerful Training: The Sequential-Iterative Model* (Milano & Ullius, 1998). We also recommend two useful books on educational program design: *Planning Programs for Adult Learners: A Practical Guide for Educators* (Caffarella, 2002) and *Mistakes Made and Lessons Learned:*

Overcoming Obstacles to Successful Program Planning (Sork, 1991). For a more concise overview, the website of Instructional Design Central (2015) provides a summary of eight popular models of instructional design.

For a more comprehensive look at Gagné's nine events of instruction, we recommend the book *Principles of Instructional Design* (Gagné, Wagner, Golas, & Keller, 2004). On the topic of backward design, we again refer readers to informative book by Wiggins and McTighe (2005). Although focused on primary and secondary education, readers can freely download the publication from the Alliance for Education and Community Development (AECD, 2010), *Introduction—The Logic of Backward Design*, which provides a concise look at backward design with example templates.

In addition to the guide by IntraHealth International (recommended also for training analysis), we also recommend the freely available WHO (2005) publication, *Effective Teaching: A Guide for Educating Healthcare Providers*, both that have practical discussion, tools, and templates for training design. The Free Management Library (2015) provides useful interactive webpages by Cater McNamara: *Complete Guidelines to Design Your Training Plan*, and *Designing Training Plans and Learning Objectives*. There are also a variety of free resources on writing learning objectives based on the three learning domains identified in Bloom's Taxonomy (discussed in Chapter 4); for example, the user-friendly guide from the International Training & Education Center for Health (2010), *Writing Good Learning Objectives*.

In the field of evaluation, there is increasing attention in the scholarly literature on the design and content of evaluation education and training. For example, the following articles from the *American Journal of Evaluation* reflect the growing research and interest in this area: Trevisan (2004) provides a valuable review of the literature for practical training in evaluation; Trevisan (2002) focuses on the use of long-term evaluation projects in training; Davis (2006) looks at methods for teaching public health evaluation; Lee et at. (2007) discusses problem-based learning to training evaluators; Oliver et al. (2008) presents a pedagogical framework to teach graduate level program evaluation; Adams and Dickinson (2010) discuss a workshop model to train community and public health workers in evaluation; Christie (2012) looks at the importance of incorporating interpersonal skills in evaluation education; and Thomas and Madison (2010) provide a compelling argument to the inclusion of social justice in evaluation education.

CHAPTER 9

Training Development and Preparation

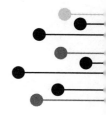

Once the training has been designed, the next step in the ADDIE sequence is to develop and test the training program and prepare it for implementation. The time, responsibilities, and what exactly needs to be developed for an M&E training event will vary according to its particular design and what existing material can be adopted or modified for training needs. Typically, materials to develop or obtain include instructional materials and guidelines for the trainer to manage, deliver, and evaluate the M&E training as well as materials the trainees will use to prepare for, during, and after the training. These resources then need to be carefully reviewed and the training piloted to ensure that they are appropriate for the training audience and learning objectives.

In addition to developing the training, there are practical logistics that need to be arranged for training implementation. To a large degree, the success of training will depend on how such details are managed. Otherwise, it can be quite disorientating for both the trainer/s and the trainees when logistics arrangements are not well planned and organized. For instance, a noisy location or insufficient space or materials for training activities can backfire and undermine a M&E workshop. Therefore, you should not underestimate the importance of preparing for training logistics. As in our prior chapter on training design, our discussion in this chapter will also be geared toward live, face-to-face training, especially the discussion of training preparation, which is based on delivering an M&E workshop.

Learning Objectives

By the end of this chapter readers will be able to . . .

✓ List examples of and related considerations for the development of M&E training materials and resources

✓ Discuss key considerations to review and pilot M&E training

✓ List key considerations for the preparation of an M&E training workshop

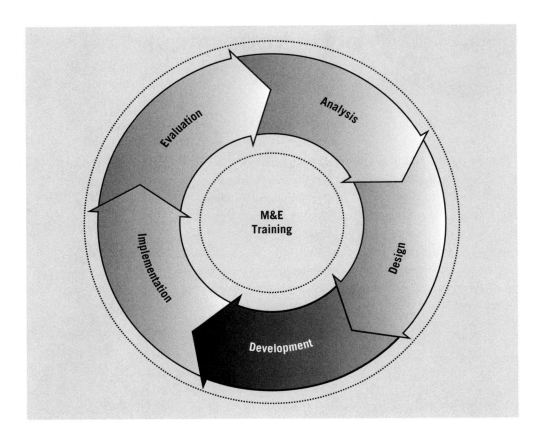

9.1 Develop Training Materials and Resources

There exists a wide assortment of training materials that may need to be developed, adopted, or adapted for M&E training—see **Table 9.1**. Consideration should be given not only to the materials required for each activity in the training curriculum but also to pre- and post-training materials for the trainees as well as those resources used by the trainer to prepare for, manage, and deliver training. Below we summarize some overall considerations to help guide the use of time and resources when developing M&E training materials:

- **Be realistic in the time for and cost of material and resource development**. Development and duplication of materials can be expensive and time consuming. Even just a few hours of actual training can equate to many hours in material preparation and development.

- **Consider adopting or adapting existing materials and resources appropriate for M&E training needs.** There may

BOX 9.1
Adopting or Adapting Materials for M&E Training?

As we noted in Chapter 2, technological breakthroughs have been tremendous in the training industry, and there are now an assortment of training resources that can be readily accessed over the Internet. From M&E webinars and self-tutorials to online learning platforms and communities of practice, there are a variety of options that can be readily incorporated into a blended approach to training. However, do not fall into the trap of adopting just because it is available—ensure that training resources are relevant for learning objectives or can be modified according to training needs (e.g., learner profiles). Below we have highlighted just a few examples of free M&E resources available online to convey the range of options that can be used adopted or adapted for M&E training:

- The AEA (2013) *Guiding Principles Training Package* includes a facilitator's guide, PowerPoint slides, and three different case studies (with worksheets) that can be adapted for a session on good evaluation practice.

- *Evaluation Flash Cards,* developed by Michael Quinn Patton, is a set of one-page factsheets on a variety of evaluation topics that can be used to build or complement M&E lessons (Otto Bremer Foundation, 2014).

- The *Equal Access Participatory Monitoring and Evaluation* toolkit consists of six modules that can be used to structure an M&E training or specific sessions (Lennie, Tacchi, Koirala, Wilmore, & Skuse, 2011).

- A variety of M&E-related webinars are available online to support learning prior to, during, or after training: for example, AEA (2014a, 2014b), MEASURE Evaluation (2015), My M&E (2014), CLEAR (2014), Oregon State University (2015).

- Browse the variety of open educational resources (OER) related to M&E that can be found on websites, such as OER Commons (2015), OpenCourseWare (OCW, 2014), and Massive Open Online Courses (MOOC List, 2015). An appropriate course can be used as a self-tutorial for pre- or post-training learning activities, such as an introductory statistics course prior to training on survey design.

be less costly solutions that can be obtained commercially or for free that meet or can be modified to meet M&E training needs, see **Box 9.1**.

- **Limit in-training materials to only what is necessary and sufficient for training purposes**. This can help reduce development time and costs as well as material overload (clutter) for the trainees.

- **Supplementary training resources can be provided electronically.** For example documents, presentation slides, videos, spreadsheets, and other training materials can be provided on a flash drive, CD, DVD, through email attachments, website, or an online hosting service or cloud (e.g., Dropbox).

- **Keep training materials and other resources organized and user friendly**. You do not want to overwhelm or confuse trainees with too much resource clutter. Whether materials are provided in a folder, binder, workbook, flash drive, or online, present them in an organized manner to help users navigate through and relate them to M&E learning topics and the overall vision for training (reinforcing learning principles for a structure approach and learner's "need to know" what is planned for training).

- **Develop training materials that can be easily revised**. Training content and delivery often have to be changed during the training itself to accommodate learners or for future training. Therefore, consider how easy and inexpensive it will be to add, delete, and rearrange training material and content.

Information about existing and required training materials can be initially identified during the training analysis (Chapter 7), and specific material requirements for each activity can be noted during the activity planning during curriculum design (Table 8.7 in Chapter 8). In addition to the training content itself, the training length, budget, and prior experience and knowledge of trainees will also steer the development of training materials.

It is also important to consider the number of trainers and their level of familiarity and experience with the training content, activities, and management. For example, if the training program is to be repeated over time, in different locations by different trainers, detailed trainer guidelines can help ensure standard and consistent delivery of M&E content. Sometimes different people design the training program (e.g., subject matter experts) and a more comprehensive trainer's guide or individual lesson plans is needed, providing detailed facilitation tips for those delivering the training. In other instances, less comprehensive trainer notes may be sufficient for trainers already familiar and comfortable with the training program, such as a printout of a detailed agenda with handwritten or slide notes.

TABLE 9.1   Example Materials and Resources for M&E Training

Training strategy (plan)	This provides overall guidance for the management of the training. Depending on the length and frequency of training, the plan can be a detailed, stand-alone document, as the example in **Table 9.2** illustrates, or consist of separate management resources, such as the training syllabus, schedule, curriculum, lesson plans, budget, checklists, and so forth. Note that if a training analysis report has been prepared, this can feed into a training strategy.
Training budget	This is an itemized list of anticipated human resource and capital expenses for all stages of training—design, development, implementation, evaluation, and follow-up. Expenses will depend on the scale and scope of the training. HR expenses can include trainers, subject matter experts, instructional designers, evaluators, and administrative staff. Capital expenses can include training materials, equipment and supplies, technology (hardware and software), facility costs, and any travel, lodging, and accommodation. For larger training programs over a longer period of time, it is also important to plan for contingency costs to cover unexpected expenses that may arise during training (i.e., because of inflation, equipment theft, or the hire of additional personnel). In addition to itemizing expenses in a spreadsheet, a narrative justifying each line item can help guard against arbitrary budget cuts.[*]
Training syllabus (description)	The training syllabus provides a summary overview of all the basic information of a training. This assists not only with the planning and management of the training but also to communicate/advertise to trainees and other stakeholders, frame expectations, and help participants prepare for training. Table 8.2 provides an example of contents for a training syllabus.
Training curriculum	The training curriculum is a detailed training agenda or outline for trainers, providing a session-by-session summary of objectives, topics, activities/methods, and materials (e.g., see Table 8.7 in our prior chapter on training design).
Training schedule/ agenda	A training schedule can be used to communicate the timing for multiple training events over a longer period (e.g., weeks or months), whereas "agenda" is used for a particular training event (e.g., a three-hour or three-day workshop), providing a session-by-session summary of the planned time, topics, and breaks. Both can include additional information, such as the location, trainers, learning objectives, training materials, and any required reading and assignments.
Trainee (participant) list	In addition to names and contact information, it may be useful to list other relevant information available about the trainees, such as their gender, age, nationality, native language, job title, experience in M&E, expectations, and so forth. Supplementary information can be obtained to note with the roster from a learner assessment (Chapter 7) or from a Personal Development Plan, if used (see below). Remember that trainees often use a participant list themselves to network, share resources, and follow-up training (potentially supporting training transfer).

(Continued)

TABLE 9.1 (Continued)

Trainer's (facilitator's) guide	This is a comprehensive resource document to support and guide the trainer/s to prepare for, deliver, and follow-up the overall training. Depending on the training needs, it can include the following: training objectives, detailed curriculum, lessons plans and facilitation tips; further background information on the subject, learners, and training context; supplemental information such as training logistics checklist; frequently asked questions; additional reading/resource list for the trainer; and so forth.
Session/lesson plan	The session/lesson plan is a detailed description and sometimes script of how the trainer should prepare for and conduct all training activities for each session on the training curriculum. **Table 9.2** below provides an example of contents for a lesson plan, and we provide an example in Part 3 of this book (p. 401).
Trainer/facilitator notes	These notes proved abbreviated guidance for trainers familiar and experienced with training program; for example, a printout of the agenda, handwritten or slide notes, and cue/prompt cards. **Table 9.3** illustrates an example of a more formal format for facilitator notes. Facilitator notes should help the trainer facilitate, and therefore the specific format and content should be tailored to each trainer. ***Often, it is simply taking the time to prepare the notes beforehand that will help facilitators organize, familiarize themselves, and prepare for training.***
Pre-workshop questionnaire— personal learning plan	While trainee information may have already been gathered during the training analysis, a pre-training questionnaire or personal learning plan can provide additional information about individual trainees. Furthermore, they can help trainees prepare and reflect on why they are taking the training and how they can best use it afterward, supporting training transfer. Information to seek can include the person's name/position, contact information, length in position, reasons and expectations for attending, their perceived level of M&E experience, how they plan to use the training afterward, any disabilities or any dietary limitations, and any questions or concerns they may have. As we will discuss in Chapter 11, information about trainee expectations, personal learning objectives, and intended use of training can also be useful for training evaluation.
Instructional materials	Also called instructional aids, we use it here to refer to the audiovisual material the trainer needs to prepare to present lessons and facilitate other training activities.** Clearly, it is helpful when instructional presentations are attractive, engaging, and well organized to spark trainee interest and clarify M&E topics. Also, a variety of instructional aids helps to enliven instructional presentations and appeal to different learning styles. Examples include slide presentations, poster diagrams, graphs, audiovisual recordings, and online resources such as webpages or webinars. Other instructional aids include any materials needed for facilitating activities, such as game pieces. We discuss these in more detail as they related to training facilitation in Chapter 10.
Learner materials	This is the collection of training material provided to and used by trainees. Learner aids are not limited to materials used during training but also include those provided prior to training to help prepare trainees, and afterward for training follow-up. Examples of learner aids include the following:

	• **Handouts**—for example, the training schedule and/or agenda, a participant roster, presentation slide printouts, lesson notes, an individual or professional learning plan, assignments, case studies, activity instructions, templates (e.g., logframe or M&E plan, terms of reference and evaluation report formats), checklists, and frequently asked questions. • **Trainee/participant information packet**—when there are many handouts, it is helpful to organize them in a binder, folder/s (paper or electronic), or a spiral bound manual or workbook for training, with a table of contents aligned with the agenda. • **Supplementary M&E resources and reference materials**—for example, M&E guidelines, standards, principles, policies, glossaries, and a resource list of additional sources of M&E resources.
Assessment and evaluation tools	Depending on training needs, there is a range of assessment and evaluation resources to develop or adapt for training—for example, pre-/post-tests, quizzes, evaluation and satisfaction forms, daily feedback forms, session feedback forms, skill observation checklists, and so forth. We will discuss training evaluation and related resources in more detail in Chapter 11, with example tools/formats in the appendices.
Miscellaneous	Inevitably, there are additional specific materials or items to prepare for training, depending on training needs. It is important not to underestimate the time additional items may take to prepare. For example, it may be appropriate to develop a certificate of participation or completion of training, which will usually need to be signed beforehand by relevant people.

* Microsoft (2014) offers generic guidance and a spreadsheet for planning the training budget that can be tailored according to training context—see Recommended Resources at the end of this chapter.

** Instructional (or teaching) aids can be defined broadly to include anything used in training delivery. However, there is a difference between instructional aids (materials) used by trainers versus learner aids (materials) used for trainees to interact with and share learning content. Instructional aids include instructional media (technology) used to communicate instructional messages to learners, such as printed material, flipcharts, computer speakers, and projectors. Here, we refer to the content and material that need to be prepared to be transmitted by the instructional media; for example, diagrams, PowerPoint presentations, or specific audio or video recordings.

TABLE 9.2 Three Example Outlines For . . .

Training Strategy (Plan)	Training Syllabus	Session/Lesson Plan[1]
1. Training description 2. Training objectives 3. Background information: description of need, casual analysis, and so forth.	1. Training title and description 2. Training objectives 3. Training prerequisites and attendance criteria	1. Session title 2. Learning objectives 3. Time—duration 4. Facilitation guidance—for example,

(Continued)

TABLE 9.2   (Continued)

Training Strategy (Plan)	Training Syllabus	Session/Lesson Plan[1]
4. Training requirements (if applicable)	4. Training logistics: location, length, and dates (schedule/agenda)	a. Introduction
5. Management team—roles and responsibilities	5. Training methods/activities	b. Presentation
6. Target audience—number, characteristics, selection criteria	6. Training assignments and follow-up	c. Practice
		d. Debrief/reflection
		e. Review
7. Training location—instructional setting	7. Training assessment and evaluation (clarifying for trainees how this will be used)	5. Session assignments (pre- or post-session)
8. Training schedule/agenda	8. Training costs or required materials (e.g., printed books or guidelines, computer, software)	6. Session assessments and evaluation (as applicable)
9. Training curriculum—outline		7. Materials for session activities
10. Training/learning methods and activities		8. Additional reference materials
11. Training materials and delivery media	9. Contact, registration, and/or application information (as applicable)	9. Additional notes/comments
12. Training assessment and evaluation		
13. Training budget/costs		
14. Training logistics and preparation		
15. Training follow-up		
16. Potential constraints and limitations		

1. Part 3 (p. 401) provides an example of a complete lesson plan.

TABLE 9.3   Example Facilitator's Notes or Training Outline for "Planning an Evaluation"

Time	Activity	Notes
8:30–9:30	• Introduction	• Welcome (training importance); introductions; trainee expectations; learning objectives (LO); training agenda and materials; training ground rules and logistics; pre-test.

Time	Activity	Notes
9:30–10:30	• Presentation—stakeholder analysis • Activity—stakeholder role-play • Debrief	• Use fruit energizer to form groups. • Have participants score role-plays and award prizes. • Debrief with plenary flipchart notes elicited from participants.
10:30–11:00	• Break	• Float around and check in with participant understanding.
11:00–12:30	• Presentation—external versus internal evaluation • Activity—debate on pros and cons • Debrief	• Hand out case study to each small group, with ample time for them to review. • Elect time keep with cue cards for each debater to present and respond.
12:30–1:30	• Lunch	• Jane L. and David F. have vegetarian meals.
11:00–12:30	• And so forth	

Clearly, there are a range of materials that can be developed for M&E training, and our examples are just that—*examples*. As already stressed, the number, type, and format of training materials will need to be tailored according to those who will use them, and other factors in the training context.

9.2 Review and Pilot the Training

Before investing the time and resources into developing training, it is recommended to validate that the training design and draft materials achieve learning objectives. Reviewing and piloting M&E training is actually an early form of formative evaluation for training, assessing its potential effectiveness prior to official delivery. It takes additional effort up front, but it can save much time, money, and headache in the long run, helping to identify otherwise costly problems associated with unmet training objectives, unfulfilled expectations, and damaged credibility.

The degree to which training can be tested will vary based on the available time and resources. The degree to which it is necessary will vary depending on whether training is newly designed or has already been used and vetted. When piloting, another consideration is whether it is necessary for trainers new to the curriculum to practice facilitation beforehand. At a minimum, the draft training curriculum and materials should be thoroughly examined by external reviewers. This can include subject matter (M&E) experts, instructional designers, and people from or familiar with the training audience and context in which M&E is to be practiced. Reviews can be conducted individually with written feedback and/or through group discussion.

Piloting M&E training can involve all or part of the training, and it can be conducted after the training has been designed or as an ongoing process during design, such as rapid prototyping—see **Box 9.2**. Despite the potential advantages of trying out the training prior to actual implementation—early deliveries of training serve to determine revisions and improvement to the design (Sanders, 1989)—there is often reluctance, because of the time and resources required. However, when a considerable investment is being made for a training program that will have a wide outreach or be sustained over a long period of time, a pilot can be well worth the investment.

Running a pilot of the entire M&E training involves not only the planned activities in the curriculum but also assessment and evaluation instruments and any pre- and post-training activities/materials. This can provide practical observation of and feedback on the appropriateness of the training content and delivery for the training audience. When a full pilot is not practical, select and test specific sessions and activities, preferably those that are being tried for the first time or the more complicated activities that you suspect may need to be adjusted.

Key questions to consider include

- Is the training understood and does it support the learning objectives?
- How complete and effective is the learning progression?
- How engaging and effective are specific learning activities?
- How realistic is the time management?
- Are there any unanticipated problems or issues with the training?

Pilots work best if they are in the actual setting the training will occur and the sample population is as representative as possible of the learners for whom the training was designed. Also, consider having an external observer present, especially someone experienced in M&E training; it can be difficult to observe the training when delivering it yourself, and an external reviewer can provide valuable feedback.

Whether early, formative feedback on the training is from trainees during a pilot or from reviewers, consider using questionnaires, forms, and/or checklists to solicit, organize, and record feedback (discussed further in Chapter 11 on training evaluation).

BOX 9.2
Rapid Prototyping

Rather than a single event, such as a pilot after training is designed, rapid prototyping involves learners and those involved in training design (instructional designers and/or subject matter experts, SMEs) interacting with training prototypes in a continuous review/revision cycle, catching problems while they are still easy to address. For example, having learners trial an online activity for e-learning, such as responding to question prompts, to see if the interface is intuitive and user-friendly. The use of rapid prototyping for training is not new (e.g., Tripp & Bichelmeyer, 1990), but it is receiving increasing attention for e-learning, such as computer-based training (e.g., Botturi, Cantoni, Lepori, & Tardini, 2007). However, the concept is also useful for face-to-face training and is combined with an ADDIE approach, illustrating an iterative approach that uses formative evaluation and feedback early in the design and development stages of training (e.g., Piskurich, 2000). For instance, if a case study or learner guide is developed for a training workshop, it can be shared with and reviewed by representative learners prior to training but separate from a full-training pilot, providing a valuable opportunity for feedback to improve the resource early on.

9.3 Preparing for an M&E Training Workshop

After developing and piloting the training, there is an assortment of practical matters that need to be ready for training delivery. These logistics will depend on the particular type of training and setting. We will consider them in the context of preparing for a face-to-face M&E workshop, outlining ten overall tasks for training preparation:

1. Develop a checklist or action plan

2. Confirm stakeholder commitment and approval

3. Schedule the training

4. Select the trainees (when applicable)

5. Select the training facility

6. Communicate with trainees

7. Select and prepare trainers (and others involved in training delivery)

8. Prepare training materials and media

9. Prepare the training facility

10. Confirm additional logistics

The extent to which the trainer/s will need to oversee everything that needs to be done before a workshop will vary, and usually responsibilities are shared with others. For example, others involved in the training preparation can include administrative staff with a sponsoring organization or personnel working with the facility hosting the workshop. Regardless, it will be important to ensure that the tasks identified for training preparation are completed and ready for the training start. Therefore, they should be well planned and confirmed before the training start, with enough time to troubleshoot any related problems.

1. Develop a checklist or action plan

There is a lot to manage for any given training event, whether it is only a half-day workshop or a multiday, integrated, or residential workshop. It can be stressful, especially for new trainers, and it is easy to forget to follow-up on everything that needs to be done. Therefore, the first step is to make a list of tasks that need to be completed before the training start. This can be in the form of a checklist or a more detailed action plan identifying tasks, responsibilities, timeline, and other relevant information according to training needs, for example, budget. In **Table 9.4**, we provide a generic example of a checklist for an M&E training workshop. If a training strategy or facilitator's guide has been developed (discussed above), pre-training logistics may be included in these resources.

However it is formatted, there should be enough detail in the logistics checklist or plan to guide the timely management of training logistics. If responsibilities are shared, you may want to use a team of appropriate people to delegate tasks. It will be essential that everyone involved in managing the workshop logistics understand their responsibilities and timeline and immediately inform others if any problems arise. Throughout the process, you should monitor and check in with others to ensure tasks will be completed on time.

2. Confirm stakeholder commitment and approval

As with conducting an evaluation, all people affected by the training workshop should be informed well in advance, and any required approval or permission obtained. Typically, this begins prior to training design, during stakeholder consultation for training analysis. However, at this this stage of the planning process, the specifics for the training will be more concrete and should be confirmed with key stakeholders. Depending on the training context, this can include managers and decision-makers in an organization, community members, local leaders, and local authorities. If possible, it is best to meet

TABLE 9.4   Training Preparation Checklist

Develop a checklist or action plan—this should be tailored according to training context/needs.

Confirm stakeholder commitment and approval

- ☐ Workshop purpose and importance
- ☐ People identified for training
- ☐ Training location, time, duration
- ☐ Training budget
- ☐ Any key resource people to support the workshop

Schedule the training

- ☐ Training urgency—when it needs to be completed
- ☐ Availability of trainees and trainers
- ☐ Availability of facilities and equipment
- ☐ Avoid scheduling conflicts with other events

Select and prepare trainers (and others involved in training delivery)

- ☐ Recruit qualified trainers, translators, or other people that may be needed for training delivery
- ☐ Orientate or provide a training of trainers (ToT) to prepare trainers

Select the trainees (when applicable)

- ☐ Prerequisite M&E knowledge
- ☐ Suitable number for workshop facilitation
- ☐ Suitable composition for workshop objectives

Select the training facility

- ☐ Location—convenience
- ☐ Sufficient floor and wall space for people and activities
- ☐ Privacy/quiet—minimal distractions
- ☐ Accessibility for physically disabled people
- ☐ Safety and security—neighborhood and facility

- ☐ Acoustics, lighting, and visibility
- ☐ Climate control—ventilation
- ☐ Electrical outlets and Internet connectivity

Communicate with trainees

- ☐ Initial training announcement or invitations
  - Acknowledgment of any sponsor/s
  - Training purpose and objectives
  - Training schedule or agenda, indicating specific time and location/s
  - Perquisite knowledge or selection criteria
  - Pre-training work or assignments, if any
  - Trainee costs/fees and required materials, if any
  - Application/registration information or forms
- ☐ Contact information—trainers, organizers, and so forth
- ☐ Pre-training packet for confirmed trainees
  - Trainee participant contact list
  - Training agenda and/or syllabus
  - Pre-training material and assignments, if any
  - Pre-training questionnaires, forms, or tests, if any
  - Logistical information—for example, detailed directions, map, and transportation and accommodation information

Prepare training materials and media materials

- ☐ Training handouts, information packet, or workbook
- ☐ Updated training agenda and participant list
- ☐ M&E resources and reference materials
- ☐ Activity pieces and props (including sweets/chocolates for game prizes)
- ☐ Audio-visual materials
- ☐ Tests and quizzes
- ☐ Feedback and evaluation forms

(Continued)

(Continued)

- □ Name tags/plates, training certificates, and so forth
- □ Any flash-drives, DVDs, and CDs to be distributed

Supplies

- □ Pens, pencils, note paper, or writing tablets
- □ White boards, colored markers, and erasers
- □ Flipcharts and colored markers
- □ Extendable or laser pointer
- □ Tape and/or blue-tack for hanging up flipcharts and other training aids
- □ Post-it notes, cards, activities/game pieces, and so forth
- □ Stapler, paper clips, thumbtacks, extra folders, or binders
- □ First aid kit

Electrical equipment

- □ Computers and software
- □ Audio-visual equipment: projector, screen (if not wall space), TV, VCR, DVD
- □ Printers, copy machines, telephones
- □ Electrical accessories: remote control, laser pointer, detachable speakers, and so forth
- □ Extension cords, power cords, adaptors, and so forth
- □ Backup equipment and spare parts: extra projector, bulbs, batteries, and so forth

Survival kit—consider preparing a "toolbox" or duffel bag with extra supply of essential items

Prepare the training facility

- □ Arrange seating with comfortable chairs (adjustable for longer training)—seats should be accessible, not cramped, so people can see and hear each other.
- □ Arrange the room so people can interact for activities.
- □ When possible, locate the entrance/exit in the rear of the room.
- □ Ensure adequate tabletop space for materials and activities.
- □ Clear wall space for displaying completed flip chart pages.
- □ Arrange table/s for training materials, podium, projector, refreshments, and so forth.
- □ Locate teaching aids so they are assessable, visible, and audible, for example, flipcharts, whiteboards, projectors, and screens.
- □ Test any audio-visual equipment and Internet.
- □ Test the lights and ventilation for the room.
- □ Place trainee materials and name tags/plates on tables.

Confirm additional logistics, for example,

- □ Transportation and accommodation
- □ Refreshments and meals—coffee, tea, juice, water, soda, fruit, cookies, cups, plates, napkins, and so forth

with key stakeholders in person or at least speak with them over the phone, to ensure they understand and approve the importance and reasons for M&E training; the people identified for training; and the training location, time, duration, and budget. Also confirm with them any key resource people to support the workshop at the training location.

3. Schedule the training

Scheduling an M&E training workshop can be an involved process with multiple days to consider or it can be more straightforward, if only for a single workshop delivered in one day. First, you will need to consider the training duration: that is, whether it has been designed to be delivered in few hours, days, or through a series of workshops over weeks or months. Another consideration is whether there is a deadline for when training needs to occur. For example, training may need to coincide with a program start, the hire of new staff, or by the end of the fiscal year. The training start will also need to be realistic to how long it will take to develop the training materials. Such information is typically drawn from training analysis.

Of course, an essential factor for scheduling a training workshop is practicality and convenience for the trainees themselves. For instance, if they are volunteering their own time for training, evenings may be preferable when they are not working. Related, it is important to ensure that training avoids potential conflicts with other events that can affect attendance, for example, other trainings, organizational meetings, holidays, political elections, and so forth. In an organizational context, it is especially important to avoid "training burnout," when people are inundated with various training and learning initiatives and unable to retain, never mind apply, new learning.

Other practical considerations that can affect training timing include the availability of the trainer/s, any guest speakers, the training facility, and any equipment needed to be rented or borrowed for training. In the end, depending on who is involved with the training, you may need to propose several options to arrive at one most suitable for the trainees and training needs.

4. Select and prepare trainers (and others involved in training delivery)

If more than one trainer is to deliver the M&E workshop, it is important to recruit and prepare qualified trainers. In Chapter 5 we discussed trainer competencies, outlined steps for recruiting M&E trainers, and provide a checklist of key trainer competencies to guide the process. Trainers should have adequate background and experience, be approved by stakeholders when the workshop is commissioned, and understand their roles and responsibilities as a trainer.

Once trainers have been selected, it will be necessary to orientate and prepare them for the training. This includes familiarizing them with the curriculum, M&E topics and activities to facilitate, materials and instructional media, and so forth. If a trainer's guide or lesson plans have been prepared, this can be very helpful at this stage. Orienting trainers may require a training of trainers (ToT), mock training sessions, or pilots where trainers practice facilitating training activities. The ToT and actual M&E workshop can also be used as an advanced training opportunity for qualified trainers—see **Box 9.3**.

In addition to trainers, it may also be necessary to prepare others involved with training, such as translators, so they are familiar with training content and how to best translate it to trainees.

BOX 9.3
Training-of-Trainers (ToT) as an Opportunity for M&E Capacity Building

As we discussed in Chapter 3, M&E training is best planned as part of a comprehensive approach to capacity building, aligned with related initiatives among the stakeholder group. This can include building the capacity within an organization or community of more advanced and qualified people to train others in M&E. The International Federation of Red Cross and Red Crescent Societies (IFRC) have successfully used this approach to build the capacity of National Society staff and local partners as part of its M&E capacity building strategy. It selects four or five qualified people who have expressed a professional interest in and have responsibilities for M&E capacity building. These trainers in training participate in an applied training combining an intensive ToT with an actual M&E workshop. The lead trainer for the workshop serves as a ToT trainer as well as a mentor for the trainers in training, who receive immediate and practical experience and feedback on their training in the real-life setting of delivering an actual M&E workshop.

5. Select the trainees

Depending on the context, training participation may be voluntary, mandatory, or *strongly encouraged*. For instance, in an organizational context, trainees may be selected by management during the training analysis phase. In other contexts, whether for an organization or the general public, training may be optional and self-selected, for which marketing and advertising will be important. However trainees are identified for a M&E workshop, three important considerations include

1. **Prerequisite M&E knowledge**. The selection of trainees should be appropriate to the level of KSA required for training. Ideally, prerequisite knowledge was noted when preparing the learning objectives (Chapter 8), and additional information about trainee M&E background and experience has been gathered during the training analysis. It may be useful to create a list of selection criteria based on required KSA and other requirements specific to the training context, for example, post-training commitments to use training in an organization.

2. **Number of trainees**. The size of an M&E workshop will be in relation to what is most appropriate for the learning objectives and type of activities planned to achieve them as well as how much space

is available in the training facility. Typically, between ten to twenty people is a good number for a workshop. This number will allow for a variety of opinions and perspectives but is small enough so people are more likely to actively participate and the trainer/s will be able to provide individual feedback and attention. There are no set rules, but the following illustrates how group size can affect discussion among participants:

- Three to 6 people—everyone usually speaks.
- Six to 12 people—most participants speak, a few are quieter or do not contribute much at all.
- Twelve to 20 people—five or six people speak out the most.
- Twenty to 30 people—only a few people speak out.
- Thirty plus people—discussion is very limited.

3. **Composition**. Is it better to have trainees from a homogenous group—for example, managers or a project team—or a heterogeneous group of participants with different levels of education, M&E backgrounds, cultures, and experience? What composition is most suitable for the desired level of peer learning, sharing, and interaction during training? Related, what gender balance is most suitable for training? Typically, it is good to have a well-balanced group, but in some contexts the presence of one group (e.g., men) may be domineering and hinder participation of others (e.g., women), in which case it may be preferable to offer separate training to different groups (e.g., single-gender training) or divide up small working groups accordingly.

Ultimately, each training event will have its own focus and dynamics for which the number and composition of trainees should be adapted. If the trainer has little experience with the particular M&E training, it is recommended to keep the number of trainees small.

6. Select the training facility

The workshop location can affect who is able or chooses to attend training, their attention during training, and what activities are possible for training. Typically, it is best if the training facility is relatively convenient and accessible for trainees; that is, near their workplace, home/accommodation, public transportation, and so forth. If the workshop will involve a site/field visit for a practicum experience, the training should be located reasonably close by. Other practical considerations include accessibility to restrooms, meal facilities or restaurants, and accommodation for residential training workshops.

In an organizational context, it will be important to determine whether it is more appropriate to have an external training event, where trainees travel to and spend time outside their normal context, which can allow trainees to better concentrate and focus on the training in a shorter period of time. However, external training will depend on available resources for venue, transport, and accommodation, and it may be preferable to offer training on-the-job or in the contexts that trainees can immediately apply and use knowledge and skills. Furthermore, there may be costs associated with removing trainees from their normal responsibilities in an organization, in which case, training may need to be provided at a different time.

It is difficult to learn when there are distractions and noise. Therefore, the location should be isolated and preferably quiet, without interruptions, so people can concentrate on training—for example, avoid common rooms, such as cafeterias, where people can wander in and distract from the training; rooms with thin walls, where noise next door can compete with the training; and rooms next to exterior traffic or other sources of noise.

Ideally, there should be plenty of space at the facility to accommodate everyone and the type of interaction required for training activities. There should be enough space for trainers to walk around and interact with trainee groups, and trainees with each other. You do not want a crowded or claustrophobic atmosphere, especially for longer workshops. Consider not only the floor space but also the presence of windows or high ceilings can help reduce a closed-in feeling. Also consider wall space to hang up flipchart paper and other visual material. Related, consider the acoustics of the room. Is it large enough so people do not need to talk over each other during small group activities and not so cavernous that they cannot hear each other speak in plenary? (Note that a microphone can help address audibility in a large room with many people.)

The lighting and configuration of the room should be adequate for everyone to see each other and visual aids and presentations. Preferable, the lighting is adjustable, and if there are windows, they can be covered to avoid distracting sunrays from projected visual presentations. Participants should be able to see the trainer as well as each other; therefore, avoid rooms with visual obstructions, such as pillars or posts, that block or limit participants' views. In addition to the lighting, consider the climate control for the room. We know how hard it can be to concentrate when the temperature is uncomfortable and distracting. Ensure there is good ventilation to keep the air moving, open windows, or adjust the temperature (thermostat).

Take the time to look into other important aspects of the training facility. Is the facility and neighborhood safe and secure? If not, you may need to take precautions like hiring security staff. Consider whether the facility is properly equipped with safety equipment (e.g., emergency alarm system, fire extinguishers), and when required it should be accessible for the physically disabled. Do not forget to check that there is adequate (and working) electrical outlets for computers, projectors, and other electrical media is to be used (e.g., microphones); in addition to audiovisual aids used by the trainer, increasingly participants use computers during training for activities or note taking. Related, the Internet is also increasingly used during training workshops—ensure there is a reliable source and bandwidth. It can be a real showstopper when a presentation or activity using the Internet gets sabotaged because of poor connectivity.

Clearly, there are a lot of considerations that can come into play when selecting the training location and facility, which are summarized in the above checklist (see Table 9.3). It is preferable if you can visit the training location yourself to confirm suitability. If you are unable to do so, see if it is possible to get a diagram or pictures of the space to best ensure it is appropriate for training needs.

7. Communicate with trainees

Pre-training communication with trainees can play a significant role attracting appropriate people, setting the initial tone and expectations, and building motivation for M&E training. It is best when the trainer/s can directly communicate with trainees beforehand. In settings where an organization is spearheading trainee communication rather than trainers themselves, they should nevertheless be aware of and advise pre-training communication as needed. Sometimes, such as a training for the general public, it may not be possible to directly communicate with trainees beforehand, in which case the training syllabus or description will play a key role.

There are a range of media and outlets to communicate with trainees: for example, flyers; posters; individually mailed, faxed, or emailed invitations; phone calls; public announcements at the workplace or on radio and TV; and the assortment of social media and network options on the Internet (e.g., M&E and organizational websites, email list-serves, and communities of practice). Multiple sources of information are useful, but keep in mind that people are busy and you do not want to overwhelm them with too much information. Related, keep communication concise and clear.

There are basically two types of pre-training communication. First, there is the training announcement or invitation, which should respond to the trainees' "need to know" what, why, and how training will occur. Keep it upbeat and positive, stimulating interest in the training content and its importance, but also include the practical, logistical details about the workshop and how to register. If a training syllabus or program has been prepared, this can be used to summarize the overall training or a website link can be provided to access it over the Internet. Be sure to provide enough lead time when first announcing or sending out workshop invitations so trainees have sufficient time to consider, plan, and prepare for training.

The second type of communication is for confirmed workshop participants, providing any material or resources trainees should be familiar with prior to the workshop (e.g., case studies), assignments to complete, detailed logistical information for attending the training, and additional items that arise. For example, confirmed trainees may be asked to complete a pre-workshop questionnaires or personal learning/development plans (described above). The checklist in Table 9.3 summarizes other considerations for these two forms of communication, and **Box 9.4** highlights some key considerations for pre-training assignments.

8. Prepare the training material, supplies, and media

We discussed earlier in this chapter the development of training resources. At this stage of the training planning, materials need to be ordered, printed, or copied and organized for the training. It also involves preparing the secondary media equipment and other supplies to deliver training activities. It is critical to take the time to carefully inventory training materials and supplies, preferably a day or week beforehand, as well as complete a thorough equipment check to ensure everything is in working order. It can be quite frustrating and disorienting, and can undermine credibility, if the training starts out with a shortage of materials for the trainees or the audiovisual equipment is not working for the presentations.

BOX 9.4
Pre-Training Assignments or Not?

Trainers sometimes ask whether assigning pre-reading or other assignments, such as viewing an online webinar on an M&E topic, is advisable prior to a face-to-face training. In short, there is no one answer, and it will largely depend on the training audience, topic, and time available prior to training. Pre-training assignments, such as reading a case study to be used during training, can be a useful strategy to familiarize learners with content and better capitalize on time during the training for learners to apply and practice knowledge gained before the training start. However, there is no guarantee that trainees will do pre-training assignments—whether due to lack of motivation or personal circumstance (e.g., job and family responsibilities that limits their time). This, in turn, can complicate training activity facilitation. One way to approach this is to try to determine the likelihood that prospective trainees will complete any pre-training assignments during training analysis—that is, ask them. Another consideration in an organizational training or work setting is to allocate time during work for trainees to prepare assignments. Of course, pre-assignments can be "required" by trainee supervisors, but as self-directed learners, this is not the best strategy to motivate and inspire adult learners for training.

9. Prepare the training facility

It is best to confirm the suitability of the training space when it was selected (discussed above) and then arrive well enough prior to the workshop to set up the room. In instances when trainers are unable to see the training facility in person beforehand, it is especially important to arrive early on the day of training to prepare the room. There are two primary considerations for preparing the workshop space.

First, the seating arrangement can have a considerable impact on training facilitation. There is an assortment of configurations, and we illustrate eight major types in **Figure 9.1**. Participants should not feel cramped, and there should be easy access to seating with adequate aisles and space. Seats should be comfortable (preferably adjustable for longer trainings) and movable, to change according to the interaction require for training activities. For example, small group tables can be used for breakout discussion sessions, followed by a large circle of chairs for plenary discussion and sharing. Theater or classroom arrangements allow for maximum seating capacity, but these arrangements are poor for participants to move around and to see and interact with each other.

For M&E training workshops, it usually works best to arrange seats in a small group format, with chairs arranged facing the focal point for plenary discussion and then facing each other for group activities. This allows the trainer/s to float around and check in on small group activities. Other seating arrangements can be made accordingly for other activities (even as an energizer with participants helping to arrange chairs). For example, while theater or classroom seating is not ideal for small group participation, they are useful for lectures or viewing a panel discussion or debate. Horseshoe or circle arrangements are useful for plenary discussion or viewing a training demonstration.

FIGURE 9.1   Seating Arrangements

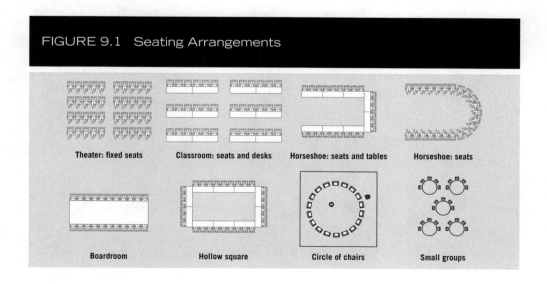

Theater: fixed seats   Classroom: seats and desks   Horseshoe: seats and tables   Horseshoe: seats

Boardroom   Hollow square   Circle of chairs   Small groups

In addition to participant seats, the furniture and teaching aids will need to be arranged for a supportive learning environment. Participant tables should have enough surface space for training materials and activities—for example, note taking, personal computers, books and supplies, game pieces, and so forth. Tables for projectors, trainers and other potential observers, and training supplies should be considered beforehand. If possible, it is best to arrange the room with the primary entrance/exit in the rear to minimize distractions. Teaching aids, such as flipcharts, white boards, projectors, and screens, should be arranged for easy access and visibility. Refer to the above checklist (Table 9.3) for additional considerations for room preparation.

10. Confirm additional logistics

Typically, there is an array of additional logistics to either do yourself or confirm they are ready. This will depend on the particular workshop setting but can include arrangements for transportation, accommodation, refreshments, and meals.

Lastly, despite the best-laid plans, the unexpected hiccup or problem will often arise. For instance, it can be a challenging start to the training if you arrive and find out there is construction going on next door, the PowerPoint projector has a burnt-out bulb, or the Internet is not functioning properly for planned activities. Indeed, it is best to expect the unexpected, and **Box 9.5** summarizes some tips to help mitigate potential problems that can arise during the training preparation.

BOX 9.5
Last-Minute Checks and Contingency Planning

- Tailor and use a preparation checklist for the workshop.
- Don't rely on verbal communication; put facility requirements in writing and provide a diagram.
- Confirm reservations a week before and again the day before the workshop.
- Confirm last-minute logistics, materials/equipment, refreshments, guest speaker/s, and so forth.
- Send a friendly reminder to participants the day before to confirm attendance.
- Arrive early with enough time to address any unforeseen problems.

- Conduct checks to ensure everything is functional and ready: equipment, instructional aids, Internet, lighting, ventilation, and so forth.

- Find out whom to contact at the facility if there is a problem, for example, with the lighting, temperature, or electrical source.

- Bring a *trainer's survival kit* (toolbox or duffle back) with extra supplies and replacement parts (e.g., bulbs), copies of handouts and other material, plug adapter, backup copy of software and presentations, and so forth. See **Figure 9.2** for one example.

- Have a back-plan or contingency plan, just in case you need to rearrange the room (e.g., for more or less attendees than expected) or relocate (e.g., due to unexpected noise or interference).

FIGURE 9.2   Example Trainer's Survival Kit

9.4 CHAPTER SUMMARY _____

This chapter offers a great deal of practical advice for the development phase of the ADDIE framework. In Chapters 6 and 7 we went into great detail about systematically analyzing the training context and, based on evidence arising from such analyses, designing the training event. During the development and preparation step, it is time to move from *what* the training is expected to accomplish to getting ready to bring that about. Much of what we have shared is grounded in practical experience and common sense. However, as is the case with most project management challenges, it is essential to have a comprehensive overview including reminders and checklists. In this chapter we important summary points include

- Plan realistically the time and costs for the development of training materials and resources and consider whether existing resources can be adopted or modified to meet training needs. Related, consider how easy it will be to revise training materials to best accommodate learners and future training needs.

- Ensure training materials, especially those provided to trainees, are organized and user-friendly and limit them to only those that are necessary and sufficient to achieve learning objectives.

- Consider the pros and cons of pre-training assignments and whether training materials can be provided to trainees beforehand (see Box 9.4).

- Although it takes additional time and resources, reviewing and piloting training can go a long way to ensure that the planned curriculum contents, activities, materials, and delivery media can be revised to best achieve identified learning objectives.

- There is an assortment of practical arrangements to prepare prior to training, and we refer readers to the Training Preparation Checklist, which summarizes key considerations for each of the following tasks:

  a. Develop a checklist or action plan.
  b. Confirm stakeholder commitment and approval.
  c. Schedule the training.
  d. Select the trainees (when applicable).
  e. Select the training facility.
  f. Communicate with trainees.
  g. Select and prepare trainers (and others involved in training delivery).
  h. Prepare training materials and media.
  i. Prepare the training facility.
  j. Confirm additional logistics.

9.5 RECOMMENDED RESOURCES _____

The development of training materials will be highly context specific, and in the preparation of this chapter we relied heavily on our own prior experience with and resources for M&E training. However, as we highlight in **Box 9.1**, readers can consider adopting or adapting existing materials for training development. In addition to those examples listed there, we refer readers to the Open Education Resources and other online resources for M&E recommended in Chapter 2. Of course, the example formats in this chapter are meant to be tailored and adapted to specific training contexts as well. For further examples, there are a variety of free templates for training planning available online, such as those available for download on the website of Trainers Advice (2015) and the *Templates for Instructional Design* on the website of Donald Clark (2015d). Lastly, many of the recommended resources books in Chapter 6 and Chapter 10 include example templates, forms, and checklists as part of their contents.

CHAPTER 10

Training Implementation

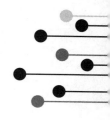

Typically, a great deal of preparation has taken place by the time you reach this stage of the ADDIE training cycle. The purpose of the training implementation is to operationalize what has been designed and developed (e.g., the training curriculum and materials) to achieve training objectives. It is when learning occurs, which involves various activities where people interact with training content and each other, experiencing, practicing, and reviewing new M&E concepts and practices. If the previous phases of training analysis, design, and development were done well, training implementation is more likely to be successful in achieving the learning objectives identified for M&E training. To the extent that these objectives were informed by training analyses, participants are likely to not only acquire new KSA but to transfer such to their own work context.

For the trainer, implementing training involves the facilitation or management of training activities, participants, the training environment, and the overall learning process. Therefore, in this chapter we provide an overview of training facilitation and then specifically at key consideration during three key stages of training delivery: the training introduction, activity facilitation, and the training closing. Building upon our prior two chapters, we again focus and illustrate our discussion as it applies to a live, face-to-face training workshop. Later, in Part 3 of this book, we will look more specifically at examples of activities and methods for training facilitation.

Our discussion of effective training facilitation is informed by a learner-centered approach to training and the adult learning principles that we introduced in Chapter 4. Facilitation can be learned and improved, but the most successful trainers truly

Learning Objectives

By the end of this chapter readers will be able to . . .

✓ Identify key signs or indicators of successful training facilitation

✓ Review key tips and considerations for different elements of training facilitation

- o Communication
- o Cultural competence
- o Using questions
- o Using training aids
- o Facilitating discussion
- o Monitoring and feedback
- o Co-facilitation
- o Handling disruptive behavior
- o Time management

✓ Review key tips and considerations for facilitating the

- o Training introduction
- o Activity facilitation
- o Training closing

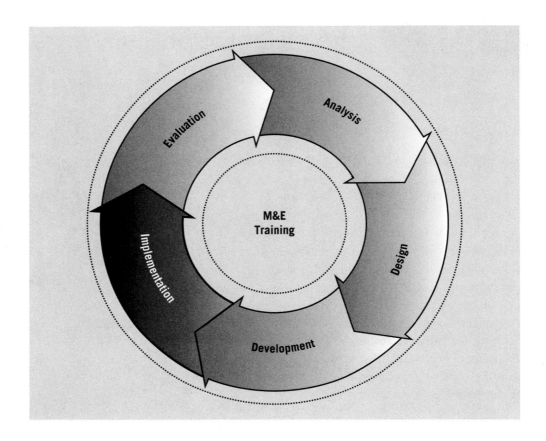

enjoy working with people. They are motivating, enthusiastic, and able to build rapport and trust with participants. Experience is also essential to anticipate and respond to group dynamics, work with different types of people, and build one's repertoire of relevant examples, anecdotes, stories, and analogies to help people understand and learn. Just as people have different learning styles, trainers will develop their own personal style and approach to training facilitation. Along this journey, authenticity and an earnest desire to help people learn will prove invaluable.

_____

10.1 Training Facilitation

In Chapter 5, we identified facilitation and group management as a key set of interpersonal skills for the M&E trainer. The extent to which newly acquired KSA transfers into practice after training will largely depend on the degree training was informed by the training analysis. As we highlighted in Section 5.2 (p. 125), the M&E trainer is not just a content expert with technical M&E knowledge (hard skills), but also a process expert (soft skills) who must effectively interact with learners for learning. During training delivery, this involves a combination of interrelated skills, including effective communication, listening, questioning, feedback, and the effective use of a mixture of media (training aids) to engage learners. Good training facilitation is informed by each of the adult learning principles that we introduced in Chapter 4, and below we highlight six signs or indicators that facilitation has been effective.

1. **People feel comfortable and safe to participate, ask questions, share knowledge, and learn** (Adult Learning Principles 1 and 14). This can begin when agreeing upon the ground rules (norms) for behavior at the training start and should be monitored throughout to ensure a safe and supportive learning environment. As participants begin to interact more, the trainer needs to know when and how to best step in to ensure that people are respectful and positively reinforced, and feel comfortable to express themselves and learn. As we shall see later in the chapter, this may involve addressing disruptive behavior.

2. **People feel the training is organized and know what is ahead and why** (Adult Learning Principles 1 and 2). Participants should have a good sense of the overall learning progression so they are able to integrate M&E topics and form a "big picture" of what they are learning. Whether at the training start, at the beginning of activities, or when questions arise in between, good facilitation regularly helps learners mentally organize and prepare for what is ahead and understand why it is relevant (worth their effort). This principle of need to know not only reinforces learning but supports a safe learning environment by reducing anxiety about what is next.

3. **People fully participate in their own learning process** (Adult Learning Principle 3). As we discussed in Chapter 4 (Section 4.7, p. 98), participation is a key principle for a learner-centered approach to adult training. The trainer is not the sole knowledge provider ("sage on stage"), and learners are not submissive recipients. Good facilitation employs a variety of approaches to encourage participation and peer learning. For instance, we shall see that including debriefs with activities is an effective method for participants to reflect upon and share with others what they

experienced and learned, relate material to their own lives and experience, and consider how they foresee using what they learned in real life. Facilitating participation is not easy: At times trainers need to nudge and prod participants, and at other times they need to pull back as people lead discussions and express themselves. We will discuss later how this can be done, but when learner-centered facilitation is poorly executed or inauthentic, it can have negative consequences for the training, as **Box 10.1** highlights.

4. **People are both mentally and physically engaged** (Adult Learning Principles 4, 7, 9, 10, 11 and 12). Good facilitation is motivating, enthusiastic, energetic, and even entertaining. It involves employing a mixture of methods and media (training aids) to add variety, fun, and humor—for example, interesting anecdotes, stories, metaphors, well-timed questions, games and team competition, and moving people around to keep learning lively. An assortment of different activities and approaches to facilitation is differentiated and more stimulating, and participants become curious to know what is next.

5. **People do not feel rushed** (Adult Learning Principles 1, 3, and 10). Activities should be facilitated so they are not hurried, and participants should have ample time for practice, trial, and error. This is closely related to time management, discussed later in this chapter. Good facilitation is a balancing act of constantly monitoring time versus people's progress with an activity and their learning. The latter should take precedence, and it may even be necessary to readjust or revise the workshop agenda to accommodate differentiated learning. Otherwise, a rushed atmosphere can threaten each of the above goals if people are stressed and frustrated because of the lack of time to fully participate in their learning.

6. **People have mutual respect and trust for the trainer/s** (Adult Learning Principle 1). Trainers do not need to be everyone's best friend, the world's greatest entertainer, or a walking M&E encyclopedia. Participants know this and are not expecting superwoman or man. What will, however, make a big difference with people is the degree of authenticity, responsiveness, patience, and hard work (evident in the delivery *and* preparation) that trainers demonstrate.

To a large degree, the above measures of success reflect the adult learning principles discussed in Chapter 4 (at times we note in parenthesis principles related to topics in this chapter, but they are interwoven throughout the various topics we discuss). How to achieve them as well as other elements of effective facilitation will be elaborated in

BOX 10.1
False Participation

In his informative book, *The Skillful Teacher*, Stephen Brookfield's (2006, p. 68) warning against "falsely participatory" teachers in the college environment also applies to adult learning in training. "Students usually come to know pretty quickly when they are being manipulated." In training, this could be falsely participatory trainers who talk about the importance of active participation, trainee opinions, and contributions but then proceed to lecture most of the time, limit questions, cut discussion short, and are more concerned with staying on time and covering planned content than actual learning. It also includes the "counterfeit critical thinker" or trainers who claim to welcome critical questioning of different viewpoints and assertions but then get agitated when this is applied to their own ideas. Clearly, false participation is counter to the principles of learner-centered training and can erode the trust in and credibility of trainers.

the remainder of this chapter. Our discussion is largely based on our own practical experience with and understanding of M&E training and how adults learn.[1]

Training communication

In Chapter 5, we identified communication as a key competency for trainers. During training delivery, this encompasses a variety of skills. Certainly it is important to speak clearly and helpful to use animated gestures, body language, and eye contact to engage learners. However, effective communication is much more than that.

Good communicators know how to read and respond to their audience. This involves not only listening to what people say but also carefully observing what they do: their body language, social interactions, and other cues as to how they are receiving information and responding to planned activities. For example, are people gazing absentmindedly into space, distracted by or in a side conversation or lost and leaning over to ask the person next for clarification? Carefully monitoring people's interest, attention, and understanding allows trainers to modify their delivery accordingly. It helps them know when to pause or speed up, ask questions, repeat key points, and ask people to paraphrase to check and reinforce understanding.

Knowing how to *read* your audience can be challenging if you have not worked with them before, even more so if they are from a different culture. It is worth the time and

---

1. This includes providing training of trainers as well as our exposure to training and education resources.

effort beforehand to get to know your training audience. This can occur during the training analysis, whether you meet directly with prospective trainees or with others familiar with them. In other instances, such as flying into another country to deliver training, trainers should do their best to understand the culture/s they anticipate will be represented at training—see the section in this chapter on cultural competence.

Of course, another key element for good communication is the ability to clearly explain things, such as M&E concepts and practices, activity instructions, and answers to questions. Whether explaining what a counterfactual is or how to determine a sample size, it is important to tailor explanations according to the audience and their level of understanding. Being familiar with the trainee background and M&E material helps to anticipate topics that will be more difficult, conceptual stumbling blocks, and challenging questions to answer.

Well-prepared presentations, facilitation notes, and a variety of instructional media (e.g., PowerPoint handouts, worksheets) will help to convey information. It is much easier to teach well-planned material from the start than to backtrack and address poorly communicated information. Explanations are most clear when they are concise and coherent, visually reinforced, and logically arranged so they are easier to follow, as opposed to haphazardly jumping from one point to another (Adult Learning Principle 3). It is also helpful when explanations are engaging and related to real-life application of M&E concepts (Adult Learning Principles 5 and 6). As **Box 10.2** highlights, consider developing some favorite "pocket examples" for M&E explanations.

BOX 10.2
M&E Pocket Examples

Pocket examples are anecdotes, interesting stories, vivid examples, or metaphors useful to illustrate and elaborate M&E concepts and practice. For example, when explaining the importance of mixed methods, one author uses a pocket example of an HIV/AIDS program distributing sexual lubricant to reduce HIV transmission.[1] In Cambodia, a baseline/endline survey was used to measure the amount of sexual lubricant distributed before and after a program as a proxy indicator of program impact. The quantitative survey showed an increase in the distribution of lubricant, but when qualitative focus groups were conducted, it was revealed that people were using the lubricant for their bicycle chains rather than sexual intercourse.

---

1. There are increasing doubts about which type of sexual lubricant is most effective, generally, some kind of lubricant is always preferable, as "dry sex" increases friction and puts extra strain on the condom.

Approaches such as referring to the training agenda, structuring redundancy into the lessons, and using periodic reviews of material help participants organize and make sense of the training content (Adult Learning Principle 12). When using repetition, also keep in mind the adult learning principles (13) of primacy and recency to help learners retain learning: Frame key learning points initially (primacy), revisit them during the presentation (repetition), and summarize them at the end (recency). Consider reinforcing these points with summary handouts and other visual aids for learners.

Metaphors and *analogies* are a particularly useful way to explain M&E concepts and practice (e.g., House, 1983; Kaminsky, 2000; Nassif & Kahalil, 2006; Patton, 2002; Smith, 1981). For example, consider Stake's metaphor for explaining the difference between summative and formative evaluation: "When the cook tastes the soup, that's formative; when the guests taste the soup, that's summative" (quoted in Scriven, 1991, p. 169). We also begin this book with a metaphor of the trainer as a chef. Such comparisons help make new and unfamiliar concepts more meaningful by connecting them with what learners already know. According to Patton (2002, p.95) good learning metaphors should be

a. Understandable for learners

b. Connect with real life experience

c. Meaningful or relevant for the learning objective

d. Express appropriate values (and be culturally appropriate) for the intended audience

e. Situationally and contextually appropriate for the audience

In actuality, Patton's advice applies to other learning examples used in M&E training. In **Box 10.3**, we highlight some examples of simple metaphors we have successfully used in M&E training.

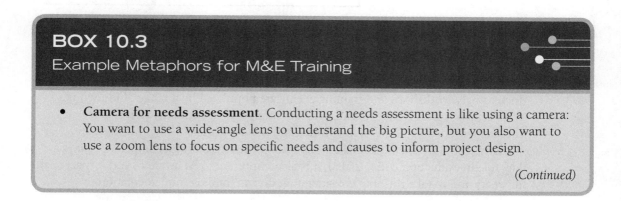

BOX 10.3
Example Metaphors for M&E Training

- **Camera for needs assessment**. Conducting a needs assessment is like using a camera: You want to use a wide-angle lens to understand the big picture, but you also want to use a zoom lens to focus on specific needs and causes to inform project design.

(Continued)

(Continued)

- **House for project design.** A logframe (or other program design framework) is like the foundation and roof of a house: Before painting the walls, laying down the carpet, and arranging the furniture and living area, you want to make sure it has a sound structure that can withstand the weather.

- **Paint-by-numbers picture for mixed methods**. Quantitative data are like the numbers on a paint-by-number picture, sketching the boundaries of the picture (what you are examining), whereas qualitative data paint in the color for a more full picture. Both are very useful for seeing the complete picture.

- **Car dashboard for indicator.** Indicators are like the instruments on a care dashboard: The speedometer measures whether you achieving your objectives on time; the fuel gauge measures how efficiently you are using resources; the odometer measures how much you have accomplished; and the oil gauge measures peoples satisfaction level. .

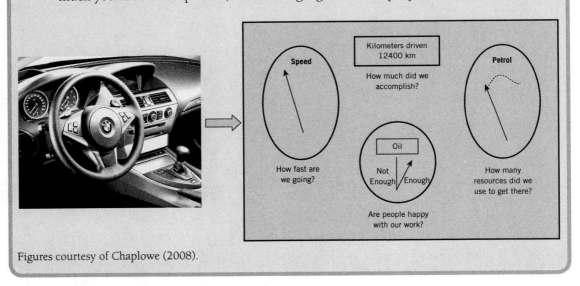

Figures courtesy of Chaplowe (2008).

Cultural competence

Increasingly workshops and training events are populated by a range of individuals from diverse cultural backgrounds. *Cultural competence*, the ability to recognize and interact with people of different cultures and socioeconomic backgrounds, is an important skill for the M&E trainer (Chapter 5). Just as cultural competence plays a key role in evaluation (AEA, 2011), it is also important to be aware of and respect such diversity and to take this into consideration during training implementation.

BOX 10.4
Culture Matters

In its workbook, *Culture Matters*, the Peace Corps (2014) identifies a variety of considerations that are very relevant for M&E trainers. Other examples identified in the workbook relevant for training include attitudes toward age, taking risks, formality, dress, respect, directness in communication, power, gender relations, responsibility, time, and being on time. When not properly understood, these factors can challenge training facilitation with misunderstanding and misinterpretation. However, the workbook also stresses that cultural awareness encompasses not only understanding other cultures represented at training but also self-awareness, to understand how your own background shapes your interactions with others.

Knowing about and respecting the norms of the local culture can be tricky business and requires an active effort. It is more than adapting delivery and visual aids to linguistic differences; it includes other subtle factors that can affect training facilitation and interactions—see **Box 10.4**. For example, in some cultures it may be considered disrespectful to challenge the instructor, or people may be reluctant or uncomfortable speaking publicly to a large group. The trainer would be remiss to insist that such persons assume the role of small-group spokesperson during a plenary follow-up activity.

Questioning

Using questions is an essential technique for training communication that deserves particular attention. Effective questioning can be used to engage learners and interest in a topic, check understanding, steer discussion, change topics, clarify and review key points, and provide feedback. It is the basis of discussion activities and can make lectures and presentations more participatory. Questioning is a flexible technique that can be planned into the training or unplanned and used spontaneously to ensure no one is lost, draw people out during a lull, and solicit opinions.

There are a variety of different forms of questions used in training. In **Table 10.1** we summarize some major types, and readers may want to refer to the description of question and answer activities in Part 3. Many evaluators may already be well versed in questioning from qualitative data collection, but in a training, the primary objective is not gathering information but learning.

Questioning is a skill, and knowing who and how to ask questions develops with time and practice. The examples we provide for each question type can be called "overhead"

TABLE 10.1 Types of Questions Used in Training

Closed questions	***What is the first column in the logframe?*** These are used when the response is limited to a single, correct answer or short phrase. Useful to clarify and check factual understanding and, therefore, sometimes called *clarifying questions*. Reply time is quick and can be used as a springboard for open questions explaining the response—that is, followed by, Why do you think? Avoid compound questions with more than one answer. As these have a "correct" answer, they may be threatening. Avoid putting someone on the spot.
Open questions	***How would you characterize the difference between monitoring and evaluation?*** These are questions that cannot be answered with a yes–no response but require explanations of concepts or opinions. Useful to elicit additional information and opinions and engage learners to articulate their understanding themselves and to share experience. Trainees can better convey understanding through open questions than through a cursive, one-word reply to a closed question. These can also be less threatening than a yes/no question, but they are more time consuming in reply.
Probing questions	***How might politics affect the reliability of an evaluation?*** These are a form of open question used to delve deeper into topics and issues, adding additional detail and explanation. They're useful to further engage participants and move the discussion forward, building on prior understanding and further exploring topics. Probing questions allow participants to more fully articulate themselves and opinions, and are therefore useful for affective learning.
Leading questions	***Would you want unreliable secondary data?*** These are used when there is a specific answer in mind to lead the discussion, guide learners, and/or suggest the correct answer. They can be effective in a disagreement when you know that there is a right answer. However, if used poorly they can seem manipulative. Leading questions are also useful to steer training facilitation; for example, *Do you want to be late for the next session?*
Funnel questions	***Who can name the two major types of evaluation we have discussed thus far? What are the primary differences between summative and formative evaluation? Can anyone give an example of when they used a formative evaluation? and so forth.*** This is a form of leading questions using open or closed questions to narrow down specific information with increasing detail. Funnel questions are a very active form of questioning, but questioning this way can make it challenging for trainees to interject with follow-up questions.
Rhetorical questions	***Do we all want our evaluations to be reliable and credible?*** Related to leading questions, these questions have obvious answers, and a response is not necessarily expected. They are useful to underscore a point that everyone should agree with, but participants do not necessarily need to answer. Rhetorical questions are best when addressed to the whole group rather than an individual.

questions, as they are asked to the whole group. However, they can also be directed to individuals. Overhead questions tend to be less threatening, but if the same person in the group continues to answer questions or if you want to check a specific person's understanding or draw them into the discussion, it may be more appropriate to use direct questions for individuals. **Box 10.5** summarizes some tips to guide effective questioning.

Remember that questioning is two-way, and trainers should encourage questions from trainees to assist their understanding and ensure no one is being left behind. As the axiom goes, "No question is a bad question, except the one that wasn't asked" (which can be discussed as part of the training introduction). Chances are that if one person has a question, others will likely share it. Participant questions allow learners to address their own learning needs, synthesize new knowledge, and help one another learn. They are also meaningful opportunities to reinforce learning, review key points, and allow the group to further discuss and explore topics. In Box 10.5 we summarize some tips for responding to questions.

BOX 10.5
Tips for Questioning

Tips for asking questions

- Begin with an overhead question, for example, "How might monitoring contribute to evaluation?" and then redirect the question to an individual if there is no immediate answer, such as "What do you think, Jane?"

- Prepare key questions to guide learning prior to training, which can then be adapted accordingly.

- State questions clearly, concisely, and audibly in a complete sentence.

- Spread questions throughout the training, at random to keep it lively, or for Q&A sessions, but do not overuse them.

- Don't interrogate or embarrass people.

- Avoid trick questions, and be sure to know the answers.

(Continued)

(Continued)

- Pause and allow people time to consider their response.

- Don't get sidetracked by answers, and be ready to use leading questions if necessary to stay on topic.

- At the same time, do not cut people short or interrupt them when they are responding.

- Don't delay the process too long if an answer is not forthcoming, and be ready to step in with an answer.

- When handling an incorrect answer, first commend them for trying and try to identify what is useful in their response.

Tips for responding to questions

- Anticipate questions learners may have and prepare draft responses.

- Thank people and validate their question, "That's a good question, Purnima." Be genuine about it, not automatic. When reformulating the question (below) explain why it is a good question.

- Paraphrase the question to check your understanding and so others in the group can hear, understand, and learn from the answer or try to answer it themselves.

- Allow the asker the first chance to answer the question. Leading questions can help in this process.

- Redirect the question to others to engage and empower them, reinforcing peer learning.

- Acknowledge when you do not know the answer but follow-up with, "But I will try to find out," and then try to get an answer in the time frame of the session or training or to be shared in correspondence afterward.

- Add unanswered questions or those to discuss in more detail later to the Parking Lot (discussed below).

Using training aids

Also called instructional aids, training aids are essential tools for training delivery and communication. They are used by trainers to present and clarify learning content and by trainees to participate in learning activities and share with each other. Often, the same training aid is used by both trainers and trainees—for example, a flipchart. Like training activities, a variety of training aids is important to engage and involve different learners, keep their energy level high, and maintain interest (Adult Learning Principles 4, 9, and 10). As we discussed in Chapter 4, learning is multisensory, and using a range of audiovisual and tactile aids is more "entertaining" to the senses than repetitive presentation and discussion.

It is beyond the scope of this book to go into detail about the selection and use of training aids, but we have summarized some of the more commonly used aids and related considerations in **Table 10.2**. With advances in technology, the range of training aids on the market is expanding; for instance, CLEAR (2013) recommends clickers for its M&E training events, allowing participants to engage (e.g., vote on poll questions) with slide presentations. In Part 3 we provide an example of a training activity using a cartoon as a visual aid for M&E learning, and Box 10.3 (as shown previously in this chapter) illustrates a visual aid in the form of an indicator dashboard.

An overall reminder about training aids is that they should be used discriminatingly; they should not distract from learning, and ultimately, they are only "aids" and not a

TABLE 10.2   Common Training Aids

- **Printed material**. Handed out or posted on the wall; for example, diagrams, drawings, photographs, maps, charts, graphs, tables, cartoons, and posters.

- **Chalkboard/whiteboard**. Cheap, easy to use, but contents are lost once erased (unless a picture is taken).[1]

- **Flipchart**. Cheap, easy to use, and output can be posted for display and saved as a record.

- **Overhead projector**. Moderately expensive; requires transparencies that are typically prepared beforehand but can be customized on the spot.

- **Computer projector** (e.g., PowerPoint projector). Expensive but versatile for projecting slides, diagrams, documents, video and online content and playing audio recording (with speaker).

- **Audio and visual recording**. Costly and require equipment; used to share prerecorded or obtained material as well as to record in-training activities for self-observation, discussion, and feedback.

- **Microphone**. Costly and requires a speaker; useful for soft-spoken people and to facilitate discussion and direct attention to speakers.

- **Computers and mobile devises**. Costly, but trainees may already have them; useful for trainees to practice with M&E software, take notes, refer to documents and online resources, and so forth.

- **Activity materials**. Game pieces or materials used to facilitate interaction with content and between learners.

1. There are now more expensive, electronic whiteboard options on the market that can print output from their writing surfaces before erasing.

substitute for good preparation and training delivery. For presenting visual aids, four specific reminders include the following:

- Do not block the displayed material (screen or flipchart).

- Talk to the audience rather than face what is displayed.

- Do not over-complicate/crowd visual presentations—for example, use key words rather than sentences.

- Ensure that displayed material can be clearly seen (and read) by everyone in the training—for example, from where people are seated, whether lights need to be dimmed for visual projection of material, and so forth.

Facilitating discussion

Facilitating discussion is one of the chief responsibilities in M&E training and can be one of the most demanding. Learning is at an optimum level when participants are given the opportunity to reflect and share their ideas, opinions, and knowledge with each other (Adult Learning Principles 4, 5, 8, 11). However, facilitating discussion can at times feel like a balancing act for the trainer between being flexible and being directive.

Good facilitators do not impose their own views on others but instead know how to maintain a neutral perspective so that people are able to articulate and reach their own understanding and learning. At the same time, they know how to step forward and provide timely feedback, challenge participants' ideas, and add relevant information for learning. At the start of a discussion, it is important to frame the topic/s and agree on the outcomes, which will provide direction and a sense of shared responsibility for the discussion (Adult Learning Principles 2 and 3).

During the discussion, it is the learners who should furnish most of the ideas. However, the trainer should help *steer* discussion in the right direction and may interject for a variety of reasons:

- Reinvigorate the conversation if it fades or loses momentum

- Draw out personal experiences and opinions from people

- Acknowledge or highlight people's contributions for others

- Compare and contrast different responses

- Avoid unnecessary detours and friction

- Distinguish between fact and opinion

- Clarify or correct misunderstanding

Toward the end of a discussion, it is best if participants can summarize and draw conclusions themselves. However, the trainer may need to help accommodate individual differences and arrive at consensus, even if it is agreement on the points of disagreement. When key learning points do not emerge from the group/s themselves, the trainer may need to identify them and relate them to the learning objectives.

There will be times when more open group discussion and process can lead to emergent, unexpected learning opportunities from the participants themselves—see **Box 10.6**. There will be other times when it is necessary to rein in and refocus a group so that it stays on task and can move forward toward its goals. This can include facilitating discussion so dominant participants do not monopolize dialogue and everyone has an opportunity to provide input and express opinions. It also includes managing conflict and difficult situations to maintain a respectful and safe atmosphere for people to participate and express themselves, which we will discuss further below.

Discussion can be an activity in itself, such as debate or small group discussions, or it can be a part of another activity, such as an activity debrief, review, or sharing feedback. The outcomes and scope of discussion can range from more defined topics to a more open format, such as brainstorming. In Part 3, we summarize some useful methods or techniques to consider when facilitating discussion. Keep in mind that the discussion format can be sitting or standing up, and moving around and mixing discussion groups can help keep discussion active and expose people to different viewpoints.

BOX 10.6
Using Emergent Challenges as Learning Opportunities

Adult learners can often challenge the learning content and process. For example, one of us (Chaplowe) was presenting a lesson of data collection methods to frame a follow-up activity, during which a participant challenged the categorization of data collection methods presented. Pursuing discussion reflected that others in the training were intrigued by this alternative viewpoint. Thus, in response, I decided to replace the follow-up activity with an unplanned activity that seemed more appropriate: Small groups were asked to list and then organize data collection methods into categories they felt best summarize them and then share and discuss their conclusions in a follow-up plenary session. This proved to be very engaging, and as the learning objective was for participants to be able to compare and contrast different data collection methods, it was accomplished, in a more meaningful and engaging manner than initially planned.

Monitoring and feedback

Monitoring lets people know and provides opportunity for feedback on how they are doing (supporting Adult Learning Principles 4 and 14 for trainee participation and feedback). This includes participants' progress toward learning objectives as well as how they feel about the learning process itself, for example, facilitation, interactions, and group dynamics. It also includes other aspects of the training, such as how participants feel about the training materials, facility (e.g., temperature or lighting), and other logistical matters, such as the meals.

Like questioning, monitoring and feedback is two way and done by both trainers and trainees. For trainers, it is important to regularly monitor and solicit feedback on people's satisfaction and comfort level to maintain a safe and effective learning environment (Adult Learning Principle 1). For the trainees, group and self-monitoring and opportunities for feedback are important elements of a learner-centered approach, empowering them to reflect upon and participate in their learning process. Adult learners want to know how well they are doing, whether from direct feedback from trainers or activities that allow them to individual or collectively check and reflect on their understanding. They also want opportunity to express concerns and problems they may confront.

Monitoring and feedback during an M&E workshop can be unstructured and structured relative to the training.

a. **Unstructured monitoring and feedback**. Techniques such as observation, questioning, and discussion can be used unplanned to check people's understanding and how they are doing. During group activities, trainers can float among participants to observe what and when they understand or are struggling with M&E concepts or to pick up on tensions or other dynamics that reflect how they feel about the learning process. Questioning, practice, and discussion are also opportunities for trainers and trainees to self-monitor and talk about areas to improve.

b. **Activities for monitoring and feedback on learning**. These include review activities structured into the curriculum as well as any formal assessment activities, such as quizzes, which can be debriefed and used as a review exercise to reinforce learning (Adult Learning Principle 12). Reviews help the trainer and trainees both check how well people understand M&E content.

c. **Activities for monitoring and feedback on the training** (Adult Learning Principle 4). These include activities that allow the trainer and trainees to express how they feel about the training facilitation and each other—for example, the training pace or group interactions. Activities include discussion and debriefs as well as questionnaires for anonymous feedback that can also be used for training evaluation.

d. **Personal feedback**. There may be times when it is most appropriate to provide individual feedback, from the trainer to the trainees or vice versa. This can help address specific conceptual or personal problems people may have, whether it is conceptual stumbling block, low level of participation, or disruptive behavior. If appropriate, longer training programs, personal feedback sessions, or interviews can be scheduled in as part of the training program.

The frequency of structured activities for monitoring and feedback typically depends on the duration of the workshop. For instance, with longer, multiday workshops, it is important to structure periodic reviews as well as feedback opportunities at the end of the day, and midday if appropriate. If there are particular sessions that are being piloted or trainers in training for whom feedback on activity facilitation is desired, debrief discussion and questionnaires can be used after an activity to solicit targeted feedback.

We will discuss monitoring and feedback in further detail in Chapter 11. One last reminder is that feedback is most effective when provided in a timely, positive, and respectful manner. As we shall see later in this chapter, it is helpful when this is discussed and collectively agreed upon at the start of a workshop or training event.

Co-Facilitation

Facilitating training can be demanding and tiring work—especially for workshops that are a day or more in length. Co-facilitation allows trainers to share responsibilities, and it is helpful to have another trainer to "lean on" when exhausted or confronting a challenging situation. With more than one trainer, it is possible to provide added attention to trainees as well as variety in facilitation to make the workshop more engaging for learners. Each trainer is able to complement the other's facilitation style, strengths, and experience. Co-facilitation can also be a valuable opportunity for a more experienced M&E trainer to mentor less experienced or apprenticing M&E trainers.

These benefits aside, if not approached properly, co-facilitation can backfire because of different theoretical, technical, or personal orientations, disagreements, and competition. Therefore, co-facilitation should be planned and enacted carefully. We summarized some suggestions in **Box 10.7**.

BOX 10.7
Tips for Co-Facilitation

- Identify who is the lead trainer—typically the more qualified person experienced in M&E and training.

- Share your M&E orientations and experiences of training in similar contexts beforehand.

- Review the material together beforehand, allocate topics and tasks and be clear about roles and responsibilities.

- Do not interrupt or challenge a co-facilitator but wait to be invited to speak. Consider establishing a signal that one facilitator has something to add and for the speaking facilitator to periodically ask, "Any questions or anything else to add?" as an opportunity for the co-facilitator (and learners) to contribute additional information.

- Consider a "tag team" approach, where you both share in delivering a session rather than a session at a time.

- When one trainer is leading an activity, the other can support with operating visual aids, taking notes, managing time, floating and checking on participants, and so forth (rather than checking their personal email).

- Regularly check in with each other, debrief, and solicit feedback, in between sessions and at the workshop end.

- Support and validate each other; if there are disagreements, resolve them promptly during a break or check in.

- Try to convey intertrainer rapport through the use of banter, good-humored comments, and the like.

Handling disruptive behavior

There are a lot of things that can go "wrong" in a workshop—for example, the projector bulb burns out or sessions go overtime—but one of the most challenging problems to handle is disruptive behavior. It is hard to anticipate the personalities who will attend training or how people will behave, but some of the more problematic characters that you may encounter include (IFRC, 2010)

- **The Bulldozer**—dominates and domineers, interrupts others, and is disrespectful of others' opinions

- **The Conspirator**—whispers in side conversations, doesn't pay attention, and distracts others

- **The Heckler**—ready to find fault and criticize you and the training

- **The Dropout**—doesn't pay attention, gazes out the window, texts on their mobile phone, or reads a magazine

- **The Know-It-All**—has something to say on every topic and at great length

- **The Overachiever**—demands to do more, even if the others are not ready

- **The "Disser"**—disrespectful, uses inappropriate language, insults others, or acts in a way to make others feel uncomfortable

These may be stereotypes, but the behaviors they represent are real. Knowing how to respond to difficult behavior will vary. Sometimes, it will be clear that inappropriate or disruptive behavior needs to be immediately and directly addressed, such as a racist, sexist, or otherwise offensive remark. In other instances, disruptive behavior may be addressed indirectly, such as eye contact with people to cut short their side conversation. Of course, the first step toward addressing inappropriate behavior is to avoid it by discussing and agreeing upon unacceptable behavior early in the workshop when establishing the ground rules (discussed later in this chapter). Nevertheless, problems arise, and in **Box 10.8**, we offer some suggestions for dealing with disruptive behavior during training.

Jessie Mountfield

Time management

Time management can be one of the most challenging aspects of training facilitation. Activities and sessions often run overtime, discussions take longer than expected, questions arise that take time to address, and unexpected technical difficulties with visual media can hold things up. There are also instances when it becomes apparent that activities and learning is taking less time than anticipated.

It is important to be flexible and ready to readjust the training agenda to learners' needs, moods, interests, and pace—an essential element of a learner-centered approach (Adult Learning Principles 3 and 10). The training agenda should not be a blueprint

BOX 10.8
Suggestions for Handling Disruptive Behavior

- Connect individually and establish rapport and respect early on. This can help curb negative behavior later on.

- Signal nonverbally to let individuals know when they are disruptive; for example, make eye contact or move closer to the person.

- Set an example by commending positive behavior and participation (but don't be patronizing).

- Circumvent dominating behavior by breaking eye contact or turn from the person and invite others to participate.

- Revisit group rules and refer to any of the agreed upon behaviors that are being disrespected (sometime just walking over to and pointing at the posted ground rules will do the trick).

- Use the group and ask how people feel about the learning environment and clarify what is needed from participants.

- Redirect disruptive behavior by giving the disruptive person a responsibility, such as managing time or recording discussion points on a flipchart.

- Sometimes disagreements or awkward moments can be defused with appropriate, nonoffensive humor: "Okay, okay, can we *pleeeze* move on to the next topic now?"

- However, immediately address negative behavior when it is personally threatening to others.

- Change gears—introduce an energizer or tell a story to shift gears form an disruptive issue.

- Avoid arguments or singling out individuals into a standoff; back off and let people cool down. Do not take challenges personally or dig in your heels on nonessential issues.

- Discuss negative behaviors with individuals in private when necessary—during a break—or call them aside during an activity to determine if there is a problem.

- Focus on the behavior and not the person when individually confronting disruptive individuals.

- Ask the person to leave the workshop if disruptive or threatening behavior continues.

and take precedence over learning. People generally understand and respect adhering to an agenda but will appreciate if you need to readjust, that is, shorten a session to focus on one or two key learning points rather than trying to cover everything or answer all questions. In **Box 10.9**, we highlight some tips that can help manage time during an M&E training.

BOX 10.9
Tips for Time Management

- **Carefully design the training curriculum with attention to timing** (Chapter 8).

- **Have a large clock visible for everyone to see.**

- **Plan activities with "cushion" time** in case it takes longer to facilitate than expected. If you finish early, the extra time can always be used for an energizer or other training activities that may go overtime.

- **Be prepared** and have activities, materials, and audiovisual aid prepped and ready to go.

- **Pilot and practice training delivery**, so that you are familiar with the content and where you should be at 15 to 30 minute intervals.

- **Prioritize training content so you know what can be shortened or skipped if necessary.** When possible, plan essential topics/activities for early in the training, so if it goes overtime, the time devoted to nonessential material can be adjusted accordingly.

- **Recruit volunteers** and other people needed for activities beforehand to avoid delays.

- **Share the responsibility of time management with participants.** Assigning a timekeeper to help manage time.

- **Agree upon time limits for group activities and presentations beforehand.**

- **Agree on a time limit (e.g., two minutes) for individual contributions** that spontaneously arise to avoid long-winded speeches; set expectations and ground rules of this sort early on (discussed below).

- **Before the start of a break, agree on (or remind) people of the allotted time** and consider agreeing beforehand on a playful *penalty* for people who return late, such as having them sing a song or dance to prerecorded music.

(Continued)

(Continued)

- **Use attention-getters to start, reconvene, and close activities and session**. Some examples include a verbal wave in which people increasingly repeat after you that "time's up"; a silent signal in which people increasingly mimic you and fall silent (e.g., make a *T* with your hands); flick a light switch; play a song, use clapping, a kazoo, bell, squeaky toy animal, or a musical instrument.

- **Count down remaining time** to remind people how much time is left for each phase of the activity they are doing—for example, 20-minute, 10-minute, 5-minute warnings. Consider using cards with time increments written on them to warn people they are nearing the end of an activity or presentation and need to wrap up.

- **Float around and check in with people during an activity** to see how much more time they think they need and, when appropriate, adjust and announce the new time frame.

- **Expedite subgroup reporting** by having trainees visually list ideas for presenting on a flipchart or cards posted on the wall. Have each successive group report on one idea at a time, only adding new points rather than repeating those already covered.

- **Utilize a "parking lot"** (discussed below) to record and keep track of important ideas, issues, or questions that may not be timely and relevant when raised but can be addressed later in the training.

- **Utilize lunch and breaks to reassess and adjust the training agenda if necessary.**

- **If changes need to be made to the training agenda and content, discuss and validate them with participants**.

10.2 Facilitating the Workshop Introduction, Activities, and Closing

Having looked at some overall guidelines for training facilitation, it is helpful to consider how they more specifically apply to key stages during an M&E training workshop. During the training design, we discussed that there are an assortment of training activities for M&E, and in Part 3, we provide more detailed descriptions of activity types that can be used for M&E training. Two types of activities that every M&E training will have are the training introduction and the closing. The activities between will vary according to the training objectives but typically include presentation, instruction, practice, reflection and discussion, fun and games, and material review or assessments. Below we provide some overall guidance to consider when facilitating these three stages of a workshop.

The training introduction

First impressions are important, and a good introduction can go a long way to lay the foundation to successfully achieve training objectives; therefore, it deserves careful planning and attention. The introduction prepares trainees to participate in the training, reinforcing a safe and respectful atmosphere (Adult Learning Principle 1). Effective introductions usually consists of a number of activities that together stimulate people's interest in the training, allow them to get to know each other, and help them feel comfortable. It should respond to people's *need to know* what, why, and how they are to learn and establish a safe and respectful learning atmosphere (Adult Learning Principles 2). Below, we have outlined eight components to consider for a workshop introduction. What to include, their order, and how much time to devote to the introduction will depend the particular training needs and duration; that is, the introduction for a three-hour workshop will typically be much shorter than a three-day workshop.

1. Getting ready

To a certain extent, conducting a workshop is like giving a performance, and it is important to ensure the stage, lighting, props, costumes, and actors (trainers) are "lights, camera, action" ready to go. How smoothly this process will be when you arrive for the workshop will depend largely on how well you prepared beforehand, which we discussed in our prior chapter. Nevertheless, the unexpected will often arise, so it is best to arrive early, especially the first day of a multiday workshop. This also allows you to unwind and get comfortable and psychologically prepared to greet and focus on people when they arrive rather than being distracted, running around doing last-minute tasks. Below we have listed some "day-of" tasks to consider when you arrive for the workshop:

- Dress appropriately and respectful for the audience and culture.

- Place any signs in the facility and outside the door identifying the workshop location and time.

- Check the room set up, seating arrangements, sight lines, lighting, ventilation, power and extension cords, and so forth.

- Do last-minute presentation checks for the audiovisual equipment, computers, microphones, and so forth.

- Confirm where any support might be in the facility in case a problem needs to be addressed.

- Place participant training materials neatly on each seat or table spot—for example, manuals, binder of handouts, workbooks, agenda, markers, pens, and additional resources.

- Supply water and refreshments (if appropriate).

- Place name tags or plates where each participant will sit if seats are to be assigned, or leave the name tags blank if they are to be used for an introduction activity (see below).

- Prepare your wall space with any teaching aids, such as posters, a large agenda, flipchart paper for a parking lot (see below), ground rules, and so forth.

- Prepare yourself—review participants' names, turn to the right page of your facilitation notes, cue the start of any presentation slides, videos, or recordings you will be using, and so forth.

2. Meet and greet

As participants arrive, the trainer should not appear disorganized, uninterested, or distracted but should warmly greet people and help to make them feel welcome. This is an opportunity to establish rapport and show genuine interest in people. A couple tips to consider for when people arrive are following:

- **Have something ready to say when you first meet participants**, even if it is something as simple as acknowledging how far they have travelled to get to the workshop, asking about their accommodation, their breakfast—was it good?—and so forth.

- **Have something for participants to do while waiting for everyone to arrive**. For example, personalizing their name cards/tags with a quote, picture, or color indicating their level of M&E experience. Participants can also prepare for an activity to follow, such as writing down on sticky notes or cards expectations or ideas for training ground rules.

3. Gain their attention

As we discussed for training design, it is good practice to begin training by gaining people's attention, stimulating their interest in the M&E topic/s and explaining why the material is worth learning. This can be particularly important for M&E, because despite the best efforts to positively frame M&E in pre-training messaging, some people may find it threatening or boring. Therefore, rather than starting off with a long-winded description of the training objectives and agenda, consider how to spark people's interest right away. A couple examples include

- **Begin with an interesting or humorous story, quote, cartoon, or video** that underscores the importance of M&E, how it can be useful, or what happens when it is not done well or is absent.

- **Kick off the training with a fun, nonthreatening icebreaker or activity** that gets people talking to one another and participating immediately. Consider an activity that helps achieve other objectives for the training, such as introductions, sharing expectations, or related to M&E content later in the training.

4. Introductions and expectations

Even if the training is under a few hours, it is helpful to give people a chance to get to know each other and share their reasons and any reservations they have about M&E training. This helps not only trainers but also trainees understand the diversity and different motives among each other. It also helps deflate initial tensions and misgivings and build a sense of community and a warm, welcoming atmosphere for learning. Also, people are often interested in getting to know each other for networking after training. When people are already familiar with themselves, introductions can be conducted in such a way that they learn something new or relevant to the training topic.

There are an assortment of icebreakers and activities for introducing people and sharing training expectations and concerns. We summarized some examples we have found useful in Part 3 (p. 319), and following are some considerations for when facilitating introductions and expectations:

- **Introductions and expectations activities can be combined or done separately**, and the time devoted to them will vary according to training need. When time is constrained, it can be as quick as the "minute intro" or more involved with people sharing their M&E experience, interests, concerns, expectations, and goals.

- **Consider whether it is appropriate for the culture/audience to use methods that stress anonymity and protect people's identify when providing information** (e.g., response cards). For many people, it is empowering to share about themselves and reassuring to discover others have similar goals or concerns for training. However, some people may be intimidated and hesitant to share personal expectations and fears, especially when just getting to know each other. Even when people are already familiar with each other, such as during an organizational workshop among colleagues, they may feel vulnerable expressing what they really think about or expect from the training (e.g., with their manager or supervisors present).

- **Trainers should participate in introductions and expectations as equals**, so participants understand who they are and that they too have personal expectations, concerns, and goals. In addition to interest and enthusiasm, this allows trainers to modestly convey their credentials and experience and establish credibility.

- **Use the training introductions and expectations to model active listening and a sincere interest in the trainees**, establishing rapport.

- **Acknowledge and reflect upon what people share and summarize similarities and differences in people's responses.** People's M&E backgrounds and expectations typically vary, which is handy to point out so people understand that the learning pace and content may also vary, and while it may feel slow for some, it may be challenging for others. In turn, this can help frame ground rules for a patient and supporting learning environment for differentiated learning (Adult Learning Principle 10).

5. Training objectives, agenda, and materials

Trainees may have already been informed of the training objectives prior to the workshop, but it is important to review them together as a group and address any questions or concerns. When training expectations have already been shared, it is useful to relate then to learning objectives to reinforce buy-in and ownership.

This is also a good opportunity to discuss the workshop agenda as it relates to each learning objectives. Keeping in mind the adult learning principle of primacy, this "big picture" provides a shared sense of direction of key M&E topics for training, helping people anticipate what to expect, reinforcing the adult learning principle "need to know." When reviewing the agenda, it is a good idea to point out that it may need to be readjusted to best meet the group's learning needs. This is also a good time to introduce the training materials and resources that have been provided to trainees to help them understand how they will be used during the training.

6. Ground rules and group work

It is useful at the beginning of a workshop to agree upon the basic norms and guidelines for how people should interact and work together. This reinforces Adult Learning Principle 1, to establish a safe and effective learning environment where people are respectful and supportive of each other and feel comfortable learning and trying new things. It is good to build a list of ground rules from suggestions from the group and ensure everyone agrees to abide by them. This can then be posted on the wall and referred to when norms are not being respected. Figure 10.1 is an example of some common ground rules used in training workshops.

This is also a good opportunity to discuss group time management and introduce the *parking lo*t (**Figure 10.1**).[2] The parking lot is a visual training aid used to keep track of or *park* important ideas, questions, and issues that may not be appropriate to

---

2. Depending on the training context, participants, and culture, other terms can be used: for example, refrigerator (to store food later to digest), water cooler (to let hot topics cool down for later discussion), and so forth.

FIGURE 10.1   Examples of a Parking Lot and Ground Rules

immediately discuss and address when they are first raised, because they can distract or sidetrack the discussion and topics at hand. Sometimes the items in the parking lot are addressed later in the training, in which case they can be checked-off, or if left unaddressed, they should be revisited at the training closing. The parking lot helps ensure people feel acknowledged and heard, noting their questions or concerns to address later in the workshop, or afterward if more appropriate.

When discussing how people will work together, it is also a good time to explain the rationale for forming groups and how they will be managed during the workshop; that is, whether groups will be reformed, why, and the importance of group composition to best support peer learning and sharing. Depending on the planned activities, initial groups or teams may be formed at this time (if not earlier as an introduction activity). Part 3 (p. 339) presents some examples of activities to form groups.

7. Housekeeping—logistics

Typically, there are additional practical matters to discuss with participants for efficiently running the workshop. This can include the locations of toilets, Internet codes, lunch arrangements (e.g., confirming who is to be served meals for restricted diets—for example, vegetarian meals), wastepaper bins, and so forth. If appropriate, identify any point person (other than the trainer) that trainees are to approach if they have an administrative or logistical question or concern.

8. Training feedback, evaluation, and pre-tests

It is also important to discuss how participants can give immediate or urgent feedback during the training about any problems or concerns they may have. Trainers should genuinely convey receptivity to feedback and explain arrangements made for workshop feedback. This can include end of session/day debriefs or feedback forms, a comment envelope located in the room for anonymous feedback, and approaching the trainer privately during breaks.

Related, this is a good opportunity to review any arrangements made for training evaluation. It is recommended to introduce beforehand any session, daily, or end-of-workshop feedback or evaluation forms so people know what to expect, understand the purpose, and give their consent. Related, trainees can begin to note feedback during the training itself on the forms, while ideas are fresh as they arise. If a pre-test is to be conducted during the workshop, this is also a good time to introduce its purpose and conduct it *before* starting on the training content.

Training Tip

When introducing any evaluation or feedback forms and procedures for training, use the time as a teaching moment to relate the process of data collection and feedback to M&E good practice. Discuss the principle of obtaining informed consent for evaluation, the use of the end-of-workshop evaluation form for *summative* evaluation, and the use of feedback during the workshop (monitoring) for *formative* evaluation of the training.

Activity facilitation

No matter what type of training is planned, there will be activities, even if only the presentation of material (e.g., lecture). During the design of the training curriculum (Chapter 8), we recommended the selection of a variety of activities, with particular attention to the learning objectives, audience, and time frame. Whether an activity is done individually, in pairs, in small groups, or as a large group, there are certain common elements that are useful to review. There is no rigid rule on how an activity is structured. Below we will take a look at some considerations for facilitating an M&E activity based on four stages often used to structure activities: an introduction, doing the activity, a debrief, and conclusion.[3]

1. Activity introduction

The activity introduction shares many common elements with the overall introduction to the training, but its focus is narrower to prepare learners for the specific learning objectives and planned activity. Key considerations include the following:

- **Gain their attention**. As during the introduction for the overall training, begin by posing a challenging question, problem, interesting story, visual, cartoon, or quote. For example, prior to an activity on data collection and analysis, display Albert Einstein's quote, "Not everything that can be counted counts, and not everything that counts can be counted," and use this to springboard a discussion to introduce the topic.

- **Clearly frame the purpose of the activity and how it relates to the learning objectives/topics** (Adult Learning Principles 2 and 6). Satisfy the need to know—why the activity is important, how it relates to real world needs, and why it is worth their time. Engage participants by asking questions like, "Why do you think we are doing this activity?" "How can this help you outside of the training?"

- **Stimulate recall of prior learning and experience** (Adult Learning Principle 5). This helps learners relate what they are to do with prior understanding and acknowledges the learners themselves as a source of learning. It also gives the trainer an idea of the level of understanding among participants so they can adjust the activity and composition of any working groups accordingly (helping to support differentiated instruction, Adult Learning Principle 10).

- **Provide clear instructions so people understand what is expected of them** (Adult Learning Principle 2). Even if the activity is only a lecture presentation, frame how people can prepare questions or comments for debrief. Include how much time should be spent on the activity and its parts, so that time management is mutually understood and can be shared. Also describe any responsibilities for group activities, such as a moderator, scribe, reporter, and so forth

---

3. To a large extent, this generic progression reflects Gagné's Nine Events of Instruction, discussed in Chapter 8.

- **In addition to oral instructions, visually reinforce directions with written instructions**—for example, a handout, projected slide, transparency, or posted flipchart paper. In this way, trainees can refer to instructions during the exercise to stay on task. Consider having participants write out activity steps on a flipchart paper for others to see and validate mutual understanding.

- **Answer questions, address concerns, and agree on the activity plan.** Ensure there is understanding and buy-in for what is planned, which can help participants manage the learning process themselves. Depending on the activity, someone may have a good suggestion to improve it—for example, during one training a participant suggested rating small group presentations at the end of the activity based on "evaluation" criteria that the group came up with themselves.

2. During the activity

The activity provides the "experience" that will be used to reflect upon, process, and learn from (Adult Learning Principle 7). Its facilitation will vary, depending on whether it is a presentation or individual, sub-group, or plenary group work. Key considerations include the following:

- **Ensure there is adequate time and carefully manage it.** A rushed activity, whether a presentation or group work, can really undermine the learning process. For hands-on experiential activities, ensure there is ample time for practice and repetition to reinforce learning, and build confidence and competence (Adult Learning Principle 12).

- **Make it fun and active** (Adult Learning Principle 8). For presentations, make them interactive with questions and more engaging, funny or entertaining by using different media (see relevant sections in this chapter above). For group activities, consider having people do stand-up discussion, rearranging or rotating sub-groups, and using games, contests, and fun interactive exercises to make learning more enjoyable.

- **Monitor people throughout the activity.** Whether the activity is a presentation or interactive group work, the trainer should be aware of how people are doing. This is especially important at the start of individual and group activities to check that people understand what is expected and do not stall, and then during the activity to see if they are on track or if the activity needs to be modified to address differentiated learning (Adult Learning Principle 10).

- **Provide feedback and positive reinforcement as appropriate** (Adult Learning Principle 14). Feedback, whether corrective or approving, is best provided when the learning moment is immediate and fresh. However, it is also important to maintain a low profile, allowing people to work with the activity themselves, experiment, and learn from their peers (Adult Learning Principle 11). When providing feedback, highlight what has been done well and frame corrective feedback positively, praising people for training regardless of accomplishment.

- **Remind participants of the "good enough" principle.** When an activity results in products, people can become very intent, anxious, or even competitive, especially when they are to share what they have done with others during the activity debrief. Remind them that within the time given for an activity you do not expect perfection or a *dissertation* but their best attempt to identify key learning points from the exercise.

- **Remember that problems can be learning opportunities.** If individuals or groups get held up and are unable to accomplish everything—to the standards they would like—consider letting them deviate and identify specific challenges and lessons to share during the activity debrief.

- **Answer questions as they arise**, and if it is a good question that others might have during individual or group activities, answer it in a plenary manner so others can learn from it.

3. Activity debrief

The activity debrief provides an opportunity for participants to reflect upon and process what has happened to support learning and to make connections (generalize) between their learning experience and real life situations. Key considerations include the following:

- **Schedule enough time to conduct the debrief.** The debrief is an important element of an activity that is often overlooked or conducted superficially; however, it is a critical part of the activity to make sense of and learn from what has happened, and adequate time should be spent on it.

- **Vary discussion methods so they do not become routine and tiresome;** see example facilitation activities in Part 3.

- **Consider whether it is appropriate to use discussion methods that let people anonymously or more equitably share their opinions and express themselves.**

- **Use questioning to lead participants to discuss what has occurred** (see above discussion in this chapter). A generic progression is *what, so what*, and *now what*. Other specific questions include What happened? What did people experience and feel? Was the activity easy or hard? What problems did you encounter and why? What did you learn? How would you do it differently? How might this apply to real life situations (with your job)? Will this be useful for you after the training? How?

- **Let participants lead the debrief** (Adult Learning Principle 4). This is an opportune time to give participants the power to participate in and make sense of their learning, supporting peer and collaborative approaches to learning. Initially, the trainer may frame and model the particular method used for the debrief but then hand it off once participants understand the process. When necessary, the trainer can step in to guide the process with leading questions, ensure equal participation, provide clarifications, and recap or summarize key points for consensus.

- **Use the debrief for feedback on each other** (Adult Learning Principles 4, 11, and 14). As people explore what and how they learned, it is a good opportunity for peer feedback and for the trainer to supplement and summarize feedback provided during the activity. Again, allow participants to take the lead, as it is more meaningful when feedback points are elicited and discussed by the participants themselves.

- **Use the debrief for feedback on the activity itself** (Adult Learning Principles 4 and 14). The debrief can also be a good opportunity to get timely and relevant input on the activity and how it might be improved for future use. Consider asking participants how they might do the activity differently in the future. This also empowers trainees as equals in the learning process, validating their experience and expertise. However, it should be used carefully, and difficulty with the activity does not necessarily mean that it was not useful or effective (per our following point).

- **Acknowledge difficulties and misgivings, but frame the debrief positively**. Even when an exercise did not achieve its intended objectives, there is still learning that can be had. Examine and discuss problems and ask participants how they can learn from them to help them in the future after training when actually applying what they have learned.

- **Take notes during the debrief to capture and validate key points**. The trainer may record points on a flipchart, or it can be participant-led, depending on the discussion method used.

- **Identify any topics, questions, or ideas to follow up on**. Often, there will be issues or ideas that arise during the activity or debrief that are relevant for learning but beyond the content scope or time allotted for the activity. For example, an activity may underscore a recommendation for an organization to improve its M&E practices. Acknowledge and validate such ideas and add them to a parking lot to follow up on later in the workshop or afterward.

4. Activity closing

The activity conclusion is used to wrap up the discussion and key learning points from the activity and is often combined seamlessly with the activity debrief. Key considerations include the following:

- Review key learning points, group consensus, or points of disagreement and how the activity relates to the overall training objectives.

- Answer any remaining questions, add any final additional points, and address any final concerns.

- Revisit how the activity relates to what has been learnt thus far in the workshop and frame how it relates to what is ahead. This is an important step to help trainees organize and integrate training content and prepare for what is next (Adult Learning Principles 2 and 3).

- Consider taking digital pictures of activity products and summary notes from the debrief as a record and review tool for later.

- Validate any parking lot ideas.

The training closing

This final session of the training shares some similarities with an activity closing, but the scope is wider to bring overall closure to the workshop, final items to conclude, and considerations for training follow-up and learning transfer in the future. The length of the closing session will depend on a variety of factors, such as the overall duration of the workshop and amount of material to review, the number of follow-up items in the parking lot, whether a post-test is planned, the detail of arrangements made for training follow-up, and so forth. Below we discuss the key elements to consider for the workshop closing.

- **Content review**. The final training review should summarize M&E topics and learning points, helping people organize and integrate what they have learned. This is an important element for Adult Learning Principle 12 to support repetition, reinforcing key learning points and building confidence and competence. It also contributes to the Adult Learning Principle 13 for recency: Information learned last (most recently) is best remembered, "fixing" in the learners' mind key messages to leave with them. Content review should be structured regularly throughout the training, but at this stage it should be more comprehensive, focusing of the major topics and learning points to underscore. It is also an important opportunity for people to ask and clarify those lingering questions.

By this time of the workshop, people may be tired, or like *horses to the barn*, they may be thinking about leaving, what they will do next, and so forth. Therefore, it is recommended to make the training review energetic and lively to ensure people are engaged. There are a variety of active and fun ways this can be facilitated, which we discuss in Part 3 (p. 375).

- **Post-test**. If a post-test is to be conducted during the training, it is a good opportunity to combine it with the review. In Part 3 (p. 380) we provide an example of how a post-test can be graded in such a manner to (a) support and reinforce learning and (b) allow people to see the level of immediate change in KSA among each other. If a post-test is to be conducted sometime after training (e.g., online), details should be clarified with trainees (supplementing any information provided about this during the training introduction).

- **Parking lot review**. Earlier we discussed the use of a parking lot to store ideas, questions, and issues appropriate to follow-up at a later point in the workshop. At this stage, any items not already checked off should be revisited with participants. This is often combined with the training follow-up discussed below.

- **Training debrief and follow-up**. Just as an opportunity for reflection and processing is recommended during a debrief for individual training activities, it is important to also allow participants to do so for the overall training itself. This helps people consider what they have learned and conceptualize how it may be used in real life after they leave the workshop. The reflection can be conducted as a separate activity from training follow-up, but obviously the two are interconnected. As people project into the future, it is helpful to have them identify potential opportunities, roadblocks, and available resources to support their M&E understanding and practice following the training.

As we discussed in Chapter 8, training follow-up can play an important role in learning transfer and should be carefully planned for during training design. Participants may have already been briefed on plans for training follow-up; for example, they have prepared a personal development plan prior to training, or other arrangements may have been made with management for an organizational training. Or this may be their first time really considering how they will follow-up. Whatever the circumstance, it is important to spend some time discussing this with participants. The range of options is wide, and we summarize some examples in Part 3 (p. 393).

At a minimal, it is recommended to review key M&E resources (people, websites, materials, etc.) available for trainees following training, for which a summary handout is very useful. It is also recommended that trainers let people know about their availability for questions immediately after the training and for additional support in the future.

- **Training feedback and evaluation** (Adult Learning Principles 4 and 14). Training feedback and evaluation can be conducted in a number of ways, depending the training need, which we will discuss in more detail in Chapter 11. In addition to individual feedback that may be provided through a written evaluation form, there are a variety of other methods for people to anonymously and openly share their thoughts on the training content, facilitation, and each other (examples of which we provide in Part 3, p. 382). To a large extent, feedback discussions and activities are also part of the training debrief, with the emphasis on feedback for the training and each other. Discussion during the training debrief on *what* they learned and *how* to follow-up often spills over into *how* they learned, focusing on the training process and each other. This is fine, and it may be preferable to combine training feedback with the debrief. We discuss it separately just to highlight it as a key component of the training closing; however, it may be structured into the closing.

- **Closing ceremony/celebration**. However formal or festive, it is worth considering having a final activity to acknowledge and thank the participants for their hard work as well as anyone involved in sponsoring and supporting the training. Related, this is a good opportunity to take any group pictures, hand out any certificates, and stage any final speakers (e.g., from organizational management) to commend and endorse the training and the trainees. In Part 3 (p. 388), we provide some examples to consider.

As this chapter reflects, there is no shortage of considerations for training implementation. For more experienced trainers, many of these may be implicit.

However, we have tried to make these tips for training facilitation more explicit, not only for those new to training but as a reminder/checklist for veteran trainers. The guidance we provide is grounded in the adult learning principles introduced in Chapter 4, and while we have identified at certain points in our discussion examples activities in Part 3 to support specific practices, the reader will find addition exercises and examples in that section of the book.

10.3 CHAPTER SUMMARY

Having "sowed the ground" during the training design and development, this chapter covers what is needed in order to bring the training to life. To the extent the training is well conceptualized, implementation will be more straightforward. This is not to say that it will be easy, because the trainer will be confronted with many challenges. It is to say that inadequate planning can only add to the intensity of challenges. Much of what we have shared in this chapter is grounded in our own practical wisdom and common sense. Key points to highlight include the following:

- A good part of this chapter focuses on effective training facilitation, and therefore we begin highlighting some key indicators for this: Trainees should feel comfortable and safe, be engaged yet unrushed, fully participate in their learning, and have mutual respect and trust for the trainer.

- Effective communication is more than just clear speaking; it also involves listening to people—both what they say and what they *do*. Careful preparation and innovative approaches, such as the use of pocket examples and metaphors, can go a long way to make presentations more successful.

- Cultural competence is an important ingredient for effective facilitation and relating to trainees.

It includes an understanding of not only other cultures but also your own in relation to them.

- Questioning is a basic but fundamental skill for effective facilitation, allowing to clarify learning points and engage learners. There are a variety of different techniques for both asking and responding to questions.

- Training aids are used by both trainers and trainees to clarify learning content and make learning more engaging, supporting a more multisensory approach to learning for different learning styles.

- Facilitating training discussions is a balancing act between guiding and not dominating discussion, supporting a safe forum for learners to equally express themselves.

- Monitoring and feedback during training can be unstructured or planned, focus on learning or the training process, and be facilitated in groups or provided individually. When well facilitated, monitoring and feedback play a critical role in empowering learners and guiding their learning process.

- Co-facilitation brings to training the expertise and energy of another trainer, but it should be carefully planned and coordinated to ensure success and avoid potential challenges.

- We do not want to plan for disruptive behavior to happen, but it is important to know how to respond if it arises so that it does not comprise a safe and supportive learning environment.

- Time management can be one of the most challenging aspects of training facilitation. In addition to careful consideration during the design of the training curriculum, we outline a variety of tips for effective time management.

- In the last section of this chapter, we provide some key considerations when facilitating a face-to-face training workshop:

  - Be prepared! As we foretold in our previous chapter, there is are myriad of logistical preparations to ensure are in place.

  - First impressions set the tone, so deliver a planned introduction, framing the workshop objectives, agenda, ground rules, and other key messages, while allowing participants to get to know each other and relax into the training.

  - Activity facilitation includes the activity introduction, implementation, debrief, and closing, employing the guidance tips summarized above. Be sure to plan adequate time for the debrief and closing to allow learners to reflect upon and generalize from the learning activity.

  - Last impressions are lasting (Adult Learning Principle 13—recency), so utilize the training closing to review key learning points and end on a positive tone. Well-planned knowledge consolidation elements help participants make connections to their own lives (workplace) after training. This is also the time to conduct any end of training assessment of learning (e.g., post-tests) and the training itself (training evaluation).

10.4 RECOMMENDED RESOURCES

This chapter provides an *overview* of training facilitation, for which there are a variety of resources available for readers to further explore this topic. Five books that we recommend on the topic include *The Skillful Teacher* (Brookfield, 2006), *The Complete Facilitator's Handbook* (Heron, 1999), *Learner-Centered Teaching* (Weimer, 2002), and *The Art of Great Training Delivery* (Barbazette, 2006).

There is also an assortment of useful publications for training facilitation available for free download online. We highly recommend the guide from the International Institute for Environment and Development, *A Trainer's Guide for Participatory Learning & Action* (Pretty, Gujit, Scoones, & Thompson, 1995), which also provides an overview of other topics related to the whole training cycle. The FAO offers a sourcebook on principles of participatory methods and approaches for trainers that can be accessed on its interactive website (Chatty, Baas, & Fleig, 2003), and we also recommend the user-friendly manual on learner-centered training from AIBD and UNESCO (McDaniel & Brown, 2001).

The website of the Free Management Library (2015) has a helpful interactive webpage, *All About Facilitation, Group Skills and Group Performance Management.* Similarly, Businessballs (2015) has an assortment of useful topics for facilitation, ranging from presentation skills and visual aids to body language and running workshops. The training toolkit on the website of I-TECH (2015) has a helpful webpage on *Training Delivery—Online Resources for Implementing Training*. On the topic of instructional aids, we found the slideshow by Margeret Pullante (2015) a very user-friendly overview on the topic.

Another source for practical guidance on training facilitation as well as other topics is training of trainer (ToT) guides. For example, we recommend the following resources freely available online: the trainer and participant guides by Pathfinder International (2007), *Advanced Training of Trainers*; the ILO's *Trainer's Toolbox of Training Techniques* (Mason, 1995); MicroSave's *Training of Trainer* manual (Frankiewiez & Parrott, 2006); and the facilitator's guide developed by Communication for Change (C-Change, 2012).

In addition to the resource highlighted in Box 10.4, *Culture Matters* (Peace Corps, 2014), we refer readers to the recommended resources in Chapter 5 to consider cultural competence for facilitation. Lastly, we also refer readers to Chapter 12, in which we profile 20 different categories of methods and techniques for training facilitation and identify additional recommended resources that are useful for training facilitation.

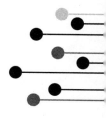

CHAPTER 11

Training Evaluation

This chapter introduces basic concepts and practices to plan for and conduct evaluations for M&E training. Although training evaluation is the last phase in the ADDIE model for training, it should be carefully considered and prepared for early as part of training design and development (as noted in Chapters 8 and 9). This will help ensure that training objectives are aligned with measurable results, and assessment tools can be prepared beforehand.

Historically, the evaluation of training has been neglected (Brinkerhoff, 1989; Goldstein & Ford, 2002; Guskey, 2000). This is because of a combination of reasons, including a fear of being held accountable; the perception that evaluation is costly and time consuming, and that it diverts resources and attention from training planning and implementation; and a lack of skill and expertise for conducting training evaluation. "The result is that they either neglect evaluation issues completely, or leave them to 'evaluation experts' who are called in at the end and asked to determine if what was done made any difference" (Guskey, 2000, p. 68). It is our aim that this chapter will help ensure that meaningful and useful evaluation is practiced for M&E training, providing readers with an understanding of the importance of and knowledge to conduct evaluations that contribute to better M&E training.

Learning Objectives

By the end of this chapter readers will be able to . . .

✓ Describe what is training evaluation

✓ Explain major methodological approaches and limitations for training evaluation

✓ Outline key steps to plan for and conduct training evaluation

✓ Determine who will conduct the training evaluation

11.1 What Is Training Evaluation?

In its Program Evaluation Standards, the Joint Committee on Standards for Educational Evaluation defines evaluation as "The systematic investigation of the worth of merit

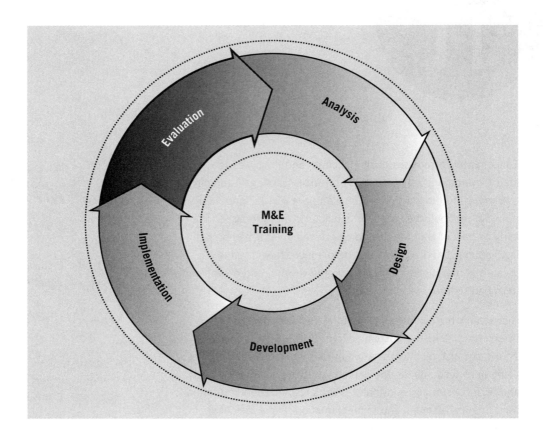

of an object" (JCSEE, 1994, p. 3). Adapting this, we can define training evaluation as the *systematic investigation of the worth or merit of training.* Similarly, the U.S. Office of Personnel Management defines training evaluation as "a continual and systematic process of assessing the value or potential value of a training program, course, activity or event. Results of the evaluation are used to guide decision-making around various components of the training (e.g., instructional design, delivery, results) and its overall continuation, modification, or elimination" (USOPM, 2015). Both definitions convey that a judgment is being made about the quality or effectiveness of the training and that the evaluation is "systematic," meaning it is intentional and planned, involving the collection, analysis, and communication of information to answer key questions to guide decision-making for M&E training.

To a large degree, training evaluation has many similarities with the debrief of a training activity we discussed in our prior chapter on training implementation. In his influential book on utilization-focused evaluation, Michael Patton (2012, p. 3) identifies the same three questions for evaluation as we identified for debriefing training activities: *what, so what*, and *now what*. Such core questions trace a sequence of inquiry of what happened during training, what difference it made, and what recommendations can be made for training. Later in this chapter we will consider how these questions can be focused to different aspects of training and its results.

There are a variety of evaluation types. For example, evaluations can be categorized according to who conducts the evaluation—such as self-evaluations—or internal versus external or independent evaluations. Evaluations can also be classified according to their method or focus, such as process, impact, or empowerment evaluations. However, the most fundamental distinction of evaluation types is according to the evaluation timing, primarily, whether it is formative or summative (Scriven, 1967):

- **Formative evaluation** occurs during training development (e.g., a pilot training) and implementation (e.g., quizzes and real-time feedback from trainees). It is typically conducted for the purpose of improving training before it is completed, helping trainers monitor the learning process and modify training to best achieve learning objectives. It helps identify and track what is and is not working, provide feedback for both trainers and trainees, and address problems immediately.

- **Summative evaluation** is conducted at the end of and/or after training implementation (e.g., post-tests, post-training surveys or interviews). Its purpose reflects our above definition of training evaluation: to determine the overall worth or merit of the training. It helps answer the *so what* question, providing decision-makers with information to make decisions about future training, for example, whether training should adopted, changed, or discontinued.

In summary, formative evaluation is more process focused and done *for* training improvement, while summative evaluation is more outcomes focused and done *of* training effectiveness. Summative evaluation encompasses the results identified for training, which includes learning as well as other training objectives, and should also include any unintended outcomes that may also arise. It is important to note that information from formative evaluation can also contribute to the summative evaluation. Both can include assessment of individual learning as well as other aspects of the training. For example, in addition to "paper-and-pencil" assessment of knowledge, daily or session evaluation forms during the workshop and after it is completed can focus on participant perception of training content, environment, and facilitation.

Terminology Tip
Comparing *Assessment, Evaluation,* and *Monitoring for Training*

In training, it is important to make the distinction between *learning assessment* and *training evaluation*. With learning assessment, the unit analysis is the individual trainees and their level of KSA and performance. This can be used to determine trainee readiness for and design of training, monitor progress during training, assess trainee readiness to perform after training, and assess long-term retention of learning after training. In comparison, the unit of analysis for training evaluation is more broadly the *entire* training and its effectiveness or worth. Individual learning assessment contributes to training evaluation, but the latter also includes judgment of other aspects of training (e.g., content, the trainer, facilitation, training planning, and follow-up). *Monitoring* is the ongoing process of tracking how well training is being implemented. This includes learning progress, the training process (facilitation), and the training context (training facility, equipment, and the overall learning environment). Monitoring can be informal observation, or it can involve structured activities to assess learning and provide feedback on the training itself. When monitoring is systematic and intentionally planned, it contributes to formative evaluation.

11.2 Training Evaluation Methods—An Overview

No evaluation methodology can be all things to all people in all situations, and the scholarly debate is contentious about the pros and cons of the various methods used in training evaluation. We will limit our discussion to two methodological approaches that we feel are appropriate for an introductory chapter on the topic: a levels approach and a logical framework approach. Both approaches reflect an approach to evaluation based on program theory, which makes explicit the theory of change and action planned for a program to bring about intended or desired results (Funnell & Rogers, 2011).

A "levels approach" to training evaluation

A good place to begin considering training evaluation methods is Kirkpatrick's "four levels for evaluating training programs" (Kirkpatrick, 1959, 1996). Since its introduction in 1959, it has become the most prominent framework for training evaluation (Falletta, 1998). In our discussion of training analysis (Chapter 7), we introduced Kirkpatrick's four levels to help elaborate the backward planning approach for training analysis. The Kirkpatrick model is based on one or more of four criteria or outcomes presented as levels, as we summarize in **Table 11.1**. It was

TABLE 11.1   Kirkpatrick's 4 Levels for Training Evaluation

Level	Guiding Questions	Example Measurement Methods
4. Results	Were longer-term outcomes achieved for trainees or the organization?	Post-training questionnaires, interviews, performance reviews, organizational assessment, program evaluation
3. Behavior	Have trainees applied what they learned after training?	Post-training questionnaires, interviews, observation, and performance reviews
2. Learning	How much did trainees learn during training (changes in KSA)?	Individual assessment at the completion of and after training, for example, written tests, demonstration
1. Reaction	How satisfied are trainees with the training?	Satisfaction survey (e.g., smile sheets)

developed for evaluating business and industry training programs, with behavioral changes (Level 3) focused on job performance and results (Level 4) on organizational outcomes. However, as we illustrate, the model can and has be adapted to evaluate both organizational and non-organizational training.

Kirkpatrick's model is sequential, with each level building upon the one that came before, with increasing complexity in measurement. Level 1 focuses on trainee satisfaction: whether they felt training was effective and worthwhile. This includes their perception of the training content and materials, trainers and facilitation, and the training setting. It is the easiest and most common form of training evaluation, typically measured by questionnaires ("smile sheets") at the completion of training. Level 2 measures the learning objectives identified for training and becomes more challenging to measure. It is typically assessed by written evidence (e.g., pre/post-tests or assignments) and observation of performance at the completion of training, and longer-term learning retention requires post-training follow-up and assessment.

Levels 3 and 4 in Kirkpatrick's model need to be measured after trainees have had time and opportunity to apply in the workplace what they learned, to determine whether it has made a difference. They are more difficult to measure as it is more challenging to verify whether a trainee is really using what they learned and to attribute any longer-term individual or organizational change to training. Consequently, these two levels are the least commonly measured.

Kirkpatrick's four levels model is not without its critics (e.g., Allinger & Janak, 1989; Bates, 2004; Holton, 1996), and while it is beyond the scope of this book to review such controversy in detail, we do want to highlight three major limitations. First, the model is simplistic in the linear causality between each level. Success at one level will not necessarily equate with outcome attainment at the next level. Participant satisfaction with training does not guarantee trainees *learned*; similarly, learning does not mean trainees will necessarily *apply* what they learned; and even if used, there is no assurance individual behavioral change will contribute to longer-term outcomes identified for training (whether for the individual or organization). These linkages among levels need to be considered as necessary but insufficient to the attainment of the next level, and the entire process is likely to be less linear than implied. Second, Kirkpatrick's approach fails to take into account the mediating value of workplace context, which may be complex and highly variable, as would be the case in organizational training. Third, the model focuses on intended outcomes and does not capture unanticipated outcomes and or changes, for good or bad, that may be attributable to the training but not aligned with its goals and objectives.

Criticism aside, since introduced in 1959, Kirkpatrick's four-level conceptualization has withstood the test of time.[1] The criticism that it is simplistic is one of the very reasons it has been so widely embraced; it is intuitive and easy to understand, helping people to think about training evaluation criteria. Further, the four levels are flexible and can be adapted to different training contexts and needs (as we illustrated for backward planning). The model has been modified in numerous ways, from the evaluation of e-learning programs (e.g., Hamtini, 2008) to higher education (Praslova, 2010), and Phillips (1994) adds a fifth level to measure return on investment (ROI), which examines whether the benefits of training were worth the cost.

One variation of Kirkpatrick's model we find particularly compelling is Guskey's five-level framework for evaluating professional development, which we summarize in **Figure 11.1** (Guskey, 2000). Developed in the education sector, Guskey's first two levels match Kirkpatrick's for reactions and learning, but the next three levels present a different configuration. Level 3 is of particular interest, as it acknowledges the mediational importance of *context* or organizational leadership, policies, and practices that can support or hinder M&E capacity building efforts (this we highlighted in Chapter 3 on the capacity building context). While Level 4 is similar to Kirkpatrick's Level 3 (transfer of learned KSA), its order in Guskey's levels underscores that organizational factors can help explain trainee use of new knowledge and skills. Any gains made at Levels 1 and 2 can be "canceled at Level 3" if organizational policies are not compatible with training implementation efforts (Guskey, 2000, p. 84). At Level 5 in Guskey's model, the emphasis is on organizational impact, defined as student outcomes, the bottom line in educational organizations. (As we discuss below, this reflects Guskey's orientation to the educational sector.)

---

1. For example, it is endorsed by the American Society for Training and Development and adopted by numerous organizations, such as the U.S. Office of Personnel Management (Falletta, 1998; USOPM, 2011).

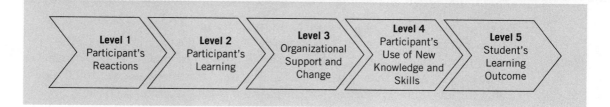

FIGURE 11.1   Guskey's Five Levels for Evaluating Professional Development

| Level 1 Participant's Reactions | Level 2 Participant's Learning | Level 3 Organizational Support and Change | Level 4 Participant's Use of New Knowledge and Skills | Level 5 Student's Learning Outcome |

Like Kirkpatrick's four levels, Guskey's five levels are hierarchical, with increasing complexity in measurement. It is also outcome focused and developed for organizational settings—schools. However, in contrast to a business/industry setting, where organizational performance and profit is typically the end goal, schools prioritize learning. Guskey's model can be easily adapted to noneducational contexts by elaborating what organizational results might be (if not classroom student outcomes). Another key distinction is that the model has more "explanatory power" (Guskey, 2000, p. 78). In addition to including important organizational effects on training transfer, Guskey stresses that unintended outcomes should be examined at Levels 2 and 5. Such an approach provides a more complete picture to help explain what is measured in training evaluation.

A logical framework approach for training evaluation

Another method for evaluating training is the use of a *logical framework* or *logframe*. A logframe is logic model in the form of a matrix (table) that provides a visual road map summarizing how to achieve intended results. It summarizes a program's logic or theory of change to make explicit how resources and planned activities are to bring about intended or desired results (outcomes). Logframes are used as much as a planning tool to design projects and programs (in our case M&E training) as to monitor and evaluate them.

The logical framework approach was initially developed in the late 1960s to guide the design and evaluation of international programs.[2] Since, it has been widely adapted for both international and domestic programming. However, developing a logframe is an involved process that may be more appropriate for M&E training programs with multiple training events and activities or when training is one component of a larger program rather than a single training event (e.g., workshop) of short duration. Logframes can be developed after (or during) training for evaluation but are most

2. The use of logframes is actually a form of program theory evaluation, for which Kirkpatrick's Four Levels of Learning Evaluation can be considered one of the earliest examples (Funnell & Rogers, 2011).

effective when developed early during training design. Knowing the intended results (as per the backward design approach) will go a long way to ensure learning objectives are relevant and make it possible to develop the methods and tools for their assessment *prior to* training delivery.

We expect many readers of a book on M&E training will be familiar with logframes; thus, our discussion is brief (and additional resources on the topic are listed at the end of this chapter). **Table 11.2** illustrates an abbreviated example of how a logframe can be used for M&E training based on a generic 4 x 5 matrix (Chaplowe, 2008). The matrix includes four columns: (1) statements summarizing the intended results, (2) indicators or evidence to assess progress toward the results, (3) means of verification to describe the sources/methods for measuring the indicators, and (4) assumptions or external factors (potential risks) that can affect the achievement of intended results. A clear understanding of the intended results is essential for logframe design, and we have adapted our example to reflect the training design objectives we introduced in Chapter 8. However, as we have noted, terminology and formats used in program designs, such as logframes, vary widely according to organization and context, and we recommend they are adapted accordingly.[3]

In comparison to the levels approach for training evaluation discussed above, a logical framework approach is potentially more comprehensive. In addition to intended results, it includes resources, activities, and other processes that contribute to the results, such as training planning, delivery, and follow-up. However, logframes also express result as levels, and the results hierarchy is also sequential with increasing complexity in measurement (i.e., it is much easier to measure activities and outputs, typically "counts," versus higher level "percentage changes" in KSA and practice).

Related, logframes also assume linear causality between results, reflecting intention rather than reality. The logframe structure lays everything out in advanced using predetermined objectives, assuming everything will go according to plan. As we pointed out in Chapter 7, such an approach risks oversimplification of reality, straightjacketing training and its evaluation. It can inhibit experimentation and risk taking, potentially excluding important emergent learner needs and objectives for training delivery and unintended outcomes for training evaluation. As Funnell and Rogers (2011, p. xx) warn,

> It can lead to monitoring systems and evaluations that produce an incomplete or distorted picture of what is happening and mistake judgments about what is effective or efficient. It can demotivate

---

3. For example, the well-received Logic Model Development Guide from the Kellogg Foundation (2004) uses "inputs, activities, outputs, outcomes and impact" for the levels of results in the left column of the logic model. A list of different terms used by some major international organizations is summarized by Rugh (2005). Often, "inputs are left out of a logframe and captured in the program (training) itemized budget.

BOX 11.1
Methodological Challenges in Training Evaluation

Early in this book, we defined learning as both a process and a change. As a process, learning is not directly observable, which makes its measurement difficult, especially the extent to which learning is sustained and transfered into practice and longer-term, desired changes or outcomes. Furthermore, it is easier to measure whether individual or organizational change occurs than it is to determine to what extent it is due to training (attribution). For example, if trainees are not using newly acquired skills after training, is it because the training failed or because of other factors, such as a lack of workplace opportunity to use new skills or a change in personal circumstances? Related, there may be unintended consequences or outcomes from training. For instance, M&E training may succeed in improving trainee KSA in an organizational context, but this may lead to staff turnover as trainees become more qualified and pursue careers elsewhere, affecting staff retainment and longer-term organizational objectives identified for training.

In short, many of the changes training seeks to achieve from improved knowledge, attitudes, and practice are long term, seldom attributable to a simple factor, and our ability to isolate, control, and measure them for simple causal inferences will be limited. These challenges present methodological limitations that are not limited to training evaluation but are inherent in the evaluation of any intervention occurring in socially complex systems (e.g. Hargreaves, 2010; Morell, 2010; Patton, 2011; Williams & Imam, 2007). Such a systems perspective recognizes there are a myriad of dynamic, interdependent factors (intervening variables) that come into play according to the specific time, place, people, and circumstances of training. However, this does not mean we give up on trying to measure and evaluate training. In the absence of irrefutable *proof*, it is still possible to collect reliable *evidence* to determine the likelihood that training is contributing to desired outcomes (Kirkpatrick, 1977; Guskey, 2000, p. 86). As we shall discuss later in this chapter, designing training evaluation with mixed methods that include multiple perspectives can help in this process.

staff and deflect attention from what is important to only what can be easily measured.

Any model of reality, such as those we discuss above, will be limited and should be carefully used. In the remainder of this chapter, we will look at specific guidelines for evaluating M&E training. As one approaches training evaluation, it is important to acknowledge methodological limitations, which we highlight in **Box 11.1**.

TABLE 11.2 Abbreviated Example of a Training Logframe*

Training Objectives (results)	Example Indicators	Means of Verification (examples)	Assumptions
Training Outcome Example: Effective training design for program implementation, M&E, and reporting	Percentage of program designed using a logframe approved by organizational management and/or donor within 1 year of training	Inventory of program logframes Interviews with organizational management/donors	Organizational leadership/management support (provide time) for staff to apply newly acquired KSA External funding remains available for training program
Learning Goal Example: Improved trainee KSA to design a program using a logical framework approach	Percentage increase in trainee KSA for logical framework development Percentage of trainees who contribute to the development of an approved program logframe within 1 year of training	Pre/post-tests Post-training interviews. Staff professional performance review records Post-training survey	
Learning Objectives By the end of training, trainees will be able to • Develop SMART objective statements • Identify appropriate indicators for objectives • Select appropriate data collection methods for their program indicators • Identify appropriate assumptions	Percentage of trainees who correctly answer relevant post-test questions Percentage of trainee groups that correctly complete the training case study logframe	Post-test Case study logframe exercise results (reported in training report)	

Training Objectives (results)	Example Indicators	Means of Verification (examples)	Assumptions
Output Program staff successfully trained in program design using a logical framework	Number of program staff having completed the complete training Percentage trainees satisfied with training	Training report Trainer self-assessment form Trainee satisfaction feedback forms	
Activities (examples) Training strategy developed by X date Training lesson plans developed by X date Training of trainers delivered by X date And so forth	Training implementation records and report		
Inputs Instructional designer, subject matter expert, trainers, evaluator, administrative staff, office supplies, training facilities	Training program itemized budget (audit)		

*The above logframe is an abbreviated illustration, and the result terminology and overall framework should be adapted according to context. Typically there are many more results and indicators, and so forth.

11.3 Training Evaluation Guidelines

The basis for successful training evaluation is established early, when the training needs are identified, objectives designed, and the criteria for their measurement identified. When backward planning is used during training analysis and design, it lays the groundwork for evaluation by asking the very questions evaluation is to examine—primarily, what are the intended results of training. This, in turn, helps ensure that careful consideration is given to the design of training objectives that are evaluable. Once training objectives are clear, it is easier to ask the right evaluation questions and determine methods to best answer them. In effect, the training objectives guide the development of the evaluation objectives.

There is another practical and important reason to design and developed training evaluation in tandem with the training itself: so learning assessment and evaluation tools can be developed *prior to* training implementation. This is necessary if these tools are to be used before (e.g., baseline data collection), during, and after training delivery as part of a systematic and coherent approach to training evaluation.

Below, we summarize five stages for planning and conducting a training evaluation. An evaluation plan (see **Box 11.2**) can be developed to help manage this process so that evaluation can meet its objectives in a timely and efficient manner. The length and detail of this document and how thoroughly to evaluate training will depend on the evaluation purpose and scope—the first step for evaluation planning. The end result is to have reliable and credible data for training evaluation that are useful and used.

BOX 11.2
What is an Evaluation Plan?

An evaluation plan is a road map to guide evaluation and to communicate about it with others. Sometimes called an evaluation strategy,[1] an evaluation plan identifies what will be evaluated, why, how, when, and by whom. It typically includes a description of the evaluation stakeholders, objectives (purpose, key questions and criteria), data sources, data collection and analysis methods, reporting and dissemination, timeline, budget, and responsibilities. It may also include monitoring guidelines as well as any other deliverables for the evaluation.

---

1. However, evaluation "strategy" is also used to refer to the long-term plan of multiple evaluations over a period of time (for which individual evaluation plans can be developed for each evaluation).

1. Determine the evaluation purpose and scope

Just as we begin the training analysis identifying training needs, training evaluation begins by identifying its needs, starting with the overall purpose for the evaluation. Foremost, this should be informed by the intended users and use of evaluation. The importance of such a utilization approach to evaluation is well established (e.g., Patton, 2012; Yarbrough, Shulha, Hopson, & Caruthers, 2011) but not always meaningfully practiced (Preskill & Torres, 2000; Weiss, 1980)—see **Box 11.3**. Learning and accountability are the most common and overarching reasons for training evaluation, but there can be other related reasons that often overlap. Below we summarize some examples for why trainings are evaluated:

- For **learning** to improve a training approach or program or overall capacity building strategy.

- For **accountability** to show that training achieved it intended objectives. Accountability can be *360°*—upward to those commissioning/funding the training, downward to the trainees themselves, and horizontal to other stakeholders (partners) affected by the training.

- Because training evaluation is mandated or required by external funders (accountability).

- To justify a new approach to or pilot of M&E training.

- To convince others to adopt M&E training.

- In response to complaints or criticism about existing training.

- Because training evaluation has been budgeted or excess funds must be used before the fiscal year closes (regardless of authentic evaluation need or intended use).

- To attract funding and support for M&E training.

- To promote and advocate (celebrate) the value of M&E training.

One especially important and practical consideration for the evaluation purpose is to determine the *evaluability* of the given M&E training. This is the degree to which training can be realistically evaluated in a reliable and credible manner. This is not only important during the early stages of evaluation planning but will also inform the later stages of evaluation design when considering realistic methods for data collection and management. Understanding the *evaluation scope* helps determine the evaluability of training and focus the evaluation purpose. The evaluation scope identifies what will be included in the evaluation: the number and location of trainings and trainees, the training time frame and budget, and the range of issues to be examined. This, in turn, will help determine what is feasible for training evaluation given the time frame, geographic spread, and available resources.

For example, one practical consideration for training evaluability is the extent to which trainees are accessible for post-training evaluation. For instance, for a single day training in a non-organizational context (e.g., a professional development training offered the general public), post-training access to trainees may not be realistic when they are independent learners, coming from disparate locations. In this instance, the follow-up necessary to evaluate longer-term impact and learning transfer with participants may not be practical in time and cost. Instead, the evaluation purpose may focus on whether participants felt the training was worth their time and money upon completion.[4] However, for organizational training, trainee access may not be a problem following the training, and the organization may prioritize the evaluation of longer-term outcomes, such as job performance and the achievement of organizational strategic objectives.

Ultimately, why and how evaluation is conducted will be distinct to the specific training context and stakeholder needs. The evaluator's role is to explore this with stakeholders (see Box 11.3), with attention to both what they want to get out of it but also what is feasible given the particular training setting and available time and resources for its evaluation.

2. Specify what will be evaluated

Having clarified the overall purpose for training evaluation, the next step is to identify the evaluation questions to be answered. The evaluation questions reflect the specific issues and information users of the evaluation need to make decisions and take action. While trainee perception of training is important, evaluation questions should go beyond this and examine actual learning and how this transfers into longer-term objectives identified for training. Thus, when training objectives have been identified as part of the training design, it will be easier to identify evaluation questions to explore whether objectives have been achieved. Evaluation criteria or standards can be used to further define the questions asked and information the evaluation will generate. In essence, the evaluation questions and criteria help focus the evaluation's objectives or what it is to achieve.

Below, we take a look at some example questions based on our foregoing discussion and our experience with training evaluation. We have organized the questions under three units of analysis that we believe are useful for training evaluation: (1) training outcomes, (2) organizational outcomes, and (3) the training program. We have *italicized* with certain questions corresponding evaluation criteria commonly used in

---

4. Alternatively, particularly for ongoing, cyclic organizational training offering a sustain program, an impact evaluation can be conducted periodically.

BOX 11.3
Stakeholder Involvement for Evaluation (and Training) Use

Evaluation can be a considerable investment in time and resources, but one of the most common complaints is that there is no follow-up to or use of the evaluation findings. For instance, in a 2006 survey of American Evaluation Association members, 68 percent self-reported that their evaluation results were not used (Fleischer & Christie, 2009). As we have stressed, stakeholder consultation and involvement can help address such a serious problem to ensure it meets their needs. However, we do not want to romanticize stakeholder involvement. The same resistance people have of evaluation that can be a barrier to M&E training can likewise undermine training evaluation; evaluation is often perceived as a threat, policing, or a waste of time. And the truth of the matter is it will be a wasted exercise if the very people intended to use the evaluation do not perceive it as useful!

When confronting stakeholder resistance to evaluation, it will be important to examine their concerns and perceived disadvantages as well as potential benefits of evaluation. This is an example where trainers' facilitation skills are not limited to training delivery but also useful for other aspects of training such as evaluation:

> Users' commitment to evaluation is typically fragile, often whimsical, and must be cultivated like a hybrid plant that has the potential for enormous yields, but only if properly cared for, nourished, and appropriately managed. (Patton, 2012, p. 16)

Stakeholder engagement may not always be easy in evaluation, but its rewards are worth the effort. In addition to evaluation, it can also help build commitment to the training itself. Why? Because when the evaluation is planned *with* the training, it can simultaneously build understanding and support for both. During training analysis, we suggested it may be useful to build a team (or committee) representative of different stakeholder groups to conduct analysis as well as other aspects of training. This same group or subgroup can also be used to form a team to lead or manage training evaluation (which we will revisit in the last section of this chapter).

program evaluation (e.g., coverage, relevance, effectiveness, impact, sustainability, efficiency, and coherence). Other criteria, such as the adult learning principles for training, can also be incorporated into evaluation questions, as reflected in those questions for the training program.

1. **Trainee outcomes**. These are immediate and longer-term results for the individuals attending the training, whether an organizational training or non-organizational training. It includes trainee satisfaction with the training, learning, behavioral changes, and any personal benefits from the training.

   - Were trainees satisfied with the training? Was the training relevant and meaningful (worthwhile) for them?
   - Did training achieve its learning objectives and improve KSA for M&E (*effectiveness*)?
   - Regardless of KSA gains, were there behavior changes and improved M&E practice by trainees (*impact*)?
   - To what degree are the observed changes among trainees due to training versus other factors (*attribution*)?
   - Was the training content (learning objectives) useful and applicable to trainees' needs and longer-term goals (*relevance*)?
   - Were there unintended outcomes (positive or negative) for the trainees?

2. **Organizational outcomes**. These are the longer-term results for organizational training. Primarily, did the organization benefit from training? It is worth noting that there may be instances where the organizational outcomes for training are focused on the individual, in which case questions framed above can be considered.

   - What is the likelihood that learning transfer will occur and M&E practice improve at the organizational level (*impact/sustainability*)?
   - Did organizational leadership, policies, and practices (related to Guskey's Level 3 for evaluation) support or hinder training transfer and use of learned KSA, and did the application of these benefit the organization?
   - Did the training achieve the longer-term objectives (results) identified for the organization (*impact*)?
   - Were the learning objectives appropriate for the training objectives identified for the organization (*relevance*)?
   - To what degree are the observed changes at the organizational level due to training versus other factors (*attribution*)?
   - Were there unintended outcomes (positive or negative) for the organization?

3. **The training program**. These focus on training processes before (planning), during (facilitation), and after the training (follow-up) that affect trainee and organizational outcomes. It also includes the trainer

performance as well as the training environment and the extent to which training supports the adult principles of learning.

Training content (M&E topics, materials, and activities/methods designed in the training curriculum)

- To what extent is the training content relevant to and support achievement of M&E learning objectives (*relevance*)?
- To what extent is the training curriculum designed to support the principles of adult learning (*effective*)? Refer to principles listed below for training facilitation.

Training facilitation

- To what extent does training facilitation realize the achievement of M&E learning objectives (*impact*)?
- To what extent is the training curriculum designed to support the principles of adult learning (*effective*):

  1. Establish a safe and respectful learning environment, where trainees and trainers have mutual respect and trust?

  2. Respond to the "need to know" *what, why,* and *how* they are learning?

  3. Provide a structured yet flexible progression appropriate for trainee level, where they are not rushed but have ample time for practice, trial, and error necessary for learning?

  4. Empower trainees with genuine participation so they can fully participate in their own learning process?

  5. Incorporate and build upon prior trainee experience (*relevance*)?

  6. Relate learning to what is relevant and meaningful to trainee's practical needs?

  7. Employ experiential learning where trainees were able to learn by doing?

  8. Incorporate active and fun activities for engaging and enjoyable learning?

  9. Use mixed and multisensory methods to address different learning styles?

10. Differentiate instruction to meet different learners' needs?

11. Support collaborative and peer learning?

12. Incorporate adequate practice and repetition to support learning?

13. Utilize primacy and recency to reinforce learning?

14. Provide opportunity for feedback and positive reinforcement?

Training processes before and after training

- Were key stakeholders actively engaged and committed to the training process?
- Was the training analysis effective, contributing to training design (content development)?
- Did the training take adequate account for and complement other M&E capacity building efforts (*coherence*)?
- Was the training follow-up effective, supporting learning transfer and use?
- Was training evaluation effectively planned and implemented, supporting learning and/or accountability?

Training setting and arrangements

- Was the training setting convenient and easily accessible (whether a physical or online setting)?
- Was the training setting comfortable and conducive to learning? (For face-to-face training, was the training facility adequate—lighting and temperature, chairs comfortable, no outside distractions, and so forth? For online training, were the Internet speed, user interface, and interactivity sufficient?)
- To what extent did the logistical arrangements meet both the trainers' and trainees' needs?

Training efficiency

- How much training was delivered (outputs) and how many people were trained (coverage)?
- Was training planned and delivered in a timely manner?
- Was training adequately budgeted and sufficient for training needs?
- Were training finances and resources cost effective (*efficiency*)?
- What was the economic return from the investment in training (ROI, in itself a form of outcome evaluation)?

Far from exhaustive, the above questions are only illustrative, and relevant evaluation questions should be identified based on a thorough understanding of the training context and the evaluation's purpose (user's needs). When planning evaluation for M&E training, a multitude of questions can be identified, and it will likely be necessary to prioritize and focus on those questions that are relevant for the evaluation purpose and realistic for the available time, budget, and resources for data collection. It is better to answer fewer questions rigorously than many vaguely. Once more, we stress that stakeholder input in any prioritization of evaluation questions to ensure that those that do remain are motivated and justified by intended users' interests.

3. Design and develop the training evaluation

After specifying what is to be evaluated, the next step is to determine how to go about doing it. The evaluation design identifies what information or evidence to collect for evaluation and the methods used to obtain and analyze this information. Ultimately, there is no single design most appropriate for training evaluation, and the sources and methods will need to be adapted to the specific questions, criteria, and objectives identified for evaluation. Once this is clearly understood, then time and resources can be invested into developing learning assessment and training evaluation tools.

Below we have identified some key reminders to help guide evaluation design for training (which reflect learning points on evaluation often included in an M&E training curriculum):

- **Design the evaluation in tandem with the training itself.** As we have emphasized, backward planning can make evaluation design more straightforward because consideration is given to training results and their measurement early when training objectives are designed. For example, in Chapter 8 we discussed how learning objectives should be written SMART (specific, measurable, attainable, relevant, and timely), specifying what trainees will be able to perform as a result of training. In turn, this informs how KSA can be measured and assessed, which we recommended documenting at the time each learning objective is written.

- **Be alert for unanticipated outcomes**. It is important to remember that training design using predetermined objectives is limited because there may be unanticipated consequences from training. The potential for unpredictable behavior and related consequences are inherent in the complex systems in which training occur. Thus, it is important that training evaluation probe for unplanned outcomes, whether positive and negative, as they provide a more accurate understanding of what occurred from training and why. Including multiple perspectives and using mixed methods, both discussed below, can help identify and analyze unanticipated training outcomes.

- **Plan to collect and analyze information from multiple perspectives**. Triangulating (combining) different data sources for evaluation provides a richer and more complete picture to understand observed changes. For example, it can be useful to compare trainer self-assessments with trainees' perceptions of the training or trainees' self-assessment of post-training performance with the opinions of colleagues or supervisors.

- **Use mixed-methods.** When possible, both qualitative and quantitative data collection and analysis methods can be used to make the evaluation design more robust. Like triangulating data sources, combining different methods can cross-check and compare results and help identify unanticipated outcomes from training. For instance, quantitative methods can be used to assess predetermined objectives, such as differences between pre- and post-measures of KSA, appropriate comparison groups, or longitudinal time series surveys of post-training results. On the other hand, qualitative methods that elicit stakeholder opinions and reflections can provide valuable insight to explain quantitatively measured results and help probe for any emergent, unplanned training consequences.

- **Be systematic, yet flexible**. The evaluation design should be carefully constructed and systematically conducted so that data collection is relevant and reliable for comparison over time and place, leading to accurate and valid analysis. Clear instructions for conducting evaluation and consistent scoring and interpretation of assessment result help support a systematic approach to training evaluation. However, just as training itself should be flexible and responsive to emergent needs, so should training evaluation. The evaluation design should not be too rigid and blindly followed, but adaptable to changing needs, especially for longer-training programs for which training objectives may evolve (often as a result of findings from formative training evaluation). When too rigid, evaluation designs can inhibit experimentation and probing different results, explanations, and solutions.

- **Keep it practical and focused**. Evaluation design is best when the methods are easily understood and realistic for the available budget,

Prior to investing in the design of training evaluation, it is important to consider what is possible given the existing expertise and financial resources available for evaluation. For example, qualitative methods can be very effective to evaluate learning transfer and use after M&E training, but interviewing and observing trainees can also be costly, as they require considerable in-person time and potentially travel and accommodation. How much money to allocate for training evaluation? There is no set formula, but a general rule of thumb is that the evaluation budget should not be so small as to compromise the accuracy and credibility of evaluation, but neither should it divert valuable resources to the extent that it impairs service delivery—for example, training or some other use of funds (Chaplowe 2008). For program evaluation, various organizations recommend between 3 to 10 percent of a project's budget (e.g., Frankel & Gage 2007; IFRC, 2011a; Kellogg Foundation, 1998; UNICEF, 2007).

time, expertise, and other capacities available for evaluation training. Be wary of *obsessive measurement disorder* (OMD), and only collect information that is necessary and sufficient to achieve your evaluation objectives. Return to and use your evaluation questions to focus your data collection. Remember that how comprehensive the evaluation design is will have important implications for people, time, and resources needed for training evaluation—see **Box 11.4**.

- **Identify and communicate methodological limitations**. As discussed earlier in this chapter, there are methodological challenges inherent in the evaluation of any intervention occurring in socially complex systems, such as M&E training. Responsible evaluation requires that we acknowledge this and make the distinction between *evidence* obtained during evaluation, versus unequivocal *proof*.

- **Uphold evaluation principles and ethics.** Ensure the evaluation design reflects the standards and principles for ethical and responsible evaluation (e.g., AEA, 2004; Yarbrough et al., 2011), including any specific evaluation policies or requirements for the training/ organizational context.

Once the training evaluation has been designed, specific data collection tools can be developed. As discussed in Chapter 9, this should occur during training development and includes not only learning assessment and evaluation instruments but also the guidelines for using them in a consistent, reliable, and ethical manner. As with other activities and tools planned for the training curriculum, it is recommended to review and pilot learning assessment and evaluation instruments when possible to ensure they are realistic and reliable for the training context.

4. Collect and analyze data

Data collection and analysis operationalize the training evaluation design. There are a variety of data-collection methods for training evaluation, and their selection should be according to the specific evaluation questions to answer as well as what is feasible given available resources and capacities. Related, data collection should be timed according to when the information is available and needs to be used. In **Table 11.3**, we list example data collection methods for training evaluation, and the appendices of this chapter provides a more detailed description of these methods (**Appendix 11.1**), as well as specific examples of forms that can be used (**Appendices 11.2–11.4**). While not rigid, we have organized the methods according to when they are commonly used during the training cycle:

1. **Data collection methods prior to training delivery**. Information collected prior to M&E training can be used to establish a baseline of conditions for later comparison to assess change. Often, this information is collected during the training analysis stage to inform training design, or it may explicitly be collected for evaluation purposes.

2. **Data collection during training delivery**. Information collected during the training (such as learning assessments—e.g., quizzes, session feedback forms, or oral feedback during activity debriefs) can be used to monitor and adjust training delivery in real time and contributes to the evaluation of immediate training results (e.g., knowledge recall and trainee satisfaction).

3. **Data collection after training delivery**. Information collected after the training can be used to assess the usefulness of training, including individual KSA retention and performance, training transfer achieving longer-term outcomes for individuals or organizations, and unanticipated outcomes resulting from training. Post-training data collection can be *proximal* (shortly after the training) or *distal* (a longer-time period after training) and can employ time series data collection.

TABLE 11.3 Example Data Collection Methods for Training Evaluation

Prior to Training Delivery	During Training Delivery		After Training Delivery
• Trainee analysis • Organizational analysis • Training pilots • Trainee development plan or contract • Training pre-test*	• Trainee feedback forms • Quizzes & structured exams • Demonstrations & simulations • Training work products • Trainee self-assessment	• Trainee peer assessment • In-training discussion and qualitative feedback • Trainer self-assessment • Co-trainer feedback • External observers	• Training post-test* • Survey questionnaires • Structure interviews • Post-training observation • Learner portfolios, logbooks, and journals • Performance reviews

*Note that training pre/post-tests can be administered outside the training or at the training prior to and after delivery of content.

The extent to which evaluation data can be collected prior to and after training will largely depend on the access to data sources, which will vary according to training context. For instance, it may not always be possible or practical to meet or communicate with trainees prior to or after training. It is also important to recognize that data collection may not be exclusively for evaluation purposes but for other aspects of training. For example, data collected during the training analysis phase that is used to inform training design can also provide relevant baseline data on pre-training conditions for later comparison and evaluation.

Sources of data for M&E training include trainees (e.g., their learning, performance, and perception of the training); trainers (e.g., their self-assessment of the training); other stakeholders, such as observers of the training, subject matter experts, colleagues, and supervisors; and reliable and relevant secondary data, such as individual or organizational performance records. Depending on resources, time, and rigor required for training evaluation, data collection using surveys questionnaires and interviews can be conducted using a census, probability (random), or nonprobability (nonrandom) sample when respondents are known beforehand.

Data analysis methods will depend on the type of data collected (whether it is qualitative or quantitative), and any related technology used to collect it (such as online surveys forms).

Data collection, analysis, and the principles of adult learning

Data collection and analysis not only lead to modification and improvement of training but can also be a valuable source for trainee learning and involvement in training, supporting key principles of adult learning. For instance, when learning assessment is conducted prior to training to establish a baseline, it can also help satisfy trainees' need to know, framing their expectations for training content. When conducted during or after training, learning assessment can be facilitated so it helps review, practice, and reinforce key learning points. Also, when conducted at the completion of a session or training, learning assessment supports the principle of recency—what is reviewed last is best remembered.

The degree to which learning assessment contributes to learning (rather than just measuring it) will largely depend on the extent trainees are involved in the analysis of their performance, helping them identify strengths, weaknesses, and areas to work on. This underscores the adult learning principle of participation in the training process, so that training assessment is done *with* rather than *to* trainees. Adults generally prefer to see evidence of and take responsibility for their learning, and when data is collected from trainees it is a golden opportunity to support this by involving them in its analysis. In **Box 11.5**, we consider trainee involvement in pre/post-testing for training evaluation.

Participatory analysis is not limited to learning assessment but also feedback and discussion about the training itself. When debriefing an activity or soliciting trainee feedback on the training program and processes (e.g., content, facilitation, and facilities), reactions and responses can be analyzed and prioritized with trainee involvement. Such a participatory approach to evaluation supports a learner-centered approach to training, where trainees critically consider and express opinion about the learning process as equals and partners in the training. In this manner, training evaluation can be empowering rather than alienating. Furthermore, when trainees are involved in the production of evaluative knowledge about the training they participate in, they stand to benefit in ways that are quite independent of the findings. Such benefits are often thought about as instances of "process use" (Cousins, 2007; Patton, 2012). Such effects are particularly of interest in the context of M&E training because some of the learning will overlap with the goals for training. Learning about data collection strategies, how to analyze data, how to think systematically, and so forth, are examples of the sorts of learning benefits that might accrue.

5. Report on and follow-up evaluations

Evaluation reporting and follow-up is the final but critical step of training evaluation, ideally contributing to the "utility standard" for evaluation. It is best planned as part of the overall training follow-up during the design phase of training, and based on careful consideration to how information will be received and used by different stakeholder groups. Hendricks (1994) identifies some key reminders for reporting evaluation results to support evaluation use:

- **Be "aggressive" or proactive and do not wait for target audiences to request information.** It is important to remember that evaluation reporting is not limited to the end of training (final, summative evaluation) but can be regular and frequent as results from formative evaluation are available. Keeping people informed and consulting about findings emerging from evaluation has the added benefit of avoiding "surprise," preparing for acceptance and use of evaluation findings.

- **"Simplify" and report in a user-friendly manner, tailoring formats and content according to the audience.** People are busy and it is important to pare down information and direct their attention to key findings.

- **Know your audience**. This should draw on the stakeholder analysis for the training evaluation, including their priorities as well as "pet peeves." Consider preparing a dissemination list as part of the evaluation plan, identifying target audience groups and frequency of reporting. Target groups include trainees, program/organizational staff and management, funders, training developers, and others in the community.

- **Focus on specific, practical actions that frame what to do next**. This can include recommended responsibilities and timelines to inform realistic action planning to follow up and use training evaluation.

- **Report in different ways**, identifying outlets and formats, tailoring content accordingly to the informational needs and uses of target audience groups. For example, reporting that target trainers and developers of training can highlight methodological lessons for training, while commissioners of training may be more interested in comparing training cost with benefits (return on investment). Evaluation dissemination can include different products in addition to written evaluation reports—for example, summary newsletters, in-person presentations and briefings, teleconferences, web-based presentations and platforms, video-graphics, and sharing findings at relevant conference and M&E/training forums.

In addition to reporting *to* stakeholders, it is critical to involve them in discussion and feedback on evaluation findings and recommended actions. Consider establishing a feedback process that actively engages people to build understanding of and consensus for actions for evaluation follow-up. This process can begin during the review and revision of the evaluation report and involve any task force or committee formed during the evaluation planning stage. As we have stressed (Box 11.3, previously in this chapter), such stakeholder involvement in evaluation helps build ownership and its use.

A final consideration for evaluation follow-up is to reflect upon the evaluation process and methodologies itself. How useful was the training evaluation, did it achieve its objectives, and what can be improved when conducting training evaluation in the future? For the training evaluator, such "reality testing" helps improve the practice of future evaluation (Patton, 2012, p.12).

11.4 Determining Who Will Conduct Training Evaluation

It is useful to determine early on who will conduct training evaluation, as they will likely lead its design and development. Below we have summarized five types of evaluators to consider for training evaluation:

1. **Trainers**. Using trainers as evaluators is a form of internal or self-evaluation, as it is conducted by those who are responsible for implementing the training to be evaluated. This is certainly useful for evaluation processes conducted during or at the end of training, as the trainer will be present (e.g., learning assessment). However, it may not be perceived as objective as an evaluation led by independent evaluators. Also, it will depend on the trainers' experience in evaluation. Of course, for training in M&E, the trainer may be well qualified to lead training evaluation. However, some trainers may be outstanding M&E facilitators, capable to administer quizzes and other forms of assessment during training, but not qualified or experienced for more complicated, impact evaluation after training. Furthermore, trainers may only be available to conduct evaluation during the training and not afterward.

2. **External evaluators**. These evaluators can be a valuable source of expertise for training evaluation and provide a degree of objectivity and credibility that may be important for evaluation stakeholders. Examples include qualified independent evaluators, educators, consulting firms, university education departments, researchers, and research centers. Depending on the context, it can take time to recruit and manage an external evaluator and incur additional costs.

3. **Organizational staff or department**. For organizational training, these evaluators will be familiar with the organizational culture, procedures, and objectives to support evaluation. Using them not only may be more affordable but also can build understanding and ownership for the evaluation among organizational stakeholders. However, the objectivity of organizational staff evaluating its own training may be questioned. Furthermore, there may be internal politics or conflicts within an organization that can complicate such an approach to training evaluation, threatening credibility among stakeholders.

4. **Trainees.** Although less common, trainees can conduct the training evaluation themselves as a form of internal, self-evaluation. This is not simply their participation as a source of information (e.g., completing satisfaction forms or answering questions in an interview), but their actual involvement in the design and implementation of training evaluation. This can not only empower trainees but also reinforce the very learning topics targeted for training on monitoring and *evaluation*. This approach requires active facilitation from the trainer, acting to a certain degree as an evaluation

team lead. Clearly, the trainer needs to be experienced in this form participatory training evaluation.

5. **"Blended" evaluation teams**. Using a combination of two or more of the above evaluator options can help bring the benefits of different people to the evaluation team, providing multiple perspectives. Pairing an external evaluator with a trainer can be useful when the trainer is unavailable or unqualified to follow up on post-training evaluation but capable to conduct evaluation activities during the training. Similarly, when both the trainer and/or external evaluator are from outside an organization for organizational training, someone from within the organization can not only contribute valuable organizational understanding but also help "open doors" and build organizational ownership of the evaluation process.

Who to select for training evaluation will depend to a large extent on its purpose and scope and the available expertise and financial resources. For example, if the primary purpose of the evaluation is accountability or to justify a training approach and/or return on investment, it may be best to use an external evaluator, which can lend the exercise more objectivity and credibility. However, if the purpose of training evaluation is learning to improve the training, it may be more appropriate to use a self-evaluation involving trainers and those involved in supporting training and its follow-up.

Of course, as with any evaluation, it is important to ensure that selected evaluators are qualified and well suited for the training evaluation purpose. As Sanders (1989, p. 59) warns, "Evaluation of training is often conducted by trainers themselves (who have, on the average, less education about and experience with program evaluation than school teachers) and by clients of the trainers, for example, target audience managers or company executives (who have even less background experience with evaluation of training programs)." This can result in reliance on trainee reactions to training for summative evaluation to the exclusion of more in-depth evaluation of learning transfer and longer-term training impact.

There is a variety of resources to inform the selection of evaluators most suitable to the specific training context and evaluation purpose. For example, credentials can be identified from the AEA (2004) Guiding Principles For Evaluators, the JCSEE Program Evaluation Standards (Yarbrough et al., 2011), and the Canadian Evaluation Society's Competencies for Canadian Evaluation Practice (CES, 2010). The Kellogg Foundation (1998, p. 63) provides a useful, generic *Checklist for Selecting an Evaluator* for program evaluation that can be adapted for training evaluation.

11.5 CHAPTER SUMMARY

Training evaluation may be the last element of the ADDIE framework but, in our view, (a) it is one of the most important and (b) it is yet another element of a larger *cycle*. That being the case, it is essential that training evaluation feed back into or otherwise connect with ongoing training analysis, design, and development. From this chapter, it is our intention that readers will understand key ideas and some of the methodological challenges faced by training evaluators. Key summary points include the following:

- Training evaluation is the *systematic investigation of the worth or merit of training*. It includes formative evaluation of ongoing training and summative evaluation of training after training has been completed.

- Training evaluation includes learning assessment, which involves the individual learner's readiness for M&E training and to perform M&E after training, whereas the evaluation of training focuses on the overall training program and its effectiveness or worth.

- Training monitoring focuses on assessing ongoing training, which includes individual learning as well as the training process (e.g., facilitation and setting).

- There are various methods used for training evaluation, and we summarize two major approaches to consider:

  o A levels approach to training evaluation includes Kirkpatrick's classic four levels to thinking about training outcomes (reaction, learning, behavior, and longer-term results), and Guskey's framework adds value through attention to the assessment of the context in which new knowledge and skill is intended to be transferred.

  o A logical framework approach to training evaluation draws upon the practice of program/project design and evaluation, identifying the intended theory of change and desired results for training, for which indicators are used to measure and assumptions identifies to monitor.

- Whatever method is used for training evaluation, it is important to have an appreciation for the inherent methodological challenges faced when trying to measure and assess changes for interventions such as training, which occur in socially complex systems.

- Training evaluation is best considered early during the training design: Knowing the intended results to assess helps ensure learning objectives are relevant, allowing the development of appropriate methods and tools for their assessment prior to training delivery.

- There is no one way to approach training evaluation, but we identify five key stages:

  a. Define the purpose and scope of the evaluation, relying on stakeholder input to help gage that and ensure the evaluation will be useful and used.

  b. Specify what will be evaluated, which can include the training outcomes, organizational outcomes, and aspects of the training program (e.g., training content, facilitation, setting, logistics, efficiency).

  c. Design and develop the training evaluation with consideration to unanticipated outcomes, multiplicity in perspectives and methods, practicality and flexibility, and professional standards of practice.

d. Collect and analyze data, which (depending on context and needs) can occur prior to, during, and after training delivery.

e. Report and follow up on training evaluation in different ways according to difference stakeholder needs so that findings are more likely to be understood and used.

- We end the chapter identifying four types of evaluators to consider for training, either separately or for a blended evaluation team: (a) trainers; (b) external evaluators; (c) organizational staff or department; and (d) trainees themselves.

This chapter brings to a close our treatment of a systematic approach to M&E training. In addition to describing the ADDIE approach to training and how it might apply to M&E training, we have deliberately made connections to the foundational ideas laid out in Part 1 of the book. Specifically, where appropriate, as we worked through the elements of the ADDIE cycle, we discussed implications for organizational or non-organizational training contexts, the relevance and importance of backward planning in training development and evaluation, demands of the contemporary M&E context, principles of adult learning, and considerations about those involved in designing and delivering training. We now move to Part 3 of the book and provide some practical and concrete examples of types of activities that M&E trainers have and continue to find productive and useful.

11.6 APPENDICES

Appendix 11.1 Example Evaluation Data Collection Methods

Method	Description
Pre-Training	
Trainee analysis	Discussed in Chapter 7, information from a trainee or learner analysis used to inform training design can also serve as an important source of baseline data for trainee KSA levels, performance, and personal objectives. This initial trainee assessment can be compared with post-training assessments to determine individual and collective changes for training evaluation.
Organizational analysis	Discussed in Chapter 6, a context analysis can include useful organizational information to establish baseline data for organization M&E training. This can include information about current M&E capacities and practice within an organization as well as other objectives related to M&E training (e.g., accountability practices, quality of

Method	Description
	program reports, and service delivery). Information can draw upon reliable and relevant secondary data (e.g., existing organizational capacity assessments) or from primary data collection during the training analysis, for example, gap analysis. When repeated after training, organizational analysis can help assess longer-term outcomes and impact from training.
Training pilots	As discussed in Chapter 8, piloting part or all of the training can be an important component of the training design. A training pilot can identify areas to adjust and improve that can later be compared with actual training delivery for evaluation purposes.
Trainee development plan or contract	A trainee development plan is a tool used to help trainees identify and monitor personal training and related professional development or career objectives. Also called a *learning development plan*, *training transfer plan,* or *training contract*, these tools help make explicit trainee expectations and how the training is to be used after training. This not only helps prepare the trainee for training but also can be used to help monitor and assess the degree to which individual training expectations and objectives have been met. Logbooks can be used to track trainee performance toward personal learning goals. The trainee development plan can be developed by trainees themselves, or for organizational training, it can be developed in collaboration with manager/supervisors as part of the staff professional development review process. A trainee contract or development plan can be revisited and revised at the conclusion of and in follow-up to M&E training. **Appendix 11.2** provides an example of a trainee development plan.
During Training	
Trainee feedback forms	Sometimes referred to as "smiley sheets" or "happiness quotients," trainee feedback forms are probably the most common and one of the easiest sources of data for training evaluation. Rather than measuring learning or longer-term outcomes from training, they are limited trainee perceptions of or initial reactions to training (corresponding to Kirkpatrick's Level 1 on training evaluation). They can be administered at the end of training to inform the design and delivery of future training or during training (e.g., at the completion individual training sessions or days) to monitor and adjust training delivery and the learning environment. In addition to closed-ended questions that can be quantitatively analyzed, it is also important to include open-ended questions for more personal comments. It is recommended that written feedback is anonymous (although trainees can opt to identify themselves), so trainees feel more comfortable being candid in their responses, especially if critical. Categories of feedback typically include training content and design, facilitation, environment, and trainee comfort. **Appendix 11.3** provides an example of a trainee feedback form or a more elaborate assessment of trainer performance can be developed—see **Appendix 11.4**. In addition to written formats, feedback can be provided electronically, for example, over the Internet, during or after training.

(Continued)

(Continued)

Method	Description
Training pre/post-tests	Training pre/post-tests provide baseline/endline data of individual and collective KSA levels and gains for training evaluation. They are often administered at the start and end of training, but depending on the training context and access to trainees, they can also be administered prior to and after training to save time (e.g., online or in person). Training pre/post-tests are valuable not only for training evaluation but also for other uses for both trainer and trainee. For example, conducting pre-tests prior to training can help trainers anticipate trainee needs to inform training design and help trainees anticipate training content and identify personal training objectives. Pre/post-tests can also be a valuable learning activity in itself, supporting the adult learning principles of participation in training, as discussed in Box 11.5 and illustrated in Part 3 (p. 380).
Quizzes & structured exams	Quizzes and formal exams given during training not only help monitor individual learning but also can serve as a data source for training evaluation. Depending on the training purpose, a practical exam (test) may be given at the end of the training, separate from or instead of a post-test, to certify trainees and determine their readiness to use new newly acquired KSA in real-world settings. Post-training exams can also be used for evaluation purposes, while also supporting training follow-up and content reinforcement.
Demonstrations & simulations	Work task demonstrations and simulations can be conducted during, at the completion of, or after training to assess trainee performance based on pre-identified criteria for training evaluation. For example, trainees' performance can be rated during a role play facilitating a focus group discussion. Demonstrations and simulations can be a good opportunity to incorporate peer assessment (discussed above) and can also be videotaped for activity debriefs, allowing trainees to view and assess themselves.
Training work products	Work products from training can be used as a record to monitor and evaluate trainee learning and performance. Work products can include written exercises, case-study work, reports, completed logframes, M&E plans, and homework assignments. Work products can come from individual or group activities and may be handed in or documented using pictures taken during training as a record for training evaluation. This evidence can also be used to start a learning profile (discussed below). For training where these products need to be graded, this can be done with an accompanying rubric to ensure consistency (and fairness).
Trainee self-assessment	Rather than or in addition to training pre-tests, trainees can conduct a self-assessment of their KSA and personal training goals prior to, during, and after training (see Box 11.5). This reinforces the adult learning principle of feedback and participation in the training process and can contribute to individual preparation for, follow-up to, and ownership of learning. Expectations can be identified and checklists used to monitor and assess individual learning areas. Self-assessment can be factored into other data collection methods as trainee involvement increases.
Trainee peer assessment	Trainees can be involved in assessing each other during training, contributing to learning as well as evaluation. Such an approach to assessment supports adult learning principles of collaborative learning, reflection, and participatory feedback. When trainees critically think about what areas to assess, it can reinforce their

Method	Description
	understanding of learning objectives related to evaluation, and feedback from peers can be meaningful in ways different from trainers. Peer feedback can be structured into training activities; for example, trainees can practice enumerating an interview with peers observing and assessing each other's performance based on criteria that they agree upon with trainer facilitation. Feedback can be facilitated orally in group or partner discussion and guided with forms or checklists that also serve as an outline of training session content. Several of the discussion activities summarized in Part 3 can be adapted for peer assessment.
In-training discussion and qualitative feedback	Training activity debriefs and other activities can be a valuable source of formative evaluation to monitor and adjust the training delivery and environment. It also supports a learner-centered approach to training, empowering trainees to critically reflect upon training and express their opinions. When recorded, this formative feedback can also be used for summative evaluation of different stages of the training delivery. In Part 3, we summarize some examples of feedback activities for M&E training that can contribute to training monitoring and evaluation.
Trainer self-assessment	Trainers can also identify their training objectives and performance areas to monitor and evaluate for effective training. In Chapter 5, we discussed trainer competencies, with a trainer assessment checklist that can be used for self-assessment. Trainees are also recommended to note during training (for instance on their lesson plans or facilitation notes) any comments, mistakes, improvements, or reminders for future training design and delivery. A trainer assessment form can be developed to support trainer self-assessment—see Appendix 11.4.
Co-trainer feedback	When training is co-facilitated, trainers can be a valuable source of feedback for formative and summative evaluation purposes. Feedback can occur informally during training through discussion and "check-ins" between trainers or structured more formally through oral debriefs and written forms or checklists based on key assessment criteria.
External observers	An external observer can be present during training to provide external feedback on the training process for formative and summative evaluation purposes. Observers can include training evaluators, subject-matter experts, training sponsors, or other training stakeholders. Feedback can be oral and/or recorded using assessment forms or checklists. A trainer assessment form can be developed to support external assessment—see Appendix 11.4.
Post-Training	
Survey questionnaires	Post-training surveys can be used to assess the relevance and usefulness of training as well as other longer-term outcomes and issues related to training as experienced by different target groups. For example, follow-up surveys with trainees can assess to what degree they have been able to apply what they learned during training. In an organizational setting, surveys can be used to identify whether training contributed to organizational strategic objectives, the degree of support and advocacy for training use, and other factors that may contribute to or impede training transfer into M&E

(Continued)

Method	Description
	practice. As with training feedback forms, it is important to include open-ended as well as closed-ended questions, which can help identify any unanticipated outcomes or consequences from training. Post-training interviews can be easy and cost-effective to administer, especially when using an online survey platform, but when voluntary the results may be biased according to those who select to participate. When possible, consider making the post-training survey a required component of training for participants and providing incentives for respondent groups identified to survey.
Structure interviews	Post-training interviews, whether individual or focus group discussions, can be a valuable way to explore the extent of training transfer and the achievement of longer-term training outcomes. Depending on the number of interviews conducted, this qualitative approach can involve considerable time and resources in both data collection and analysis. However, the information can be rich in helping to understand not only what occurred as a result of M&E training but why. Interviews are also very effective to identify unintended outcomes and consequences from training that may otherwise be overlooked in survey questionnaires structured on pre-identified assessment areas.
Post-training observation	In settings where it is possible to follow up with trainees in person, performance observation can be used to assess the uptake and practice of M&E practices. In addition to contributing to training evaluation, this can be an important part of training follow-up, helping the trainees reflect on their M&E learning and practice. However, individual observations can require considerable time and resources, and trainee buy-in as well as the support from management in organizational settings is critical.
Learner portfolios, logbooks, and journals	When it is possible to follow up with trainees, a systematic collection of trainee work and/or reflections following training can provide useful evidence to assess trainee performance and the usefulness of M&E training. The contents of a learner portfolio can be diverse, including examples of logframes, M&E plans, or evaluation ToRs developed by trainees; job performance assessments; and mentor or supervisor reports. A learning journal or logbook can be used to document learning accomplishments as well as problems encountered, solutions, and lessons learned. More than tools for training evaluation, learner profiles and journals are an effective way to engage trainees to support training follow-up and transfer. However, they entail time, careful planning, and buy-in by trainees and other potential stakeholders that may contribute to or support the use of such processes.
Performance reviews	In organizational training contexts, any individual performance or professional development review process can be an additional data source of training evaluation. These reviews can include assessment of progress toward M&E core competencies related to training learning objectives and personal goals. Depending on the context, it can include work examples (e.g., see learner profile), personal reflections (e.g., learner journal), and feedback gathered from supervisors, peers, and subordinates (360-degree feedback).

Appendix 11.2 Example M&E Learning Development Plan[5]

> **Instructions**
>
> - This form is required by all trainees. Please send to "John Smith" at <email address> upon completion. If you have any questions or concerns, please use the email to contact "John Smith."
> - The purpose of this plan is to support trainees to reflect upon and get the most from training and to provide background information about trainees to assist in training planning.
> - This should be completed as part of a consultation between individual trainees and their managers—specifically for the sections related to *Learning Objectives, Training Utilization and Further Development,* and *Further Assistance.*

Participant name:	**Job title:**
Organization and address:	
Email:	**Skype:**
Landline phone #:	**Mobile phone #:**
Manager/supervisor name, email, and phone number:	
Gender: male female	**Native language:**
Other language & level (<u>h</u>igh, <u>i</u>ntermediate, <u>l</u>ow): *[Example "French (I), Spanish (L)"]*	
Any dietary restrictions—for example, vegetarian or allergies?	

PMER Experience	Mark with X
1. **Level of experience in project design (logical framework) development** <ul><li>Worked with logframes or similar design models but have not developed them</li><li>Developed logframes but not often</li><li>Regularly develop logframes and/or guide others to do so (more than three times a year or ten times total)</li></ul>	
2. **Level of experience in M&E planning** <ul><li>Worked with M&E plans (or similar models) or data collection and analysis but not developed them</li><li>Developed M&E plans (or similar) and/or worked with data collection and analysis but not often</li><li>Regularly develop M&E plans (or similar) and/or worked with data collection and analysis or guide others to do so (more than three times a year or 10 times total)</li></ul>	

(Continued)

---

5. Note that space in this form for written answers has been abbreviated. Some of the data in this example form may not be necessary as it may already be obtained from training analysis. The form is adapted from IFRC (2015c).

(Continued)

3. **Level of experience in managing or conducting evaluations**
• Participated in an evaluation but not as an evaluator or the manager
• Conducted or managed evaluations but not often
• Regularly participate in either conducting or managing evaluations and/or guide others to do so (more than twice a year or 10 times total)

Pre-Training Expectation & Objectives

- **Overall expectation.** Summarize your primary expectations from this training (how you plan to put it to use).
- **Learning objectives.** Summarize any specific knowledge, skills, or attitudes you want from this training.
- **Training utilization and further development.** Specifically, in what ways do plan to apply and integrate learning form this training into practice (e.g., your job)?
- **Let us know anything else you want us to know about you.**

Post-Training Reflection (to be completed AFTER the training workshop)

- **Overall expectations,** Now that some time has passed, do you feel the training has met you expectations? Please explain your answer.
- **Learning objectives,** Do you feel you met your originally stated learning objectives? Please explain your answer.
- **Training utilization and further development.** Have you been able to apply what you have learned into practice, and what would help you to do so? Please explain your answer.
- **Further assistance.** Do you need further assistance, and if so, what kind of assistance?

Appendix 11.3 Example Trainee Feedback Form[6]

Training name:
Date/Location:
Trainers' names:
Please note!
• Your feedback is confidential and greatly appreciated, and will help improve future training. ***Thank you!***
• Please check the appropriate box, and comments explaining your answers will be very appreciated.
• We will share with you analysis of training feedback via email the week after training.

---

6. Note that space in this form for written answers has been abbreviated. This is just an example and the content can drill down to more specific questions about the training and trainer. This form is adapted from IFRC (2015d).

Overall Rating Scale ⇒	☺ Excellent	☺ Good	😐 Average	☹ Poor
1. What was the training's overall value to you?				
Comments/explanation:				
2. Will the training help you to be more effective in your work?				
Comments/explanation:				
3. Did the balance of theory and practice help you understand the topics?				
Comments/explanation:				
4. Was the training facilitation clear and effective?				
Comments/explanation:				
5. How was the length and timing?				
Comments/explanation:				
6. How was the quality of the materials/handouts?				
Comments/explanation:				
7. How were the logistics & admin arrangements prior to and during training?				
Comments/explanation:				
8. How were the training facilities?				
Comments/explanation:				
9. Would you recommend this training to your colleagues?				
Comments/explanation:				

(Continued)

(Continued)

10. **What was the best part of the training? Please explain your answer.**

11. **What was the worst part of the training? Please explain your answer.**

12. **Do you have any suggestions to improve this training in the future (e.g., on session timing, facilitation/ presentation methods, practical issues, etc.)?**

13. **Please use the space below and on the back of this form to provide any additional feedback.**

Appendix 11.4 Example Trainer Assessment Form

Trainer's name:

Training title:

| **Date completed:** | **Reviewers (if applicable):** |

Instructions

The purpose of this form is to reflect upon and record assessment of a trainer's performance. It can be used for trainer professional development and/or as a record for future reference for those recruiting trainers. It can be modified to be used for trainer self-assessment, co-trainer assessment, trainee assessment of trainers, and/ or external observer assessment of trainers. It can also be used to assess candidates when recruiting trainers (see Chapter 5).

This is only a generic example and the identified criteria should be aligned to the specific training and purpose of assessment. The example criteria are many, and the content should be weighed and revised relative to the degree of rigor and time required. For example, criteria can be rewritten as self-reflection questions for trainers without rating. On the other hand, a rubric can be developed to more consistently rate candidates on each criteria according to training/job needs. Note that space in this form for written answers has been abbreviated and should be tailored accordingly.

Written and oral instructions for this form should include informed consent according to the reviewer and assessment purpose.

Assessment Criteria	🙂 Excellent	🙂 Good	😐 Average	🙁 Poor
Standards and ethics				
• Degree the trainer observed and upheld ethical and professional conduct. Explain:				

Assessment Criteria	😊 Excellent	🙂 Good	😐 Average	🙁 Poor
Pre-training				
• Stakeholder consultation and involvement. Explain:				
• Training planning and preparation (design, materials, logistics, pre-assignments). Explain:				
• Pre-training communication with trainees. Explain:				
Training delivery				
Adult learning principles				
1. Establishes a safe and respectful environment to support learning. Explain:				
2. Responds to the "need to know" *what*, *why*, and *how* they are learning (frames expectations, learning objectives, and activity instructions clearly). Explain:				
3. Provides a structured yet flexible progression appropriate for trainee level. Explain:				
4. Empowers trainees with genuine participation so they can fully participate in their own learning process. Explain:				
5. Incorporates and builds upon prior trainee experience (*relevance*). Explain:				
6. Relates learning to what is relevant and meaningful to trainee's practical needs. Explain:				
7. Employs experiential learning where trainees were able to learn by doing. Explain:				
8. Incorporates active and fun activities for engaging and enjoyable learning. Explain:				
9. Uses mixed and multisensory methods to address different learning styles (effectively incorporates a variety of training aids). Explain:				

(Continued)

(Continued)

Assessment Criteria	😊 Excellent	🙂 Good	😐 Average	🙁 Poor
10. Differentiates instruction to meet different learners' needs. Explain:				
11. Supports collaborative and peer learning. Explain:				
12. Incorporates adequate practice and repetition to support learning. Explain:				
13. Utilizes primacy and recency to reinforce learning. Explain:				
14. Provides opportunity for feedback and positive reinforcement. Explain:				
Facilitation				
• Subject matter expertise and comfort with training content (practical examples, respond to unanticipated questions). Explain:				
• Training communication (explanations, demonstrations, use of metaphors, use of examples, pronunciation, audibility, eye contact, body language, movement and gestures). Explain:				
• Cultural competence (aware of, respects, and effectively interacts with different people of different cultures). Explain:				
• Use of questions (and responding to them). Explain:				
• Facilitation and group management (lead discussion, consensus reaching, listening and rephrasing, summarizing). Explain:				
• Administers learning assessment and training evaluation. Explain:				
• Co-facilitation (effectively interacts with other trainers in a positive manner). Explain:				
• Handling disruptive behavior (recognizes and effectively responds to negative or distractive behavior). Explain:				

Assessment Criteria	☺ Excellent	☺ Good	😐 Average	☹ Poor
• Time management (smoothly follows training agenda or adjusts accordingly as needed so learners do not feel rushed). Explain:				
Post-training follow-up (as appropriate)				
• Post-training communication				
• Post-training activities to support training transfer				
• Post-training learning assessment				
• Summative training evaluation				
Management Skills (as appropriate)				
• Organization, planning, and logistics				
• Resourcing and budgeting				
• Recruitment and supervision of personnel				
• Contractual and legal agreements				
Personal Attributes, for example . . .				
• Organized and prepared				
• Results orientated				
• Versatile and flexible				
• Patient and accepting				
• Energetic and enthusiastic				
• Humorous and fun				
• Creative				
• Empathetic				
• Authentic				
• Responsive				
• Other...				
Additional Comments—Use this space to record any additional points worth noting, etc.				

11.7 RECOMMENDED RESOURCES _____

Training evaluation is best considered during the analysis and design stages; thus, we again recommend three resources on backward planning identified earlier: AECD (2010), Clark (2015c), and Wiggins & McTighe (2005). For further reading on Kirkpatrick's four levels for evaluating training programs, we recommend his book *Evaluating Training Programs: The Four Levels*, for a technical discussion, and the companion book *Implementing the Four Levels: A Practical Guide for Effective Evaluation of Training Programs* for a more practical guide—(both largely focus on business contexts) (Kirkpatrick, 1996; Kirkpatrick & Kirkpatrick, 2007). The freely available *Training Evaluation Field Guide* by the U.S. Office of Personnel Management (USOPM, 2011) is an example of the application of the Kirkpatrick's model for training evaluation and effectiveness in federal agencies.

For further reading on Guskey's five-level framework for evaluating professional development, we recommend his book, *Evaluating Professional Development* (Guskey, 2000), which includes sample evaluation forms, checklists, as well as practical guidance tips. Available online, the Evaluation Exchange (2005) published a useful conversation with Thomas Guskey, which provides a concise overview of his model.

For a logical framework approach to training evaluation, there are a variety of publications and guidelines on logic modeling for program and project design. Two books we recommend are *Purposeful Program Theory* (Funnell & Rogers, 2011) and *The Logic Model Guidebook* (Wyatt & Phillips, 2013). There are also a variety of freely available publications on logic modelling, of which we recommend the *Logic Model Development Guide* by the Kellogg Foundation (2004). We refer readers to the online M&E resources identified in Chapter 2 for further links to logic modelling resources, such as the webpage on BetterEvaluation (2015), *Develop Programme Theory/Logic Model*, which includes links to related topics and resources.

Other freely available resources on evaluation in general that are useful for training contexts include the *Evaluation Handbook* by the Kellogg Foundation (1998), which is a useful complement to their logic model guide recommended above; the guide from the Robert Wood Johnson Foundation for engaging stakeholders in developing evaluation questions (Preskill & Jones, 2009); and the guide from the Centers for Disease Control and Prevention (CDC, 2013) on evaluation reporting that supports the use of findings.

There is an array of other publications specifically on training evaluation. For example, Leslie Rae has written extensively on the topic, and his book, *Using Evaluation in Training and Development*, provides a user-friendly overview of different approaches (Rae, 1999). Readers may also be interested in the *Handbook of Training Evaluation and Measurement Methods* by Phillips (1997), noted for their work on return on investment (ROI) for training design and evaluation.

Recommended in earlier chapters, the freely available training guides by IntraHealth International (2007) and WHO (2005) each include useful sections on training evaluation. The website of HELVETAS Swiss Intercooperation (2015) offers a useful online publication for evaluating vocational education and training (VET) interventions. Businessballs (2015) offers a variety of useful topics for training evaluation, and we recommend its webpage on *Training Programme Evaluation*, by Leslie Rae, as well as the webpage on Kirkpatrick's Learning and Training Evaluation Theory. The Free Management Library (2015) provides a useful summary of *Evaluating Training and Results (ROI of Training)*, with links to additional resources by Carter McNamara. We also recommend the Training and Development Policy Wiki on the website of the U.S. Office of Personnel Management (USOPM, 2015), which provides links to a variety of resources for training evaluation as well as links to several other models for training evaluation. We found the online *Clinical Educator's Resource Kit* (QOTFC, 2007) to have useful interactive webpages on feedback, reflection and self-evaluation, and evaluation.

Lastly, there are also a variety of books on program evaluation in general that are useful to consider training evaluation. Four volumes in our bookshelves that we found useful in the preparation of this chapter include: *Evaluation: A Systematic Approach* (Rossi, Lipsey, & Freeman, 2004); the *Essentials of Utilization-Focused Evaluation* (Patton, 2012); *Real World Evaluation* (Bamberger, Rugh, & Mabry, 2012), as well as *A Practical Guide to Program Evaluation Planning* (Holden & Zimmerman, 2009).

M&E Training Methods and Techniques

Effective M&E trainers require an arsenal of methods and techniques that they can use and adapt in multiple and varied training contexts. We consider Part 3 of the book to be a compendium of practical resources and ideas for M&E training, and for that reason, it departs from the structure of the book that we adopted for Parts 1 and 2. Rather than a sequence of chapters, we have organized Part 3 as a single, admittedly lengthy section, which lays out a large collection of practical training methods and techniques that have and can be used for M&E training. We organize our discussion into 20 different categories of activities for M&E training facilitation, with an additional category on supporting training follow-up to reinforce learning transfer after training.

While our list of methods and techniques is quite lengthy, we do not claim that it is exhaustive. It is, we would suggest, comprehensive in that it covers a wide and encompassing range of possibilities. Where it makes sense, we have provided links to sources and other resources, but by and large, this collection arises out of our own practical experience from M&E training and education in various contexts. Indeed, there is a wealth of additional, practical resources on instructional methods and facilitation, for which we identify key examples in the Recommended Resources (p. 404).

Readers will note a *loose* temporal sequencing of the 21 identified categories with elements ranging from (a) opening activities designed to "hook" or engage learners, (b) content-oriented training activities designed to enhance cognitive and skill development, (c) assessment activities intended mostly for formative knowledge consolidation purposes, (d) closing activities designed to wrap up the training event

Learning Objectives

By the end of this part of the book readers will be able to . . .

✓ Identify primary methods and techniques for M&E training, including their

- Advantages
- Disadvantages
- Key tips or considerations for facilitation
- Specific examples illustrating each activity method

PART 3 Road Map to Categories for Example M&E Training Activities

1. Icebreakers	p. 318	8. Guest Speakers	p. 356	15. Practicum Experiences	p. 370
2. Energizers	p. 323	9. Panel Discussions and Debates	p. 358	16. Independent Learning Activities	p. 372
3. Lectures	p. 326	10. Role-Playing	p. 361	17. Review Activities	p. 375
4. Discussion Activities	p. 330	11. Simulations	p. 363	18. Learning Assessment Activities	p. 379
5. Subgroup Formations	p. 339	12. Demonstrations	p. 364	19. Training Monitoring and Evaluation Activities	p. 382
6. Case Studies	p. 342	13. M&E Software Activities	p. 366	20. Training Closing Activities	p. 388
7. Learning Games	p. 348	14. Learner Presentations	p. 367	21. Training Follow-up Activities	p. 393

and gather information for future considerations, and (e) follow-up activities concerned with the transfer of knowledge and skill into practice.

We begin each category description with a definition and explicit link to the adult learning principles covered in Chapter 4 and then summarize key advantages, disadvantages, and additional considerations. This is followed by one or more specific examples to illustrate more concretely methods and techniques—99 examples altogether. For instance, after our general overview of Discussion Activities, we provide specific example activities to illustrate how discussion can be facilitated, such as the used of snowballing, discussion stations, and visual response activities. It is important to note that many of the illustrative examples overlap in method; for instance, we present Hot Seat as a discussion activity, but it also has elements of case study work as well as learning games.

This final section of the book is grounded in and consistent with the principles that we covered in Part 1 and the systems approach for M&E training laid out in Part 2. In particular, we refer readers to Chapters 8 and 10 for overall considerations for the selection of training activities and their facilitation to best achieve training objectives.[1] For example, consider the following:

---

1. Consequently, there is some duplication of considerations for activity facilitation, but we felt it useful to reinforce key guidance as it applies to specific activity types.

- In Chapter 8, Box 8.3 summarizes guiding questions for activity selection when designing training curriculum. This includes the relevance of activities for learning objectives, the profiles and experience of learners as well as trainers, the principles of adult learning, and other context specific factors, such as the training duration, number of trainees, and available resources for training delivery. Particular attention should be given to the level and type of interaction suitable for learning objectives and the extent to which activities can draw upon actual examples, tools, and practices realistic to the context in which M&E learning is to be applied.

- Our focus on training implementation in Chapter 10 covers many considerations related to activity facilitation, such as the use of questions, training aids, facilitating discussions, co-facilitation, handling disruptive behavior, and time management during training. On page 260, we provide a summary of three general stages of a training workshop: the introduction, activity facilitation, and the closing. Many of the activity types we discuss in this part of the book illustrate more concretely how these stages can be facilitated.

Before getting underway, we want to highlight two other important clarifications for readers about our selection and discussion of activity methods and techniques.

First, the activities are primarily for live, face-to-face M&E training, especially training workshops. However, many can be adapted to an e-learning training context, and there are exciting possibilities to complement face-to-face training with e-learning for a blended approach to training (which we highlight in several of our activity descriptions). Yet it is important to recognize that developing quality activities to promote engaging distance and online learning involves a separate set of considerations, which deserves more detail than is possible in this book. For example, attention should be given to technological literacy and access as well as implications for interaction, feedback, and coordinating group work using a synchronous or asynchronous instructional setting. While activity development for distance and e-learning is beyond the scope of this book, we refer readers to our discussion in Chapter 2, which examines the potential of these delivery mediums for M&E training (with recommend resources for their design).

Second, our focus is on activity methods rather than M&E topics or methodological stages of the M&E process. As discussed in our introductory chapter, we use M&E broadly in this book to encompass a variety of interrelated processes in the overall RBM system. This underscores a systems perspective of M&E as a subsystem that is interdependent on other program management systems. As such, there is an assortment of potential topics that can be included in M&E training, which lie beyond the scope of this book. We would refer readers to the recently updated resource produced by Preskill and Russ-Eft (2015), which offers a comprehensive compendium of activities for evaluation education to consider for M&E training—see **Box 12.1**.

Therefore, rather than attempting to provide specific examples that encompass the array of potential topics for M&E training, our objective is to provide relevant examples to illustrate key elements of each category of activity method. Related, we have kept our descriptions of each activity method and related examples concise. Our primary aim is to provide user-friendly summaries with sufficient information for readers to adapt activities to specific training contexts and needs. The succinct descriptions of illustrative activities and techniques also allow us to include more examples within the space limitations of this book. In **Appendix 12.1** at the end of this part of the book, we provide an example of a more complete activity lesson plan to illustrate how activity planning can be further developed and detailed according to training context.

The possibilities for M&E training activities are boundless, and we hope our discussion and examples inspire readers to innovate for M&E training that makes a positive difference. We also hope it will foster a spirit of creativity among trainers to develop, adapt, invent, or otherwise create additional methods that are engaging and effective for specific M&E training context.

1. Icebreakers

Description

An activity intended to welcome and warm up conversation among learners at the start of M&E training.

Advantages

Icebreakers help establish the learning environment, can contribute to learners' need to know, and make training more active and fun (Adult Learning Principles 1, 2, and 8; Chapter 4, Table 4.4). They are useful to relieve inhibitions or tensions that people may have at training start and can help establish rapport and a positive learning atmosphere. They are also useful to gauge training participants early on and how they interact.

Disadvantages

Icebreakers can distract from learning time when unrelated to learning content, and they may be unnecessary when learners are already familiar with one another. When poorly facilitated, icebreakers can set a damaging tone for the training.

Additional considerations

Consider developing icebreakers that reinforce and contribute to the training's learning objectives. For instance, capitalize on the activity to identify learner's expectations and M&E experience. This can be useful to support mutual understanding of and patience for the diversity of individual goals and levels present during the training. Of course, icebreakers help people get to know each other, so consider adding something fun, such as an interesting fact about the person (e.g., their favorite food or animal or nickname) to help learners relate to and remember individual names or characteristics.

Planning and clearly framing instructions and outcomes is critical; participants will want to know if they are to reveal certain things about themselves. Be careful so that icebreakers do not inadvertently insult or negatively affect individuals. Related, it is important that trainees are not forced to participate in ways that may be inappropriate for their learning styles or cultural context. For example, more inhibited or shy people may be more comfortable sharing expectations using more confidential activities.

Below we present some example activities for icebreakers for which the underlying approach can also be adapted for discussion activities of M&E topics and activity debrief and feedback.

1.1 Minute (or less) Introductions

This is a useful activity when time is of essence, such as a half-day or less training. People quickly go around and introduce essential information about themselves. It is helpful for the trainer to model it first and to visually display information to include in the introduction: for example, name, job title, organization, where they are from, where they currently live, M&E background, one thing they want to get out of the training, something interesting to remember the person (e.g., favorite food, pastime, animal).

A variation is to allow participants to introduce themselves in whatever manner they want, whether it is a song, dance, or just speaking. However it is facilitated, a firm timekeeper is recommended, as this activity is usually used when time constraints are a priority. One caveat to keep in mind is that some people are quite shy about having to speak publicly to a large group of strangers and might feel anxious as their "turn" approaches. Consider asking for a hand signal to indicate when participants are ready to self-introduce.

1.2 Popcorn Introductions

This is an active way to help people get to know each other while avoiding lengthy introductions. The trainer calls out, "Stand (pop) up if you . . . ," and then completes the statement with a (funny) fact about people's backgrounds, interests, and motivations for training. For example, "English is not your native language . . . ," "Have travelled more than X hours to attend this training event . . . ," "Have developed an M&E plan . . . ," "Have been part of an evaluation team . . . ," "Have lead a focus group . . . ," "Knows what RCTs are . . . ," and so on. It is useful to include statements that help the group scope the diversity of people, M&E experience, and other relevant information for training. If appropriate, participants can call out their own statements as well.

1.3 Paired Introductions

This is a common icebreaker for introductions. Participants pair up and interview each other, gathering information to introduce their partners to the group in plenary discussion. Questions can be prepared prior or agreed upon by the group, related to participants' background, M&E experience, training expectations, something interesting or funny to remember the person, and so forth. Consider arranging seats or standing in a circle for plenary sharing.

1.4 Name Tag/Card Jumble

This is a quick but active way for people to intermingle and get to know each other. The trainer shuffles and passes out name cards, and everybody needs to find the person whose name matches that on the card they were given. A short interview can ensue, where name tag givers get key background information to introduce to the group their name tag recipients—see Paired Introductions above.

1.5 M&E Level Tree

This is a useful activity to visually reinforce names and get an idea of everyone's M&E background (IFRC, 2011c). Prepare a sketch of a tree on a flipchart paper displayed on the wall (or on the floor) where everyone can see it. Place a card in the lower part of the trunk of the tree labeled "beginner," the lower branches labeled "intermediate," and in the higher branches labeled "advanced." Each participant introduces themselves by legibly writing their name on a Post-it note (or small index card) and affixing it on the tree according to how they rate their level of M&E experience. It is helpful to provide criteria to guide people in their self-rating; for instance, beginner for no prior experience with evaluations, intermediate for experience on an evaluation team, and advanced for experience leading evaluations. As people introduce themselves, they can also state other useful background information, such as their expectation for training. Another option, as illustrated, is to have people write their expectations for training on the Post-it note, which they affix on the M&E tree according to their level of experience. Consider taking pictures of the tree as a training record.

Courtesy of Chaplowe (2015)

1.6 Confidential Cards

This is a useful way for people to anonymously provide information that they may feel personally threatened to disclose; for example, training expectations, concerns, or their level of M&E experience. Questions are presented to people (e.g., on a flipchart) who anonymously write as many answers as appropriate, one per card—for example, "I took this workshop because . . . ," "By the end of this workshop I hope I can . . . ," "After this workshop I plan to use what I learn for . . . ," "My greatest fear for this workshop is. . . ." Cards can be collected, shuffled, and read by the trainer or participants or posted on the wall or floor for stand-up viewing and discussion. This can also be done while participants are arriving for the start of training to give people something to do when it is likely the training start will be delayed because of stragglers coming in late. When posted on the wall, walls can be named according to question focus, for instance, an "expectations wall" or an "experience wall." An expectations wall can later be used at the end of training to reflect on achievement of personal expectations. Consider taking pictures of posted answers as a training record.

1.7 Self-Portraits

This is a fun, humorous way to engage people when they first arrive and set up for an introduction activity. Each person is provided a sheet of paper or index card and colored markers, pencil, or pen to draw a self-portrait (e.g., artistic, cartoon, stick-figure, abstract) of something they feel represents themselves. Portraits are used for participants to introduce themselves, and they can post them for display on the wall or floor. A key element is the oral description/explanation to the group that accompanies the portrait. An entertaining variation is to combine this with paired introductions, with partners drawing and introducing each other. Another variation is to have participants personalize their name tags or cards, which they use to introduce themselves. Again, drawings can be used to convey useful information to complement training, such as M&E experience and expectations. Consider taking pictures of artwork.

1.8 Group Resumes

This is a fun team-building method when forming groups and for people to introduce themselves and their backgrounds. Participants are divided into subgroups and asked to prepare a group resume of their experience and combined resources. It can be framed as if they are applying for a consultancy or job. Resume categories can be suggested, such as the group's objectives, combined years of education, M&E experience, positions held, publications, other skills or accomplishments, hobbies, and so forth. Resumes can be shared by reading and/or posting on the wall using flipchart paper. A fun variation is to combine with group self-portraits, a variation of self-portraits described previously.

1.9 Bio Wall

This activity can be used when participants have prepared a one-page bio or learning development plan appropriate to share with others. It is useful when these are sent into trainers beforehand, so they can learn more about the trainees, and then trainers can post bios on one wall prior to the training start for people to preview while waiting for others or during breaks. Participants can use the bios to introduce themselves or with paired introductions (described previously).

1.10 Diversity Welcome

This can be a useful exercise when discussing ground rules for how people should interact and work together. Participants are asked to welcome different types of people into the room to help make everyone feel accepted and included and to acknowledge and demonstrate respect for individual differences. Write or post the statement, "I'd like to welcome into the room," clearly where everyone can see it. Then go around and have people complete the sentence—for example, "People of all sexual orientations . . . ," "People of all colors and races . . . ," "People of all ages . . . ," "People who speak English, Spanish, Chinese, and so forth . . . ," "People who are from (name the different geographical origins in the room) . . . ," "People native to this land . . . ," and so forth. In addition to prepared statements, participants can add their own statements to the activity.

2. Energizers

Description

A brief activity intended to increase the energy level among trainees, typically involving physical movement and laughter.

Advantages

Energizers help make training more active and fun (see Adult Learning Principle 8, Chapter 4, Table 4.4). They are useful to liven up the atmosphere during tedious M&E topics or when there is a lull in the group energy (e.g., after a lunch break). They are also useful for breaking down barriers, teambuilding, and reinforcing group cohesiveness.

Disadvantages

As with icebreakers, energizers can distract from learning time when unrelated to learning content. Also, when poorly facilitated, they can backfire and set a damaging tone for the training.

Additional considerations

When possible, use energizers that reinforce M&E learning content. Trainers should select energizers that they are comfortable and enjoy: If their enthusiasm is low, then the groups' enthusiasm will probably be low as well. Consider letting participants introduce and facilitate energizers, or if one is prepared beforehand, select and brief a participant to lead or co-lead the energizer with the trainer. It is important to anticipate time not just for activity but to move to and from an appropriate location. With this in mind, it may be useful to time energizers with toilet breaks or periods when trainees are already up and moving about. It is especially important with energizers that people are not forced to participate in ways that may be inappropriate for their learning styles or cultural context, especially with regards to physical contact. There are a variety of energizers from which to choose and these can easily be located with a keyword search on the Internet; one useful resource freely available on the Internet is from the International HIV/AIDS Alliance (2002): *100 Ways to Energise Groups*. Below we illustrate energizers we have found to be useful with an M&E theme and a couple of examples of quick, popular energizers with more general application. Several of the game activities described later can also serve as energizers.

2.1 Chocolate Estimates

This is a useful energizer to help participants understand that people have different opinions and that sharing and consultation can help arrive at a more complete picture (e.g., for evaluation or stakeholder analysis). Prepare a large glass bowl (or another clear container) with *counted* chocolate pieces or some other individually packaged candy or treat. Explain to participants that whomever comes closest to estimating the number of chocolates in the jar "wins." Place the jar in the middle of the room and instruct participants to walk around but to remain within three feet or a meter from the jar (i.e., beyond touching distance).

Each person divides (folds or draws) a piece of paper into three sections, and during the first stage of the activity, they write down their own estimate of the number of chocolates. Next, have participants pair up with an individual, preferably someone with whom they have not yet interacted, and have them compare estimates; then allow individuals to adjust their initial estimate if desired and write the revised estimate in the second space on the paper. During the third stage, individuals form (or return to) small groups and share/discuss estimates and agree upon a number to nominate from their group, which each individual writes in the third space on their paper.

After elected representatives from each group share their groups' estimates, reveal the actual number in the jar, which should be pre-written on a piece of paper (i.e., in the trainer's back pocket or on an overhead slide) to reassure people of a fair process. The "winning" group then gets the honor of serving the chocolate to others in the training before serving themselves. As chocolate is served, debrief with the group and ask how many people changed their individual estimates after (a) conferring with the person they paired with and/or (b) discussing in a small group. This can be used as a springboard to discuss the value of listing to different perspectives and opinions. The debrief can also explore how people conducted their discussions, consensus raising, the importance of listening to different viewpoints, and the like.

2.2 If . . . Then

While the connection is "light" and not direct, this is a fun way to consider theory of change, the logical hierarchy in a logframe, or the use of assumptions in program design (IFRC, 2011b). Split the group into two and have people stand in two lines facing each other. Individuals in one line pre-write phrases on scrap paper that begin with an "if clause," such as, "If I attend this training. . . ." The other line then prepares the other half of a clause statement—for example, "I will be able to leap tall buildings in a single bound." Starting with participants in the first line, each individual reads their if clause and then the person in the line across from them reads the completion of the clause statement with the phrase they have prepared. It is fun to see if it makes sense, and it often results in a humorous statement. The activity can be framed to narrow down clauses to a particular area, or it can be left open to people's imagination.

2.3 Hunter—Rabbit—Wall

This can be a fun activity to frame strategic planning or project design. This activity is a group variation of widely known game, "rock-paper-scissors." Split the group into two and explain that each subgroup will have one minute to huddle up and decide on a hand gesture to hold up representing either a hunter (gun), rabbit (fingers place on their head like rabbit ears), or wall (hands placed open and palms facing outward in front of people like against a wall). It is helpful to lead everyone in mimicking these gestures together first. Then each group faces each other in two lines and on the count of three they are to hold up their agreed hand gesture: hunters win over rabbits, rabbits win (hop) over walls, and walls win over (backfire on) hunters. It is good to do three rounds, and if there is any inconsistency in gestures from one group line, they automatically lose that round. A fun variation is to require all planning and agreement on hand gestures to be done in silence. Use the activity debrief to springboard into reflecting on group dynamics, the importance of having a plan, the potential challenges of consensus reaching, what worked and did not work (the value of assessment and learning from it), and so forth. **Caution**: this activity may not be appropriate in contexts where hunting animals or "shooting" may offend people, in which case other alternatives can be used, such as rock-paper-scissors.

2.4 WEM3

This is a quick activity that can be used to reinforce understanding that people may have very different but legitimate perspectives. Place on the ground a rope or cord in the shape of W and have the group stand in a large square around it, corresponding with the bottom, top, and sides of the W (if a rope is unavailable, a large W can be written on a flipchart paper instead). One at a time, ask people standing at each of the square's sides what they see. One side will say they see a W, another a M, another an E, and another a 3. Use the activity debrief to reflect on how each perspective is valid, and then consider lessons for M&E, such as stakeholder involvement and consultation during assessment and triangulating sources during data collection for a more complete picture.

2.5 Songs

Songs can be a fun way to take a break and engage learners, and there happens to be a variety of M&E-related songs to choose from, often written to the tune of a familiar melody—for example, see Susan Kistler's AEA365 Tip-a-Day post on "Songs with an Evaluation Message" (Kistler, 2013). In training in southern Africa, where there is a strong tradition of singing, we found the use of songs particularly effective. It is very useful to accompany songs with an instrument (when possible) or even something as simple as tapping, snapping fingers, or clapping to help maintain the rhythm.

2.6 Rain

This energizer can be renamed to "thunderstorm" to energize a group or "gentle rain" to de-energize a group and gain everyone's attention. Standing or sitting, ask everyone to follow the leader in tapping the palm of one hand with one finger of the other hand, then two fingers, then three, then four, then the whole hand, then back again—four fingers, three fingers, two fingers, one finger, then quiet. The sound mimics that of a light drizzle into rain into downpour into thunderstorm and then the reverse. The activity can also serve as a quick way to gain people's attention.

2.7 Exercises that Involve Contact

Energizers that involve contact can be fun, but it is important to be careful that they are appropriate for individuals, especially when men and women are involved. An example of an easy contact energizer is to have people stand in a circle and then hold hands with someone across from them, allowing people to cross arms; then the group tries to untangle themselves (which can involve people ducking under or stepping over each other's arms). Another example is to have people stand in a circle and hold the hand of the person next to them; then have alternate people lean in or out from the circle but be careful as people place their weight into their leaning! Such energizers can then be debriefed to reflect on teamwork, how people are all interconnected, and so forth. As with all contact energizers, careful attention should be given to physical and emotional safety of each person.

3. Lectures

Description

Typically one-way delivery of training content from a presenter, but can be accompanied by questions, answers, and discussion.

Advantages

Lectures are useful to convey a large amount of information in a short period of time, without interruption, and to a large group of people. They are also useful because they can be prepared beforehand to ensure all learning points are covered in a structured manner, supporting a structured progression (Adult Learning Principle 3, Chapter 4, Table 4.4). This helps ensure learning content is consistently covered when repeating training to different audiences and for reliable learning assessment of key learning points. Another potential advantage of lectures is that they can be recorded to be used later for consistent messaging and greater outreach (e.g., using online webcasts of the lecture).

Disadvantages

Lectures have low interaction, are instructor centered (rather than learner centered), and involve passive learning. They can be boring if the lecturer is not engaging and can be disempowering because of limited learner participation. They are also susceptible to content overload with poor memory recall for learners.

Additional considerations

Lectures can be effectively used as lessons that are combine with and used to frame learning activities. It is important that lectures are well structured, rehearsed, and relevant to learning objectives. Consider handing out an outline to respond to learners' need to know and try not to cram too much information. Of course, a key element of lectures is to keep them interesting and learners engaged. Toward this end, it is helpful to relate the delivery to real-life application or use and use engaging visual aids and props to reinforce learning (see Chapter 10). Effective delivery includes well-timed pauses and the use of questions and answers to check understanding, review key learning points, and reinforce learning (also discussed in Chapter 10). One way to engage learners is to encourage note taking and allow people to summarize for themselves key learning points. Another strategy to reinforce learner participation is to have trainees present lectures on key topics they prepare for beforehand (see "Learner Presentations").

There are a variety of resources available to support effective lecture presentations. Rather than activities, the examples below are presented more as techniques that can be used during lectures to make them more engaging for learners. As we explain, they can often be used as stand-alone activities as well.

3.1 Storytelling

As we discussed in Chapter 10, storytelling can be an effective way to kick off a training or presentation, capturing people's attention. Stories work best when they are authentic and the storyteller is comfortable with the storyline or plot. They can be humorous or serious and are best when they are relevant to real-life situations. Short stories can be useful to highlight key learning points, such as the "pocket example" illustrating the importance of mixed methods presented in Box 10.2 in Chapter 10. There is an abundance of resources available online that can be found with a keyword search of "storytelling and learning." For example, Koppett and Richter (2013) provide a useful, generic guide to storytelling for learning. One way to liven up a lecture is for the trainer to model a story illustrating a learning point from their own experience and then "throw it back" to the audience to see if any of them have an account drawn from their own experience.

Master storyteller Michael Quinn Patton (winner of the university of Minnesota storytelling competition) explains how he uses children's stories to open up evaluating dialogues:

The four short stories in *Sneeches and Other Stories* are brief and loaded with evaluation metaphors. "What was I scared of?" is about facing something alien and strange—like evaluation, or an EVALUATOR. "Too Many Daves" is about what happens when you don't make distinctions and explains why we need to distinguish different types of evaluation. "Zaks" is about what happens when people get stuck in their own perspective and can't see other points of view or negotiate differences. "Sneeches" is about hierarchies and status, and can be used to open up discussions of cultural, gender, ethic, and other stakeholder differences. I use it to tell the story, metaphorically, of the history of the qualitative-quantitative debate. (Patton, 2014)

It is worth noting that storytelling is also a technique used for M&E itself, allowing stakeholders to make sense of the past and possible futures for planning, monitoring, or evaluating interventions. See also Mayne (2004), who talks about telling an evidence-based "performance story" as an approach M&E.

3.2 Metaphors

Also discussed in Chapter 10 (see Box 10.3), metaphors and analogies have a strong tradition in M&E training, helping learners relate new concepts to familiar ones. For example, many readers will be familiar with the metaphor of an elephant, helping people understand that different parts can be part of the same system (for one blind person the trunk feels like a big snake, for another the tusk like a spear, for another the leg feels like a tree, etc.). The key points covered above for storytelling also apply to metaphors, and many of the best metaphors we have collected have resulted from "throwing-it-back" to trainers and allowing them to create a metaphor for an M&E concept during a lecture.

For instance, during one training activity a participant used the metaphor of whitewater rafting to explain the importance of risk assessment to inform project design (assumptions): Scouting the river beforehand helps identify potential stationary and transitory risks, such as rapids, rocks, and *strainers* (submerged trees that can tear a rubber raft). Another example developed spontaneously by the trainer with trainees is the use of buckets to help disaggregate and manage data: that is, separate buckets according to geographic, demographic, or temporal differences for the collection and management of data.

A separate activity can be developed as a short break from lectures in which people sitting next to each other or in small groups create metaphors that they feel convey the key learning point. Whether provided by the trainer, elicited from trainees during lecture, or facilitated as a separate activity, metaphors are useful to refer back to during training, providing "conceptual scaffolding" for learners to relate covered material to new topics. Hubelbank (2012) provides useful summaries on metaphors for evaluation that can be adopted for training, and there is even a book devoted to the metaphors for evaluation (Smith, 1981).

3.3 Cartoons and Other Visual Aids

In Chapter 4, we discussed the importance of vision as a learning style, and in Chapter 10, we looked at visual aids as one of several instructional aids useful for training. Books have been written on the use of visual aids, and it is beyond the scope of this one to review all the good advice and resources available. However, one example to highlight the potential of visual aids to energize a lecture is the use of cartoons. Whether projected using an overhead slide or presented on a flipchart, a cartoon can provide a useful pause from lecture delivery for interaction. For instance, **Figure 12.1** illustrates

FIGURE 12.1   Example M&E Cartoons

Source: Cartoons by Julie Smith, courtesy of IFRC (2011a).

cartoons related to M&E content. Try first displaying the cartoon with the caption removed or covered. Ask people what they think it is about or to write an appropriate caption. Then share the original caption (but be prepared for someone in the audience to come up with a better caption). Like metaphors, "cartooning" can be facilitated as a non-lecture activity (M&E game), with small groups comparing captions or creating their own illustrations themselves (i.e., similar to the self-portraits icebreaker described previously in this chapter). Prizes can be awarded for learner-generated cartoons, making the activity a game-break during a lecture.

Cartoons, comics, funny pictures, or illustrations can be located in print or on the Internet (observe copyright laws), developed by trainers beforehand, or created freehand during training. Kistler (2010) provides a nice summary of the use of humor and cartoons for evaluators. In addition to freehand illustrations, an online, keyword search for "comic generator" will provide a variety of links for free and pay-for software for developing one's own illustration, or readers can take a look at Sara Vaca's useful post on four easy and free comic-generator tools for evaluation (Vaca, 2013).

4. Discussion Activities

Description

People exchange ideas or questions on a given topic, either as a whole group, in subgroups, or in pairs. Discussion can focus on the learning content or the process of learning itself for training monitoring and feedback.

Advantages

Discussion activities encourage participation and can be used to support peer learning (Adult Learning Principles 4 and 11, Chapter 4, Table 4.4). The very act of people asking and answering questions, providing explanations, or expressing opinions helps them articulate learning points in their own words. Plenary discussion is useful to explore a topic together to ensure everyone is "on the same page." In our discussion of subgroup forming below, we highlight some advantages of using smaller group sizes.

Disadvantages

Discussions can be challenging to facilitate, stay on topic, and manage time. Outspoken group members may dominate while quiet-spoken members may be reluctant to participate. There is also a risk that discussion can diverge from the primary learning topic.

Additional considerations

Discussion plays a critical part in learner-centered training, engaging people to participate. It can be facilitated as a standalone activity or as part of another activity—that is, discussion is a critical aspect of an activity debrief. In Chapter 10, we discuss facilitating discussion. It is important to frame discussion topics beforehand and agree on outcomes and time to devote to discussion so there is a clear understanding and expectation that can support mutual facilitation and time management. Leading questions (Chapter 10, Table 10.1) are useful to guide discussion and stay on topic. It is helpful to call on less-outspoken individuals to draw them out for their input and participation. Build upon any ground rules identified during training start to encourage equal participation and respect for different viewpoints. Training aids, such as flipcharts and whiteboards, can be used for plenary summarizing and organizing key points and help arrive at consensus. Group ownership and management of discussion can be enhanced when participants are elected to serve as moderators and timekeepers for discussion facilitation. Discussion group size can be adjusted according to the level of desired interaction (which we look at next for subgroup forming).

Many of the other activities described in this part of the book are activities designed to encourage discussion and reflection among learners through case studies, games, and problem solving. Below we highlight some additional examples for facilitating discussion.

4.1 Question and Answer

Question and answer (Q&A) is one of the simplest forms of interaction for learning, which can be planned or incidental. It is a useful technique to gauge the level of understanding and interest and clarify complex learning points. It also contributes to active and peer learning, because formulating questions or answers reinforces learners' understanding for themselves and others. Q&A can be planned to debrief activities, or review learning content, or as part of another activity, such as questions to ask during a panel discussion.

In Chapter 10, we discuss the use of questioning for training facilitation. However, we include Q&A as a separate activity here because we believe it is such a basic but essential technique to underscore for effective training delivery. We encourage readers to refer to Table 10.1 on different types of questions that can be used during training and Box 10.5 on tips for questioning and responding to questions.

There are a variety of ways to facilitate planned Q&A activities. One example of a participatory approach is Pass the Question. This is a useful technique for both reviewing material and debriefing activities. Rather than the trainer asking questions, one person is called upon to ask another participant a question related to the discussion topic. The person who answers then asks a different person in the group (who has not responded yet) a new question related to the topic. If the respondent gets stuck, they can pass the question to someone else or the trainer can assist by paraphrasing the question and adding leading questions. Time can be provided for participants to prepare a variety of questions beforehand to support the activity and in case one of their questions has already been asked. This technique also forms the basis of a variety of review games, with teams developing questions/problems to challenge other groups to respond to or correct.

4.2 Brainstorming

Brainstorming can be used for open plenary or small group discussion where participants freely exchange ideas and opinions on a topic. It can be used to elicit new ideas and viewpoints; generate and organize lists (e.g., of stakeholders from a case study), steps or procedures, and problems or solutions; break a stalemate; or narrow down options in a short period of time. Participants can be encouraged to suspend judgment and criticism for a later stage, so they feel more comfortable to express innovative or alternative ideas or viewpoints. Brainstorms are unstructured by design, but facilitation (whether trainer or participant led) should support equal opportunity for input and participation. It is helpful to review relevant ground rules discussed at the start of training. Agree upon time limits for discussion, and when subgroups are used, provide time at the end of the brainstorm for each group to summarize and report back in plenary.

It is useful during brainstorming to have people capture and summarize key ideas using a flipchart or other visual aid for collective viewing, which can help organize them and reach consensus. A "graffiti wall" (using mural or flipchart paper) can be used where different people write down or visually display their ideas, summarizing key points, differences, and so forth.

We have coined the term *brain hurricane* to refer to a rapid brainstorm activity where subgroups have two minutes to write as many things they know about a topic, such as different examples of data collection methods. Within the short time allotted, key ideas or conclusion are written clearly on flipchart paper for sharing. Each group has one minute to display and explain their flipcharts. This can be used on a rolling basis throughout training to gauge the learners' understanding of a topic and validate prior experience when new topics are introduced.

4.3 Snowballing

As a snowball gets bigger when it is rolled down hill, this technique is used to increase the size of discussion as more people are added (in warmer countries where people are less familiar with snow, it can be called the "dung beetle method"). A question or topic is posed, such as, "What are the key elements of evidence-based reporting or effective evaluation reporting and follow-up?" Participants first individually consider the topic, then discuss and refine their responses or opinions with partners, then in small groups, and finally in plenary with the whole group (a similar format to the icebreaker, Chocolate Estimates). At each stage, responses and ideas can be summarized orally or written down on cards or notepads to bring to the next level, arriving at a master list representing the group's viewpoints. This approach takes more time than an open, plenary discussion, and it can be difficult to ensure each level is properly incorporated into the next. However, it is an effective approach for more active participation by everyone and allows people to experience differing degrees of interaction for different learning styles. A variation is to reverse the order, beginning with plenary discussion and working to individual reflection. With short-time limits for each stage, it can be repeated both ways.

4.4 Discussion Stations (gallery walk)

This is a useful technique for small discussion groups to share their ideas or conclusions with each other on a variety of topics. Each subgroup starts out a discussion on a particular topic or question assigned to the discussion station, for example, What are the elements of a good monitoring report? Evaluation report? Donor report? and so forth. They have a certain amount of time (e.g., 15 minutes) to discuss and record their ideas on a flipchart or whiteboard, after which each group rotates (counter clockwise) to a different station or spot to discuss the topic assigned there. However, one person nominated by each small group remains at their station (with their flipchart), as a "host" for rotating groups. Their role is to provide a short summary (2–5 minutes) of what has been discussed thus far (opinions/ideas) and then moderate the visiting group's discussion on the station's topic, recording any new ideas/opinions. When all groups have rotated to each station, the exercise can be followed by each host summarizing in plenary the discussion and key ideas/opinions shared at their station.

This technique takes more time than subgroup discussion and reporting without any rotations, but it is a good way to give everyone a chance to actively discuss a variety of different topics. Moving around and covering different topics is energizing for learners. A variation of this activity is rapid learning stations, where rotating groups each work on an exercise or task to be completed in a set period of time (similar to brain hurricanes, discussed above). Activity debriefs are used to identify challenges, solutions, and other lessons at each station.

4.5 Visual Response Activities

This activity uses visual aids created by participants to initiate discussion. Subgroups are asked to prepare a word collage (or cloud), graffiti drawing, picture, cartoon, or comic strip reflecting their views or opinion on a given topic—for example, "What are the components of a good M&E system? What are the key elements of a good (or bad) focus group discussion?" **Figure 12.2** illustrates subgroup drawings of what makes a good M&E officer on a project team. Combined with Snowballing, learners can first create individual sketches, then subgroup artwork, followed by plenary sharing, and then even a large group "masterpiece" can be prepared summarizing key lessons or conclusions. Artwork can be prepared and displayed in varying sizes using flipchart, poster, construction paper, or index cards. Different walls or floor space can be used to display individual, subgroup, and plenary group drawings. The value of the exercise is the thought and discussion that goes into creating drawings and then the explanations and discussion when it is shared with others. This can be a fun and entertaining activity, especially when participants are asked to portray something undesirable—for example, "What makes a bad evaluator?" A variation is to have small groups role-play different stakeholder group using visual response. Consider taking pictures of artwork as a record of training.

4.6 Mapping Activities

Mapping is another activity for training that is also used in the field of M&E, for example, community mapping, problem trees, and outcome mapping. It can be used in both plenary and subgroup settings for a range of learning objectives, including mapping M&E concepts, processes and procedures, good or bad practice, needs and resources, stakeholder viewpoints, and casual relationships. (The organization of opinions described below in the Four Walls activity is a form of mapping.) In contrast to linear, hierarchical tables or lists, it is easier to represent interdependent relationships using mapping. Maps can be done on the wall, floor, flipcharts, construction paper, and notebooks (see **Figure 12.3**). Index cards with reusable adhesive (e.g., putty) can be used to record key ideas or concepts that can be repositioned on the wall to show relationships or priorities. Consider taking pictures as a record of training.

Graduated mapping can be used at different stages during M&E training for reflection and discussion before introducing the next lesson. For example, for M&E training for a project, people begin by preparing a map of key components they identify for their own project M&E system; this is used as a segue into a lesson on the what is M&E. Later, they can then develop a second map of key problems or challenges for their M&E systems (e.g., tardy project reports that are antidotal and lack evidence-based data). This can build appreciation for upcoming lessons and learning objectives on M&E good practice. Toward the end of training, after people have a better understanding of M&E and good practice, they can then prepare a final map of solutions to the problems they mapped earlier in training. At each stage, key points can be mapped to show interrelationships. With such a graduated approach, each map can inform the other and highlight the relevance of other lessons.

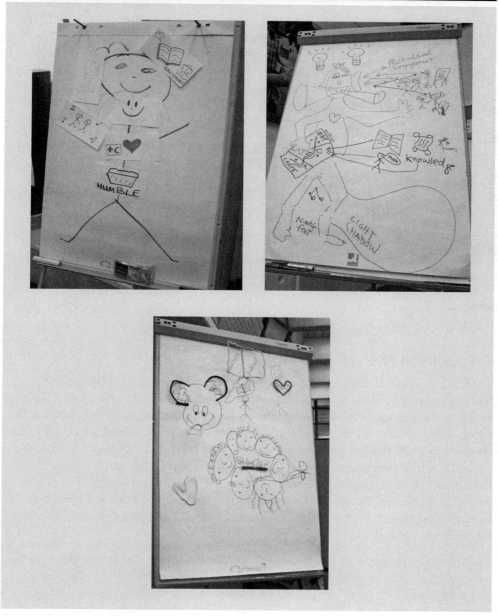

FIGURE 12.2   Example Drawings—*What makes a good M&E officer?*

Courtesy of Chaplowe (2015)

FIGURE 12.3 Examples of Wall Mapping

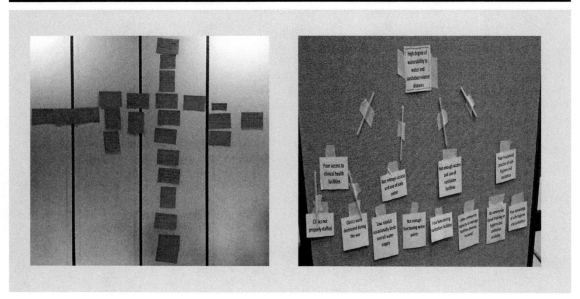

Courtesy of Chaplowe (2015)

4.7 Opinion Rating

There are a variety of ways to elicit and then rate people's opinions, which many trainers working in M&E will be familiar with for qualitative data collection. For example, the Kellogg Foundation describes two techniques for group interviewing, the nominal group technique and the Delphi technique. These techniques are used to pose specific questions that people consider and use to generate a list of responses that are ranked according to importance (or other criteria). "These techniques were developed to facilitate efficient group decision-making by busy executives, but they may also be useful in evaluation, particularly when groups composed of experts, community members, or project staff are making recommendations for ongoing projects" (Kellogg Foundation, 1998, p. 77).

Such mapping methods are also useful for eliciting discussion on various topics during training, ranging from M&E topics and practice to reflection on training processes and group dynamics. For example, we have adapted a "Four Walls" activity used for experiential education with young adults in California. Key questions, statements, or topics from trainers (or participants) are displayed on four walls or in the four corners of a room for people to walk around and silently read and consider. Some example questions include the following:

- What sources are there for evidence-based data for your project?

- What methods can be used to collect evidenced-based data for your project?

- What are the biggest obstacles for collecting evidenced-based data for your project?

- What can help address obstacles for collecting evidenced-based data for your project?

Participants write down (legible and anonymous) their responses on cards or Post-it® notes for group viewing. It is helpful to encourage people to abbreviate responses to one statement summarizing one primary idea. Each person then reads a response card and either places it on the floor or affixes it to the wall with reusable adhesive (e.g., putty). Confidentiality is reinforced when cards are used to write down ideas or opinions, collected, shuffled, and then handed out again before they are read and displayed.

People agree on a time limit for discussion and to collectively consolidate and group any similar responses. Each person is then given a few minutes for individual reflection on how they want to use a given number of votes. This is determined by dividing the number of individual or groupings of responses by a number providing a sufficient amount to distribute voting (e.g., dividing sixteen responses by four to provide four votes each person). Check marks or sticky dots (or small Post-it notes) can be used for wall voting, or small objects, such as beans, rice kernels, or coins, for floor-voting. It is best if voting is silent as people distribute votes among choices for prioritization.

Evaluators familiar with Empowerment Evaluation (Fetterman, 2001) will be familiar with this approach to prioritizing group ideas and opinions. It takes time and careful facilitation but can be an empowering method to engage people, allowing them to anonymously respond to and then analyze their responses as a group before individually prioritizing. The key elements of this approach are also used in wall or floor mapping to prioritize needs and potential solutions in participatory project design. The activity should provide ample time to discuss and debrief voting results. Consider taking pictures as a record of training.

4.8 Opinion Ballots

Opinion ballets are a safe, anonymous way to elicit and examine opinions in a group setting. Invite all participants to write down clearly and anonymously on a notecard or piece of paper key topics, learning points, definitions, personal or group lessons, good or bad practice, and questions or problems appropriate for the learning objectives. Opinion ballots are then neatly folded in half and placed in a large jar, hat, or bowl. One at a time, opinion ballots are then read out loud to stimulate discussion. An adapted version of Opinion Rating can be used for people to prioritize items. Opinion ballets can also be used to elicit different discussion topics on rolling basis throughout training or to monitor feedback on the facilitation and learning environment (discussed later).

4.9 Hot Seat

This learner-centered activity is an oral version of learner-generated, mini case studies, using one panelist who responds to questions about a real-life problem. People are provided time to reflect on an actual problem they have personally encountered related to learning topics or to fabricate one likely to encounter. For example, determining the best sampling method for a household survey or responding to a threat to the independence of an evaluation. Instruct people to clearly write their problems or scenario in a clear statement on a card to discuss with others. Problem cards are folded and placed in a box, hat, or other container. In this manner, problems can be selected randomly to facilitate for the activity (allowing the trainer to use as many as time allows). The selected problem is clearly read out loud, and the person who prepared it is asked to come to the front and sit in the "hot seat." The audience is provided a time limit for questions and discussions to explore the problem and consider solutions. (An added outcome of this approach is that it can complement key informant interviewing skills.) At the conclusion, plenary discussion can seek consensus on the best solution. If the problem is based on a real experience, the person in the hot seat can describe how it was actually handled—lessons can then be identified for future M&E practice.

A variation of this activity is to draw problem cards at different points during the training to facilitate as a break to pause or energize the group between other learning activities. Another option, although it takes more time, is to conduct the activity with interview questions rotated between subgroups, which are given a moment to consider and prepare their next question. After a period of questioning, subgroups are then provided a moment for reflection and discussion before they explain how they would address the problem. Solutions can be rated or compared with what actually happened for reality problems. Hot Seat is a flexible activity that can also be adapted for guest speakers or learning games (see "trouble sharing," following).

4.10 Kneesies

Kneesies is an activity fashioned after speed dating, an American formalized matchmaking process or dating system, the purpose of which is to encourage people to meet a large number of new people. Originally developed by Peter Walker (University of Ottawa), Kneesies is a great way to solicit participants' reactions or opinions or otherwise explore complex questions in short order. The activity works best with groups in multiples of eight (or six, as the case may be). Four stimulus questions are printed at the top of sheets of colored paper. In a session on participatory evaluation the questions might be the following:

- Who should decide who participates? Why?

- Can participatory evaluation serve accountability AND learning demands? If yes, how?

- Should intended program beneficiaries be involved as participants? Why/not?

- What are possible unintended consequences of participatory evaluation?

Two groups (A & B) of four participants are seated facing one another, close enough that their knees are touching, each group member having a different colored sheet of paper (stimulus question). The timer allows Group A 30 seconds to pose the question and record their counterpart's response. When time has elapsed, the Group B member reciprocates after which Group A members shift one seat to the right with the first member moving to fourth position (Group B members remain seated throughout the activity). The cycle repeats until each member has posed their respective stimulus question and recorded responses four times. The participants are then divided into color groups where the responses to stimulus questions are content analyzed (usually with the aid of a flip chart), and subsequently, the results are shared with the larger group.

4.11 Cocktail Party

A variation of Kneesies developed by Jenepher Lennox-Terrion (University of Ottawa) is called Cocktail Party. Participants move from table to table where a host greets them and introduces a question or problem. As a group, the participants discuss and respond to the question, while the host facilitates and takes notes. After a set time, participants move around the room to a different table (not as a group and, ideally, the composition of each new grouping is different from the previous ones). This can be a fun and productive exercise for active peer sharing and learning.

5. Subgroup Forming
....

Description

Activities that divide learners into subgroups to prepare for the facilitation of one or a series of learning activities.

Advantages

Subgroups are useful to vary the level of interaction for different activities and provide more opportunity for individual participation, input, and peer learning (Adult Learning Principles 4 and 10, Chapter 4, Table 4.4). It can be empowering for subgroups to accomplish tasks and solve problems as a team and motivating when combined with sharing and reporting back activity outcomes and lessons in plenary discussion. Subgroups are also useful for arranging learners according to different criteria, such as gender, language, prior experience, abilities, interests, learning topics, or problem solving (supporting Adult Learning Principle 10 for differentiated instruction).

Disadvantages

Like plenary discussion, outspoken group members can also dominate in small groups. When different activities (topics and material) are assigned to each subgroup, exposure to topics will be limited among participants, and plenary debrief can be time consuming. For face-to-face training, the possibilities and arrangements for subgroups will often depend on the training setting. Also, it can be challenging to circulate and facilitate different groups conducting different activities to ensure learners remain on task. Lastly, small group work can backfire if there is negative chemistry between any of the group members.

Additional considerations

The formation of groups will depend on the training audience and learning objectives. Subgroups can be homogenous; for example, by gender, M&E experience, or project teams. Or they can be heterogeneous, used to mix learners for a composition that will best support learning. Consideration should be given to the desired level of interaction, sharing, and peer learning. For example, learners with prior experience or language skills can be distributed with others to help explain concepts and processes. It is often good to have a well-balanced group, but in some contexts the presence of dominant members may be domineering and hinder the participation of others, in which case, it may be preferable to tailor subgroups accordingly. It is a good idea to ensure that group members are not highly familiar with one another; friends can easily wander off topic.

Frame individual subgroups' activities, objectives, and overall process clearly beforehand, including recommended timing for different stages of the activity. Clarify any questions beforehand about the process, and circulate during subgroup activities to support discussion or troubleshoot any problems that arise. More content can be covered by assigning different topics to each subgroup. Depending on the activity, it can be helpful to have groups assign different responsibilities, such as note takers or timekeepers. Consider debriefing activities first in subgroups and then in plenary. For plenary debrief, it is helpful to have groups elect who will present the results beforehand, assign a time limit for each presentation, and encourage presenters not to repeat but add to what has already been discussed.

Many of the other activities discussed in this part of the book can be used for different kinds of subgroup work, such as case studies and learning games. Below, we limit our examples to some approaches for forming subgroups. Whichever method is used, it is recommended to frame a group-forming activity beforehand so people understand the rationale and how they will be managed.

5.1. Prearranged Subgroups

Subgroups can be prearranged based on background information from trainee analysis to identify individual differences and commonalities. For instance, subgroups can be formed to support graduated learning objectives for different levels of knowledge and experience. Such approaches are useful to differentiate learning instruction and challenge; for example, the level of difficulty can be varied by using different case studies or problem-solving activities. Seating can be pre-assigned, or name tags can be color coded for or include subgroup names. This activity can be made more "tasty" when facilitators use candies (preferably individually wrapped) to randomly arrange groups, handing out different colors or flavors according to the desired number of groups (e.g., four different flavors for four subgroups).

5.2 Quick Random Selection

Different activities can be used to randomly arrange subgroups. "Count-offs" are a quick way to arrange subgroups with people of the same number. Participants count off in sets of numbers according to the desired number of subgroups (e.g., one through five), with people of the same number arranging themselves into subgroups. A deck of playing cards can also be used, shuffling and dealing one per trainee, who are then grouped according to shared suits or numbers (this group forming activity can also contribute to a discussion on random sampling).

5.3 Fruit Salad

A variation of count-offs, this can be a fun way to form subgroups with an equal number of learners. Standing or sitting in a circle, ask one person to name a fruit, then the person to their right to name another fruit, and continue until you have as many different fruit groups as you want subgroups. Then assign each named fruit group in repetitive order to each successive person until everyone in the circle is assigned a fruit group. This activity can be facilitated as an energizer, with the trainer standing in the middle calling out for all people of the same fruit group (e.g., apples) to change positions (or seats). While everyone is racing around, the trainer sits down, leaving one "apple" in the middle. To turn it up a notch, *everyone* needs to change position when "fruit salad" is called out. Variations of this activity can be used with animal names, M&E topics (e.g., different types of evaluation), or other desired categories.

6. Case Studies

Description

A form of problem-based learning (PBL) in which learners are presented with a problem, need, or challenge to address.

Advantages

Case studies are a useful method to make learning meaningful and relevant, using real-life examples or fabricated situations for which M&E practice is to be used (supporting Adult Learning Principle 6, Chapter 4, Table 4.4). They help convey how and why to apply a concept or skill, thus supporting the potential for training transfer. They are useful to consider complex scenarios and problem solving, and to frame group discussion and related activities. They also can be used for team building, as group members work through different opinions, methods, and perspectives to solve problems.

Disadvantages

Insufficient or poorly communicated information in a case study can backfire during facilitation; learners may not be able to interpret the story or "case" and how to accomplish the activity. Therefore, case study development requires time and careful consideration in preparation. It also requires additional time for trainees to read and familiarize themselves with the content prior to using the case study for the activity. Depending on circumstances (e.g., cross-cultural context) nuances of case studies may not be entirely accessible or understood.

Additional considerations

Many M&E trainers will be familiar with the use of case studies or stories for conveying findings and conclusion in evaluation. Case studies are an especially useful method for real-world M&E preparation and a great opportunity to use the needs analysis to develop a scenario that reflects the contexts in which M&E practice is to be applied. This can include using actual examples of M&E, such as a real needs assessment report, logic model, or terms of reference (ToR). Case study activities can be built around actual templates, tools, or software that learners are expected to work with after training.

Case studies can be presented in written, oral, audio, or video formats, or a combination of each for different learning styles. They can vary in length and detail according to learning objectives and available time, but it is usually best to keep case studies as concise as possible, focusing on key points: for example, problem or need, context, stakeholders, timing, and budget. It is particularly important to clarify and answer any questions about the case study beforehand to avoid misinterpretation. When activities involve working with case studies that are shorter in length, that is, a page or less, it can be useful to clarify that learners can elaborate or "color in" the situation to help achieve the learning activity and objectives.

Distributing case studies prior to training can be an effective time saver, allowing learners to familiarize themselves with and prepare to use the information when they arrive for training. For example, trainees can view an online video or read an emailed copy of a written case study. Case studies are very useful to frame and complement other activities, such as group discussions, role-playing, panel discussion, debates, and independent study/reading.

Below we summarize some examples of activities based on case studies, illustrating some different M&E topics, and end with a discussion of participant-driven case studies. The topics are illustrative, and approaches in each example can be adapted and used for a variety of M&E topics and learning objectives.

6.1 Stakeholder Analysis

There are a variety of ways to practice stakeholder analysis. This activity works well after key concepts and a process and tool are introduced to guide stakeholder analysis. Teams are asked to identify key stakeholder groups from a given case study using mapping to consider relationships. Small cards or tables can then be used to identify stakeholder needs, priorities, assets, and deficits. **Table 12.1** illustrates a table format for learners to analyze different stakeholders identified from a case study. Subgroups can be assigned the same stakeholder groups to compare analysis during plenary discussion or different stakeholder groups. This activity can also be used to inform stakeholder role-playing (discussed later). Consider taking pictures as a record of training.

6.2 Needs or Problem Analysis

This is a mapping activity where learners develop a conceptual diagram in a form of a problem (or needs) tree to identify the causes and effects to identified problems presented in a case study. This can then inform a solution analysis to select desired changes, such as behaviors to target in a project. Using the case study, small or plenary groups prepare key phrases or statements of problems, effects, and underlying causes, writing them clearly on index cards, which they can then arrange on a wall or flipchart similar to the profile of a tree: the core problem at the height of the branches, the effects or consequences above at the height of the leaves (or fruit), immediate and underlying (secondary) causes at the level of the trunk, and the roots representing underlying causes. **Figure 12.4** illustrates a couple example products from this activity as well as

TABLE 12.1 Examples of Stakeholder Analysis Table

Stakeholder Analysis Example – (RCRC)

STAKEHOLDER	Institutions		Potential target groups			
	Government	UNICEF, Oxfam, Helpage	Children	Women	Elderly	Others
						Water committee
Problems	Limited power	Difficult relations with government	Easily affected by unclean water	Have to walk far to get water	Easily affected by unclean water	*Need* training and support
Interests	Regaining control in the South	Providing support to clinical health care	Be healthy, be able to study	Health of their family	Health of their family	Health of the community
Potential	Provide basic infrastructure for health, education	Provide expertise and resources for health care	Learn and promote hygiene & sanitation practices	Learn and promote hygiene sanitation practices	Learn and promote hygiene & sanitation practices	Maintain new or repaired water/sanitation facilities
Interaction	Work through established channels	Inter-agency coordination meeting	Regular focus group meetings	Regular focus group meetings	Regular focus group meetings	Community meetings
Other's action	Working with UNICEF & Oxfam & JRC S	Working together, and with Govt. and JRC S	Targeted by Unicef & Oxfam (for health)	Targeted by Oxfam (for health)	Targeted by Helpage International (for health)	Previously supported by Govt.
Red Cross Red Crescent Action	Good relations, auxiliary status	Coordinates through IA platform	JRC S/Federation Malaria programme	JRC S/Federation Malaria programme	Community-based First Aid	None

Courtesy of IFRC (2011b)

FIGURE 12.4   Examples Problem Trees

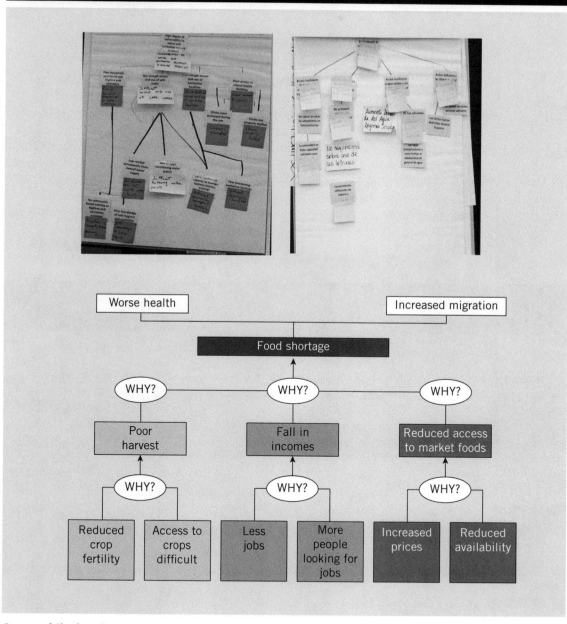

Courtesy of Chaplowe (2015, 2008)

an example of a trainer-prepared visual to explain the process. This vertical form of mapping can then be reversed with learners preparing solution trees, with objectives statements to address the problem and the underlying causes targeted by the project as well as the desired effects or longer-term outcomes the project seeks to achieve. Consider taking pictures as a record of training.

6.3 M&E Plans

This activity allows learners to practice mapping indicators in a data collection or M&E plan. After a lesson introducing key concepts, teams are given or identify different level indicators from their case study. They prepare on a flipchart a table with columns for each indicator and its definition, data sources, measurement methods, data collection frequency, responsibilities, and reporting audience—see **Figure 12.5**. Rather than each team preparing a whole M&E plan, which may not be practical given the time, good learning examples of indicators at different levels of measurement can be selected from the case study for people to practice with (i.e., process versus outcome indicators). Similar to the SMARTer Indicator Game, discussed later, this activity can be adapted into a team competition, with scoring of team products. Consider taking pictures as a record of training.

FIGURE 12.5 Example M&E Plan Format

Example Data Collection Plan

✓ *A road map that guides you on how to actually collect data on [and monitor] your indicators & assumptions.*

Indicator Or Assumption	Definition (& Unit of Measurement)	Data Collection Sources -Method	Frequency & Schedule	Responsibilities	Information Use & Audience
OUTCOME 1:					
Indicator 1a:					
Indicator 1b:					
OUTPUT 1a:					
Indicator 1a:					
Indicator 1b:					
Output 2a:					
Indicator 2a:					
ETC.					

Courtesy of Chaplowe (2008)

6.4 M&E Bad Examples

Examples of what not to do are especially useful for considering the quality of M&E practice and products, such as monitoring or evaluation reports, logframes, ToR, and so forth. For example, after a presentation on the key elements of a well-prepared ToR, subgroups can each be provided with an example of a poorly prepared ToR. They can then identify problems and how they would address or "rescue" the ToR, which can then be shared and discussed in a plenary forum. The same problem ToR can be given to each subgroup to compare their conclusions and recommendations, or different bad examples can be provided (the more examples, the more time will be required to debrief in plenary discussion). A variation is to give each subgroup a bad and good example of a ToR for the same assignment and let groups identify which ToR is better and why; having a good example for comparison assists learners to identify solutions.

6.5 Participant-Driven Case Studies (scenarios)

Participant-drive case studies can be an effective approach for learners to work with real-life M&E situations or fabricated scenarios that reflect those that they are likely to encounter after training. This helps to make learning more practical and relevant to real-world application. This learner-centered approach can be used with plenary or subgroups and in combination with any of the other example activities discussed for case studies. For example, subgroups can create mini case study scenarios highlighting specific M&E problems, which they then exchange with each other to develop solutions or strategies. During plenary discussion and debrief, learners are exposed to a variety of learner-generated scenarios and how each group decided how to address the problem. The subgroup that prepared the scenario can comment on whether the problem was correctly analyzed and solutions identified as they envisioned, and often unexpected strategies or solutions arise.

As with most activities, it is important to clearly frame learning objectives and instructions beforehand. It is helpful if participants have experience working with case studies before, either in the current or prior training. It is also useful to have an example case study to guide and discuss key elements of a good case study according to the specific learning objectives. During a single-day, in-person training, it may not be practical for groups to prepare a detailed written case study but instead to summarize key elements for a scenario on a flipchart. For multiple day training or when using social media for e-learning, more elaborate case studies can be collaboratively written as an assignment prior to the training session/s. Another consideration is to ask participants in pre-training communication to bring examples of M&E that can potentially inform case study development.

Participant-driven case studies typically take more time than prepared case studies provided to learners. However, it can be very empowering for learners to create scenarios or situations based on their own real-life experience and context in which M&E is to be used.

7. Learning Games

Description

Activities designed to make learning fun, typically involving group interaction and often team competition.

Advantages

Learning is enhanced when it is more engaging and enjoyable (Adult Learning Principles 8, Chapter 4, Table 4.4). Learning games are useful for more tedious M&E topics, and they support participatory peer learning and team-building (Adult Learning Principles 4 and 11). Like energizers, they can be used to "lighten" up the training atmosphere with humor and play and help energize people during a lull in the training, such as after a lunch break or toward the end of the day when people are tired.

Disadvantages

Play or competitive elements of certain games may not be suitable for certain cultures and/or individuals. Competition and winning can also take precedence over and distract from learning. Game activities with pieces require additional preparation time and resources.

Additional considerations

M&E learning games are a great way to energize a group while also achieving learning objectives. The tone for games and play can be largely influenced by the trainers, so it is important they have the proper attitude and approach to support the planned activity (or it can easily backfire). It is helpful to frame exercises clearly on a flipchart, projected slide, or handout beforehand, visually reinforcing game rules.

When competition is involved, identify scoring criteria relevant to the learning objectives and remind learners that winning is secondary to learning. Consider assigning judges to each team to support activity management—that is, not only to help score team products or performance but also to moderate good sportsmanship. For training that takes place over hours or days, consider sequencing game activities throughout training and keeping a running score board.

Teams can be periodically mixed up to expose learners to each other and different experience and viewpoints (see subgroup forming, above). If competition and scoring becomes distractive, playfully remove scored points for poor "sportsmanship" or discontinue scoring altogether. When prizes are given (e.g., peanut-free candy), have consultation prizes for teams that do not "win," or create different categories of winners to reward everyone.

Many of the activities discussed in this part of the book can be tailored into a game by simply using teams to compete in presentations of activity products and performance. For example, the M&E matching exercises introduced for individual learning activities or Oscar Commercial role-plays, both discussed later, can easily be adapted as a game. We have also use team development of M&E Metaphors or captions for M&E Cartoons (discussed early as techniques for lectures) as fun "breakout games" interspersed during training.

Below we present some other examples of games that we have used for M&E training. Really, the possibilities are endless, and with a good mix of ingenuity and a fun attitude, trainers can design learning games for most M&E topics. As these particular activities reflect careful consideration to and preparation of game pieces and time management during facilitation is essential.[2]

7.1 M&E Masterpiece

We use "masterpiece" loosely to refer to a variety of learning games where teams work together to produce M&E products that they compare and rate according to different criteria. We begin with this generic example, as we believe it is one of the most basic and flexible approaches that can be adapted for almost any small group learning game where learners develop outputs to share with others. Outputs can vary from lists, outlines, key components or processes, best (or bad) practices, diagrams and other visual products, role-plays, and other performances. For examples, teams can be asked to develop a list or diagram of the key components of a M&E system for a given case study, a conceptual diagram showing the relationship between key stakeholders to consider for project design or evaluation, an outline of the recommended contents of a monitoring or evaluation report, the key steps for conducting an evaluation, interview, survey, and so forth.

The game element of these activities is introduced by judging or scoring subgroup M&E outputs, which can be done by trainer or the learners themselves. Judging criteria for learning products should be clearly framed beforehand; for example, relevance to learning objectives, completeness of key ideas, innovation and entertainment of team presentation or display, timeliness (efficiency) in completing the task, and so forth.

---

2. We also refer readers to the useful activity summarized by Nicole Vicinanza (2010) in an AEA365 "tip-a-day" post for a fun way to train people in random sampling using candy to illustrate the use of different sampling methods.

Prizes are a fun way to liven up these activities, which can be awarded at the end of each activity or at various points during training based on a running score board. It is recommended to set a time limit for teams to prepare their masterpiece as well as how much time they will have to present it to others. Related, it is recommended to brief teams to determine who will present or explain the learning product during plenary sharing and judging.

M&E masterpiece activities can be introduced prior or after a lesson covering M&E concepts. The Logical Bridge activity (following) illustrates an M&E masterpiece activity used to segue into a lesson on the use of logframes for project design using logframes. Other pre-lesson activities, such as identifying the key elements of an evaluation terms of reference (ToR), are a good way to determine and validate learners' prior knowledge and experience on the topic. When conducted after a lesson introducing M&E topics, these team activities allow learners to apply their newfound knowledge. For instance, the SMARTer Indicator Game (following) is a form of an M&E masterpiece game (with the product being and indicator).

One technique that works well to liven up a lesson presentation is to introduce a brain hurricane activity (discussed previously in this chapter) prior to a lesson covering a new topic, with teams generating a list of key elements, steps, or components related to the learning topic. At the completion of the team work, the trainers present their prepared list for comparison with and scoring of each team's generated list. Teams score points for every matching item on their list, subtract for any inappropriate items, and are awarded bonus points for any correct item that are on their list but overlooked by the trainers (which is a good safeguard to build into the activity). This approach helps to engage participants with the learning content and draw upon their experience and prior knowledge rather than just presenting out key learning points in lecture presentation.

7.2 Logical Bridge

This is a fun activity that introduces the basic concepts of the hierarchy of results in a logframe table. Everyone can relate to a bridge, and this activity is a springboard into a lesson on logic models. We profile this activity as our example of a completed lesson plan for an M&E activity in Appendix 12.1 at the end of Part 3 of this book. It was also featured in a "top ten" AEA365 "tip-a-day" in 2011 on Fun and Gamers in M&E Training (Chaplowe, 2011).

7.3 The "SMARTer" Indicator Game

Also dubbed the "Dumb Indicator Game," this is a fun example of an M&E masterpiece activity to reinforce learners understanding of well-designed indicators. The general approach to team preparation and play can be tailored for other M&E learning objectives, such as team development of results (objective) statements, or definitions for key M&E terms or concepts. After introducing the M&E concept, in this case the acronym of SMART (specific–measurable–attainable/achievable–relevant–timely/time bound) as it applies to indicators, teams are provided with examples of "dumb" indicators that are purposefully prepared for learners to identify their problems and correct. It is important to display dumb indicators so everyone can view them at the same time. Related, an appropriate results or objective statement should also be displayed with each indicator as it is required for learners to access indicator relevance.

Similar to a popular U.S. game show *Family Feud*, each team is provided a set time to discuss their given indicator (and results statement), identify which element of SMART is a problem, and rewrite the indicator to be SMARTer. When the time is up, they get the first attempt to present their SMARTer indicator to the group. Other teams can challenge and "steal" points if they provided a better explanation and rewritten indicator. Points are awarded after the trainer reveals the correct answer. Be prepared for trainees to come up with answers that may not necessarily match the prepared answer but are nevertheless valid. If there is more than one trainer, this is a fun activity to use a panel of judges scoring with numbers similar to Olympic diving (judges can adopt personalities similar to those on popular talent competition TV shows, such as *American Idol*).

As with other learning games based on good examples, ensure that corrected indicators are indeed appropriate and model the SMART criteria (otherwise, it can undermine credibility when trainees identify points that were missed by the trainers!). It is recommended to design the game using examples relevant to the program areas that trainees will apply M&E learning. A fun variation is to have learning teams prepare dumb indicators (and solutions) to challenge other groups with. Another variation is to facilitate this as a baseball game or cricket match with each team coming up to "bat" or take a swing at their indicator problem.

7.4 M&E Puzzle Games

Puzzle activities are fun ways to engage learning teams to correctly complete a puzzle of M&E products, processes, or steps. We will use a "logframe puzzle" example to illustrate this approach, with learners working with a prepared logframe based on a real project or fabricated case study. The trainers prepare different parts of the example logframe on individual pieces of paper or cardboard to fit in a large logframe table (template) on flipchart or mural paper: results statements, indicators, means of verification, and assumptions—see **Figure 12.6**. If time allows, learning teams can prepare the logframe table themselves, reinforcing their understanding of the template format, or it can be prepared beforehand by trainers to save time (this latter option also helps ensure the table is the correct size with column width and row height to

FIGURE 12.6   Logframe Puzzle Examples

Courtesy of Chaplowe (2015)

accommodate prepared puzzle pieces). Trainees work in small groups, which are provided prepared statements of the different logframe elements that they piece together in the logframe table.

The activity is best phased with logframe pieces for each element handed out progressively, after lessons introducing concepts related to each column in the logframe. For example, after a lesson on the results hierarchy of a logframe, teams are given the results statements to put into order in their logframe template; this process is repeated for after lessons on indicator statements, means of verification, and assumptions. Such an approach helps to break up lecture presentations with fun interaction and practice of concepts.

After each stage, correct puzzle arrangement can be debriefed by the trainer using an animated slide presentation or their own flipchart table with answers incrementally revealed. If team competition and scoring is incorporated, it can be co-managed with monitors from each team selected and assigned to other teams to check and confirm correct puzzle piece placement as the trainer reveals the answers. As with other game activities, prizes (candies) can be awarded.

This activity is especially useful when working with a project team or organization (Type 1 training) for which there is an existing logframe. Project managers are typically very pleased that trainees walk away from the activity with a considerably better understanding of their project logframe. Whether an actual or fabricated logframe is used, it is critical to ensure that it models the correct learning points and good practice for logframe design according to the desired format (different organizations and donors use various logframe formats). Variations of this activity can be used for other M&E products and practices that lend themselves to puzzle games, such as data collection (M&E) plans (discussed previously in this chapter).

7.5 M&E Definition or Concept Cards

This is a basic matching activity that can be facilitated in a fun, competitive manner where learners match M&E terms, concepts, or key practices with descriptions provided on cards. For example, key M&E terms can be selected from the OECD's trilingual *Glossary of Key Terms in Evaluation and Results-Based Management* (available in English, French, and Spanish) (OEDC, 2002). Key terms and descriptions or definitions are prepared on separate cards and handed out to teams to compete to match. Teams can all be provided with the same sets of concepts to match, or different sets can be provided to different teams to cover more concepts. This activity lends itself well to snowballing, with learners first conducting matching individually, then in pairs, then teams, and followed by plenary sharing and scoring. Cards can be organized on tables, the wall with removable adhesive, or on the floor. Plenary debrief and discussion of the activity can involve stand-up, rotating viewing, and scoring of team work.

7.6 M&E Dating Game

This is a fun, interactive matching activity that can be adapted to support a variety of M&E learning objectives, ranging from M&E terms and concepts to best practices. Similar to Roaming Role-Playing (discussed later in this chapter), it is also a fun way to energize training and to get people moving around, meeting and interacting with each other on an individual level. Statements are prepared on index cards that match key learning points; for example, evaluation types or criteria with corresponding definitions, indicators with corresponding objective statements, data collection or analysis methods with corresponding indicators, and so forth. Each person randomly selects a dating card from the shuffled or mixed group of cards and then walks around the training space to find their "date," introducing themselves by reading and comparing what is on their cards with the people they meet. When they feel they have met their "match," the couple then has a brief discussion about why they feel they are a good match, any related considerations for their matched learning point. They then prepare a short summary of the lessons from their date to present in plenary discussion and debrief. During the activity debrief, any mismatched couples are rearranged, with reasons for these mismatches and related learning is shared among trainees. If the concept of dating is culturally inappropriate for trainees, M&E "buddy" or "partner" can be substituted. One limitation with this activity is that, if there is not an even number of participants, one date will need to be a threesome. Related, the number of matched learning points must be considered in relation to the number of potential pairs in the group.

7.7 M&E Trouble Sharing

Problem solving based on actual scenarios helps make learning more practical and relevant for real-life application of concepts and processes. This activity can be tailored and facilitated in a variety of ways. We will illustrate it using two rounds based on a "do one, share one" format using mini case studies. During the first round, learning teams are provided a mini case study highlighting an actual or fabricated problem describing real-life problems or challenges one may encounter in M&E practice. Each scenario is prepared, clearly and concisely written on an index card, summarizing the challenge or problem to troubleshoot. During the second round (or as a substitute to trainer-prepared problem scenarios), teams prepare their own problem cards and solutions to challenges other teams (similar to the Hot Seat activity discussion activity described earlier).

This exercise works best after introducing guidelines of good practice. For example, scenario cards can be prepared for each team describing challenges to troubleshoot when managing an evaluation, such as disagreement among stakeholders when recruiting an external consultant, a threat to evaluation independence, disagreement or different opinions regarding evaluation findings, poorly produced evaluation reports, evaluation follow-up and use, and so forth. Teams then identify solutions by referring to a given organization's evaluation policy or other source of evaluation standards, ethics, and good practice. It is recommended to display the written scenario in plenary discussion for activity debrief (e.g., on a flipchart or projected slide), which can involve scoring or assessment of team solutions.

7.8 M&E Jeopardy

Styled after the well-known American TV game show *Jeopardy*, M&E Jeopardy provides a fun knowledge consolidation activity and is particularly useful to review basic M&E terms and concepts. (The game can be greatly aided by the use of a template designed using standard presentation software, such as PowerPoint.)

Teams of "contestants" are formed, each participating in turn in a clockwise fashion. Each team begins with a set amount of play currency (e.g., $1000). In turn each team selects a problem from one of five categories (e.g., see **Figure 12.8** template) and specifies the amount of currency they wish to wager. Teams have 30 seconds to come up with a response, which is stated in the form of a question, such as the following example:

- **Stimulus Problem**: An audio recorded conversation between two people in a private space with one person directing the discussion.

- **Correct Response**: What is a data collection interview?

If the response is correct (within reason), the team wins the amount specified; if the response is incorrect, the team forfeits that amount. By chance, teams may encounter DOUBLE JEOPARDY opportunities (usually 2 such opportunities per game), and the team must write down a secret bid *before* they see the stimulus problem. That is the amount of currency the team will win or lose. When all responses have been given, the FINAL JEOPARDY question will be revealed. Each team will wager as much as they wish up to a specified maximum. All wagers will be written down *before* the problem is revealed. That is the amount of currency each team will win or lose.

M&E Jeopardy is a fun way to reinforce understanding of basic terms and concepts. The facilitator should take opportunities to elaborate on misunderstood concepts as the game proceeds. It is best to award prizes to the winning team and consolation prizes to the others: "Everyone is a winner in M&E Jeopardy."

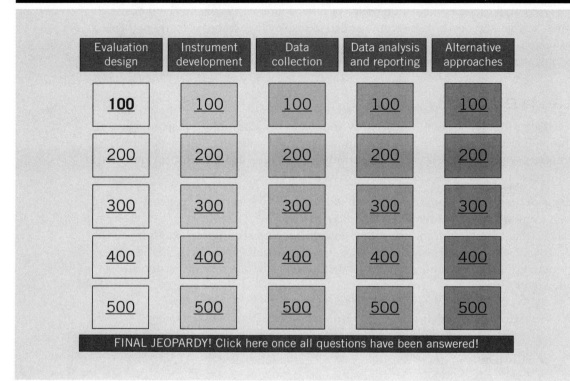

FIGURE 12.8   Evaluation Jeopardy Template

Evaluation design	Instrument development	Data collection	Data analysis and reporting	Alternative approaches
100	100	100	100	100
200	200	200	200	200
300	300	300	300	300
400	400	400	400	400
500	500	500	500	500

FINAL JEOPARDY! Click here once all questions have been answered!

8. Guest Speakers

Description

People external to the training provide a presentation or answer questions to support learning objectives.

Advantages

External speakers are useful to introduce practical expertise or different viewpoints relevant to M&E to make learning more relevant and real (Adult Learning Principle 6; Chapter 4, Table 4.4). Guest speakers can be stimulating and engaging for learners and add credibility to the training. As with lectures, they work well with large groups.

Disadvantages

Guest speakers share many of the disadvantages of a lecture activity (discussed earlier), such as low-level audience participation. Another consideration is that trainers have less control over the training content and delivery, which will depend on the individual speaker. Scheduling is dependent on speaker availability, and other costs may be required to engage the speaker.

Additional considerations

Consider inviting speakers form a university, research center, public agency, voluntary organization for professional evaluation (VOPE), or a qualified M&E consultant or practitioner. Guest speakers can also include clients or stakeholders of M&E for their perspective. Whoever is invited, ensure they are prepared with a description of the training, the specific activity learning objectives, and how they can best highlight their experience to achieve the objectives. Also, clearly go over the time frame, facilitation, and any other expectations with guests beforehand. It is also useful to have guest speakers prepare a bio beforehand highlighting experience and information relevant to learning objectives.

The facilitation for guest speakers can use a similar format to lecture and presentation or it can be conducted similar to a panel discussion (discussed below) but with only one panelist. Q&A is a good way to make activities with guest speakers more interactive. It is helpful to have trainees prepare questions based on the guest's bio and M&E topic, which they can ask before, during, or after the presentation or talk. Individual and group note taking can be used to summarize key points and steer activity debrief of lessons learned.

Below we provide a brief example of using video conferencing to conduct a guest speaker activity.

8.1 TV Interview

This is a participatory approach involving audience questions to interview a guest speaker who is inaccessible in person by using video conference. Have the guest speaker prepare a one page bio as it relates to the training focus. In preparation for the interview, learners individually read the guest speaker's bio and then discuss in small groups, preparing questions and other points to discuss. The interview is conducted using the Internet and telecommunications software (e.g., Skype, Adobe Connect), projecting the video synchronously onto a screen or wall using a computer projector. (Be sure to confirm time and test Internet connectivity beforehand.) The interview can begin with a short speech, provocative statement, story, or reflection from the guest followed by questions that are shared among the audience. It may be necessary to have each person asking a question to do so near the computer microphone, and depending on the training facility acoustics, a loudspeaker may be required so people can hear the guest. Also allow the guest to ask questions of the audience. Depending on the software used, visual media, such as example work products (e.g., a data collection tool) can be displayed by the guest. The activity debrief can involve the guest speaker or be conducted separately after the conference call has concluded.

9. Panel Discussions and Debates

Description

A moderated discussion or debate in which external experts or trainees themselves explore different viewpoints for a relevant topic, situation, or problem.

Advantages

Panel discussions or debates are useful for controversial topics, opinion sharing, and affective learning. They can also be entertaining for the audience. External panelists can introduce expertise, and other viewpoints, and can help make learning more relevant and real (Adult Learning Principle 6; Chapter 4, Table 4.4). Using trainees as panelists can be empowering and highlight their own knowledge and experience (Adult Learning Principles 4 and 5).

Disadvantages

Participation prioritizes panelists over audience (although audience participation can be facilitated through questions and debriefs). Quiet-spoken members may be reluctant to participate.

Tips

Depending on the learning objectives, example external panelists include people who conduct household surveys, facilitate focus group discussions, design results-based management systems, manage evaluations, or use M&E information to inform decision-making. As with guest speakers, it is important to properly brief external panelist about the activity facilitation and objectives beforehand and have them prepare relevant bios of themselves to share with learners.

An alternative to external panelists is to use learners themselves. As a group activity, this is a useful approach to accommodate active and pragmatic learning styles as panelists, and reflectors and theorists as audience. It is especially useful for affective learning objectives, providing a structure to allow people to express different opinions. Panel discussion and debates are also well adapted for role-playing.

It is important to clearly agree on ground rules at the start of panel discussion or debate. It is especially important for debates to stress respectful listening and patience among participants. Clarify any procedural questions on how the activity will be moderated as well as topic questions and activity learning objectives. Participation is increased when the audience is allowed to ask questions, which can be prepared individually or collectively by learners prior to the event. Capable moderation is important, including the use of time limits for questions, responses, and statements. When appropriate, learners can be engaged as timekeepers or moderators, allowing them to support activity management. Individual and group note taking can be used to engage the audience, to identify follow-up questions, and to capture key points for the activity debrief.

Below we provide two examples illustrating the use of external panelists and trainees themselves.

9.1 Three M&E Guests

This is a participatory approach for facilitating an external panel discussion. Rather than a moderator asking panelists questions, the audience leads and directs the questioning. Invite three guests who use and work in real-life with the M&E practices covered in training; for example, three evaluators or people who commission and use evaluations to inform decision-making. Similar in format to the TV Interview discussed earlier for guest speakers, each panelist prepares a short bio related to the training focus, which are given to trainees beforehand for individual reflection or a group-facilitated activity to prepare different questions for panelists based on their bios. The moderator's role is to rotate questioning between subgroups (or individuals) and the panelists, who can ask the groups questions as well. With the guest present in-person, it is useful to involve them in the activity debrief. For instance, provide time for small group discussion and reflection following the panel phase of the activity. Groups can list key reflections or conclusions, which they report back in plenary discussion with the guests. Lastly, allow the guests to each leave a reflection or take-away message for the group.

9.2 Trainee Panel Debate

This activity is moderated in a similar manner as a panel discussion, but without external panelists. Instead, trainees are provided (or generate themselves) issues related to training that have two or more sides. For example, people can represent different stakeholder perspectives based on a case study or debate the advantages and disadvantages of different M&E practice (e.g., external vs. internal evaluation, evaluation for accountability vs. learning, logframes vs. outcome mapping, the use of qualitative vs. qualitative methods). Teams are first provided time to reflect upon and discuss the selected debate topic and key talking points: This includes preparing responses to defend and questions to challenge viewpoints. Two teams debate at a time in plenary, with three people nominated to represent each team for a panel of six (having more than one person per team reduces anxiety). Careful time management is essential, and a timekeeper is recommended.

Role-playing can be encouraged to represent different opinions. A variation is to provide time for learners to identify and debate issues in pairs first, before snowballing into small groups and then plenary debate. A fun addition to the exercise is to have a panel of judges comprised of one person from each subgroup, who score debate teams; this is a useful springboard for debriefing key lessons. Scoring can model Olympic diving, holding up a number score and providing an explanation of the merits or weaknesses of a team's argument or position. In **Box 12.2** we provide a concrete example of a debate that we routinely use.

BOX 12.2
Should Evaluators Be Accountable for Use?

In 2008 Michael Patton was president of the American Evaluation Association and scheduled to make a keynote address on the Saturday of the annual conference in Boston. Carol Weiss, in her keynote address on the Thursday before, implied that given evaluation's political nature, the use of evaluation is beyond the evaluator's control. Word has it that Patton took exception to the message delivered by Weiss and substantially rewrote his presidential address to be delivered two days hence. His message, loud and clear, was that as evaluators, we know enough about how to conduct useful evaluations that we should be accountable for their use. Weiss' speech, Patton's presidential address, and Weiss' subsequent written rejoinder were all published in sequence in *Evaluation Practice* (Patton, 1988; Weiss, 1988a, 1988b).

This scenario provides a perfect opportunity for trainee-led simulated debate, illustrating how training reading material and content can be made more engaging and meaningful. Here is how we have structured it for training groups of up to about 20 members.

a. Have participants prepare for the session by reading in chronological order the relevant material articles. Instruct them to prepare for the debate of the question, "Should the evaluator be held accountable for the use of evaluation findings?" However, let them know that they will NOT know their role in the debate (pro, con, or judge) until the session begins.

b. In their review of readings, participants ought to identify five reasons why evaluators should be held accountable for the use of evaluation findings AND five reasons why evaluators should NOT be held accountable for use. Participants are also provided with a set of rules governing the debate from Musgrave (1957).

c. In the session, randomly assign participants to one of three equal-sized groups: pro, con, or judges. Review the rules for debate and then provide ample time for groups to prepare for the debate (30–45 min.). The pro and con teams need to prepare their assertions and be able to anticipate and rebut from their counterpart team. The judges need to develop a scoring rubric to be used during the debate.

d. Run the debate (according to the guidelines) including assertions, rebuttals, and questions/answers with the trainer serving as timekeeper and moderator.

e. Following the debate, the judges meet privately to review the scoring and determine a winner. They are instructed to provide constructive feedback to both groups followed by an announcement of their choice. The winning group receives a prize and consolation prizes are awarded to everyone else (including the judges).

10. Role-Playing

Description

Participants are provided a scenario, script, or instructions to act out and assume the perspective of a particular viewpoint or opinion for group learning.

Advantages

This has many of the advantages of a plenary group discussion activity (discussed previously) and can be very engaging, lively, and fun (Adult Learning Principle 8; Chapter 4, Table 4.4). It is empowering (Adult Learning Principle 4), encouraging people to explore other viewpoints they otherwise might not hold. Similar to debates, it is useful for affective learning and can prepare trainees for more real-life situations, especially work with M&E stakeholders (Adult Learning Principles 6 and 7).

Disadvantages

Role-plays share many of the shortcomings of plenary group discussion (above), especially in that quiet-spoken or reserved members may be reluctant to participate. Depending on the scenario, there may be a limited amount of roles for large groups. Role-playing takes time and consideration for the trainer to prepare case studies or scenarios to inform roles and additional time for trainees to prepare to act out.

Additional considerations

Roles can be played by individuals, small groups, and even as a whole group. Carefully prepare and brief participants about the scenario, roles, and activity instructions beforehand. Written handouts are recommended, and it may be useful to model or demonstrate the technique of role-playing for learners. Provide role-play descriptions to trainees beforehand, with adequate time for preparation. Roles can be randomly distributed, or allow trainees to select roles they are comfortable with. It is useful to encourage participants to build or elaborate their characters and use exaggeration and humor (when appropriate). Provide time limits to encourage equal participation, and consider conducting the activity as a panel discussion or debate. As with panel discussion and debates, learners can be engaged to support activity management as timekeepers or moderators. Likewise, individual and group note taking can be used to engage learners and identify learning points and reflections for debrief. Activity debrief can highlight not only what participants learned but also what they *felt*, reinforcing affective learning.

Below we provide three types of formats that can be adapted for and used to inspire other variations.

10.1 Group Role-Playing

This is a useful activity to support actors as a team in preparation for the role-play (which can help reduce inhibition). Provide or generate with participants a scenario, such as an evaluation with difficult findings or a poorly prepared monitoring report. Identify key characters (stakeholders) in the scenario and then ask for the same number of volunteers to role-play these characters: for example, an evaluator who needs to share bad findings with different people in an organization that has commissioned the evaluation. The actors then leave the room to discuss their roles, performance, and order of appearance. Actors can enter the room one at a time and act for the same scenario representing their role or viewpoint, or they can have different "acts," with one or more actors representing different aspects of the scenario (e.g., representing the beginning, middle, and end of the scenario). The activity debrief can begin with audience questions and actors still playing their role in response. They can then switch over to explain what they really thought and felt during the role-play.

10.2 Oscar Infomercials (mini-skits)

This is a fun activity that can be done individually or in groups. People are given (or generate themselves) an M&E concept, viewpoint, or good and bad practice for which they are to provide a one- or two-minute advertisement promoting their topic. As with debates, a panel of judges can be used or plenary judging where everyone in the audience can score commercial performances to determine who gets the "Oscar." It is helpful to frame scoring criteria to help ensure that commercials have learning content and are not just fun spoofs. These criteria can mimic evaluation criteria, for example, relevance (related to learning points), effectiveness (well delivered), efficiency (good time management), and so forth. The judging using the criteria facilitates debriefs of each infomercial and learning points.

10.3 Roaming Role-playing

This is a useful activity to involve everyone in a role-play. Prepare or have participants identify and prepare descriptions representing different roles for a given case study or scenario. For example, an evaluation commissioner, evaluation team leader, evaluation team members with different opinions, a donor requiring the evaluation, organizational management using evaluation findings, and different viewpoints of the intended beneficiaries of the program being evaluated. Each description is prepared clearly and concisely on a role card, which can be shuffled and handed out to participants or read with participants allowed to select their role. People then roam around and approach each other, one at a time, to discuss different topics or issues related to the scenario while representing the roles or viewpoints that they have been given or selected. This can take time with a large group, and it is recommended to provide time limits (e.g., one minute) for each paired discussion. A debrief can be conducted in a plenary format, highlighting the variety of different perspectives and feelings encountered.

11. Simulations

Description

An activity designed to imitate a realistic scenario or situation for trainees to experience and learn from.

Advantages

Simulations are active and engaging, and stress experiential learning from doing (Adult Learning Principles 6, 7, and 8; Chapter 4, Table 4.4). Learning is relevant and meaningful to real-life application, preparing trainees to apply new KSA in a safe environment. Simulations can also be useful to assess learners' level, of understanding and practice of M&E content (Adult Learning Principle 14).

Disadvantages

Simulations can cause anxiety and discomfort for certain learners, especially when used for assessment. They are ultimately limited in imitation of reality and can inflate learner confidence.

Additional considerations

Simulations are typically conducted later in the training, after people have learned key concepts and practices. It is critical to clearly frame the simulation objectives and how it will work beforehand, addressing any questions or concerns learners may have. Consider developing simulations with trainee input, helping them to anticipate the real-world elements to consider. If the simulation is being used to assess learners, be sure to use a consistent rubric to rate performance; this can be a useful teaching aid to share with learners to frame the activity and then afterward to debrief.

There are ranges of simulations that can be conducted during M&E training, ranging from key informant interviews and focus group discussions to phone calls from the field asking for M&E assistance on a particular topic. Below we provide an example using a fishbowl technique for observation and feedback to encourage peer learning.

11.1 Fishbowl Simulations

The "fishbowl" technique is a form of peer review that can be used for other training activities in addition to simulations, such as discussions and role-playing. This example illustrates how it can be used to train volunteers to use mobile phones to enumerate household surveys. Simulations are conducted after having covered the content of the enumerator training and letting participants practice with each other and their phones. A portion of the group (e.g., three members) perform the simulation in the center of the training space with the remaining training participants forming a listening circle around them. One person is the respondent, while the other two obtain informed consent, enumerate the survey, and enter data into their mobile phone (if the survey is long, an abbreviated portion that is sufficient to review performance can be used by different groups). Learners are rotated into the fishbowl so everyone gets a chance inside "doing" and outside "observing."

Peer rating and feedback encourage active listening from the observers as well as meaningful peer feedback on individual performance. The group can be given or prepare a rubric handout to consistently rate each other's performance based on key criteria. As with role-plays, in addition to debriefing how people perform, participants are asked how they felt. The activity can conclude asking people what they learned and how it can help them in the future when enumerating surveys using mobile technology. The generic approach to this activity can be used with different size groups for a range activity simulating different M&E practices.

12. Demonstrations

Description

A visual display of how to do something or how something works, either by trainers, an external guest, or recorded media (e.g., video).

Advantages

Demonstrations utilize visual learning to help clarify complex tasks or procedures. They can be meaningful for learners to see the practical application of concepts, and introduce examples into a classroom or online setting that mimic real-world application (Adult Learning Principles 6; Chapter 4, Table 4.4).

Disadvantages

Demonstrations take time to prepare and practice, as they need to model correct performance. Technology and the understanding of how to use it will be required for recorded demonstration. If demonstrations are too long, it can become passive and boring for learners.

Additional considerations

It is best if demonstrations are not too long (five to ten minutes), because they are more passive (viewing) than interactive. As they may be meant to model appropriate performance, it is essential to ensure they are accurate and clear. Whether provided in a live, in-person format or through recorded media, it is also prudent to ensure that the demonstration is visually and audibly accessible to all learners. It is useful to brief trainees to share expectations beforehand and to note important elements, additional questions, and key lessons during the demonstration to share/discuss afterward. This can be used for the activity debrief to further explore the practice being observed and frame the actual application of learning for learners to practice themselves what has been demonstrated. Live demonstrations can be recorded for referral and consistent messaging for future learning and reinforcement.

Below we provide an example activity to illustrate the use of recorded media with live demonstration combined with learner simulations.

12.1 Sequenced Demonstration Into Simulation

This is an example of a generic progression for demonstrations that utilizes recorded demonstration with live demonstration and can be tailored to different learning needs (i.e., see simulations above and M&E software activities below). Depending on the learning objectives, a recorded video of the demonstrated skill is provided to learners prior to or during the training. Video can be recorded using technology ranging from a mobile phone to sophisticated video equipment. Participants are asked to identify key questions and lessons while viewing the video, which are discussed prior to a live demonstration.

For example, video clips of specific moments in a focus group discussion can be used to highlight key learning points for trainees. This is used to frame an actual in-training demonstration of a focus group. Participants can be used as focus group members, with the trainer or other experienced focus group facilitator demonstrating the discussion. A generic topic for which trainees are familiar can be used, and trainees who will participate in the demonstration assemble in a central place for the demonstration—the fishbowl technique described above can be used for observation. An example of a semi-structured questionnaire for the focus group is provided beforehand, so the audience can follow the sequence and adaptation of questioning. This phase of the activity is again debriefed, highlighting key lessons and addressing any questions.

The third phase of the activity is a simulation (see above) in which trainees practice facilitating different parts of a focus group discussion themselves. A topic can be assigned, and groups can prepare questions for the focus group discussion. Interviewee and interviewers can be periodically rotated to give participants opportunity to practice facilitation, with debriefing involving peer feedback, discussion of how people felt, and what they learned that can inform real-life focus group facilitation.

13. M&E Software Activities

Description

Activities in which trainees use software relevant to M&E practice.

Advantages

Activities using relevant M&E software in training are applicable and useful for real-life M&E practice (Adult Learning Principles 6 and 7; Chapter 4; Table 4.4). They provide opportunity for practice with timely troubleshooting and feedback to ensure correct understanding and use (Adult Learning Principle 14).

Disadvantages

M&E software has acquisition and licensing costs as well as hardware (computer or mobile) costs to operate the software. These costs as well as the training setting (primary delivery medium) may limit trainee access for individual practice. The use of M&E software also requires a certain degree of prerequisite technical literacy, which can vary among learners and challenge facilitation.

Additional considerations

Today, software is playing an increasing role in M&E practice, from mobile data collection applications, such as survey design and enumeration, to software for program design and management, data analysis, and reporting. For example, Raftree and Bamberger (2014) provide a useful overview of M&E in a "tech-enabled world," and *Monitoring and Evaluation News* (2015) provides an online list of M&E software. It is essential to pilot software and equipment beforehand, and trainers should ensure they themselves are competent with their use. Consider providing software and self-directed tutorials beforehand, allowing learners to familiarize themselves with the software and bring to training questions and issues to address. It is useful to demonstrate software use with the aid of a digital projector, capitalizing on shared learning and reflection. It is also recommended to accompany the activity with a handout of key steps, frequently asked questions, and troubleshooting steps. Pair work among trainees is useful for peer learning and support, with trainers circulating to check and troubleshoot software use.

Following we illustrate a training activity for M&E software using a "screencast" to frame learner hands-on practice using the software.

13.1 Screencast Into Practice

As discussed in Chapter 2, a screencast is basically a "moving" screenshot of actions taking place on the computer screen using software, which can be handy to demonstrate the steps to complete a task—in this case the operation of software for M&E. For example, participants can be taken through the steps using an Excel spreadsheet to enter data into an indicator-tracking table using formulas to aggregate actual measures with percentage of targets reached to calculate variance. There is a variety of free and real-cost software available online. These can be obtained with a keyword search of "screencast software," and examples of free versions include Snagit, Screener, Microsoft Expression Encoder, Community Clips, and Apple QuickTime Player. It is important to provide adequate time for learners to practice with the software and useful to bring to plenary discussion and debrief common problems and solutions encountered to inform real-world application following training. It is also useful to provide additional resources for learners to follow up and improve software proficiency after training. There is a variety of online, self-directed tutorials available— for example, using pivot tables in Excel.

14. Learner Presentations

Description

Activities in which learner's themselves present training content.

Advantages

Learner presentations allow learners to organize and articulate learning content for their own understanding and retention. These activities are learner centered and empowering, drawing upon learners' own experiences and background, encouraging peer learning and cooperative group work (Adult Learning Principles 4, 5, and 11; Chapter 4, Table 4.4). When planned with recommended time limits, they are useful to equally distribute and ensure learner participation and engagement

Disadvantages

Learner presentations are limited to smaller groups, as it take time for everyone to prepare and participate. They may be intimidating for certain learners, and accuracy and effectiveness of presentations and learning may be compromised. As with lecture activities, learner presentations can have low interaction and passive learning for non-presenters.

Additional considerations

Learner presentations can be facilitated with individual, paired, or group presentations. They can be used before or after material has been introduced, or when learners may already be experienced in the training content. Learner presentations need not be one-way transmissions of information; more interactive formats such as round tables and poster sessions are potentially effective alternatives to a "talking head" approach. It is important to provide adequate background information to ensure presentations address learning objectives. Consider providing or generating with participants guidelines for good presentations beforehand to frame the activity. Also consider providing or suggesting visual aids (e.g., example M&E formats, lists, or tools), upon which presentations can be based. It is best to keep topics specific and presentations short, setting a time limit. Presented content can be corrected during the presentation or afterward to encourage peer feedback and learning during the activity debrief. Audience participation can be increased through the use of Q&A during and at the end of the presentation, note taking to identify key learning points and follow-up questions, and rating or scoring presentations to increase audience participation.

Many of the activities outlined in this part of the book illustrate how learner presentation can be used during M&E training—for example, see plenary presentations and debrief components of discussion and case study activities.

14.1 Multiple Session Group Projects

In a multiple session training workshop it is often useful to include an ongoing (daily) group project with a specific focus or product in mind. For example, groups can be formed to work on the development of a logic model or an evaluation design matrix for a particular case study example. The training design may call for all groups to work on the same case example in which related materials are provided. Alternatively, participants might self-select into meaningful groups, such as practice domains (e.g., education, health, community development), and be charged with a particular task and product expectations.

Groups typically require breakout rooms or suitable space (e.g., corner of large room) to work together on their task in a focused manner. Groups should be supplied with needed resources, such as flip chart paper and markers, blackboard/whiteboard space, Internet access, and relevant documents. The trainer's role during group work sessions is to facilitate by routinely checking in with groups to ensure they are on task, have the required resources, and answer any questions of clarification.

With a final product being required, it is essential that groups are given ample opportunity to present to the plenary group, during which they receive constructive feedback on their final product. **Figure 12.9** shows the results of a multi-day group activity in Senegal, where practice-based groups spent time considering challenges

FIGURE 12.9 Winning Poster From Senegalese Short Course on M&E

Courtesy of Cousins (2015)

for M&E in their respective domain (e.g., community development, environment, education) and potential solutions to address the challenges. The groups were required to produce posters complete with content, symbols, and artifacts to communicate their results, and everyone took part in an end-of-training poster session. During this final session, all participants visited all (in this case six) poster stations and conversed with group members about identified challenges and solutions and poster displays. All members were assigned anonymous peer-evaluation responsibilities; peer evaluations were ultimately used to identify a winning poster (shown in Figure 12.9) with the winning group receiving prizes (and everyone else receiving consolation prizes).

15. Practicum Experience

Description

Activities conducted in the actual context in which learning is to be applied—for example, on-the-job or during a field visit/exercise working with actual M&E stakeholders.

Advantages

Practicum activities are a form of active learning that can be engaging, stressing experiential learning from "doing" in real-life settings, allowing learners to practically learn M&E concepts under the guidance/support of an experienced trainer or mentor (Adult Learning Principles 4, 6, and 7; Chapter 4, Table 4.4).

Disadvantages

Practicum activities can cause anxiety for certain learners. They also require considerable time, resources, and logistics to arrange and conduct. Substandard performance can impact M&E task, service delivery, and any stakeholders who are involved.

Additional considerations

A practicum activity is a valuable approach to incorporate an actual program or project M&E needs with practical learning. However, it is essential to carefully select appropriate contexts for a practicum activity and to obtain informed consent and approval of all stakeholders beforehand, ensuring they understand how the exercise will be used for learning and any project or program outputs/outcomes. Likewise, it is important to frame this for the trainees themselves, address any questions and concerns beforehand, and carefully ensure they understand how the practicum experience is planned and how they will be supported if any problems arise. If consent is forthcoming by all parties involved, the practicum activity can be recorded for learning purposes afterward. Whether recorded or not, it is important to carefully debrief the activity, which can involve non-trainees (service recipients and/or external observers) if appropriate. Similar to role-plays, activity debriefs should highlight not only lessons learned but how learners felt during the practicum experience and how their experience can inform future M&E practice after training.

Practicum activities may vary considerably in scope. Below we highlight an example of practicum activities combined with service earning, and in **Box 12.3**, we illustrate an example of this approach with an integrated M&E capacity building initiative that took place over 3.5 years in India.

BOX 12.3
Integrated M&E Capacity Building in the Indian Education Sector

In the period 2009 to 2012, an integrated M&E capacity building initiative was implemented in India, illustrating the combination of training that also contributed to an actual project focused on the evaluation of elementary education quality initiatives associated with Sarva Shiksha Abhiyan (SSA), the national Indian elementary education reform policy. The training was sponsored by the UK's Department for International Development (under the auspices of Cambridge Education Ltd through the Technical Cooperation Fund) and involved several consultants from North American and Europe in training more than 30 Indian professors and educators from the National Council for Educational Research and Training (NCERT) and associated organizations. In the first cycle, four state-level evaluations of SSA initiatives were implemented (Andrea Pradesh, Himachal Pradesh, Orissa, Tamil Nadu) with centralized workshops on evaluation planning, instrument development/data collection, data analysis, and reporting and in-person coaching expertise being provided along the way. The evaluations were guided by a steering committee and peer reviewed by external experts as a measure of quality control.

In a second cycle, which included a mix of original participants and a range of new ones, four more evaluations were undertaken, this time addressing crosscutting SSA initiatives and issues (e.g., Midday Meal; Continuous, Comprehensive Evaluation, Teacher Training). This integrated activity culminated in an end-of-project conference in New Delhi in September 2012. For more details see http://www.ssatcfund.org/Home.aspx.

15.1 Service Learning

Service learning is an approach to education that combines formal instruction with meaningful community service (National Geographic, 2006, provides a concise overview with a list of additional, online resources). It is increasingly used in K–12 education and even post-secondary educational contexts in North America, but the general concept also lends itself to M&E training with adults. M&E trainers can prepare for an appropriate service-learning activity by consulting with community organizations or initiatives where the training is to be provided. For instance, if training is a Type 1 training for an organization, there may already be an initiative underway for which an M&E practicum experience can be provided. If training is a Type 2 training for individuals with whom pre-training communication is possible, actual initiatives that they are working with may lend themselves to a service-learning practicum exercise. For example, a community project may address a need, such as beachside or roadside pollution, for which M&E trainees can help collect both quantitative and qualitative data to contribute to project outcomes. The possibilities are endless, but underscored above, it is essential to obtain informed consent beforehand of all relevant stakeholders involved and affected by the activity, to frame the activity process and objectives clearly with learners, and to ensure it follows adequate training in content and practice beforehand. Assign experienced supervisors or mentors to support learners during the activity, and if learners will be participating in pairs or subgroups, consider mixing skills and backgrounds accordingly.

16. Independent Learning Activities

Description

Activities in which individuals are responsible to complete a given learning exercise or task.

Advantages

Incorporating independent learning activities into M&E training accommodates a wider range of learning styles, providing opportunity for learners who prefer individual time to reflect and organize content themselves (Adult Learning Principles 9; Chapter 4, Table 4.4).

Disadvantages

Independent learning activities are limited in learning from trainers and other learners. This absence of interaction can be discouraging for people who prefer more timely assistance and reassurance (although in an in-person setting, trainers can circulate to provide assistance). Individual activities also require a greater degree of self-motivation and responsibility from learners and may not be the best option for the people who procrastinate and have bad study habits.

Additional considerations

One of the advantages of in-person training is the opportunity for learners to directly interact and learn from the trainers and each other. However, independent learning activities can be a powerful complement to M&E training. It can be used to (a) prepare learners beforehand by individually familiarizing them with training material, (b) during training as a break from plenary and subgroup activities to address different learning styles while framing or reflecting on group activities, (c) and for training follow-up to reinforce learning objectives and training transfer.

It is especially important to anticipate potential questions or problems prior to the activity and clearly frame the learning objectives and instructions, as learners will be working independently. When conducted during a face-to-face training with other trainees, consider combining with interactive activities, using a snowballing technique (discussed earlier). Circulate among learners to assist with any questions and monitor progress and encourage them to identify key learning points, questions, and viewpoints to later share with others.

In Chapter 2 we discuss distance-training options that can readily be adapted for individual learning activities, such as the use of printed and e-learning media. For instance, assigned reading, online webinars, and screencasts can be used prior to training to prepare learners, followed by individual assignments shared using an online blog or community of practice to share (see training follow-up techniques, discussed later in this chapter). The distance and e-learning media discussed in Chapter 2 lend themselves especially well for independent learning activities that can be incorporated into M&E training.

Below we provide one example of an independent learning activity with which many people are familiar from formal education contexts.

16.1 M&E Matching Exercise

Matching exercises can be used effectively to practice or review new learning as well as for learning assessment. In addition to self-directed activities, they work equally well in pairs, and for group work and team competition games. The example we discuss here is used with a handout to review and reinforce key learning points by matching M&E related vocabulary, concepts, or practices with descriptions. For example, a list of M&E types on the left (stimulus) side of a handout, with potential definition answers to match them with on the right (response) side. It is important to ensure matching items are singular (i.e., do not contain more than one element). There are different ways to design matching exercises, varying the level of difficulty: An equal number of items to match in each list is easiest as learners can use the process of elimination as clues to the correct response, a greater number of items in the response list than in the stimulus list will be devoid of such clues and therefore more challenging to answer, and matching can also be configured so that there is more than one answer to an item.

An example activity that has an unequal number of items to match is a "data collection matching activity." A handout (see **Figure 12.10**) is provided to learners with numbered example indicators on the left side and an alphabetized list of data collection methods on the right side. Learners are first asked to individually consider and write the letter of the most appropriate data collection method on the right side of the handout next to the given indicator on the left side. When more than one

FIGURE 12.10 Example Data Collection Matching Exercise Handout

Match Indicator with Data Collection Method

1. ___.#/% of participating schools successfully conduct a minimum of one mock crisis drill per year.
2. ___.# of community volunteers trained and certified as Psychological Support Programme (PSP) Community Facilitators.
3. ___. % of teachers reporting that PSP activities have been helpful.
4. ___. % of community members who report a sense of place (belonging/identity) in their community.
5. ___. # of non-PSP events in which PSP project team participated to disseminate program approach
6. ___. # of ARC PSP community and school projects designed with the Host NS.
7. ___. # of specific types of community PSP promotion materials developed and used.

A. Survey Questionnaire
B. Self Administered Questionnaire
C. PRA—Participatory Rapid Assessments (Participatory Rural Appraisal)
D. Key Informant Interviews
E. Focus Group Discussions
F. Case Studies
G. Field Observations
H. Secondary Data Sources
I. Checklist/Event Form
J. Attendance/Certification Records
K. Proposal and Approval Sign Off
L. Meeting Minutes
M. Inventory of Materials

data collection method can be used, people can prioritize their answers according to which method is most appropriate, followed by other methods that can be used for triangulation of methods (mixed methods). For instance, the indicator, "Number of targeted communities that successfully conduct one disaster drill every six month," can involve a variety of data collection methods, including the following: observation and recording performance using a checklist rubric, a survey questionnaire, qualitative interviews, and review of secondary data (project records).

This activity can be combined with case study work to inform the matching process. Snowballing can also be used where learners progress from solo to paired to small group and then plenary discussion of responses. Discussion and debrief should not simply focus on right or wrong answers but also explanations for learners' selections.

17. Review Activities

Description

Activities designed to reinforce learning through repetition, practice, recall, and feedback.

Advantages

Review activities reinforce key learning points for trainees, helping them to organize and clarify material for better understanding and retention (Adult Learning Principle 12; Chapter 4; Table 4.4). Review activities are especially important for longer training or complex topics. In addition to reinforcing learning, they are also valuable to assist both learners and trainers to monitor learning progress and give and receive feedback on areas to improve (Adult Learning Principle 14).

Disadvantages

Review activities take time away from the introduction of new material, and advanced participants might find them to be redundant or of low interest.

Additional considerations

Learning review can be planned as a specific activity or incorporated as part or another activity. They can also be conducted as an individual, paired, subgroup, or plenary activity. Keep in mind the adult learning principle of recency and conduct review activities to highlight key messages at the end of individual lessons. Questions and answer checks can be incorporated into lessons and presentations for immediate review and feedback, and group discussion and debrief activities support peer review and feedback. Use not only reviews to highlight areas to improve, but also learning accomplishments to provide positive reinforcement and encouragement. When reviews are conducted collectively, remind learners of key guidelines (ground rules) for supportive, positive participation. It is helpful to accompany reviews with a handout summarizing key learning points/answers.

Review activities can be made more engaging and entertaining when lead by the learners themselves (peer review) and conducted as a learning game. Many of the activities already discussed lend themselves well to learning review. For example, activity debrief discussions are worth mention again, as they are not only useful to review training content, but also to provide feedback as well as opportunity for people to discuss how they felt or experienced learning, and to consider how learning can transfer into practice after training. Q&A, brainstorming, opinion rating, and visual response can each be adopted to review key learning points. Related, many of the learning games are also very suitable to review learning content, such as M&E masterpiece, puzzle, and definition/concept cards. Other examples that readers will likely be familiar with include matching exercises, hangman, and crossword puzzles (for which there is an assortment of crossword puzzle makers available online).

Below we summarize some additional some additional examples for learning review that are relatively easy to prepare and facilitate. Note that M&E Jeopardy, described previously in this chapter, would also fall into this category.

17.1 Who Wants to Be an M&E Millionaire (billionaire)?

This is a fun learning game to review key learning points similar to the popular TV game show of the same name. Teams elect a representative as a game panelist to sit in front of everyone and respond to learning questions related to covered material. The moderator presents each panelist with a question one at a time, which they answer to the best of their ability. A given amount of "phone calls" are provided to each panelist for the duration of the game, which they can use to call their team members for support if they get stuck. If their answer is incorrect, the next panelist in order can steal the point if they provide the correct answer. Questions can be multiple-choice or open-ended (for which answers should still be prepared by trainers to confirm correct response). As questions increase in difficulty, so does the amount of money awarded for correct answers. Questions and then answers should be displayed using media appropriate for plenary viewing. The use of projected, animated slides (see example) is useful to display questions and answers sequentially and can be accompanied by recorded sound clips using a computer speaker to introduce the money value for each question (e.g., a cash register ring), the choices (e.g., prompt sound), time management sounds (e.g., clock ticking followed by buzzer), and the answer (applause).

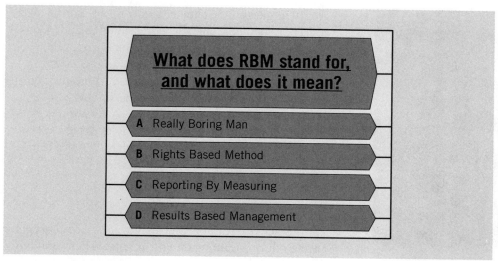

IFRC 2011b

17.2 Pass the Question (learner-generated quizzes)

This is a simple and flexible way for learners themselves to reflect upon training content, identify key learning points, and then quiz each other in a learning tournament with review questions. Rather than the trainer asking review questions, the learners themselves prepare and ask each other. Learners are provided time to reflect upon training content and prepare questions and answers. It is helpful to forewarn learners to note key learning points during the presentation of M&E lessons, so they can later use them to develop questions for the review activity. The activity can be facilitated with individuals or teams posing questions to each other and as a learning game with scoring and prizes awarded. It is helpful if questions are written down, ideally on media suitable for plenary display, such a flipchart or whiteboard. People can steal points by answering correctly questions that stump others. Questions are rotated among learners, with each individual or team that has been asked a question selecting the next individual or team to respond and providing the question. This is a similar format to the SMARTer Indicator Game described earlier.

17.3 M&E Charades

This is a fun version of role-playing to review key M&E concepts and practices. It can be conducted in plenary or with teams. Individuals or pairs are provided with a word (e.g., written on a card) that represents a key learning point from previously covered material. They then nonverbally act out the meaning for others (team or plenary

Courtesy of Chaplowe (2015)

group) to guess: for example, following a lesson on data collection methods, charade words could include focus group discussion, observation, randomly controlled trials, selection or measurement bias, and so forth. Learning points to act out can increase with difficulty, and scoring can be used based on the amount of time taken to correctly guess the answers. A variation is to have individuals or teams identify key terms or concepts to challenge each other with. Each charade word can be debriefed by highlighting related learning points.

17.4 Recap Hat

For this activity, learners prepare key topics or concepts covered during training on Post-it notes. Then, standing in a large circle, people take turns wearing a hat to which other participants stick their topics, one at a time. The person wearing the hat cannot see the topic but must guess it using verbal explanations and hints (without stating the given word!) provided by the other surrounding learners. A variation is to have topics stuck to the person's back.

17.5 M&E Hot Potato

This fun activity uses a ball that can be passed around to learners to answer questions related to key learning points covered in training. Questions are prepared by the trainer or learners themselves on small pieces of paper or index cards, which are folded and affixed to the hat using removable adhesive. Learners sit or stand in a circle and the ball is passed around randomly, accompanied by music. When the music stops, the person stuck with the ball removes a question, reads it aloud, and tries to answer. Others can help or elaborate provided answers. Resume the music and procedure until questions on the ball have been addressed.

17.6 Floor Cards

This activity helps visually reinforce the learning progression of key topics covered in training. It is a useful method after multiple topics have been introduced, such as at the end of the day or to begin the day reviewing topics covered the prior day/s during a multiple-day, in-person training. Learners are first asked to individually reflect upon the material covered and clearly write down on an index card one topic they felt was especially important. Everyone then stands up and moves to a place in the training space where there is adequate space for everyone to put his or her topic card on the floor. Then, as a group, people move the topics around to chronologically reflect the order in which they were introduced during the training. For a twist to the activity, it can be conducted in silence. After group consensus is reached, any topic covered that was not identified by the group (topic gaps) can then be elicited in group discussion and added to the floor map of topics. In addition to learning review, this activity can help trainers assess which parts of prior training left an impression on learners.

18. Learning Assessment Activities

Description

Activities during training to measure and assess individual learning, providing feedback for both the leaner and instructor. They can be written or observations of performance and either summative or formative. (Learning assessment can also occur prior to or after training, but we focus on training delivery here.)

Advantages

Similar to review activities, learning assessment assists learners and trainers to monitor learning progress and identify areas to improve (Adult Learning Principle 14: Chapter 4; Table 4.4). Related, they are goal oriented and can be used to motivate learners. When appropriate, they can also be used to assess or certify learners' readiness to perform skills after training. Learning assessment is also useful to evaluate training effectiveness.

Disadvantages

Learning assessments can intimidate certain learners and be seen as a threat. Their reliability and validity may be questioned. Poorly constructed or ambiguous items not only affect reliability/validity but also can cause resentment and frustration. Therefore, preparation of learning assessment tools takes time to develop (and should be governed by principles of instrument development and data quality assurance).

Additional considerations

Learning assessment activities are very similar to review activities, but we discuss them as a separate category of activity, as they are often required to rate learners and evaluate the training. Recognizing this, a review activity can be adapted as a learning assessment activity when a consistent and reliable rubric is used to rate or score trainee performance. As discussed in Chapter 8, learning assessment is best considered early during training design to ensure assessment criteria and tools are well aligned with learning objectives and can be developed prior to training for any pre/post-comparison. It is important to ensure that assessment tools only measure content covered during training, and it is recommended to pilot all written assessment instruments to address any ambiguous items. Assessment criteria and rubrics should be specific and measurable for consistency when observing and appraising performance.

Clearly frame the purpose and use of learning assessment activities with trainees beforehand and address any related questions and concerns. Some participants might feel uncomfortable, for example, completing a pre-test before training has even begun; they may need to be reminded of the purposes of the pre-test. If assessment will be recorded individually and used for certification or professional development, this should be communicated to trainees prior to training, and written consent should be provided when required. When appropriate, use learning assessment to meet other training needs, such as review and feedback. For example, peer assessment can be a very effective approach to support learning and meaningful feedback. Consider the use of recorded video to review and assess nonwritten performance.

Some of the activities already covered can be adapted for informal learning assessment and monitoring; basically, whenever learners present their work or understanding. When learning assessment needs to be more formally recorded for individual rating and/or training evaluation, rubrics can be created for consistent scoring. For example, simulation, learner presentations, or practicum activities can be used for learning assessment when properly prepared. Remember to use the same assessment tools and methods when learning assessment is to be compared between different training events with different people, locations, and timing. Another consideration is that learning assessment activities can be used to model, discuss, and reinforce topics related to measurement and assessment often covered in M&E training.

In Chapter 11, we discuss learning assessment as part of training evaluation, and Appendix 11.1 summarizes different methods for training evaluation that can be used for learning assessment prior to, during, and after training. Below, we summarize how pre/post-tests can be facilitated for learning assessment that supports participatory review and learning.

18.1 Participatory Pre/Post-Tests

In Box 11.5 in Chapter 11, we highlighted the potential advantages of self-assessment to traditional pre/post-tests. This activity illustrates such an approach. We suspect most readers will be familiar with the overall approach from peer grading during formal K–12 education. However, it is surprising how often this method is overlooked when training pre/post-tests are administered (which are often handed out, collected afterward, and graded by trainers without learner involvement).

A clear explanation should be provided to learners beforehand explaining the purpose of the pre/post-tests. This typically includes one or more of the following: (a) assess learning progress and areas to improve, (b) contribute to training evaluation, (c) and help frame beforehand (pre-test) and review afterward (post-test) selected learning points. Also critical for this activity, learners should understand that it is not necessary to write down their names on the test, as they will be anonymous and not identified with specific individuals. This will go a long way to defuse anxiety and support the activity as a welcome learning opportunity. However, this highlights an important caveat for this activity; in M&E practice it is imperative that pre- and post-test data are linked to enable the disaggregated analysis of learning change. Limiting such analyses of change to an aggregated comparison implies a loss of valuable information. This point ought to be reinforced by trainers if the anonymous approach is taken. Peer grading in this exercise only applies to the post-test phase. Pre-tests are graded by trainers (or assistants) after administrated at the start of training. A large table is prepared on flipchart paper (as illustrated) to aggregate scores according to grade percentiles: A (90%–100%), B (80%–89%), C (70%–79%), D (60%–69%), F (50%–59%), and the like. Percentile categories should go as low as individual grades (hopefully lower for pre-tests grades). The grade levels are listed in the first column of the table, followed by a column for pre-test scores and a column for post-test scores. After administrated, pre-tests can be graded with the total number of tests (people) achieving each grade category entered into the respective column. The table summarizing pre-test grades can be shared with learners once completed, to help them understand the varying levels of understanding and experience and help frame mutual patience and support for differentiated learning.

100		2
90	1	7
80	3	8
70	3	6
60	8	3
50	6	
40	3	
30	1	

Courtesy of Chaplowe (2015)

Post-tests are administered as a training review and debrief activity, used to frame (and hopefully celebrate) what has been achieved, and highlight areas to explain and work on following training. This is accomplished by collecting completed post-tests, mixing them up, and handing them back to learners to be corrected in plenary review. Have learners read each question and identify the correct answer (which trainers verify); they leave correct answers alone, and put an X over the number of any questions answered incorrectly. The value of the exercise is the pursuing discussion of any problem questions during peer grading. After all post-tests have been graded, the trainer stands in front of the flipchart with the half-completed pre/post-test table. Ask peer graders to count up how many correct answers on the post-test they graded and calculate the percentage correct (it is helpful if there is an even number of questions, such as 10 or 20). They then write the total number correct at the top of the post-test and circle it. Starting from the lowest percentile category, the trainer calls out each category and asks peer graders to raise their hand if the post-test they graded falls within that percentile. Trainers count and write the total number of post-tests graded for each percentile and write the number in the respective space in the post-test column of the table.

Typically (and hopefully) there will be a noticeable improvement in the column of post-test versus pre-test grades, which is visually powerful for learners to see before them. A debrief of overall group performance can also be used to discuss differences between pre- and post-test scores. For springboarding into discussion about training follow-up and transfer, ask learners how well they expect they will retain their knowledge (perform on the same test) sometime after training (three or six months later) and what can be done to reinforce learning.

Remember that the purpose of a written pre/post-test is not to assess everything presented during the training, but to be a sufficient representation of learning content to generalize about learning progress, determine readiness to perform M&E skills, and assess training delivery. For instance, one sheet of paper (two sides) with concise, clear multiple-choice or true/false questions can be used. Write-in answers can also be used but only when there are specific words or answers that can be graded consistently. Open-ended questions with learner explanation will not be suitable for the peer-grading component of this exercise, but can be read out loud for peer review and learning afterward and for trainers to better evaluate individual performance and training.

19. Training Monitoring and Evaluation Activities

Description

Activities during training to assess trainee perception of training. (Note: M&E activities *during* training are one of several methods to evaluate training—see Chapter 11.)

Advantages

These activities help monitor trainee satisfaction and comfort, which are useful to make adjustments and improvements during training and improve future training (supporting Adult Learning Principles 1; Chapter 4: Table 4.4). Training monitoring and evaluation activities can help determine whether training has achieved its objectives (i.e., trainees felt it was worthwhile, that they learned something). These activities help to uphold and demonstrate accountability and value for trainee feedback/information. They can also be empowering for trainees, providing an important vehicle to express negative or positive feedback (Adult Learning Principles 4 and 14).

Disadvantages

Monitoring and evaluation activities take time away from the learning content. As we discuss in Chapter 11, they are also limited in ability to assess training effectiveness and longer-term impact for training evaluation, such as trainee retention and use of KSA. Participants need to have confidence that the information they provide will be put to good use; otherwise, they are likely to resent evaluation activities they perceive to only be symbolic of compliance with accountability demands.

Additional considerations

Planned training M&E can be used to obtain feedback during (formative) or at the end (summative) of training. They can be used to obtain feedback on individual sessions, training content, trainer facilitation and participant dynamics, and people's comfort with the physical training environment. Feedback activities focused on specific training activities can be used when they are piloted for the first time. It is useful to pilot any M&E instruments and activities beforehand and ensure activities are well framed to trainees, obtaining informed consent and explaining how feedback will be used.

Training M&E activities can involve written and oral feedback. Feedback forms are useful for consistent and reliable measurement for later comparison, sharing and upholding accountability with other training stakeholders not present during training. While individual, written feedback using forms is less interactive than participatory discussion, it is more confidential, and people may feel less inhibited to provide candid feedback.

Participatory feedback activities can be empowering for trainees to express themselves, and the group process can provide more in-depth discussion and explanation of feedback areas. If written products are produced (e.g., key points prioritized on flipcharts or cards) this can later be used as a record for training evaluation and comparison. Pictures can be taken of any written, group feedback, and video or audio recording can even be used to capture nonwritten feedback.

It is important to remember that training monitoring can also be informal and unplanned, with trainers observing and checking in with trainees individually or collectively. For example, many of the discussion and debrief activities already examined are useful opportunities for feedback on the training process and trainee experience to monitor training. Related, discussion and debrief activities can be adapted to explicitly focus on training feedback; for instance, the "Four Walls" activity for opinion rating can be used for a qualitative discussion on and prioritization of different aspects training.

As with learning assessment, training M&E activities often employ the very principles and practices that may be covered in M&E training: data collection, measurement, analysis, and use. Therefore, consider discussing and using these activities to reinforce any relevant M&E learning points.

In Chapter 11, we discuss trainee feedback as part of training evaluation, and many of the methods in Appendix 11.1 can be used to obtain trainee feedback during and after training. Below we provide some key reminders for the use of written feedback forms and then summarize a variety of participatory approaches we have found useful for obtaining training feedback. Just as other activity methods already discussed can be used for training M&E, several of the examples we provide below can also be used for discussing training content.

19.1 Written Evaluation/Feedback Forms

Also called "smiley sheets," "happiness quotients," or satisfaction forms, Appendix 11.1 in Chapter 11 summarizes this method for training monitoring and evaluation, and Appendix 11.4 provides an example with simple instructions for trainees. We again highlight this method here, as it is such a popular approach for obtaining trainee feedback, and we want to direct readers to the appropriate part of the book for further information. Consider providing, explaining (including informed consent), and reviewing the use of written feedback forms at the beginning of training, clarifying and answering any questions and concerns. In this way, trainees can begin to complete the forms during training, taking notes and recording feedback while impressions and recall are fresh. Reassure trainees of confidentiality, and consider whether it would be best for written feedback to be submitted anonymously. In addition to closed-ended questions, include open-ended questions for respondents to explain and elaborate their feedback. While obtaining written feedback using forms is less interactive than participatory discussion, one way to increase participation is to have trainees discuss the form and feedback areas in pairs, small groups, or plenary before having them individually complete feedback forms.

19.2 Small Group Feedback

We have already discussed a variety of activities for subgroup discussion, but the use of these for training feedback is so valuable that we want to specifically flag this approach for training monitoring and evaluation. We encourage readers to peruse activities already covered above and consider how they can be adopted with the focus on training feedback rather than learning content. One example is simply to have subgroups discuss a series of predetermined (or, alternatively, learner-generated) questions pertaining to the training, such as the following examples:

a. What did you like best or find most interesting? Why? Can it be improved upon?

b. What did you like least or find least interesting? Why? How could it be improved?

c. Is there anything you would do differently if you were to conduct training like this in the future?

d. What would you like to see included or removed from this training for the next people who do the training?

After subgroup discussion, each group can report back in plenary using visual display of key feedback points or another method to facilitate plenary debrief already discussed above. Consider taking pictures of any written products as a record for training evaluation.

19.3 Pair 'n Share

This is a common partner discussion activity that can be used as an icebreaker (see paired introductions), as part of a learning activity (see snowball discussions), or to solicit feedback as we discuss here. Participants partner up to discuss training feedback in general or provided feedback topics on which to focus. A similar sequence of questions can be used as presented for small group feedback activities above. Paired discussion can then be followed by larger group discussion about the share opinions and feedback discussed by partners. This approach is useful for training feedback because it provides an opportunity for people to first explore and discuss opinions with a partner, allowing them to reflect and refine their viewpoints before sharing with the whole group.

19.4 Sweet 'n Sour

This is a simple feedback activity that can be conducted at the end of individual training sessions or overall training. Also called Roses and Thorns, training participants are asked to write down, anonymously, on Post-it notes or index cards, one high point and one low point during training (or overall positive and negative feedback point). Additional Post-it notes can be provided to record more than one high or low point. These can then be affixed on each side of the door as trainees depart the training, allowing for mutual viewing by all. However, it is more effective to designate one wall as the "sweet" wall and another as the "sour" wall for participants to post their feedback and to debrief comments as a group. Posted comments can be grouped together into similar categories and even prioritized if appropriate, similar to opinion rating (discussed earlier).

19.5 Incomplete Sentences

This technique is useful to help direct the type of feedback sought for training monitoring and evaluation. Incomplete sentences are provided for participants to complete, allowing them to express their opinions on different aspects of the training. For example, "I found this activity useful because . . . ," "I found this activity difficult because . . . ," and so forth. Incomplete sentences can be provided on a handout to be anonymously completed to ensure confidentiality, collected, and then shared for small group or plenary discussion. Sentences can also be displayed on a flipchart, whiteboard, or projector for all to view and complete orally as a discussion activity. After having worked with some provided sentences to complete, it is useful to elicit from participants their own incomplete sentences for others to complete; this is an effective way to allow participants to pinpoint feedback areas they feel are important. (It is worth noting that in addition to training feedback, this activity can also be used to cover learning content; that is, "Bias is a problem with data collection for my project because . . .")

19.6 Before and After Cards/Posters

This is a useful technique to revisit trainee expectations identified before training or specific training activities. Similar to the icebreaker Confidential Cards, individuals can write down expectations on provided index cards before training or activities start. Then, at the conclusion, they compare and discuss their actual experience of and reflections on the activity or training with their initial expectations. Another version is to use flipchart or poster paper for individuals, pairs, or small groups to visually prepare and compare pre- and post-expectations (a variation of a visual response, discussed earlier). Reasons and potential remedies for unmet expectations can be discussed, and those expectations that were met or exceeded celebrated. Consider taking pictures as a record for training evaluation.

19.7 Reflection Role-Playing

This is another example of an activity type already discussed but tailored for training monitoring and evaluation. It can be especially useful as a fun energizer to solicit training formative feedback to monitor and adjust training facilitation or highlight areas (ground rules) for learners to better work together for a mutually supportive learning environment. Participants are asked to prepare a short skit that says something about what has been happening in the training. It can be something that went well, that could go better, or was funny or challenging. Role-plays can involve pairs or groups. Preparation, presentations, and debrief can follow guidelines already discussed for role-plays, emphasizing how feedback and reflection can inform lessons to bring back to current or future training. This activity also works very well as a fun closing activity to reflect on training.

19.8 Forward and Backward Feedback

Like Reflection Role-Play, this is a good activity for formative monitoring of participant reactions, perceptions, or feeling about different aspects of training.

While it is not confidential, it is quick, easy, and an alternative approach for soliciting nonverbal feedback. All trainees (and trainers) stand in a line. The trainer calls out different topics for training feedback, such as quality of facilitation, specific activities, level of difficulty, relevance of content, or the training environment (temperature, distractions, lighting, etc.) Topics can be expressed as a statement: for example, "That was a really cool activity," or "I feel like the training is too easy (or hard) for me." Trainees then step forward if they agree with the statement, backward if they disagree, or remain where they are in the line if they are neutral. Each statement can be debriefed by asking people to share why they are standing where they are after each statement. After modeling a few statements and process, the trainer can turn it over to learners and let them call out statements for the group to "step to." In addition to soliciting feedback, this activity acts as an energizer as it gets people out of their seat and moving.

19.9 Basketball Feedback (debrief)

This is a fun way to allow people to confidentially provide feedback on training, which can be adapted for a variety of activities where the objective is to solicit candid opinions (this activity is actually adapted from facilitating experiential education for adolescents to safely share emotions they would otherwise be hesitant to do in an open, verbal forum). Similar to the Forward and Backward Feedback activity discussed above, statements are provided to participants one at a time for reflection. It is best if this phase is conducted in silence, with statements visually displayed for group viewing and individual reflection. Participants anonymously write on a piece of paper (best handed out to ensure everyone uses the same size paper) their response or opinion to the given statement in clear handwriting.

The next phase is a surprising but fun twist to the activity. They are asked to sit in a circle around or stand in a line before an empty (and clean) paper bin. Next, they are told to crumple up their paper into a ball and take a shot into the bin. Candies can be awarded to make the activity even more fun (two for scores and one for misses so nobody feels left out because of their lack of basketball skills). People can get additional shots if they miss, but in the end, all paper balls should be in the water paper bin.

During the final phase of the activity, the facilitator (either a trainer or appropriate trainee) takes out each ball one at a time and reads it aloud, stressing that it need not be identified with its author. This is used as a springboard to share and discuss feedback (opinions) to the initial statement or question presented to the group. The phases can be repeated with separate pieces of paper used for each provided statement. A variation is to provide more than one question during the initial phase for people to respond, writing all responses on one piece of paper folded into boxes according to the number of questions. This latter technique is a quicker way to facilitate multiple questions but ensure participants all write the answer to specific questions in the same box (i.e., top left, top right, bottom left, and bottom right box for four questions).

20. Training Closing Activities

Description
Activities used to bring closure to training.

Advantages
Training closing activities are useful to review and help trainees organize and remember training content (Adult Learning Principles 3 and 13: Chapter 4, Table 4.4). They can also support training evaluation and training transfer and celebrate individual and group accomplishments resulting from training. They help recognize what has been covered and accomplished and identify what can be done to best meet longer-term training outcomes (Adult Learning Principles 14).

Disadvantages
If poorly facilitated—that is, rushed due to limited remaining time—closing activities can leave a bad final tone or impression with trainees.

Additional considerations
Planned activities for training closing are an important opportunity to reinforce the adult learning principle of recency for both learning content and parting impressions and considerations for trainees. Specific closing activities and the time devoted to them will depend on the overall length, objectives, and other aspects of training particular to the training context. In addition to training review, M&E, and discussion of training transfer, the closing should discuss any pending topics or actions identified but not addressed during training (i.e., unaddressed items remaining in the parking lot). While these pending items may not be resolved during the training closing, recommended individual or group actions for follow-up can be discussed.

The training closing is also a good opportunity to recognize trainee accomplishments, award any certification or recognition of training participation, and thank key stakeholders involved in supporting and providing training. It is useful to keep the tone upbeat and celebratory as well as respectful and authentic. Consider inviting outside guests, such as senior management during training for an organization (Type 1), to help recognize and celebrate training accomplishments.

Chapter 10 summarizes key considerations for this final session of M&E training. Also, many of the activities already discussed in this part of the book can be used for the training closing: for example, training review, monitoring and evaluation, and debrief discussion activities. Therefore, we encourage readers to refer to them when planning the closing session for training. Below we provide some additional examples that are specifically useful for training closing.

20.1 Envision Role-Play

This can be a fun way for trainees to "project" into the future how they envision practicing M&E topics after training. Participants are asked to prepare a short skit that highlights the use of newly found M&E skills, the context in which they expect to use them, key stakeholders they will interact with, or any challenges they may encounter. Readers can refer to Reflection Role-Play (a monitoring and evaluation activity discussed above) as well as the other examples provided earlier of role-playing to consider different ways to facilitate this activity. The activity debrief is a useful platform to realistically consider training transfer.

20.2 Stakeholder Constellation

This is a variation of role-playing adapted from Jean-François Goulay, a trainer with over 20 years of experience at IFRC. It is designed to help trainees consider interests and perceptions of key groups, decision-makers, "gatekeepers," and other stakeholders they need to interact with in their M&E practice following training. Frame the activity stating something like, "So, you have taken this training and hopefully learned a lot of new information and good practice. How will you take this back to where you are coming from and put it to use? Which stakeholders can help you achieve or block your M&E practice (learning goals)?" People stand or sit in a circle, with a diagram of a big, happy face in the middle of the circle. Explain that the happy face is to represent them, and ask participants to name key types of stakeholders they will need to interact with after the training: for example, their supervisor, colleagues, an M&E specialist or mentor, HR personnel, and even family, friends, or "enemies." (Care should be taken when facilitating the activity with people from the same organization not to offend or insult anyone.)

People then pair up to represent and discussed different stakeholder groups identified: What are their priorities? How do they feel? Are they champions, followers, or obstacles to M&E practice and why? After a timed period of discussion, pairs return to the circle and position themselves closer or further from the happy face according to the degree they concluded their assigned stakeholder will be supportive and helpful for M&E practice (i.e., those stakeholders who are champions would stand closer to the happy face than those who are roadblocks or obstacles). Each paired group explains their rationale for why the stakeholder they represent is standing where they have positioned themselves.

The last phase of the activity involves people sharing with others how they would deal with the various stakeholder groups represented in the constellation. Each time a person makes a suggestion, they first move to the center of the circle and stand on the happy face to represent the perspective of the trainee returning to the real world.

20.3 Emptying the Parking Lot

As the name implies, this activity can be used to address any pending items in the parking lot or that trainees otherwise identify. People are first provided time to individually and collectively reflect on and discuss pending items, removing and adding any items, if needed. Consider debrief discussion activities covered earlier for facilitation, such as opinion rating, to elicit and prioritize items. A table can then be used to organize and analyze items according to different criteria—for example, columns rating importance, urgency, time frame, responsibilities, and resources/funding. This can then be used in any training report that will be prepared after training. Consider taking pictures as a record of training.

20.4 M&E Capacity Assessment and Planning

Training is a valuable opportunity to consider organizational capacity building needs and potential solutions while M&E content and issues is fresh in people's mind. For organizational training (Type 1), it is a useful chance to capitalize on the presence of key stakeholders to assess organizational M&E needs and strategic planning to address them. For Type 2, individual training, this activity can be tailored for trainees to reflect upon any organizational context they currently or expect to work in. The rigor and degree to which this can be achieved as a training activity will vary according to training context, but at a minimum, it can serve as a valuable opportunity for reflection and discussion to inform any M&E capacity assessment and strategic planning exercise following training.

Readers can refer to Chapter 3 for further discussion and resources to support this activity. One basic example for activity facilitation is to hand out a generic organizational capacity building assessment checklist for M&E. This can be used for people to individually and collectively reflect on and discuss capacity needs and potential solutions. Participation does not need to be limited to trainees, as it is a valuable opportunity to draw upon the experience and insights of trainers. Example checklists include Preskill and Torres (2015), Stufflebeam (2002), and Volkov and King (2007).

20.5 Senior Management Debrief

This is a useful activity for training for organizations (Type 1) to help convey to senior management training content and priorities and support training transfer.

Simply having key decision-makers and other relevant stakeholders present to observe and potentially participate in closing activities, such as emptying the parking lot or M&E Capacity Assessment and Planning, discussed above, can go a long way to build stakeholder understanding and support for training. As a specific activity, trainees can prepare a presentation summarizing key learning points and practices to highlight in a presentation to senior management and other relevant stakeholders attending the training closing. This can be used as a springboard to involve decision-makers in discussion and planning to support training transfer as part of a coherent strategy for M&E capacity building and practice. Such an activity will likely be more successful if stakeholder involvement begins early in the training process.

20.6 Elevator Speech

This is a quick but useful way for trainees to individually summarize and share key "take-away" lessons or the value of training. Each person is provided an opportunity to reflect on training and compose a short, concise summary of the value of the training that can be delivered in the time span of an elevator ride. Frame the length of the elevator speech by agreeing whether it is an elevator in a building with multiple floors (e.g., New York's Empire State Building) or a shorter ride. Depending on the number of trainees and remaining time for closing activities, one, two, or three minutes can be used. People can preface their speech identifying who they envision is in the elevator with them: for example, a stranger who knows nothing about M&E, a manager or colleague, a donor, or a community member receiving project services. This activity can be combined with an awards ceremony, discussed later.

20.7 Affirmation Mingle or Web

This is an easy and energizing way to end the training on a positive note, allowing everyone to recognize each other's contribution to training with affirmative feedback. People walk around and stop in front of someone to share with him or her one way that they valued their participation in the training. This can be tailored as part of an awards ceremony, discussed next.

A variation is to use a ball of yarn to create an "affirmation web." People stand in a circle, with one person holding the end of the yarn to begin the activity. They then pass the ball of yarn to another person, saying something positive about their contribution to the training. In turn, the affirmed person holds a piece of the yarn and passes the ball to yet another person, and the process is repeated until everyone is holding a piece of the yarn and an affirmation web is formed within the circle. Scissors can be passed around afterward for each person to cut a piece of yarn to tie onto their wrist as an "affirmation bracelet."

20.8 Awards Ceremony

Courtesy of Chaplowe (2015)

This is a flexible activity to recognize individuals for completing training. It is especially useful when certificates or "recognition of training" are to be provided to trainees; in place of or in addition to this, small gifts can be awarded, such as a candy bar or memento of the place/culture where training occurred. When possible, it is fun to accompany the awards ceremony with appropriate music (i.e., using a computer speaker); check beforehand what style of music may be most suitable for the audience (e.g., while "Pomp and Circumstance Marches" is often used in the United States, other songs may be more meaningful in other cultures). Below we summarize some simple ways that a rewards ceremony can be facilitated:

- **Participatory certificate giving**. With this activity, certificates (or written recognition) of training participation are randomly handed out to trainees. Then, one at a time, they come to the front of the room, read aloud the name on the certificate, and that person comes forward to receive it. The giver of the certificate can recognize the receiver with an affirmation (as described above) and/or the receiver can provide an elevator speech when be awarded the certificate.

- **High fives walk**. This is a fun and energetic way for trainees to receive training certificates. Trainees form two equal and parallel lines that face each other. At one end of the lines, the trainers and any other relevant people, such as a visiting guest, stand to hand out certificates. As names are called out, individuals walk to the opposite end of the lines and then walk down between them to receive the award at the other end, raising both hands to slide (or slap) their palms across other raised hands from people on each side as they walk. (Handshakes or other gestures can be substituted.) Upon awarding their certificate, affirmations can be provided, and/or an elevator speech made. A variation is to have each person walk through the lines in a different manner (backward, skipping, hopping) or using a different gesture than the prior people.

- **Group picture**. Often people want a picture to remember each other, and this can also be useful for any training report that may be prepared after training. Have participants prepare beforehand in clear, bold writing on a large piece of paper a sign stating the name, date, and place of the training; it is fun to encourage animation and illustrations on the sign. People then gather in an appropriate spot and configuration to frame the picture (with attention to lighting) and holding the sign (so it does not block anyone's face). Typically, an external person is used to take the picture, often multiple times, as people want a picture using their own camera.

A fun variation is to shuffle and place certificates on a chair at the spot pictures are to be taken. Everyone, including trainers, then gathers to be in the picture with the exception of the person whose certificate is on the top of the pile. This person is the first photographer and can make a comment or affirmation as they pick up their certificate and prior to using their own camera to take a group picture. (The chair can leave the trainer's camera for people who do not have their own cameras, although with mobile phones today this is seldom the case.) After snapping the shot, this person reads off the next person whose certificate is on the top of the pile, returns to the group, and the process is repeated until everyone has received their certificate and taken a picture. Often this can result in some fun pictures if each person calls something out to evoke funny behavior from the group.

21. Training Follow-Up Activities

Description

As the title of this last category reflects, the following are not necessary activities but actions or techniques to support training objectives after training.

Advantages

When effectively conducted, training follow-up supports continued learning and transfer of learning into practice (training transfer).

Disadvantages

Training follow-up requires an additional investment of time and resources, and trainers may not always be available to support. It can also risk "overkill" or trainee "burnout" and interfere with other responsibilities or learning trainees have after training.

Additional considerations

In Chapter 8, we discussed the importance of planning for training evaluation and follow-up as part of training design. We recommend readers refer to this discussion for key considerations for training follow-up (p. 200) as well as Chapter 11 on training evaluation. The underlying message is to plan for training follow-up to support training objectives as part of a coherent approach to M&E capacity building. Below, we summarize some key approaches that can help sustain continued learning and training transfer after training has been completed.

21.1 Social Media Platforms/Forums

Social media offers a variety of different options for post-training interaction, and we highlight it first because it can be used to support many of the other training follow-up actions we discuss next. As discussed in Chapter 2, there are assortments of social mediums that can be used to support training, ranging from Internet forums and online communities to email lists, weblogs, and microblogs. When used for training follow-up, these options can be framed at the training closing (if not already initiated prior to or during training as part of the training program). Social media can be used to share learning, experiences, lessons, and work products, while building a sense of community to motivate people to sustain their learning goals after training. Following are three brief examples illustrating the use of social media to support training transfer:

1. If a suitable "community of practice" does not already exist, consider establishing a LinkedIn interest group for trainees, trainers, and others to join. This can be set up so members have to be approved to ensure the shared information is not public. When information is not proprietary, a Facebook page or group can also be used (but be careful as permissions, privacies, and other features often change with this service). A word of warning is that people nowadays are inundated with a variety of social media forums, and while optimism may initially be high, actual use in the long run may be low. Thus, consider scheduling regular reports or assignments beforehand with trainees to keep it active. For instance, identify trainees who will be using learning after training and are willing to report back or share drafted or completed products for comment and lesson learning (see peer-reviewed work samples below).

2. Using an email list or weblog, have learners share and solve problems online. People can list and prioritize problems to work on together or in subgroups and set up a schedule to coordinate follow-up. If a particular problem generates a lot of interest, or seems to require more

than asynchronous, online communication to discuss, consider using a group videoconference call to allow people to report back to others and explore topics.

3. Have participants create Twitter accounts or provide their existing Twitter username, which can be used to send short M&E tips after training. Accounts can be configured so that when a tweet is directed to or mentions them, it will also be emailed to them. In this manner, people who may not be interested in regularly using their Twitter accounts will still receive tweets. Using this medium, the trainer (or others) can tweet regular M&E tips and resources supporting ongoing learning and support for training objectives. Of course, the drawbacks with Twitter is the messages will need to be very concise (although a link can be attached for more comprehensive information), and it can be difficult to message or mention more than one person at a time.

21.2 Share a Training Report

A training report can be an effective way to raise wider support for training transfer, while also upholding accountability. The contents and tone of the training report should be tailored to the target audience, but key elements typically include a summary of the training objectives and outcomes, the curriculum and key topics covered, any training evaluation results and pre/post-test scores, training highlights (and any low points), and other items that can help convey what occurred (e.g., how many trainees), why it is important, and how it can be supported—for example, key quotes or testimonies from trainees as well as colleagues or supervisors, pictures of training activities and work products, and a list of additional resources and events to support for additional M&E capacity building. Training reports can be disseminated in print, and through social media, or posted in public spaces (cafeteria bulletin board) for viewing. They can also be presented orally with a slideshow and recorded for further dissemination. It can be very effective when trainees are involved in preparing and sharing training reports, and below we illustrate two examples using trainee-generated reports and presentations.

21.3 Trainee-Generated Reports

Trainee-generated reports are a learner-centered approach where trainees themselves take the initiative to summarize and report on the training or their experience with practicing M&E following training. The frequency and level of detail can vary according to trainee context, ranging from two or three key points they took away from training to more detailed accounts of applying training KSA and identifying related lessons. Some examples of questions to consider for trainee-generated reports include the following:

a. What did you learn from training that you didn't already know?
b. What have you accomplishment as a result of training that you are most proud of?
c. How did you modify your approach to make it work better?
d. What related questions or challenges do you confront using what you have learned?
e. How can you address those challenges?
f. Are there any other additional resources or recommendations you have?

Social media is useful to exchange reports, and individual accounts can be consolidated and shared with trainees and other training stakeholders as an overall, collective report. In an organizational context, lessons and anecdotes can be posted in a central, public place in the organization, such as a physical bulletin board in the cafeteria or meeting room or an online discussion board or learning platform. This type of sharing not only supports training transfer for trainees but also informs and builds M&E understanding among others who view trainee reports.

21.4 Trainee Post-Training Presentations

This is an especially effective way to empower trainees and reinforce their understanding of training content, while promoting learning among others who did not participate in training. Similar to trainee-generated reports, post-training presentations are live presentations where trainees share what they learned and key resources with others. They are especially well suited for training in an organization (Type 1), capitalizing on the investment of training by having trainees share training content with and teach other colleagues. Presentations can be during regular departmental meetings, "bag-lunch" affairs in a conference room, or even online using videoconferencing. One of the best ways to reinforce understanding is to explain to others what has been learned.

21.5 Post-Training Quizzes or Tests

Certainly this may not sound like the most exciting way to support training follow-up, but with a little ingenuity, pot-training tests or quizzes can be facilitated in a non-threatening way in which learners genuinely appreciate the opportunity they provide to reinforce learning. As discussed in Chapter 11, post-training learning assessment can also be a valuable source of data for training evaluation. They can be administered online through surveys or sent out via email or in person through a written format.

Good practice for learning assessment should be followed (e.g., informed consent), and particular attention should be given to reviewing correct answers, addressing pending questions, and identifying lessons learned. When appropriate, trainee performance can be publically posted, either in an anonymous format or identifying individual performance to inspire trainees (and others).

One way to decompress test or quiz anxiety is to change their names and call them contests or tournaments. Awarding prizes or even just recognition can help boost motivation. Teams can be used, tallying individual performance (let participants select team names that coincide with sporting events that are in season). Another consideration is, rather than administering tests at one time, spread out the questions over a period of days or weeks with sequenced grading—this can help to make testing seem less ominous. Of course, there may be contexts, typically organizational, where post-training performance assessment may be required as part of professional development or quality control.

21.6 Peer-Reviewed Learning Assignments or Work Samples

Like tests or quizzes, the word "assignment" can conjure up negative associations of required homework during schooling. However, when assignments are peer reviewed and presented as an optional opportunity for learners to sign up for, it puts a different spin on the process, empowering people to take advantage of and support each other. It also helps when people select or identify assignments appropriate to their post-training needs. Often, it may be possible to have people review actual samples of their work after training for which they apply their M&E knowledge and skills (this has the added benefit to defuse the perception of assigned "extra" work). The use of work samples for training follow-up is a nice complement to trainee work portfolios (discussed below). Depending on the context, peer reviews can be conducted in person or online through social media.

21.7 Incremental Trainer Follow-Up

This approach will depend on trainer availability but is a very straightforward way to support training follow-up. In short, the trainer periodically communicates with trainees via email or discussion board, the day after training, a week later, two weeks, one month, three months, and so forth. This can include supporting many of the follow-up actions discussed in this section, such as sharing M&E tips, resources, calendars of events, and answering trainee questions.

21.8 Share Additional M&E Resources

People will generally be more receptive and appreciative of M&E resources for further learning and practice after they have already been introduced to topics in training.

In addition to providing a list or bibliography of additional resources at the end of training, additional resources can be shared *after* training to help keep the training momentum alive. Certainly trainers can do this as part of incremental follow-up (above), but another approach is "peer-identified resources." It can be very meaningful when trainees themselves identify and share M&E resources that they have found especially useful. This can be a review of a book, guide, website, software, checklist, template, and so forth. This can be combined with post-training learning assignment (above), and reviewed resources can be shared using a variety of social media options.

21.9 Distance and e-Learning Follow-Up

As discussed in Chapter 2, distance and self-directed learning is on the rise, especially with the technological advances of e-learning. In addition to training delivery itself, e-learning and other distance learning options are valuable resource to follow up training, with an assortment of online outlets, mobile applications, and recorded media to reinforce and sustain M&E learning and practice. Appendix 2.1 in Chapter 2 summarizes some key examples of different types of these delivery options, and the Recommended Resources at the end of Part 3 provides examples of online learning sources for M&E.

21.10 Post-Training Learning Events

Many of the options we discuss in this last section of the book can be an "event," but here we refer to more formal, live activities for M&E learning that can support training follow-up. When training is approached as one of a variety of learning sources within a larger learning system, other events can be used to complement training, and vice versa. Examples include other training events, videoconference calls between trainees and trainers, webinars and field and exchange visits. These can be planned explicitly to support trainees after training, or they may already be separately planned by others but open for trainee participation. Trainees can be informed about them by the trainer or each other using a variety of social media.

21.11 Trainee Logbooks and Work Portfolios

Also discussed as a method for training evaluation (Chapter 11), trainee logbooks and work portfolios are useful tools to track trainee performance toward personal learning goals. The content of logbooks includes written reflections on and assessment of progress towards learning goals, key areas to work on, and specific actions that can be taken. A key component of work portfolios is examples of work products. For instance, if training objectives include the ability to develop logframes or conduct evaluations, examples of completed logframes and evaluation reports can be included in the portfolio. This not only supports training transfer by considering concrete follow-up but can also help trainees prepare a professional portfolio to serve them in their career advancement.

21.12 Trainee Development Plan or Learning Contract

Trainee development plans and learning contracts are tools used to help learners identify and monitor personal training and related professional development or career objectives. Also called *learning development plans, training transfer plans,* or *training contracts*, these tools help make explicit trainee expectations and how learning is to be used after training. As such, they should be planned and implemented prior to training so that trainees can identify expectations and goals. Trainee development plans can be developed by trainees themselves, or for organizational training they can be developed in collaboration with manager/supervisors to ensure personal goals are aligned with organizational-wide performance management and development processes. A trainee contract can be revisited and revised at the conclusion of or in follow-up to M&E training. As discussed in Chapter 11 (Appendix 11.1), trainee development plans and learning contracts can be used for training evaluation, and in Appendix 11.2, we provide an example of a M&E learning development plan, with accompanying instructions. Trainee logbooks and work portfolios discussed above are a useful complement to development plans and learning contracts.

21.13 Coaching, Mentoring, and On-the-Job Training

As discussed in Chapter 2 (Table 2.3), coaching, mentoring, and on-the-job training are each intentionally planned approaches for individual capacity building. They are valuable approaches to complement face-to-face M&E training and support training transfer. They tend to be more appropriate for organizational contexts, although independent trainees can locate experienced M&E practitioners to serve as professional mentors. When used in an organizational setting, trainee development plans, learning contracts, logbooks, and work portfolios can also be used as part of a coaching, mentoring, or on-the-job training arrangement.

21.14 Package M&E Training as Part of a Larger M&E Capacity Building Exercise

This is an approach to M&E capacity building for training for organizations (Type 1). As discussed in Chapter 3, organizational M&E training is best provided as part of a coherent, integrated approach to building M&E capacity. We will illustrate this with an example from the International Federation of Red Cross and Red Crescent Societies (IFRC). Often, the global planning and evaluation department (PED) is asked to provide onsite M&E training to Red Cross and Red Crescent National Societies. Rather than providing M&E training as an isolated event, PED has responded to such requests with an "M&E capacity building field visit." The exercise capitalizes on the resources invested in a field visit for a M&E training workshop to include other capacity building activities.

As represented in **Figure 12.11**, the field visit consists of three components that are planned collaboratively with National Societies according to their organizational and country contexts and needs. The M&E capacity assessment and planning component is an opportunity for the National Society to take inventory of its M&E assets and deficits to inform a strategic planning for future M&E capacity building and practice. In this way, the M&E training workshop component of the field visit can be designed to support M&E strategic objectives. The third component in the field visit is an applied training of trainers (ToT), which begins prior to the M&E training workshop, for which appropriate National Society staff participate. They then co-facilitating the actual M&E workshop planned for National Society staff and volunteers, with the guidance and mentorship of the experienced M&E trainers who provided the ToT. In this way, an additional outcome of the field visit is a cadre of apprentice M&E trainers to support future M&E training and related capacity building needs.

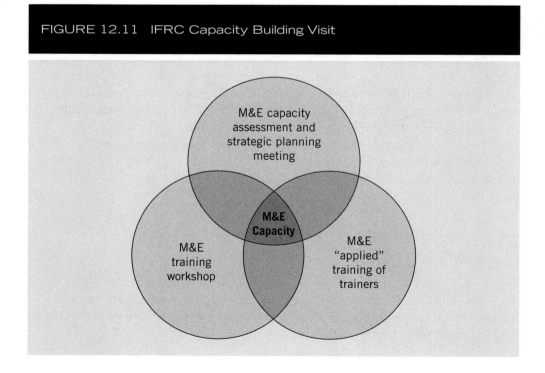

FIGURE 12.11 IFRC Capacity Building Visit

PART 3 APPENDICES

Appendix 12.1 Example Activity Lesson Plan

Learning Objective

By the end of this activity, trainees will be able to explain the key levels in the objective (results) hierarchy of the logframe format used by the IFRC (International Federation of Red Cross and Red Crescent Societies).

Time

~30 minutes for preparation; ~45 minutes for facilitation

Facilitation Guidance

This activity is a fun, energizing way to introduce trainees to the first (objectives) column of the logframe. It is appropriate for learners new to logical frameworks or to reinforce understanding for more experienced learners.

1. **Activity preparation.** Prepare activity slides and obtain required materials. If not already done, arrange trainees into balanced learning teams of four to eight people. Place on each small group table a package of 50 straws, role of masking tape, about one meter (yard) of string, and scissors.

2. **Activity introduction (5 minutes).** Brief trainees that they will be doing an activity that will help them understand the results hierarchy in a logframe. To further engage their interest, tell people that the activity is a game/contest and prizes will be awarded. Display on a projected slide the exercise instructions. Read them out load and clarify any questions or concerns people may have. Explain that groups do not need to use all of each material to build their bridge. Leave the slide displayed during the activity for people to refer to.

Logical Bridge Game

1. Your team will be provided with straws, tape, string, and scissors.
2. You have <u>20 minutes</u> to build a bridge that is:
   - Self-standing.
   - Wider than the bottom of the glass.
   - Higher than a glass.
   - Should be able to hold the glass.
3. When done, your team should do a cheer!
4. Points will be awarded for:
   - 1st team finished, Most sturdy; Most creative; Most artistic,etc.

---

3. **Activity practice (20 minutes).** Float around and check in with groups as they construct their bridges. Provide a time countdown, announcing when 10 minutes are left, 5 minutes, and then announce a final 2-minute warning. Below are some example bridges from prior activities:

(Continued)

(Continued)

Courtesy of Chaplowe (2015)

4. **Activity awards/debrief**. After time is up, debrief in plenary each team's bridge, one at a time. Ask each team what they experienced. What worked well and didn't? How was their teamwork? Awards can be provided according to different criteria for each bridge—for example, first to complete their bridge, sturdiest bridge, most innovate bridge, strangest bridge, funniest bridge, and so forth. In this manner, each team can "win" and receive a prize. Edible prizes work well, such as candy, fruit, or beverage. It is also fun to take team pictures with each bridge (which can be later used in any training report).

5. **Activity lesson.** The follow-up lesson for this activity is actually a further debrief, allowing learners to reflect on and apply the activity to the learning objective. Following the sequences of slides below, the first provides a visual overview of the Objectives (results) hierarchy. Introducing the question first best facilitates the next set of five slides; eliciting answers with plenary discussion; and then providing the abbreviated definition for each objective, which can be elaborated by the trainer. The lesson can be accompanied by a handout summarizing definitions or referral to pages 29 through 31 in the *IFRC Project/Program Planning Guidelines.* Point out that other organizations or donors often use other terminology but do not get drawn into a long discussion on which terminology is "better." Instead, you can explain that different terms can be used as long as they are used consistently and the core logic or theory of change holds.

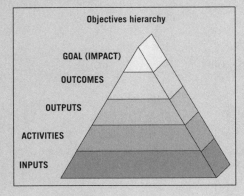

Objectives hierarchy

GOAL (IMPACT)

OUTCOMES

OUTPUTS

ACTIVITIES

INPUTS

INPUTS

Question: *What may be the inputs needed to build a bridge?*

Answer: Completed bridge connecting two different towns.

Definition: Resources needed to implement activities (financial, materials, human).

Activities	**Outputs**
Question: *What may be the activities involved in building a bridge?* **Answer:** Identify plan, lay foundation, build structure, etc. **Definition:** Tasks needed to be done to achieve the outputs (and then outcomes and goal).	**Question:** *What may be the product you want in building a bridge?* **Answer:** Completed bridge connecting two different towns. **Definition:** The tangible products, goods and services, and other immediate results that lead to the achievement of outcomes. The *deliverables* needed for higher change.
Outcomes	**Goal**
Question: *What may be the primary outcome you want to achieve with the bridge?* **Answer:** Increase trade and between two towns. **Definition:** Primary result/s (desired changes) that contribute to the achievement of the Goal. Changes are often in knowledge, attitudes, and practices (KAP).	**Question:** *In real life, what may be the overall reason you want to build a bridge between 2 communities?* **Answer:** Improved economy in two towns. **Definition:** Desired long-term result (impact), which factors outside the intervention may contribute to.

6. **Additional facilitation tips**. If presentations using projected PowerPoint slides are not possible, these components of the activity can be adapted using flipchart, whiteboard, or prepared handouts as an alternative. If other team games will be conducted during training, points can be recorded on a plenary score sheet and prizes later awarded. If team scoring becomes a distraction when debriefing the bridges, this aspect of the activity can be dropped.

Learning assessment
Recommended is observation and monitoring of trainee participation. Learning assessment of logic framework key elements can include written quiz and/or completion of case study logframe following addition lessons on key elements of the IFRC logframe.

Lesson assignments
Pre-lesson assignments are not necessary for this activity, although pre-reading from the pages 29 through 31 in the IFRC *Project/Program Planning Guidelines* can be assigned.

Lesson materials
Computer, PowerPoint slides, projector, screen, or wall space for projected images. Per each team, provide 50 straws, roll of masking tape, about one meter (yard) of string, and scissors.

(Continued)

(Continued)

PART 3 RECOMMENDED RESOURCES _____

In the preparation the Part 3 of the book, we found the following books useful to consider the categorization and description of different training methods and techniques: *Experiential Learning* (Beard & Wilson, 2006), *Training Fundamentals* (Chan, 2010), *Training in Organizations* (Goldstein & Ford, 2002), *Approaches to Training and Development* (Laird, 2003), and *Building Evaluation Capacity* (Preskill & Russ-Eft, 2015). We also recommend the ILO's freely available *Trainer's Toolbox of Training Techniques* (Mason, 1995).

For readers interested in more examples of active training techniques and activities, Mel Silberman is an authority, having authored and edited a variety of book on the subject, and we recommend *Active training: A Handbook of Techniques, Designs* and *101 Ways to Make Training Active* (Silberman, 2005, 2006). There are also an increasing number of books on training games, including *The Gamification of Learning and Instruction* (Kapp, 2012), *101 More Games for Trainers* (Pike, 1995), and *Training Games* (Sugar & Whitcomb, 2006). The publication, *100 Ways to Energize Groups: Games to Use in workshops, Meetings and the Community*, is a useful publication

freely available from International HIV/AIDS Alliance (2002).

There are also an array of online resources for ideas and examples for training activities and games. Notably, the website of Thiagi (*aka* Sivasailam Thiagarajan) contains more than 400 free, ready-to-use training games and activities (The Thiaga Group, 2015). Similarly, the websites Training Bubble (2015) and 350.org Workshops (2015) provide free energizers, icebreakers, training games, and resources.

As noted in the preface to this book, we believe there is a scarcity of general books on M&E training (and thus a gap this book seeks to address). One exception is the recently updated book *Building Evaluation Capacity: Activities for Teaching and Training* (Preskill & Russ-Eft, 2015), which we highlight in Box 12.1. There is also an assortment of organizational and sector-specific guides for M&E training, with example activities and related facilitation guidance. For example, freely available publications we recommend include *Developing a Logic Model: Teaching and Training Guide* (Taylor-Powell & Henart, 2008) from the

University of Wisconsin-Extension; the *Monitoring and Evaluation Training Curriculum 2009* from John Snow, Inc. (2012); the *Monitoring and Evaluation Training Manual for CBOs and NGOs* from the International Rescue Committee (IRC, undated); the *Monitoring and Evaluation Training Guide* from the UNDP (undated); and *Evaluation Training* from WHO (2010). These examples are only illustrative and far from exhaustive, and we encourage readers to explore and share other resources available for M&E training activities.

Lastly, another useful source of example activities and facilitation tips that can be adapted for M&E training are training of trainer (ToT) guides, which we identify in the recommended resources section in Chapter 10.

References

350.org Workshops. (2015). *Facilitation tips, games, and energizers.* Retrieved from http://workshops.350.org/facilitation/

Adams, J., & Dickinson, P. (2010). Evaluation training to build capacity in the community and public health workforce. *American Journal of Evaluation, 31*(3), 421–433.

AEA (American Evaluation Association). (2004). *Guiding principles for evaluators.* Retrieved from http://www.eval.org/p/cm/ld/fid=51

AEA (American Evaluation Association). (2011). *American Evaluation Association statement on cultural competence in evaluation.* Retrieved from http://www.eval.org/p/cm/ld/fid=92

AEA (American Evaluation Association). (2013). *AEA guiding principles training package.* Retrieved from http://www.eval.org/p/cm/ld/fid=105

AEA (American Evaluation Association). (2014a). *AEA coffee break webinar—International series.* Retrieved from http://comm.eval.org/coffee_break_webinars/coffeebreak/internationalseries

AEA (American Evaluation Association). (2014b). *AEA eStduy* and *AEA Coffee Break Webinars.* Retrieved from http://comm.eval.org/coffee_break_webinars/estudy and http://comm.eval.org/coffee_break_webinars/CoffeeBreak/

AEA (American Evaluation Association). (2015). *AEA website.* Retrieved March 1, 2015 from http://www.eval.org

AECD (Alliance for Education and Community Development). (2010). *Introduction—The logic of backward design.* Retrieved on March 1, 2015 from www.ascd.org/ASCD/pdf/books/mctighe2004_intro.pdf

AHRD (Academy of Human Resource Development). (1999). *Standards on Ethics and Integrity.* Baton Rouge, LA: AHRD.

AIMEnet. (2015). *HIV/AIDS monitoring and evaluation network or AIMEnet community of practice.* Retrieved from https://knowledge-gateway.org/aimenet

Allinger, G. M., & Janak, E. A. (1989). Kirkpatrick's levels of training criteria: Thirty years later. *Personal Psychology, 42,* 331–342.

Ally, M. (Ed.). (2009). *Mobile learning transforming the delivery of education and training.* Edmonton, Canada: AU Press, Athabasca University.

ALNAP (Active Learning Network for Accountability and Performance in Humanitarian Action). (2015). Retrieved from http://www.alnap.org

Anderson, T., & Elloumi, F. (Eds.). (2004). *Theory and practice of online learning.* Athabasca, Canada: Athabasca University.

ASCD. (2014). *Differentiated instruction.* Association for Supervision and Curriculum Development (ASCD) website. Retrieved from http://www.ascd.org/research-a-topic/differentiated-instruction-books-and-articles.aspx

ASTD (American Society for Training & Development). (2013). *State of the industry.* Alexandria, VA: ASTD Research.

ASTD (American Society for Training & Development). (2014). *Online glossary.* Retrieved from https://www.td.org/Publications/Newsletters/Learning-Circuits/Glossary

ASTD (American Society for Training & Development). (2015). *Website.* Retrieved from https://www.td.org

Bakken, L. L., Nunez, J., & Couture, C. (2014). A course model for building evaluation capacity through a university–community partnership. *American Journal of Evaluation, 35*(4), 579–593.

Baldwin, T. T., & Ford, J. K. (1988). Transfer of training: A review and directions for future research. *Personnel Psychology, 41,* 63–105.

Bamberger, M., Rugh, J., & Mabry, L. (2012). *RealWorld evaluation: Working under budget, time, data, and political constraints* (2nd ed.). Thousand Oaks, CA: Sage.

Barbazette, J. (2006). *The art of great training delivery*. San Francisco: John Wiley and Sons.

Barnette, J. J., & Wallis, A. B. (2003). Helping evaluators swim with the current: Training evaluators to support mainstreaming. *New Directions for Evaluation, 99,* 51–61.

Bates, R. (2004). A critical analysis of evaluation practice: The Kirkpatrick's model and the principle of beneficence. *Evaluation and Program Planning, 27,* 341–347.

Beard, C., & Wilson, J. P. (2006). *Experiential learning: A best practice handbook for educators and trainers* (2nd ed.). London: Kogan Page.

Beasley, M., Valerio, A., & Bundy, D. (Eds.). (2008). *A sourcebook of HIV/AIDS prevention programs*. Washington DC: The World Bank

Bell, B. S., & Kozlowski, S. W. J. (2009). Toward a theory of learner-centered training design: An integrative framework of active learning [Electronic version]. In S. W. J. Kozlowski & E. Salas (Eds.), *Learning, training, and development in organizations* (pp. 263–300). New York: Routledge.

Bersin, J. (2004). *The blended learning book*. San Francisco: Pfeiffer.

BetterEvaluation. (2015). Website. Retrieved from http://betterevaluation.org

Bloom, B. S., Engelhart, M. D., Furst, E. J., Hill, W. H., & Krathwohl, D. R. (1956). *Taxonomy of educational objectives: The classification of educational goals. Handbook I: Cognitive domain*. New York: Longman. Copyright renewed 1984 by B. S. Bloom and D. R. Krathwohl.

Botturi, L., Cantoni, L., Lepori, B., & Tardini, S. (2007). Fast prototyping as a communication catalyst for e-learning design. In M. Bullen & D. Janes (Eds.), *Making the transition to e-learning: Strategies and issues* (pp. 266–283). Hershey, PA: Idea Group.

Boud, D. (2002). What is peer learning and why is it important? In D. Boud, R. Cohen, & J. Sampson (Eds.), *Higher education: Learning from & with each other*. London: Kogan Page Limited.

Bourgeois, I., & Cousins, J. B. (2008). Informing evaluation capacity building through profiling organizational capacity for evaluation: An empirical examination of four Canadian Federal Government organizations. *Canadian Journal of Program Evaluation, 23*(3), 127–146.

Bourgeois, I., & Cousins, J. B. (2013). Understanding dimensions of organizational evaluation capacity. *American Journal of Evaluation, 34*(3), 299–319.

Bourgeois, I., Toews, E., Whynot, J., & Lamarche, M. K. (2013). Measuring organizational evaluation capacity in the Canadian Federal Government. *Canadian Journal of Program Evaluation, 28*(2), 1–19.

Brinkerhoff, R. O. (1989). Using evaluation to transform training. *New Directions for Evaluation, 44,* 5–20.

Brookfield, S. D. (1986). *Understanding and facilitating adult learning*. San Francisco, California: Jossey-Bass Inc.

Brookfield, S. D. (2005). *The power of critical theory: Liberating adult learning and teaching*. San Francisco, CA, Jossey-Bass.

Brookfield, S. D. (2006). *The skillful teacher* (2nd ed.) San Francisco: Jossey-Bass.

Burke, A. B., & Hutchins, H. M. (2007). Training transfer: An integrative literature review. *Human Resource Development Review September, 6,* 263–296,

Businessballs. (2015). Website. Retrieved from www.businessballs.com

Butcher, N. (2011). *Basic guide to open educational resources (OER)*. Commonwealth (Vancouver) of Learning and UNESCO (Paris). Retrieved from www.col.org/OERbasicguide

C-Change (Communication for Change). (2012). *C-modules supplemental facilitator's guide: Training of facilitators*. Washington, DC: FHI 360/C-Change.

Caffarella, R. S. (2002). *Planning programs for adult learners: A practical guide for educators.* San Francisco: Jossey-Bass.

Capacity for Health. (2015). *M&E capacity assessment tool.* Retrieved from www.capacity4health.org

Capacity.org. (2015). Retrieved from http://www.capacity.org

CDC (Centers for Disease Control and Prevention). (2013). *Evaluation reporting: A guide to help ensure use of evaluation findings.* Atlanta, GA: US Department of Health and Human Services.

CDC (Centers for Disease Control and Prevention). (2014). *Practical strategies for culturally competent evaluation.* Atlanta, GA: US Department of Health and Human Services.

CDC (Center for Disease Control and Prevention). (2015). Program Performance and Evaluation Office (PPEO) website. Retrieved from http://www.cdc.gov/eval

CES (The Canadian Evaluation Society). (2010). *Competencies for Canadian evaluation practice.* Retrieved from http://www.evaluationcanada.ca/txt/2_competencies_cdn_evaluation_practice.pdf

CES (Canadian Evaluation Society). (2014). *Professional designation program.* Retrieved from http://www.evaluationcanada.ca/site.cgi?en:5:6

Chambers, R. (1997). *Whose reality counts? Putting the first last.* London: Intermediate Technology Publications.

Chan, J. F. (2010). *Training fundamentals.* San Francisco: John Wiley and Sons.

Chaplowe, S. G., & Engo-Tjega, R. B. (2007). Civil society organizations and evaluation. Lessons from Africa. *Evaluation, 13*(2), 257–274.

Chaplowe, S. G. (2008a). *Monitoring and evaluation planning.* American Red Cross/CRS M&E Module Series. Washington, DC and Baltimore, MD: American Red Cross and Catholic Relief Services.

Chaplowe, S. G. (2008b). Training slides: *Fun and games with logframes.*

Chaplowe, S. G. (2011). *Scott Chaplowe on fun and games in M&E training.* AEA365 | A Tip-a-Day by and for Evaluators. Retrieved from http://aea365.org/blog/archive

Chaplowe, S. G. (2012). *Monitoring and evaluation planning for projects/programs.* American Evaluation Association Coffee Break Webinar International Series. Retrieved from http://comm.eval.org/coffee_break_webinars/coffeebreak/internationalseries

Chaplowe, S. G. (2015). Personal photo collection from trainings.

Chatty, D., Baas, S., & Fleig, A. (2003). *Participatory processes towards co-management of natural resources in pastoral areas of the Middle East. A Training of Trainers Source Book Based on the Principles of Participatory Methods and Approaches.* Rome: Food and Agriculture Organization of the United Nations (FAO). Available online as an interactive webpage of

as a PDF download. Retrieved from http://www.fao.org/docrep/006/ad424e/ad424e01.htm, and ftp://ftp.fao.org/docrep/fao/006/ad424e/ad424e00.pdf

Christie, N. V. (2012). An interpersonal skills learning taxonomy for program evaluation instructors. *Journal of Public Affairs Education (JPAE), 18*(4), 739–756.

Claremont University. (2015). Free Online Training in International Development Evaluation. Retreived from http://www.cgu.edu/pages/10314.asp

Clark, D. (2006). *Gagne's nine dull commandments.* Retrieved from http://donaldclarkplanb.blogspot.ch/2006/09/gagnes-nine-dull-commandments.html

Clark, D. R. (2015a). *Big dog & little dog's performance juxtaposition.* Retrieved from http://www.nwlink.com/~donclark

Clark, D. R. (2015b). *ISD versus ID.* Retrieved from http://www.nwlink.com/~donclark/hrd/sat1.html

Clark, D. R. (2015c). *Backwards planning model.* Retrieved March 1, 2015 from http://www.nwlink.com/~donclark/hrd/sat2.html

Clark, D. R. (2015d). *Templates for instructional design.* Retrieved from http://www.nwlink.com/~donclark/hrd/templates/templates.html

Clark, R. E. (1994). Media will never influence learning. *Educational Technology Research and Development, 42,* 21–29.

CLEAR (Centers for Learning on Evaluation and Results). (2013).

Interactive course manual: A manual on organizing and running a successful training course on evaluation methods. CLEAR South Asia.

CLEAR. (Centers for Learning on Evaluation and Results). (2014). *CLEAR South Asia M&E series.* Retrieved on from http://www .povertyactionlab.org/south-asia/ clear-me-roundtable

CLEAR (Centers for Learning on Evaluation and Results). (2015). Retrieved from http://www .theclearinitiative.org

Clinton, J. (2014). The true impact of evaluation: Motivation for ECB. *American Journal of Evaluation,* 35(1), 120–127.

Collins, A., & Halverson, R. (2009). *Rethinking education in the age of technology: The digital revolution and schooling in America.* New York: Teachers College Press.

Commonwealth of Australia. (2001). *Training package assessment materials kit.* Retrieved from www .det.act.gov.au/__data/assets/pdf_ file/0006/456351/Guide-1.pdf

Compton, D., Baizerman, M., & Stockdill, S. H. (Eds.). (2002). *New Directions for Evaluation Series: Vol. 93. The art, craft and science of evaluation capacity building* (pp. 1–120). San Francisco: Jossey Bass.

Constantinidou, F., & Baker, S. (2002). Stimulus modality and verbal learning performance in normal aging. *Brain and Language,* 82(3), 296–311.

Cooksy, L. J. (2008). Challenges and opportunities in experiential

learning. *American Journal of Evaluation, 29*(3), 340–342.

Coombs, P. H., Prosser, C., & Ahmed, M. (1973). *New paths to learning for rural children and youth.* New York: International Council for Educational Development.

Corporation for National and Community Service. (2015). *Performance measurement module series.* Retrieved from http://www .nationalservice.gov/resources/ online-courses

Coursea. (2015). Retrieved from www.coursera.org/about

Coursetalk. (2015). Retrieved from www.coursetalk.com

Cousins, J. B., & Leithwood, K. A. (1986). Current empirical research on evaluation utilization. *Review of Educational Research, 56,* 331–364.

Cousins, J. B. (2015). Personal photo collection from trainings.

Cousins, J. B., & Chouinard, J. A. (2012). *Participatory evaluation up close: An integration of research-based knowledge.* Charlotte, NC: Information Age Publishing.

Cousins, J. B., Goh, S., Clark, S., & Lee, L. (2004). Integrating evaluative inquiry into the organizational culture: A review and synthesis of the knowledge base. *Canadian Journal of Program Evaluation, 19*(2), 99–141.

Cousins, J. B. (2007). *New Directions for Evaluation Series: Vol. 116. Process use in theory, research and practice.* San Francisco: Jossey Bass.

Cousins, J. B., Whitmore, E., & Shulha, L. M. (2013). Arguments

for a common set of principles for collaborative inquiry in evaluation. *American Journal of Evaluation, 34*(1), 7–22.

Cousins, J. B., & Bourgeois, I. (Eds.). (2014). *New Directions for Evaluation Series: Vol. 141. Organizational capacity to do and use evaluation.* San Francisco: Jossey Bass.

Cousins, J. B., Goh, S. C., Elliott, C. J., & Bourgeois, I. (2014). Framing the capacity to do and use evaluation. *New Directions for Evaluation, 141,* 7–23.

Creative Commons. (2015). Website. Retrieved from http:// creativecommons.org

Cuban, L. (1986). *Teachers and machines: The classroom use of technology since 1920.* New York: Teachers College Press.

Damon, W. (1984). Peer education: The untapped potential. *Journal of Applied Developmental Psychology, 4*(5), 331–343.

Darabi, A. (2002). Teaching program evaluation: Using a systems approach. *American Journal of Evaluation, 23*(2), 219–228.

Davenport, J., & Davenport, J. (1985). A chronology and analysis of the andragogy debate. *Adult Education Quarterly, 25*(3), 152–159.

Davis, M. (2006). Teaching practical public health evaluation methods. *American Journal of Evaluation, 23*(2), 219–228.

Dewey, J. (1938). *Experience and education.* The Kappa Delta Pi Lecture Series. New York: Macmillan.

DFID (United Kingdom's Department for International Development). (2011). *DFID's approach to value for money (VfM)*. London: DIFID.

Dick, W., & Carey, L. (1996). *The systematic design of instruction* (4th ed.). New York: Harper Collins College Publishers.

Donella Meadows Institute. (2015) Retrieved from http://www.donellameadows.org/systems-thinking-resources/

ECDG (Evaluation Capacity Development Group). (2015). Retrieved from http://www.ecdg.net

EdITLib. (2015). Website. Retrieved from http://www.editlib.org

Edmunds R., & Marchant, T. (2008). *Official statistics and monitoring and evaluation systems in developing countries: Friends or foes?* Paris: PARIS21.

Edutech Wiki. (2015). Website. Retrieved March 1, 2015 from http://edutechwiki.unige.ch/en/Main_Page

eLearning Industry. (2015). *Free e-Learning books*. Retrieved from http://elearningindustry.com/free-elearning-and-instructional-design-books

Emmi, A., Eskiocak, O., Kjennerud, M., Rozenkopf, I., & Schatz, F. (2011). *Value for money: Current approaches and evolving debates*. London: London School of Economics.

ERIC (Education Resources Information Center). (2015). Retrieved from http://eric.ed.gov

Estrella, M. Blauert, J., Campilan, D., Gaventa, J., Gonsalves, J., Guijt, I. Johnson, D., & Ricafort, R. (Eds.). (2000). *Learning from change: Issues and experiences in participatory monitoring and evaluation*. London, UK, and Ottawa, Canada: Intermediate Technology Publications, and International Development Research Centre.

Estrella, M., & Gaventa, J. (1998). *Who counts reality? Participatory monitoring and evaluation: A literature Review*. IDS Working Paper 70. Brighton, England: Institute of Development Studies.

European Commission. (2006). *Classification of learning activities—Manual*. Luxembourg: European Commission.

Evaluation Center. (Western Michigan University). (2015). Retrieved from http://www.wmich.edu/evalctr/

Evaluation Exchange. (2005). *A conversation with Thomas R. Guskey*. Retrieved from http://www.hfrp.org/evaluation/the-evaluation-exchange/issue-archive/professional-development/a-conversation-with-thomas-r.-guskey

Evaluation Toolbox. (2015). Retrieved from http://evaluationtoolbox.net.au

EvalPartners. (2015). Retrieved from http://mymande.org/evalpartners

Experiential Training and Development Alliance. (2000). *ETD Alliance guiding principles* and *ETD Alliance code of ethical conduct*. Retrieved from http://www.etdalliance.com/page-761464

Falletta, S. V. (1998). Evaluating training programs: The four levels [Review of the book *Evaluation training programs, The four levels*, by Donald L. Kirkpatrick]. *American Journal of Evaluation, 19*(2), 259–261.

FAO (Food and Agriculture Organization of the United Nations). (2011). *E-learning methodologies. A guide for designing and developing e-learning courses*. Rome: Food and Agriculture Organization of the United Nations.

Faure, E., Herrera, F., Kaddoura, A.-K., Lopes, H., Petrovsky, A. V., Rahnema, M., & Ward, F. C. (1972). *Learning to Be* (prepared by Faure, E. et al). Paris: UNESCO.

Fetterman, D. M. (2001). *Foundations of empowerment evaluation*. Thousand Oaks, CA: Sage.

Feuerstein, M. (1986). *Partners in evaluation: Evaluating Development and Community Programmes with Participants*. London: Macmillan Education Ltd.

Fleischer, D. N., & Christie, C. A. (2009). Evaluation use. Results from a survey of U.S. American Evaluation Association Members. *American Journal of Evaluation, 30*(2), 158–175.

Fleming, N., & Baume, D. (2006). Learning styles again: VARKing up the right tree! *Educational Developments, SEDA Ltd, Issue 7*(4), 4–7.

Frankel, N., & Gage, A. (2007). *M&E fundamentals: A self-guided minicourse*. Washington, DC: United States Agency for International Development (USAID).

Frankiewiez, C., & Parrott, L. (2006). *Training of trainers: A guide to key content and resources* (Participants Manueal). Retrieved from http://www.microsave.net/files/pdf/Training_Techniques_TOT_Participant_s_Manual.pdf

Free Management Library. (2015). Website. Retrieved from http://managementhelp.org/systems

Free Online Education. (2015). Retrieved from www.class-central.com

Freire, P. (1970). *The pedagogy of the oppressed*. New York: The Seabury Press.

Fukuda-Parr, S., Lopes, C., & Malik, K. (Eds.). (2002). *Capacity for development: new solutions to old problems*. New York: United Nations Development Programme (UNDP) with Earthscan Publishing.

Funnell, S. C., & Rogers, P. J. (2011). *Purposeful program theory: Effective use of theories of change and logic models*. San Francisco, CA: Jossey-Bass Wiley & Sons.

Gagné, R. M. (1985). *The conditions of learning and theory of instruction*. New York: Holt, Rinehart and Winston.

Gagné, R. M., & Driscoll, M. P. (1988). *Essentials of learning for instruction* (2nd. ed.). Englewood Cliffs, NJ: Prentice Hall.

Gagné, R. M., Wagner, W., Golas, K., & Keller, J. M. (2004). *Principles of instructional design* (4th ed.). Stamford, CT: Cengage Learning.

Gardner, H. (1983). *Frames of mind: The theory of multiple intelligences*. New York, New York: Basic Books.

Gardner, H. (1999). *Intelligence reframed: Multiple intelligences for the 21st century*. New York, New York: Basic Books.

Gaventa, J., & Blauert, J. (2000). *Learning to change by learning from change: Going to scale with participatory monitoring and evaluation*. In M. Estrella, J. Blauert, D. Campilan, J. Gaventa, J. Gonsalves, I. Guijt, D. Johnson, & R. Ricafort (Eds.), *Learning from change: Issues and experiences in participatory monitoring and evaluation*. London, UK and Ottawa, Canada: Intermediate Technology Publications, and International Development Research Centre.

George Mason University. (2015). *Instructional design knowledge base*. Retrieved from http://cehdclass.gmu.edu/ndabbagh/Resources/IDKB

Ghere, G., King, J. A., Stevahn, L., & Minnema, J. (2006). A professional development unit for reflecting on program evaluator competencies. *American Journal of Evaluation*, 27, 108–123.

Global Social Change Research Project. (2015). Retrieved from http://gsociology.icaap.org/methods

Goldstein, I. L., & Ford, J. K. (2002). *Training in organizations. Needs assessment, development and evaluation*. Belmont, CA: Wadsworth, Cengage Learning.

Goleman, D. (1995). *Emotional intelligence: Why it can matter more than IQ*. New York, New York: Bantam Books.

Gordon, E. E., & Boumhart, J. E. (1997). *Ethics for training and development*. Alexandria, VA: ASTD.

Gordon, J., & Zemke, R. (2000). The attack on ISD. *Training*, 37(4), 43–53.

Görgens, M., & Kusek, J. Z. (2009). *Making monitoring and evaluation systems work. A capacity development toolkit*. Washington DC: The World Bank.

Guba, E., & Lincoln, Y. (1989). *Fourth Generation Evaluation*. London and California: Sage Publications.

Guskey, T. (2000). *Evaluating professional development*. Thousand Oaks, CA: Corwin Press, Inc.

Gustafson, K., & Branch, R. M. (2002). *Survey of instructional development models* (4th ed.). Syracuse, NY: Syracuse University. (Eric Document Reproduction Service No. ED 477 517).

Hamtini, T. M. (2008). Evaluating e-learning programs: An adaptation of Kirkpatrick's Model to accommodate e-learning environments. *Journal of Computer Science*, 4(8), 693–698.

Hargreaves, M. (2010). *Evaluating systems change: A planning guide*. Cambridge, MA: Mathematical Policy Research.

HELVETAS Swiss Intercooperation. (2015). Measuring education's path to prosperity. A practical toolkit for VET tracer studies. Retrieved from http://www.helvetas.org/topics/working_areas/skills_development_and_education/tracer_studies_tool_kit.cfm

Hendricks, M. (1994). Making a splash: Reporting evaluation results effectively. In J. S. Wholey, H. P. Hatry, & K. E. Hewcomer (Eds.),

Handbook of practical program evaluation (pp. 549–575). San Francisco: Jossey-Bass.

Heron, J. (1999). *The Complete facilitator's handbook*. London: Kogan Press.

Herrmann, N. (1999). *The theory behind the HBDI and whole brain technology*. Retrieved from www.hbdi.com

Hieder, C. (2011). *Conceptual framework for developing evaluation capacities: Building on good practices in evaluation and capacity development*. In R. Rist, M.-H. Boily, & F. Martin (Eds.), *Influencing change: Evaluation and capacity building* (pp. 85–110). Washington, DC: The World Bank.

Hodell, C. (2011). *ISD from the ground up: A no-nonsense approach to instruction design*. Danvers, MA: American Society for Training Development (ASTD).

Holden, D. J., & Zimmerman, M. A. (2009). *A practical guide to program evaluation planning*. Thousand Oaks, CA: Sage.

Holton E. F., III. (1996). The flawed four-level evaluation model. *Human Resource Development Quarterly, 7*, 5–21.

Honey, P., & Mumford, A. (1992). *The manual of learning styles*. Maidenhead: Honey Publications.

Horton, W. (2011). *e-Learning by design*. San Francisco: John Wiley & Sons.

Horton, D., Alexaki, A., Bennett-Lartey, S., Brice, K. N., Campilan, D., Carden, F., . . . Watts, J. (2003).

Evaluating capacity development: Experiences from research and development organizations around the world. The Netherlands: International Service for National Agricultural Research (ISNAR); Canada: International Development Research Centre (IDRC); the Netherlands: ACP-EU Technical Centre for Agricultural and Rural Cooperation (CTA).

Houle, C. (1980). *Continuing learning in the professions*. San Francisco: Jossey-Bass.

House, E. R. (1983). How we think about evaluation. In E. R. House (Series Ed.). *New Directions for Program Evaluation Series: Vol 19. Philosophy of evaluation*. San Francisco: Jossey-Bass, 1983.

Huba, M. E., & Freed, J. E. (2000). *Learner-centered assessment on college campuses: Shifting the focus from teaching to learning*. Boston: Allyn and Bacon.

Hubelbank, J. (2012). *Jeanne Hubelbank on using metaphors in evaluation*. A message posted to AEA365 | A Tip-a-Day by and for Evaluators. Retrieved on from http://aea365.org/blog/archive

Huebner, T. A. (2010). What research says about differentiated learning. *Educational Leadership, 67*(5), 79–81.

Hutchins, H. M. (2009). In the trainer's voice: A study of training transfer practices. *Performance Improvement Quarterly, 22*(1), 69–93.

IDEAS (International Development Evaluation Association). (2015). Retrieved from http://www.ideas-int.org/home/index.cfm

IEG. (2015). *Evaluation capacity development (ECD)*. Independent Evaluation Group and the World Bank Group. Retrieved from https://ieg.worldbankgroup.org/evaluations/evaluation-capacity-development-ecd

IFRC (International Federation of Red Cross and Red Crescent Societies). (2010). *Project/programme planning Guidance manual*. Geneva: IFRC Planning and Evaluation Department.

IFRC (International Federation of Red Cross and Red Crescent Societies). (2011a). *Project/programme monitoring and evaluation (M&E) guide*. Geneva: IFRC.

IFRC (International Federation of Red Cross and Red Crescent Societies). (2011b). *Framework for Evaluation*. Geneva: IFRC.

IFRC (International Federation of Red Cross and Red Crescent Societies). (2011c). M&E Training of Trainers workshop presentation. Geneva: IFRC.

IFRC (International Federation of Red Cross and Red Crescent Societies). (2012). *Strategic Planning Guidelines for National Societies*. Geneva: IFRC.

IFRC (International Federation of Red Cross and Red Crescent Societies). (2015a). *Monitoring and evaluation* website and learning platform. Retrieved from http://www.ifrc.org/mande, and http://www.ifrc.org/en/get-involved/learning-education-training/learning-platform1

IFRC (International Federation of Red Cross and Red Crescent

Societies). (2015b). *M&E training curriculums*. Geneva: IFRC.

IFRC (International Federation of Red Cross and Red Crescent Societies). (2015c). *M&E learning development plan*. Geneva: IFRC.

IFRC (International Federation of Red Cross and Red Crescent Societies) (2015d). *Trainee feedback form*. Geneva: IFRC.

ILO (International Labour Organization). (2015). *External resources*. Retrieved from http://www.ilo.org/eval/Informationresources/external/lang--en/index.htm

Infed. (2015). Retrieved from http://www.infed.org

Instructional Design Central. (2015). *Instructional Design Models*. Retrieved from http://www.instructionaldesigncentral.com/htm/IDC_instructionaldesignmodels.htm

InterAction. (2015). Retrieved from http://www.interaction.org

International HIV/AIDS Alliance. (2002). *100 ways to energise groups: Games to use in workshops, meetings and the community*. Retrieved from http://icaso.org/vaccines_toolkit/subpages/files/English/energiser_guide_eng.pdf

International Training & Education Center for Health (2010). *Writing good learning objectives*. I-Tech Technical Implementation Guide #4. Retrieved from http://www.go2itech.org/resources/technical-implementation-guides

INTRAC (International NGO Training and Research Centre).

(2014a). *Monitoring and evaluation blended learning—core content aeas*. Retrieved from http://www.intrac.org/events.php?action=event&id=551

INTRAC (International NGO Training and Research Centre). (2014b). *Advanced monitoring and evaluation—Core content areas*. Retrieved from http://www.intrac.org/events.php?action=event&id=545

IntraHealth International. (2007). *Learning for performance: A guide and toolkit for health worker training and education*. Chapel Hill, NC: IntraHealth International.

IntraHealth International. (2012). *Training and learning standards: A checklist and tool for developing and implementing high-quality training and learning interventions*. Chapel Hill, NC: IntraHealth International.

IOCE (International Organization for Cooperation in Evaluation). (2015). Retrieved from http://www.ioce.net/en/

IPDET (International Program for Development Evaluation Training). (2015a). Resource Center. Retrieved from http://www.ipdet.org/page.aspx?pageId=resourceCentre

IPDET (International Program for Development Evaluation Training). (2015b). *Core course topics*. from http://www.ipdet.org/page.aspx?pageId=coreCurriculum

IRC (International Rescue Committee). (n.d.). *Monitoring and evaluation training manual for CBOs and NGOs*. Thailand: IRC. Retrieved March 1, 2015 from http://cboresourcecenter.

com/phocadownload/Manuals/MinitoringEvaluation/me-00004.pdf

I-TECH (International Training & Education Center for Health). (2010). *Writing good learning objectives*. Retrieved from www.go2itech.org/resources/technical-implementation-guides/TIG4.WritingLrngObj.pdf/view

I-TECH (International Training & Education Center for Health). (2015). Training Toolkit website. Retrieved from http://www.go2itech.org/resources/Training-Toolkit

Jackson, E., & Kassam, T. (Eds.). (1998). *Knowledge Shared. Participatory Evaluation in Development Cooperation*. West Hartford, CT: Kumarian Press, IDRC.

James, R. (n.d.). *How to do strategic planning: A guide for small and diaspora NGOs*. Retrieved on March 1, 2015 from http://www.intrac.org/data/files/resources/729/Strategic-Planning-A-PLP-Toolkit-INTRAC.pdf

Jarvis, P. (1987). *Adult learning in the social context*, London: Croom Helm.

Jarvis, P. (2004). *Adult education and lifelong learning: Theory and practice*. London: Routledge.

JCSEE. (2015). *Program evaluation standards statements*. The Joint Committee on Standards for Educational Evaluation. Retrieved from http://www.jcsee.org/program-evaluation-standards-statements.

John Snow, Inc. (2012). *Monitoring and evaluation training curriculum 2009*. Boston: John Snow.

Johnson, D. (2000). Laying the foundation: Capacity building for participatory monitoring and evaluation. In M. Estrella et al. (Eds.), *Learning from change: Issues and experiences in participatory monitoring and evaluation* (pp. 217–228). London, UK, and International Development Research Centre, Ottawa, Canada: Intermediate Technology Publications.

Johnson, D. W., & Johnson, R. (1999). *Learning together and alone: Cooperative, competitive, and individualistic learning* (5th ed.). Boston: Allyn & Bacon.

Kaminsky, A. (2000). Beyond the literal: Metaphors and why they matter. *New Directions for Evaluation, 86,* 69–80.

Kapp, K. (2012). *The gamification of learning and instruction.* San Francisco: John Wiley & Sons.

Kellogg Foundation. (1998). *W.K. Kellogg Foundation evaluation handbook.* Battle Creek, MI: W. K. Kellogg Foundation.

Kellogg Foundation. (2004). *Logic model development guide.* Battle Creek, MI: W. K. Kellogg Foundation.

Kelly, M. A, & Kaczynski, D. (2008). Teaching evaluation from an experiential framework. Connecting theory and organizational development with grant making. *American Journal of Evaluation, 29*(4), 547–554.

King, J. A. (2007). Developing evaluation capacity through process use. *New Directions for Evaluation, 116,* 45–59.

Kingsbury, N., & Hedrich, T. E. (1994). Evaluator training in a government setting. *New Directions for Evaluation. 62,* 61–14.

Kirkpatrick, D. L. (1959, November). Techniques for evaluating training programs. *Journal of the American Society for Training Development.*

Kirkpatrick, D. L. (1977). Evaluating training programs: Evidence vs. proof. *Training and Development Journal, 31*(11), 9–12.

Kirkpatrick, D. L. (1996). *Evaluating training programs: The four levels.* San Francisco. Berrett-Koehler Publishers.

Kirkpatrick, D. L., & Kirkpatrick, J. D. (2007). *Implementing the four levels: A practical guide for effective evaluation of training programs.* San Francisco: Berrnett-Koehler Publisher.

Kirkpatrick, J., & Kirkpatrick, W. K. (2009). *The Kirkpatrick four levels: A fresh look after 50 years 1959–2009.* Kirkpatrick Partners. Retrieved from http://www.kirkpatrickpartners.com/Portals/0/Resources/Kirkpatrick%20Four%20Levels%20white%20paper.pdf

Kistler, S. (2010). *Susan Kistler on humor and cartoons for evaluators.* AEA365 | A Tip-a-Day by and for Evaluators. Retrieved on January 30, 2015 from http://aea365.org/blog/archive

Kistler, S. (2013). *Susan Kistler on songs with an evaluation message.* AEA365 | A Tip-a-Day by and for Evaluators. Retrieved on January 30, 2015 from http://aea365.org/blog/archive

Klein, P. D. (1997). Multiplying the problems of intelligence by eight: A critique of Garder's theory. *Canadian Journal of Education, 22*(4), 377–394.

Knowles, M. S. (1970). *The modern practice of adult education: Andragogy versus pedagogy.* New York: Association Press.

Knowles, M. S. (1980). *The modern practice of adult education: From pedagogy to andragogy.* Englewoods Cliff, NJ: Cambridge Adult Education.

Knowles, M. S. (1989). *The making of an adult educator: An autobiographical journey.* San Francisco: Jossey-Bass.

Knowles, M. S. (1995). *Designs for adult learning.* Alexandria, VA: American Society for Training and Development.

Knowles, M. S., Swanson, R. A., & Holton, E. F., III. (2011). *The adult learner: The definitive classic in adult education and human resource development* (7th ed.). California: Elsevier Science and Technology Books.

Ko, S., & Rossen, S. (2010). *Teaching online: A practical guide.* Routledge. New York.

Kolb, D. A. (1984). *Experiential learning: Experience as the source of learning and development.* Englewood Cliffs, NJ: Prentice Hall.

Kolb. D. A., & Fry, R. (1975). Toward an applied theory of experiential learning. In C. Cooper (Ed.), *Theories of Group Process.* London: John Wiley.

Koppett, K., & Richter, M. S. (2013). *How to use storytelling to increase learning.* Retrieved from http://www.koppett.com/how-to-use-storytelling-to-increase-learning

Kusek, J. Z., &. Rist, R. E. (2004). *Ten steps to a results-based monitoring and evaluation system: A handbook for development practitioners.* Washington, DC: World Bank.

Labin, S., Duffy, J. L., Meyers, D. C., Wandersman, A., & Lesesne, C. A. (2012). A research synthesis of the evaluation capacity building literature. *American Journal of Evaluation, 33*(3), 307–338.

Laird, D. (2003). *Approaches to training and development* (3rd ed.). New York: Persus Books Group.

LaVelle, J. M., & Donaldson, S. I. (2010). University-based evaluation training programs in the United States 1980–2008: An empirical examination. *American Journal of Evaluation, 31*(1), 9–23.

LDPride.net. (2014). *What is your learning style? Learning styles self-assessment.* Retrieved from http://www.ldpride.net/learning-style-test.html

Lee, J., Wallace, T. L., & Alkin, M. (2007). Using problem-based learning to train evaluators. *American Journal of Evaluation, 28*(4), 536–545.

Lennie, J., Tacchi, J., Koirala, B., Wilmore, M., & Skuse, A. (2011). *Equal access participatory monitoring and evaluation toolkit.* Washington DC: United States Agency for International Development (USAID).

Leviton, L. C. (2014). Some underexamined aspects of evaluation capacity building. *American Journal of Evaluation, 35*(1). 90–94.

Lombardo, M. M., & Eichinger, R. W. (2000). *The Leadership Architect Suite: Career architect development planner* (3rd ed.). Minneapolis: Lombinger Limited.

Lopez-Acevedo, G., Krause, P., & Mackay, K. (Eds.). (2012). *Building better policies: The nuts and bolts of monitoring and evaluation systems.* Washington, DC: The World Bank.

Loud, M. L., & Mayne, J. (Eds.). (2014). *Enhancing evaluation use: Insights from internal evaluation units.* Thousand Oaks: Sage.

Lusthaus, A., & Murphy, E. (1995). *Institutional assessment: A framework for strengthening organizational capacity for IDRC's research partners.* Ottawa: International Development Research Centre.

Mackay, K. (2002). The World Bank's ECB experience. *New Directions for Evaluation, 93,* 81–99.

Mackay, K. (2007). *How to build M&E systems to support better government.* Washington, DC: IEG and the World Bank.

Mager, R. F. (1984). *Preparing instructional objectives* (2nd ed.). Belmont, CA: Lake Publishing.

MandE (Monitoring and Evaluation News). (2015a). *MandE NEWS training forum.* Retrieved from http://pub45.bravenet.com/forum/static/show.php?usernum=3858098953&frmid=8118&msgid=0

MandE (Monitoring and Evaluation News). (2015b). Website home. Retrieved from http://mande.co.uk/

MandE (Monitoring and Evaluation News). (2015c). *M&E software: A list.* Retrieved from http://mande.co.uk/2011/lists/software-lists/me-software-a-list

Margerison, C. (2001). *Managerial consulting skills.* Hampshire, England: Gower Publishing.

Marsick, V. J., & Watkins, K. (1990). *Informal and incidental learning in the workplace.* London and New York: Routledge.

Mason, D. J. (1995). *Trainer's toolbox of training techniques.* Nairobi: International Labour Organisation (ILO).

Mathison, S. (2005) *Encyclopedia of evaluation.* Thousand Oaks, CA: Sage.

Mayne, J. (2004). Reporting on outcomes: Setting performance expectations and telling performance stories. *Canadian Journal of Program Evaluation, 19*(1), 31–60.

Mayne, J. (2012). Contribution analysis: Coming of age? *Evaluation, 18*(3), 270–280.

McCawley, P. F. (2009). *Methods for consulting educational needs assessment.* Moscow, Idaho: University of Idaho.

McDaniel, D. O., & Brown, D. H. (2001). *Manual for media trainers. A learner-centred approach.* Kuala Lumpur: AIBD and UNESCO.

McNamara, C. (2015). *Developing your nonprofit strategic plan.* Retrieved from http://managementhelp.org/freenonprofittraining/strategic-planning.htm

MEASURE Evaluation. (2015). Retrieved from https://training.measureevaluation.org

Merriam, S. (2001, Spring). Andragogy and self-directed learning: Pillars of adult learning theory. *New Directions for Adult and Continuing Education, 89.*

Merriam, S., Caffarella, R., & Baumgartner, L. (2007). *Learning in adulthood. A comprehensive guide.* San Francisco: John Wiley & Sons.

Microsoft. (2014). *Developing a training budget.* Retrieved from http://office.microsoft.com/en-us/excel-help/developing-a-training-budget-HA001122873.aspx

Milano, M., & Ullius, D. (1998). *Designing powerful training: The sequential-iterative model.* San Francisco, CA: Jossey-Bass.

Mind Tools. (2015). *McKinsey 7-S framework.* Retrieved from http://www.mindtools.com/pages/article/newSTR_91.htm

MIT (Massachusetts Institute of Technology). (2015). *Training delivery guide* (online). Retrieved 2015 from http://web.mit.edu/training/trainers/guide

Mittenthal, R. (2015). *Ten keys to successful strategic planning for nonprofit and foundation leaders.* Retrieved from http://www.tccgrp.com/pdfs/per_brief_tenkeys.pdf

Molenda, M. (2003). In search of the elusive ADDIE model. *Performance Improvement, 42*(5), 34–36.

MOOC List. (2015). Retrieved from www.mooc-list.com

Moodle (Modular Object-Oriented Dynamic Learning Environment). (2014). Retrieved from https://moodle.org/

Moore, M. G., & Kearsley, G. (2012). *Distance education: A systems view of online learning.* Belmont, CA: Wadsworth, Cengage Learning.

Morell, J. A. (2010). *Evaluation in the face of uncertainty: Anticipating surprise and responding to the inevitable.* New York, NY: Guilford.

Morra, L., & Rist, R. (2009). *The road to results: Designing and conducting effective development evaluations.* Washington, DC: World Bank.

Morrison, G., Ross, S., Kemp, J., & Kalman, H. (2011). *Designing effective instruction* (6th ed.). Hoboken NJ: John Wiley & Sons, Inc.

Musgrave, G. M. (1957). *Competitive debate: Rules and techniques.* New York: H. W. Wilson.

My M&E. (2015). Retrieved from http://www.mymande.org

Myers, I. B., McCaulley, M. H., Quenk, N. L., Hammer, A. L. (1998). *MBTI manual (A guide to the development and use of the Myers Briggs type indicator).* Consulting Psychologists Press.

Naidu, S. (2006). *e-Learning. A guidebook of principles, procedures and practices.* New Delhi: Commonwealth Educational Media Center for Asia (CEMCA).

Nassif, N., & Khalil, Y. (2006). Making a pie as a metaphor for teaching scale validity and

reliability. *American Journal of Evaluation, 27*(3), 393–398.

National Geographic (2006). *Service-learning guide for educators.* Retrieved from www.nationalgeographic.com/xpeditions/lessons/09/g68/servicelearnguide.pdf

NEA (National Education Association). (2015). *Code of ethics.* Retrieved from http://www.nea.org/home/30442.htm

NOAA Office for Coastal Management. (2015). *Needs assessment guide: Overview.* Retrieved from http://coast.noaa.gov/needsassessment/#/

NSAW (National Association of Social Workers). (2008). *Code of ethics of the National Association of Social Workers.* Retrieved http://www.socialworkers.org/pubs/code/code.asp

NSDTA (National Staff Development and Training Association). (2004a). *Instructor Competency Model. Human Services Staff Development And Training Roles and Competencies: Instructor.* Washington, DC: American Public Human Services Association.

NSDTA (National Staff Development and Training Association). (2004b). *Code of ethics for training and development professionals in the human service.* Washington, DC: American Public Human Services Association.

NSDTA (National Staff Development and Training Association). (2010). *A new key to success. Guidelines for effective staff development and training programs in* human service agencies. Washington, DC: American Public Human Services Association.

NSDTA (National Staff Development and Training Association). (2015). Series of competency guides. Retrieved from www.aphsa.org/content/NSDTA/en/resources.html

Nunley, K. F. (2006). *Differentiating the high school classroom: Solution strategies for 18 common obstacles*. Thousand Oaks, CA: Corwin.

Oblinger, D. G. (Ed.). (2012). *Game changers: Education and information technologies*. EDUCAUSE. Creative Commons. Retrieved from http://www.educause.edu/research-publications/books/game-changers-education-and-information-technologies

OCW (OpenCourseWare Consortium). (2014). Retrieved from http://www.ocwconsortium.org/about-ocw/

OECD (Organisation for Economic Co-operation and Development). (2002). *Glossary of key terms in evaluation and results-based management*. Paris: OECD.

OECD (Organisation for Economic Co-operation and Development). (2006). *The challenge of capacity development: Working towards good practice*. Paris: OECD.

OECD (Organisation for Economic Co-operation and Development). (2014a). *Supporting evaluation capacity development*. Paris: OECD.

OECD (Organisation for Economic Co-operation and Development).

(2014b). *Evaluation of development programmes. Developing evaluation capacities*. Retrieved from www.oecd.org/dac/evaluation/evaluatingcapacitydevelopment.htm

OECD (Organisation for Economic Co-operation and Development). (2015). Website. Retrieved from http://www.oecd.org/dac/evaluation

OECD & World Bank (Organisation for Economic Co-operation and Development). (2006). *Emerging good practice in managing for development results* (First issue). Paris: OECD.

OER Commons. (2015). Retrieved from http://www.oercommons.org

OERL (Online Evaluation Resource Library). (2015). National Science Foundation website. Retrieved from http://oerl.sri.com

Oliver, D. E., Casiraghi, A. M., Henderson, J. L., Brooks A. M., & Mulsow, M. (2008). Teaching program evaluation: Three selected pillars of pedagogy. *American Journal of Evaluation, 29*(3), 330–339.

Ongevalle, J. V., Maarse, A., Temmink, C., Boutylkova, E., & Huyse, H. (2012). *Dealing with complexity through planning, monitoring & evaluation (PME)* (Praxis Paper 26). PSO and HIVA.

OpenCourseWare Consortium. (2014). Retrieved from http://www.ocwconsortium.org/about-ocw/

Oregon State University. (2015). *Program evaluation capacity building webinar series*. Retrieved from http://oregon.4h.oregonstate.edu/evaluation-landing-page-0

Orey, M. (Ed.). (2001). *Emerging perspectives on learning, teaching, and technology*. Retrieved from http://projects.coe.uga.edu/epltt

Orr, S. K. (2010). Exploring stakeholder values and interests in evaluation. *American Journal of Evaluation, 31*(4), 557–569.

Otto Bremer Foundation. (2014). *Evaluation flash cards: Embedding evaluative thinking in organizational culture*. Developed by Michael Quinn Patton. St. Paul, Minnesota: Otto Bremer Foundation. Retrieved from http://www.ottobremer.org/sites/default/files/fact-sheets/OBF_flashcards_201402.pdf

Pashler, H., McDaniel, M., Rohrer, D., & Bjork, R. (2008). Learning styles: Concepts and evidence. *Psychological Science in the Public Interest, 9*, 105–119.

Patton, M. Q. (1988). The evaluator's responsibility for utilization. *Evaluation Practice, 9*(2), 5–24.

Patton, M. Q. (1994). Developmental evaluation. *Evaluation Practice, 15*(3), 311–320.

Patton, M. Q. (1997). *Utilization focused evaluation: The new century text*. Thousand Oaks, CA: Sage.

Patton, M. Q. (2002). Teaching and training with metaphors. *American Journal of Evaluation, 23*(1), 93–98.

Patton, M. Q. (2011). *Developmental evaluation: Applying complexity concepts to enhance innovation and use*. New York, NY: Guilford.

Patton, M. Q. (2012). *Essentials of utilization-focused evaluation*. Thousand Oaks, CA: Sage.

Patton, M. Q. (2014). *Best of aea365 week: Michael Quinn Patton on using children's stories to open up evaluation dialogues*. AEA365 | A Tip-a-Day by and for Evaluators. Retrieved from http://aea365.org/blog/archive

Peace Corps. (2014). *Culture matters: The Peace Corps cross-cultural workbook*. Washington, DC: Peace Corps Information collection and Exchange.

Pelican Initiative. (2015). *Pelican initiative: Platform for evidence-based learning & communication for social change*. Retrieved from https://dgroups.org/groups/pelican

Penelope, P., Baker, E., & McGaw, B. (2010). *International encyclopedia of education*. Oxford: Eldevier.

Phillips, J. J. (Ed.). (1994). *Measuring return on investment* (Vol. 1). Alexandria, VA: American Society for Training Development.

Phillips, J. P. (1997). *Handbook of training evaluation and measurement methods*. Oxon, London: Routledge.

Phillips, J. P., Phillips, P. P., & Hodges, T. K. (2004). *Make training evaluation work*. Alexandria, VA: American Society for Training & Development.

Pike, R. W. (1995). *101 more games for trainers*. Amherst, MA: Lakewood Publications.

Piskurich, G. M. (2000). *Rapid instructional design. Learning ID fast and Right*. San Francisco: Jossey-Bass.

Praslova, L. (2010). Adaptation of Kirkpatrick's four level model of training criteria to assessment of learning outcomes and program evaluation in higher education. *Educational Assessment, Evaluation and Accountability, 22*(3), 215–225.

Prelove, L. (2010). Adaptation of Kirkpatrick's four level model of training criteria to assessment of learning outcomes and program evaluation in higher education. *Educational Assessment, Evaluation and Accountability, 22*(3), 215–225.

Preskill, H. (1992). Students, client, and teaching: Observations from a practicum in evaluation. *Evaluation Practice, 13*, 39–46.

Preskill, H. (1997). Using critical incidents to model effective evaluation practice in the teaching of evaluation. *Evaluation Practice, 18*, 65–71.

Preskill, H. (2008). Evaluation's second act: A spotlight on learning. *American Journal of Evaluation, 29*(2), 127–138.

Preskill, H. (2014). Now for the hard stuff: Next steps in ECB research and practice. *American Journal of Evaluation, 35*(1), 116–119.

Preskill, H., & Boyle, S. (2008). A multidisciplinary model of evaluation capacity building. *American Journal of Evaluation, 29*(4), 443–459.

Preskill, H., & Jones, N. (2009). *A practical guide for engaging stakeholders in developing evaluation questions*. Princeton, NJ: Robert Wood Johnson Foundation.

Preskill, H., & Russ-Eft, D. (2015). *Building evaluation capacity: Activities for teaching and training*. Thousand Oaks: Sage.

Preskill, H., Torres, R., & Martinez-Papponi, B. (1999, November). *Assessing an organization's readiness for learning from evaluative inquiry*. Paper presented at the annual conference of the American Evaluation Association, Orlando, FL. Readiness for Organizational Learning and Evaluation Instrument (ROLE) instrument available at http://dmm.cci.fsu.edu/IADMM/iowaDmm/materials/ImplementationTeams/Survey/ROLESurvey.pdf

Preskill, H., & Torres, R. (2000). The learning dimension of evaluation use. *New Directions for Evaluation, 88*, 25–37.

Preskill, H., & Torres, R. (2015). *Readiness for organizational learning and evaluation (ROLE)*. Retrieved from http://www.fsg.org/Portals/0/Uploads/Documents/ImpactAreas/ROLE_Survey.pdf

Pretty, J. N., Gujit, I., Scoones, I., & Thompson, J. (1995). *A trainer's guide for participatory learning and action*. London: International Institute for Environment and Development.

PREVAL (Regional Platform for Evaluation Capacity Building in Latinamerica and the Caribbean). (2015). Retrieved from http://preval.org/en

PRIA. (1981). *Participatory research and evaluation: Experiments in research as a process of liberation*. New Delhi: Society for Participatory Research in Asia.

PRIA. (1995). *Participatory evaluation: Issues and concerns*. New Delhi: Society for Participatory Research in Asia.

Pullante, M. I. (2015). *Teaching aids slideshow*. Retrieved from https://prezi.com/kbfcvai9gkp5/copy-of-teaching-aids

QOTFC (Queensland Occupational Therapy Fieldwork Collaborative). (2007). *Clinical educator's resource kit*. Retrieved from http://www.qotfc.edu.au/resource

Rae, L. (1999). *Using evaluation in training and development*. London: Kogan Pate Limited.

Raftree, L., & Bamberger, M. (2014). *Emerging opportunities: Monitoring and evaluation in a tech-enabled world*. New York: The Rockefeller Foundation.

Rallis, S. F. (ED.). (2014). Evaluation capacity building. *American Journal of Evaluation, 35*(1), 1–159.

Ramage, M., & Shipp, K. (2009). *Systems thinkers*. London: Springer.

Reigeluth, C. M., & Carr-Chellman, A. A. (Eds.). (2009). *Instructional-design theories and models. Building a common knowledge base*. (Vol. III). New York: Routledge.

Reiser, R. A. (2001). A history of instructional design and technology, part II: A history of instructional design. *Educational Technology Research and Development, 49*(2), 57–67. (Eric Document Reproduction Service No. EJ 629 874).

Revans, R. W. (1982). *The origin and growth of action learning*. Brickley, UK: Chartwell-Bratt.

Rogers, C. R. (1969). *Freedom to learn*. Columbus, OH: Charles E. Merrill.

Rossi, P. H., Lipsey, M. W., & Freeman, H. E. (2004). *Evaluation: A systematic approach* (7th ed.). Thousand Oaks, CA: Sage.

Rothwell W. J, & Kazanas H. C. (2008). *Mastering the instructional design process* (4th ed.). San Francisco: Jossey-Bass/Pfeiffer.

Rotondo, E. (2012). Lessons learned from evaluation capacity building. *New Directions for Evaluation, 134*, 93–101.

Rubin, F. (1995). *A basic guide to evaluation for development workers*. Oxford: Oxfam.

Rugh, J. (2005). The Rosetta Stone of logical fameworks. *MandE NEWS*. Retrieved from http://www.mande.co.uk/logframe.htm#Information%20sources

Rugh, J., & Segone, M. (Eds.). (2013). *Voluntary organizations for professional evaluation (VOPEs). Learning from Africa, Americas, Asia, Australasia, Europe and Middle East*. EvalPartners, UNICEF, IOEC.

Russ-Eft, D. F., Bober-Michel, M. J., Koszalka, T. A., & Sleezer, C. M. (2013). *Fieldbook of evaluator competencies*. Charlotte, NC: IAP.

Russei, T. (2001). *The no significant difference phenomenon*. Chicago: The International Distance Education Certification Center.

Russon, C., & Russon, G. (Eds.). (2004). International perspectives on evaluation standards. *New Directions for Evaluation, 104*.

Sanders, N. M. (1989). Evaluation of training by trainers. *New Directions for Evaluation, 44*, 59–70.

Scriven, M. (1967). The methodology of evaluation. In R. W. Tyler, R. M. Gagné, & M. Scriven (Eds.), *Perspectives of curriculum evaluation* (pp. 39–83). Chicago, IL: Rand McNally.

Scriven, M. (1991). *Evaluation thesaurus* (4th ed.). Newbury Park, CA: Sage.

Scriven, M. (1994). *Duties of the teacher* checklist. Based on text in article published in 1994 in *Journal of Personnel Evaluation in Education, 8*(2), 151–184. Retrieved from http://michaelscriven.info/images/DUTIES_OF_THE_TEACHER.pdf

Segone, M., & Rugh, J. (Eds.). (2013). *Evaluation and civil society. Stakeholders' perspectives on national evaluation capacity development*. UNICEF, IOCE, and EvalPartners.

Segone, M., Heider, C., Oksanen, R., Silva, S., & Sanz, B. (2013). Towards a shared framework for national evaluation capacity development. In M. Segone & J. Rugh (Eds.), *Evaluation and civil society stakeholders' perspectives on national evaluation capacity development*. UNICEF, IOCE and EvalPartners.

Sen, A. (1999). *Development as freedom*. New York: Alfred A. Knopf.

Senge, P. M. (1990). *The fifth discipline: The art and practice of the learning organization*. New York: Random House.

SenGupta, S., Hopson, R., & Thompson-Robinson, M. (2004). Cultural competence in evaluation: An overview. *New Directions in Evaluation, 102*, 5–19.

Shelton, K., & Saltsman, G. (2007). Using the Addie model for teaching online. *International Journal of Information and Communication Technology Education, 2*(3), 14–26.

Silberman, M. (2005). *101 ways to make training active.* San Francisco: John Wiley & Sons.

Silberman, M. (2006). *Active training: A handbook of techniques, designs, case examples, and tips.* San Francisco: Pfeiffer.

Simister, N., & Smith, R. (2010). *Monitoring and evaluating capacity building: Is it really that difficult?* (Praxis Paper 23). International NGO Training and Research Center (INTRAC).

Skinner, B. F. (1974). *About behaviorism.* New York: Alfred A. Knopf.

SlideShare. (2015). Retrieved from http://www.slideshare.net

Sloman, M. (2002). *The E-learning revolution: How technology is driving a new training paradigm.* New York: American Management Association.

Smith, M. K. (2002, 2008). Howard Gardner and multiple intelligences. *The encyclopedia of informal education.* Retrieved from www.infed.org/mobi/howard-gardner-multiple-intelligences-and-education

Smith, M. K. (2003, 2009). Jean Lave, Etienne Wenger and communities of practice. *The encyclopedia of informal education.* Retrieved from www.infed.org/biblio/communities_of_practice.htm

Smith, N. L. (Ed.). (1981). Metaphors for evaluation: Sources of new methods. *New Perspectives in Evaluation Book 1.* Thousand Oaks, CA: Sage.

Social Research Methods. (2015.) Retrieved from http://www.socialresearchmethods.net

Society for Organizational Learning. (2015). Retrieved from https://www.solonline .org/?page=SystemsThinking

Soloman, B. A., & Felder, R. M. (2014). *Index of learning styles questionnaire.* NC State University. Retrieved from http://www.engr.ncsu.edu/learningstyles/ilsweb.html

Sork, T. J. (1991). *Mistakes made and lessons learned: Overcoming obstacles to successful program planning.* San Francisco: John Wiley & Sons

Stevahn, L., King, J. A., Ghere, G., & Minnema, J. (2005). Establishing essential competencies for program evaluators. *American Journal of Evaluation, 26*(1), 43–59.

Stockdill, S. H., Baizerman, M., & Compton, D. W. (2002). Toward a definition of the ECB process: A conversation with the ECB literature. *New Directions for Evaluation, 93,* 7–25.

Stloter, C., Duc, P. T. M., & Engelbrech, S. M. (2007). *Advanced training of trainers* (Participant and trainer guides). Watertown MA: Pathfinder International. Retrieved from http://www.pathfinder.org/publications-tools/Advanced-Training-of-Trainers-Participants-Guide.html

Stufflebeam, D. L., & Wingate, L. A. (2005). A self-assessment procedure for use in evaluation training. *American Journal of Evaluation, 26*(4), 544–561.

Stufflebeam, D. L. (2002). *Institutionalizing evaluation checklist.* The Evaluation Center at Western Michigan University. Retrieved from www.wmich.edu/evalctr/checklists/evaluation-checklists

Sugar, S., & Whitcomb, J. (2006). *Training games.* San Francisco: Pfeiffer.

Swan, K. (2003). Learning effectiveness: What the research tells us. In J. Bourne & J. C. Moore (Eds.), *Elements of quality online education, Practice and direction* (pp. 13–45). Needham, MA: Sloan Center for Online Education.

Tarsilla, M. (2014, March). *Evaluation capacity development in Africa: Current landscape, lessons learned and the way forward.* Keynote speech presented at the African Evaluation Association Conference, Yaoundé, Cameroon.

Taut, S. M., & Alkin, M. C. (2003). Program staff perceptions of barriers to evaluation implementation. *American Journal of Evaluation, 24*(2), 213–226.

Taylor, B., & Kroth, M. (2009). Andragogy's transition into the future: Meta-analysis of andragogy and its search for a measurable instrument. *Journal of Adult Education, 38*(1), 1–11.

Taylor-Powell, E., & Henert, E. (2008). *Developing a logic model: Teaching and training guide.* Madison: University of Wisconsin-Extension, Program Development and Evaluation. Retrieved from http://www.uwex.edu/ces/pdande/evaluation/pdf/lmguidecomplete.pdf

The Thiaga Group. (2015). *Training games*. Retrieved from http://thiagi .net/archive/www/games.html

Thomas, V. G., & Madison, A. (2010). Integration of social justice into the teaching of evaluation. *American Journal of Evaluation*, 31(4), 570–583.

Tomlinson, C. A., & Strickland, C. A. (2005). *Differentiation in practice: A resource guide for differentiating curriculum, grades 9–12*. Alexandria, VA: ASCD.

Trainers Advice. (2015). *Free training plans templates, as well as other resources for free or to buy*. Retrieved from http:// trainersadvice.com/resources/ training-plans-templates

Training Bubble. (2015). *Free energizers, icebreakers, training games and resources*. Retrieved from http://www.trainerbubble.com/ energisers.aspx

Trevisan, M. (2002). Enhancing practical evaluation training through long-term evaluation projects. *American Journal of Evaluation*, 23(1), 81–92.

Trevisan, M. (2004). Practical training in evaluation: A review of the literature. *American Journal of Evaluation*, 25(2), 255–272.

Tripp, S., & Bichelmeyer, B. (1990). Rapid prototyping: An alternative instructional design strategy. *Educational Technology Research and Development*, 38(1), 31–44.

Tyler, R. W. (1949). *Basic principles of curriculum and instruction*.

Chicago: University of Chicago Press.

UNAIDS (Joint United Nations Programme on HIV/AIDS). (2010). *Standards for a competency-based approach to monitoring and evaluation curricula & trainings*. Geneva: UNAIDS.

UNDG (United Nations Development Group). (2011). *Results-based management handbook*. New York: UNDG.

UNDP (United Nations Development Programme). (1993). *Human development report*. Oxford: Oxford University Press.

UNDP (United Nations Development Programme). (n.d.). *Monitoring and evaluation training guide*. Retrieved on March 1, 2015, from http://web.undp.org/ evaluation/documents/MandE-Tranining-package-English.pdf

UNEG. (2015). *National evaluation capacity development: Practical tips on how to strengthen national evaluation systems*. New York: United Nations Evaluation Group. Retrieved from www.unevaluation .org/document/detail/1205

UNESCO (United Nations Educational, Scientific, and Cultural Organization). (1997). *International standard classification of education (ISCED)*. Paris: UNESCO.

UNICEF (United Nations Children's Fund). (2007). *UNICEF evaluation policy*. New York: UNICEF Executive Board.

UNICEF (United Nations Children's Fund). (2015). *M&E training modules*. Retrieved from http://

www.ceecis.org/remf/Service3/ unicef_eng

University of Texas, College of Education. (2015). *Mobile learning portal* website. Retrieved from http:// www.mobilelearningportal.org

USAID (United States Agency for International Development). (2003). *Training that works*. Baltimore: JHPIEGO.

USAID (United States Agency for International Development). (2015a). *Systemic M&E interviews with Dave Snowden, Shamim Bodhanya, and Jeanne Downing*. Retrieved from http:// www.microlinks.org/learning-marketplace/news/systemic-me-interviews-dave-snowden-shamim-bodhanya-and-jeanne-downing

USAID (United States Agency for International Development). (2015b). *Learning lab*. Retrieved from http://usaidlearninglab.org

USOPM (U.S. Office of Personnel Management). (2011): *Training evaluation field guide. Demonstrating the value of training at every level*. Washington, DC: U.S. Office of Personnel Management.

USOPM (U.S. Office of Personnel Management). (2015): *Training and development policy wiki*. Retrieved March 1, 2015, from http://www .opm.gov/wiki/training/Training-Evaluation.ashx

Vaca, S. (2013). *DVR Week: Sara Vaca on 4 easy free comic-generator tools*. Retrieved from http://aea365 .org/blog/archive

Veletsianos, G. (2010). *Emerging Technologies in Distance Education*.

Edmonton, Canada: Athabasca University.

Vicinanza, N. (2010). *Nicole Vicinanza on explaining random sampling to stakeholders.* AEA365 | A Tip-a-Day by and for Evaluators. Retrieved from http://aea365.org/blog/archive

Volkov, B., & King, J. A. (2007). *A checklist for building evaluation capacity.* The Evaluation Center at Western Michigan University. Retrieved from www.wmich.edu/evalctr/checklists/evaluation-checklists

Wageningen University. (2015). PPM&E resource portal. Retrieved on March 1, 2015 from http://portals.wi.wur.nl/ppme

Ware, C. (2013). *Information visualization: Perception for design* (2nd ed.). San Francisco CA: Morgan Kaufmann.

Watkins, R., Meiers, M. W., & Visser, Y. L. (2012). *A Guide to assessing needs.* Washington, DC: The World Bank.

Weimer, M. (2002). *Learner-centered teaching: Five key changes to practice.* San Francisco: Jossey-Bass.

Weiss, C. H. (1980). Knowledge creep and decision accretion. *Knowledge: Creation, Utilization, Diffusion, 1,* 381–404.

Weiss, C. H. (1988a). Evaluation for decisions: Is anybody there? Does anybody care? *Evaluation Practice, 9*(1), 5–19.

Weiss, C. H. (1988b). If program decisions hinged only on information: A response to Patton. *Evaluation Practice, 9*(3), 15–28.

Werquin, P. (2010). *Recognising non-formal and informal learning: Outcomes, policies and practices.* Paris: OECD Publishing.

WHO (World Health Organization). (2005). *Effective teaching: A guide for educating healthcare providers.* Geneva: WHO.

WHO (World Health Organization). (2010). *WHO training evaluation guide.* Geneva: WHO.

Wiggins, G., & McTighe, J. (2005). *Understanding by design.* Alexandria, VA: Association for Supervision and Curriculum Development (ASCD).

WikiEducator. (2015). Retrieved on March 1, 2015, from https://wikieducator.org

Williams, B., & Imam, I. (Eds.). (2007). *Systems concepts in evaluation: An expert anthology.* Point Reyes, CA: EdgePress.

Williams, B., & Hummelbrunner, R. (2009). *Systems concepts in action: A practitioner's toolkit.* Stanford, CA: Stanford University Press.

Williams B., & van 't Hof, S. (2014). *Wicked solutions: A systems approach to complex problems.* Publishers Bob Williams, Sjon van 't Hof.

World Bank. (2004). *Evaluation capacity development: OED self-evaluation.* Washington, DC: The World Bank.

World Bank. (2014a). *Participatory monitoring and evaluation.* Retrieved from at http://web.worldbank.org/WBSITE/EXTERNAL/TOPICS/EXTSOCIALDEVELOPMENT/EXTPCENG/0,,contentMDK:20509352~menuPK:1278203~pagePK:148956~piPK:216618~theSitePK:410306,00.html

World Bank. (2014b). *Evaluation capacity development (ECD).* Independent Evaluation Group and the World Bank Group. Retrieved from https://ieg.worldbankgroup.org/evaluations/evaluation-capacity-development-ecd

World Bank. (2015). *The nuts and bolts of M&E system* webpage. Retrieved from http://web.worldbank.org/WBSITE/EXTERNAL/TOPICS/EXTPOVERTY/0,,contentMDK:22632898~pagePK:148956~piPK:216618~theSitePK:336992,00.html

Wyatt, L., & Phillips, C. (2013). *The logic model guidebook. Better strategies for great results.* Thousand Oaks, CA: Sage.

XCeval. (2015). *Cross cultural evaluation listserv.* Retrieved from https://groups.yahoo.com/neo/groups/xceval/info

Yarbrough, D. B., Shulha, L. M., Hopson, R. K., & Caruthers, F. A. (2011). *The program evaluation standards: A guide for evaluators and evaluation users* (3rd ed.). Thousand Oaks, CA: Sage.

Youngman, F. (2000) *The political economy of adult education.* London: Zed Books.

Index

Subgroup forming, 339–342
Subject matter knowledge and experience as
    trainer competency, 119
Summative vs. formative evaluation, 273.
    See also Evaluation phase (training
    evaluation)
Surveys, post-training, 303–304
Sweet 'n Sour, 385
Syllabuses, 211 (box), 213–214 (box)
Synchronous training, 33 (table), 34 (table),
    39–41
Systems approach
    delivery options and, 35
    origins and evolution of, 5–6
    RBM and, 13
    training objectives and, 181 (box)

Tarsilla, M., 60 (box)
Task analysis, 164–169, 167 (table)
Technological innovation, 38–39
Technological literacy, 120
Terms of reference (ToRs), 126–128, 190
Theorist learning style, 91
Three M&E Guests, 359
Tiered activities and resources, 107
Time management
    during activities, 262
    activity planning and, 196
    facilitation and, 251, 253, 254–255 (box)
    parking lot and, 258–259
Tomlinson, C. A., 94–95
Topic analysis, 165 (box)
Trainee analysis, 107, 157–158,
    159–160 (table), 300
Trainee (learning) development plans, 301,
    305–306, 399
Trainee outcomes, evaluation questions on, 286
Trainee panel debates, 359–360
Trainees
    capacity building and, 60–61
    delegation to, 102
    as evaluators, 297–298
    expected number of, 152
    learner aids, 212–213 (box), 213
    learner-centered approach and, 98
    list of, 211 (box)
    needs assessments and preliminary
        consultations with, 103

number of, 222–223
post-training evaluation, accessibility for, 284
pre-training communication with, 225–226
profile of, 152
reports, trainee-generated reports, 395–396
scheduling for, 221
selection of, 222–223
Trainer-centered vs. learner-centered approach,
    96, 97 (table)
Trainer guides, 212 (box)
Trainers
    capacity building and, 63–64
    context familiarity, 120
    curriculum development, 115
    defined, 17
    diversity of people involved, 17, 18 (figure)
    as evaluators, 297
    external, working with, 130 (box)
    facilitators vs., 18
    interpersonal skills, 120–122
    learner-centered approach and, 97–98
    learning domains, hard vs. soft skills, and,
        83–84
    modeling responsible and respectful
        behavior, 100
    number of, 210
    performance appraisal and management, 115
    professional trainers as learners, 23 (box)
    recruitment and preparation of, 125–129,
        127 (box), 221, 222 (box)
    recruitment checklist, 131–133
    self-assessment and professional
        development, 115
    standards and ethics, 116–118, 117 (box)
    technical skills, 118–120
Training, definition and key aspects of, 27–28
Training aids, 212 (box), 213, 244–246,
    245 (table)
Training analysis. *See* Analysis phase
    (training analysis)
Training design. *See* Design phase
    (training design)
Training development. *See* Development and
    preparation phase (training development)
Training evaluation. *See* Evaluation phase
    (training evaluation)
Training implementation. *See* Facilitation and
    implementation (training implementation)